Readings in

ORGANIZATIONS

Behavior, Structure, Processes

Readings in

ORGANIZATIONS

Behavior, Structure, Processes

Edited by

JAMES L. GIBSON
Professor of Business Administration
University of Kentucky

JOHN M. IVANCEVICH
Professor of Organizational Behavior and Management
University of Houston

JAMES H. DONNELLY, JR.
Professor of Business Administration
University of Kentucky

Third Edition • 1979

BUSINESS PUBLICATIONS, INC. Dallas, Texas 75243

Irwin-Dorsey Limited Georgetown, Ontario L7G 4B3

© BUSINESS PUBLICATIONS, INC., 1973, 1976, and 1979

ISBN 0-256-02247-X
Library of Congress Catalog Card No. 78–70961

Printed in the United States of America

2 3 4 5 6 7 8 9 0 ML 6 5 4 3 2 1 0 9

Preface

THE study of organizations is of vital concern to many groups in society. Behavioral and social scientists have led the way in observing that modern men and women work, learn, play, worship, heal, and govern in larger and more complex institutions than their ancestors. Modern society is characterized by the existence of intricately organized firms, universities, clubs, churches, hospitals, and agencies, each carrying out specialized social functions through the combined efforts of individual specialists. The effectiveness of these organizations determines the quality of modern life.

The achievement of effective organizational performance is the essence of the managerial process. As a consequence of history and tradition, society delegates authority to use its scarce resources to the managers of its institutions. And, in return, it holds managers accountable for their actions. Thus, managers of organizations are crucial to the manner in which a modern society functions. More particularly, the decisions of managers determine to an important degree the effectiveness of society in achieving its economic, educational, leisure, religious, health, and political goals.

The subject of this Third Edition is the management of organizational behavior, structure, and processes. Our purpose is to bring together a selection of articles that bear directly on the process by which managers achieve effective organizational performance. The contributors of these articles are representative of a variety of behavioral and social sciences, including psychology, sociology, and social psychology. Though diverse in background and training, the contributors share a common interest in bringing their theory and research to bear on the practical problems of managing organizations.

The framework which we use to present the articles identifies three aspects of organizations: behavior, structure, and process. Organizational behavior emphasizes the human element of organizations and relates to the aspects of motivation, groups, and leadership. The analysis of organization is enhanced through an understanding of each of these aspects. Organizational structure refers to the relatively fixed relationships among tasks

v

and it derives from managerial decisions which define jobs, group jobs into departments, and assign authority. Two important features of structure are job descriptions and chains of command. Organizational processes are the activities of people in the organization. These activities consist of such important elements as evaluating performance, rewarding behavior, communications, and decision making.

However, analysis of organizations implies some definite purpose. Our point of view is that the modern manager's purpose must be organizational improvement. Thus we identify a fourth aspect: modification of organizations. This aspect refers to the process by which managers improve the organization's effectiveness through the development of behavior, structure, and process. Organizational development requires knowledge of these three elements. The bases for acquiring this knowledge are provided by the articles that appear in this book.

The book is divided into five parts. The first part is introductory in that it presents articles on organizational behavior and theory, and on managerial practice. This part provides an overview of the direction and content base of these readings. Part II presents nine articles which discuss behavior in organizations. The articles focus on individuals, motivation, managing stress, leadership, and conflict. Part III includes six articles, each dealing with one or more aspects of organizational structure. This section includes articles dealing with the quality of work life, matrix organizations, and information systems. Part IV is comprised of six articles which discuss problems and strategies of performance appraisal, rewards, participation, and communications. Part V includes six articles which discuss organizational change and development and goal setting.

The articles which we included in this book were selected for a number of reasons. Of particular importance is that they are recent discussions of organizational behavior, structure, and process issues. Moreover, they are of high professional quality and readable by students. Yet, ultimately we had to make choices and in numerous instances excellent articles were omitted which would have been included in a larger collection. Although not arbitrarily selected the articles do represent our judgment.

We wish to especially thank the authors and publishers of the included readings. We also wish to acknowledge Mildred Waxler and Cheryl Willis for handling all the typing details in a prompt, accurate, and understandable manner.

February 1979

James L. Gibson
John M. Ivancevich
James H. Donnelly, Jr.

Contributors

Blanchard, Kenneth H.
Bluestone, Irving
Burck, Charles G.
Davis, Stanley
Deci, Edward L.
Donnelly, James H., Jr.
Fein, Mitchell
Fry, Fred L.
Galbraith, Jay R.
Gibson, James L.
Gray, Edmund R.
Greiner, Larry E.
Hall, Jay
Harvey, Jerry B.
Hersey, Paul
Ivancevich, John M.
Kahn, Robert L.
Kerr, Steven
Latham, Gary P.

Lawler, Edward, III
Lawrence, Paul R.
Levinson, Harry
Locker, Allan H.
Matteson, Michael T.
Miles, Raymond E.
Mintzberg, Henry
Mosher, Craig
Owens, James
Perrow, Charles
Pfeffer, Jeffrey
Porte, de la, Andre P. C.
Roy, Donald
Snow, Charles C.
Steers, Richard M.
Tell, Kenneth J.
Wallick, Franklin
Yukl, Gary A.
Zaleznik, Abraham

Contents

Cross Reference Table xii

PART I. INTRODUCTION AND MANAGING ORGANIZATIONAL PERFORMANCE

    Editors' Summary Comments 1

1. The Short and Glorious History of Organizational Theory,
   Charles Perrow 5
2. When Is an Organization Effective? A Process Approach to
   Understanding Effectiveness, Richard M. Steers 19
3. Managerial Work: Analysis from Observation,
   Henry Mintzberg 34
4. Work with Dignity, Franklin Wallick 52

PART II. BEHAVIOR WITHIN ORGANIZATIONS: INDIVIDUALS, GROUP, MANAGERIAL

    Editors' Summary Comments 59

5. The Individual Organization: Problems and Promise,
   Edward E. Lawler III 63
6. Woodworker, Craig Mosher 76
7. Banana Time: Job Satisfaction and Informal Interaction,
   Donald F. Roy 80
8. Organizations and Coronary Heart Disease: The Stress Connection,
   John M. Ivancevich and Michael T. Matteson 103
9. Operant Conditioning in Organizational Settings: Of Mice or Men?
   Fred L. Fry 114
10. Group Norms: Key to Building a Winning Team,
    P. C. André de la Porte 121
11. The Abilene Paradox: The Management of Agreement,
    Jerry B. Harvey 128
12. The Uses of Leadership Theory, James Owens 147
13. Managers and Leaders: Are They Different? Abraham Zaleznik   158

PART III. STRUCTURE AND ORGANIZATIONAL BEHAVIOR

Editors' Summary Comments 177

14. Should the Quality of Work Life Be Legislated?
     Edward E. Lawler III 181

15. The Myth of Job Enrichment, *Mitchell Fein* 189

16. Organization-Environment: Concepts and Issues, *Raymond E. Miles,
     Charles C. Snow, and Jeffrey Pfeffer* 196

17. How G.M. Turned Itself Around, *Charles G. Burck* 218

18. Problems of Matrix Organizations, *Stanley M. Davis* and
     Paul R. Lawrence 228

19. Organization Design: An Information Processing View,
     Jay R. Galbraith 244

PART IV. PROCESSES WITHIN ORGANIZATIONS

Editors' Summary Comments 257

20. Performance Appraisal—A Survey of Current Practices,
     Alan H. Locher and *Kenneth S. Teel* 259

21. Appraisal of What Performance? *Harry Levinson* 268

22. Paying People Doesn't Always Work the Way You Expect It to,
     Edward L. Deci 282

23. On the Folly of Rewarding A, While Hoping for B, *Steven Kerr* 289

24. Worker Participation in Decision Making, *Irving Bluestone* 305

25. Communication Revisited, *Jay Hall* 317

PART V. DEVELOPING INDIVIDUAL, GROUP, AND
ORGANIZATIONAL EFFECTIVENESS

Editors' Summary Comments 337

26. Organizational Development: Some Problems and Proposals,
     Robert L. Kahn 341

27. Red Flags in Organization Development, *Larry E. Greiner* 357

28. The Management of Change Part Three: Planning and
     Implementing Change, *Paul Hersey* and *Kenneth H. Blanchard* 368

29. The Non Linear Systems Experience: A Requiem, *Edmund R. Gray* 379

30. A Review of Research on the Application of Goal Setting in
     Organizations, *Gary P. Latham* and *Gary A. Yukl* 387

31. Behavior, Structure, and Processes in Two Organizations,
     James L. Gibson, John M. Ivancevich, and *James H. Donnelly, Jr.*   411

CROSS-REFERENCE TABLE

For Relating the Articles in This Reader to the Authors'
Organizations: Behavior, Structure, Processes, 3d ed.,
and Other Similar Textbooks

Selected Organizational Behavior Oriented Textbooks	Parts in *Readings in Organizations*				
	Part I Introduction and Managing Organizational Performance	*Part II Behavior within Organizations: Individual, Group, Managerial*	*Part III Structure and Organizational Behavior*	*Part IV Processes within Organizations*	*Part V Developing Individual, Group, and Organizational Effectiveness*
Gibson, James L.; Ivancevich, John M.; and Donnelly, James H., Jr., *Organizations: Behavior, Structure, Processes*, 3d ed. (Dallas: Business Publications, Inc., 1979)	Chaps. 1, 2, 3	Chaps. 4, 5, 6, 7, 8, 9	Chaps. 10, 11, 12	Chaps. 13, 14, 15	Chaps. 17, 18, 19
Filley, Alan C.; House, Robert J.; and Kerr, Steven, *Managerial Process and Organizational Behavior* (Glenview, Ill.: Scott, Foresman and Co., 1976)	Chaps. 1, 2, 3, 4	Chaps. 4, 5, 6, 8, 9, 10, 11, 12	Chaps. 13, 15, 16, 17, 18	Chaps. 7, 19	Chaps. 20, 21, 22
Hamner, W. Clay, and Organ, Dennis W., *Organizational Behavior* (Dallas: Business Publications, Inc. 1978)	Chaps. 1, 2	Chaps. 3, 4, 5, 6, 7, 8, 9, 10, 11, 12, 13, 14, 15, 16, 17			Chap. 18
Hampton, David; Summer, Charles E.; and Webber, Ross A., *Organizational Behavior and the Practice of Management* (Glenview, Ill.: Scott, Foresman and Co., 1978)		Chaps. 1, 2, 4, 8, 10, 11	Chaps. 6, 7	Chaps. 3, 5, 9	Chap. 12

Source					
Hellriegel, Don, and Slocum, John W., Jr., *Organizational Behavior: Contingency Views* (St. Paul: West Publishing Co., 1976)	Chaps. 1, 2,	Chaps. 3, 4, 5, 6, 7 8, 9, 10	Chap. 11		Chaps. 12, 13
Korman, Abraham K., *Organizational Behavior* (Englewood Cliffs, N.J.: Prentice-Hall, Inc. 1977)	Chaps. 1, 2, 6, 14, 15	Chaps. 3, 4, 5, 7, 8, 9		Chap. 10	Chaps. 11, 12, 13
Luthans, Fred, *Organizational Behavior* (New York: McGraw-Hill, 1977)	Chaps. 1, 2, 3, 4, 5	Chaps. 11, 12, 13, 14, 15, 16, 17, 18	Chaps. 6, 7, 19	Chaps. 8, 9, 10	Chaps. 20, 21, 22
Porter, Lyman W.; Lawler, Edward E., III.; and Hackman, J. Richard, *Behavior In Organizations* (New York: McGraw-Hill, 1975)	Chap. 1	Chaps. 2, 4, 5, 6, 13, 14	Chaps. 3, 8, 9, 10	Chaps. 11, 12	Chaps. 7, 15, 16, 17
Reitz, H. Joseph, *Behavior In Organizations* (Homewood, Ill.: Richard D. Irwin, 1977)	Chaps. 1, 2	Chaps. 3, 4, 5, 6, 9, 10, 11, 12, 13, 16, 17, 18, 19		Chaps. 7, 8, 14, 15	Chap. 21
Tosi, Henry L., and Carroll, Stephen J.; *Organizational Behavior* (Chicago: St. Clair Press, 1977)	Chaps. 1, 2	Chaps. 3, 4, 5, 8	Chaps. 6, 7	Chaps. 9, 10, 11, 12	Chaps. 13, 14, 15, 16, 17, 18

PART I

INTRODUCTION
AND MANAGING
ORGANIZATIONAL
PERFORMANCE

I N this part, articles are presented which serve to introduce the remaining selections in the book to provide the reader with a broad overview as a foundation for understanding and appreciating what follows. Our major interest in this book will be the behavioral sciences which have produced theory, research, and generalizations concerning the behavior, structure, and processes of organizations. The articles in this book recognize these three major organizational variables which are used to classify the selections included in the book.

One of the major themes of this book is the contribution that the behavioral sciences can make to our understanding of management and organizations. The literature of psychology, sociology, social psychology, and anthropology is the source of many of the articles chosen. Other articles from the broader literature of management and business administration which use behavioral science theories, concepts, or methods of inquiry have also been included. Our purpose is to demonstrate that the behavioral sciences are rich sources of understanding about the way people behave in organizational settings.

1

Another major theme is that managers of organizations must come to know and to appreciate the behavioral science contributions. To this end, we have included a selection of articles which deals with the practical problems of modifying organizations. The literature of organizational development and the management of change has increased substantially in the past several years through the efforts of behavioral scientists in particular. The articles in this part are concerned with the issues that managers must confront as they engage in the process of developing the capability of their organizations.

A final important thread and one which is seemingly more concrete is that of organizational effectiveness. In fact this thread pervades the entire book. The authors whose work is represented here are concerned with various aspects of organizational effectiveness. They write about leadership effectiveness, group effectiveness, communication effectiveness, structural effectiveness, and the like. They also are concerned with conceptual and measurement problems of effectiveness. What is effectiveness? How should it be measured? These questions are not easily resolved, as the reader will come to realize as he or she reads the articles in the following part of the book.

Two articles in the introductory section set the stage for the major themes of the book.

Charles Perrow's article, "The Short and Glorious History of Organizational Theory," traces the development of thinking from the advocates of the mechanical school of organizational theory—those who treat the organization as a machine—to the human relations school, which emphasizes people rather than machines as well as the contributions made by other groups along the way to the current "systems" view. Unfortunately, Perrow concludes that the ". . . systems theory itself had not lived up to its heady predictions." Where does all this leave us? Perrow provides five very important conclusions.

The second article by Richard M. Steers, "When Is an Organization Effective?" introduces the notion of multiple and often conflicting goals in organizations. He emphasizes the need to assess and to develop criteria of effectiveness. Steers presents a model for analyzing what is called effectiveness.

The next article examines the attributes of managers. "Managerial Work: Analysis from Observation" by Henry Mintzberg describes some of the main features and characteristics of managerial work. The picture painted by the author illustrates the multiple roles a manager must play to get the job done.

Franklin Wallick in "Work with Dignity" discusses the humanization of work. The author describes managerial actions which he believes are in some instances anti-union. Whether behavioralists would consider work enlargement and enrichment as anti-union or managers consider them anti-union is not the issue discussed. Wallick believes that at the worker or blue-collar level there is skepticism but hope about humanization efforts. He recommends management and unions joining together to implement procedures to give work dignity.

The Short and Glorious History of Organizational Theory*

CHARLES PERROW

F ROM the beginning, the forces of light and the forces of darkness have
polarized the field of organizational analysis, and the struggle has been
protracted and inconclusive. The forces of darkness have been represented by the mechanical school of organizational theory—those who treat
the organization as a machine. This school characterizes organizations in
terms of such things as: centralized authority, clear lines of authority,
specialization and expertise, marked division of labor, rules and regulations,
and clear separation of staff and line.

The forces of light, which by mid-20th century came to be characterized as the human relations school, emphasizes people rather than machines, accommodations rather than machine-like precision, and draws its
inspiration from biological systems rather than engineering systems. It has
emphasized such things as: delegation of authority, employee autonomy,
trust and openness, concerns with the "whole person," and interpersonal
dynamics.

THE RISE AND FALL OF SCIENTIFIC MANAGEMENT

The forces of darkness formulated their position first, starting in the
early part of this century. They have been characterized as the scientific
management or classical management school. This school started by parad-
ing simple-minded injunctions to plan ahead, keep records, write down

---

* Reprinted by permission of the publisher from *Organizational Dynamics*, Summer
1973. Copyright 1973 by AMACOM, a division of American Management Association.

policies, specialize, be decisive, and keep your span of control to about six people. These injunctions were needed as firms grew in size and complexity, since there were few models around beyond the railroads, the military, and the Catholic Church to guide organizations. And their injunctions worked. Executives began to delegate, reduce their span of control, keep records, and specialize. Planning ahead still is difficult, it seems, and the modern equivalent is Management by Objectives.

But many things intruded to make these simple-minded injunctions less relevant:

1. Labor became a more critical factor in the firm. As the technology increased in sophistication it took longer to train people, and more varied and specialized skills were needed. Thus, labor turnover cost more and recruitment became more selective. As a consequence, labor's power increased. Unions and strikes appeared. Management adjusted by beginning to speak of a cooperative system of capital, management, and labor. The machine model began to lose it relevancy.

2. The increasing complexity of markets, variability of products, increasing number of branch plants, and changes in technology all required more adaptive organization. The scientific management school was ill-equipped to deal with rapid change. It had presumed that once the proper structure was achieved the firm could run forever without much tampering. By the late 1930s, people began writing about adaptation and change in industry from an organizational point of view and had to abandon some of the principles of scientific management.

3. Political, social, and cultural changes meant new expectations regarding the proper way to treat people. The dark, satanic mills needed at the least a whitewashing. Child labor and the brutality of supervision in many enterprises became no longer permissible. Even managers could not be expected to accept the authoritarian patterns of leadership that prevailed in the small firm run by the founding father.

4. As mergers and growth proceeded apace and the firm could no longer be viewed as the shadow of one man (the founding entrepreneur), a search for methods of selecting good leadership became a preoccupation. A good, clear, mechanical structure would no longer suffice. Instead, firms had to search for the qualities of leadership that could fill the large footsteps of the entrepreneur. They tacitly had to admit that something other than either "sound principles" or "dynamic leadership" was needed. The search for leadership traits implied that leaders were made, not just born, that the matter was complex, and that several skills were involved.

ENTER HUMAN RELATIONS

From the beginning, individual voices were raised against the implications of the scientific management school. "Bureaucracy" had always been a dirty word, and the job design efforts of Frederick Taylor were even the subject of a congressional investigation. But no effective counter-force developed until 1938, when a business executive with academic talents named Chester Barnard proposed the first new theory of organizations: Organizations are cooperative systems, not the products of mechanical engineering. He stressed natural groups within the organization, upward communication, authority from below rather than from above, and leaders who functioned as a cohesive force. With the spectre of labor unrest and the Great Depression upon him, Barnard's emphasis on the cooperative nature of organizations was well-timed. The year following the publication of his *Functions of the Executive* (1938) saw the publication of F. J. Roethlisberger and William Dickson's *Management and the Worker*, reporting on the first large-scale empirical investigation of productivity and social relations. The research, most of it conducted in the Hawthorne plant of the Western Electric Company during a period in which the work force was reduced, highlighted the role of informal groups, work restriction norms, the value of decent, humane leadership, and the role of psychological manipulation of employees through the counseling system. World War II intervened, but after the war the human relations movement, building on the insights of Barnard and the Hawthorne studies, came into its own.

The first step was a search for the traits of good leadership. It went on furiously at university centers but at first failed to produce more than a list of Boy Scout maxims: A good leader was kind, courteous, loyal, courageous, etc. We suspected as much. However, the studies did turn up a distinction between "consideration," or employee-centered aspects of leadership, and job-centered, technical aspects labeled "initiating structure." Both were important, but the former received most of the attention and the latter went undeveloped. The former led directly to an examination of group processes, an investigation that has culminated in T-group programs and is moving forward still with encounter groups. Meanwhile, in England, the Tavistock Institute sensed the importance of the influence of the kind of task a group had to perform on the social relations within the group. The first important study, conducted among coal miners, showed that job simplification and specialization did not work under conditions of uncertainty and nonroutine tasks.

As this work flourished and spread, more adventurous theorists began to extend it beyond work groups to organizations as a whole. We now knew that there were a number of things that were bad for the morale and loyalty of groups—routine tasks, submission to authority, specialization of tasks, segregation of task sequence, ignorance of the goals of the firm, centralized decision making, and so on. If these were bad for groups, they were likely to be bad for groups of groups—i.e., for organizations. So people like Warren Bennis began talking about innovative, rapidly changing organizations that were made up of temporary leadership and role assignments, and democratic access to the goals of the firm. If rapidly changing technologies and unstable, turbulent environments were to characterize industry, then the structure of firms should be temporary and decentralized. The forces of light, of freedom, autonomy, change, humanity, creativity, and democracy were winning. Scientific management survived only in outdated text books. If the evangelizing of some of the human relations school theorists were excessive, and, if Likert's System 4, or MacGregor's Theory Y, or Blake's 9×9 evaded us, at least there was a rationale for the confusion, disorganization, scrambling, and stress: Systems should be temporary.

BUREAUCRACY'S COMEBACK

Meanwhile, in another part of the management forest, the mechanistic school was gathering its forces and preparing to outflank the forces of light. First came the numbers men—the linear programmers, the budget experts, and the financial analysts—with their PERT systems and cost-benefit analyses. From another world, unburdened by most of the scientific management ideology and untouched by the human relations school, they began to parcel things out and give some meaning to those truisms, "plan ahead" and "keep records." Armed with emerging systems concepts, they carried the "mechanistic" analogy to its fullest—and it was very productive. Their work still goes on, largely untroubled by organizational theory; the theory, it seems clear, will have to adjust to them, rather than the other way around.

Then the words of Max Weber, first translated from the German in the 1940s—he wrote around 1910, incredibly—began to find their way into social science thought. At first, with his celebration of the efficiency of bureaucracy, he was received with only reluctant respect, and even with hostility. All writers were against bureaucracy. But it turned out, surprisingly, that managers were not. When asked, they acknowledge that they preferred clear lines of communication, clear specifications of authority and responsibility, and clear knowledge of whom they were responsible to. They were as wont to say "there ought to be a rule about this," as to say "there are too many rules around here," as wont to say "next week we've got to get organized," as to say "there is too much red tape." Gradually, studies began to show that bureaucratic organizations could change faster than nonbureaucratic ones, and that morale could be higher where there was clear evidence of bureaucracy.

What was this thing, then? Weber had showed us, for example, that bureaucracy was the most effective way of ridding organizations of favoritism, arbitrary authority, discrimination, payola, and kickbacks, and, yes, even incompetence. His model stressed expertise, and the favorite or the boss's nephew or the guy who burned up resources to make his performance look good was *not* the one with expertise. Rules could be changed; they could be dropped in exceptional circumstances; job security promoted more innovation. The sins of bureaucracy began to look like the sins of failing to follow its principles.

ENTER POWER, CONFLICT, AND DECISIONS

But another discipline began to intrude upon the confident work and increasingly elaborate models of the human relations theorists (largely social psychologists) and the uneasy toying with bureaucracy of the "structionalists" (largely sociologists). Both tended to study economic organizations. A few, like Philip Selznick, were noting conflict and differences in goals (perhaps because he was studying a public agency, the Tennessee Valley Authority), but most ignored conflict or treated it as a pathological manifestation of breakdowns in communication or the ego trips of unreconstructed managers.

But in the world of political parties, pressure groups, and legislative bodies, conflict was not only rampant, but to be expected—it was even functional. This was the domain of the political scientists. They kept talking about power, making it a legitimate concern for analysis. There was an open acknowledgment of "manipulation." These were political scientists who were "behaviorally" inclined—studying and recording behavior rather than constitutions and formal systems of government—and they came to a much more complex view of organized activity. It spilled over into the area of economic organizations, with the help of some economists like R. A. Gordon and some sociologists who were studying conflicting goals of treatment and custody in prisons and mental hospitals.

The presence of legitimately conflicting goals and techniques of preserving and using power did not, of course, sit well with a cooperative systems view of organizations. But it also puzzled the bureaucratic school (and what was left of the old scientific management school), for the impressive Weberian principles were designed to settle questions of power through organizational design and to keep conflict out through reliance on rational-legal authority and systems of careers, expertise, and hierarchy. But power was being overtly contested and exercised in covert ways, and conflict was bursting out all over, and even being creative.

Gradually, in the second half of the 1950s and in the next decade, the political-science view infiltrated both schools. Conflict could be healthy, even in a cooperative system, said the human relationists; it was the mode of resolution that counted, rather than prevention. Power became reconceptualized as "influence," and the distribution was less important, said Arnold Tannenbaum, than the total amount. For the bureaucratic school— never a clearly defined group of people, and largely without any clear ideology—it was easier to just absorb the new data and theories as something else to be thrown into the pot. That is to say, they floundered, writing books that went from topic to topic, without a clear view of organizations, or better yet, producing "readers" and leaving students to sort it all out.

Buried in the political-science viewpoint was a sleeper that only gradually began to undermine the dominant views. This was the idea, largely found in the work of Herbert Simon and James March, that because man was so limited—in intelligence, reasoning powers, information at his disposal, time available, and means of ordering his preferences clearly—he generally seized on the first acceptable alternative when deciding, rather than looking for the best; that he rarely changed things unless they really got bad, and even then he continued to try what had worked before; that he limited his search for solutions to well-worn paths and traditional sources of information and established ideas; that he was wont to remain preoccupied with routine, thus preventing innovation. They called these characteristics "cognitive limits on rationality" and spoke of "satisficing" rather than maximizing or optimizing. It is now called the "decision making" school, and is concerned with the basic question of how people make decisions.

This view had some rather unusual implications. It suggested that if managers were so limited, then they could be easily controlled. What was necessary was not to give direct orders (on the assumption that subordinates were idiots without expertise) or to leave them to their own devices (on the assumption that they were supermen who would somehow know what was best for the organization, how to coordinate with all the other supermen, how to anticipate market changes, etc.). It was necessary to control only the *premises* of their decisions. Left to themselves, with those premises set, they could be predicted to rely on precedent, keep things stable and smooth, and respond to signals that reinforce the behavior desired of them.

To control the premises of decision making, March and Simon outline a variety of devices, all of which are familiar to you, but some of which you may not have seen before in quite this light. For example, organizations develop vocabularies, and this means that certain kinds of information are highlighted, and others are screened out—just as Eskimos (and skiers) distinguish many varieties of snow, while Londoners see only one. This is a form of attention-directing. Another is the reward system. Change the bonus for salesmen and you can shift them from volume selling to steady-account selling, or to selling quality products or new products. If you want to channel good people into a different function (because, for example, sales should no longer be the critical functions as the market changes, but engineering applications should), you may have to promote mediocre people in the unrewarded function in order to signal to the good people in the rewarded one that the game has changed. You cannot expect most people to make such decisions on their own because of the cognitive limits on their rationality, nor will you succeed by giving direct orders, because you yourself probably do not know whom to order where. You presume that once the signals are clear and the new sets of alternatives are manifest, they have enough ability to make the decision but you have had to change the premises for their decisions about their career lines.

It would take too long to go through the dozen or so devices, covering a range of decision areas (March and Simon are not that clear or systematic about them, themselves, so I have summarized them in my own book), but I think the message is clear.

It was becoming clear to the human relations school, and to the bureaucratic school. The human relationists had begun to speak of changing stimuli rather than changing personality. They had begun to see that the rewards that can change behavior can well be prestige, money, comfort, etc., rather than trust, openness, self-insight, and so on. The alternative to supportive relations need not be punishment, since behavior can best be changed by rewarding approved behavior rather than by punishing disapproved behavior. They were finding that although leadership may be centralized, it can function best through indirect and unobtrusive means such as changing the premises on which decisions are made, thus giving the impression that the subordinate is actually making a decision when he has only been switched to a different set of alternatives. The implications of this work were also beginning to filter into the human relations school, through an emphasis on behavioral psychology (the modern version of the much maligned stimulus-response school) that was supplanting personality theory (Freudian in its roots, and drawing heavily, in the human relations school, on Maslow).

For the bureaucratic school, this new line of thought reduced the heavy weight placed upon the bony structure of bureaucracy by highlighting the muscle and flesh that make these bones move. A single chain of command, precise division of labor, and clear lines of communication are simply not enough in themselves. Control can be achieved by using alternative communication channels, depending on the situation; by increasing or decreasing the static or "noise" in the system; by creating organizational myths and organizational vocabularies that allow only selective bits of information to enter the system; and through monitoring performance through indirect means rather than direct surveillance. Weber was all right for a starter, but organizations had changed vastly, and the leaders needed many more means of control and more subtle means of manipulation than they did at the turn of the century.

THE TECHNOLOGICAL QUALIFICATION

By now the forces of darkness and forces of light had moved respectively from midnight and noon to about 4 A.M. and 8 P.M. But any convergence or resolution would have to be on yet new terms, for soon after the political-science tradition had begun to infiltrate the established schools, another blow struck both of the major positions. Working quite independently of the Tavistock Group, with its emphasis on sociotechnical systems, and before the work of Burns and Stalker on mechanistic and organic firms, Joan Woodward was trying to see whether the classical scientific principles of organization made any sense in her survey of a hundred firms in South Essex. She tripped and stumbled over a piece of gold in the process. She picked up the gold, labeled it "technology," and made sense out of her otherwise hopeless data. Job-shop firms, mass-production firms, and continuous-process firms all had quite different structures because the type of tasks, or the "technology," was different. Somewhat later, researchers in America were coming to very similar conclusions based on studies of hospitals, juvenile correctional institutions, and industrial firms. Bureaucracy appeared to be the best form of organization for routine operations; temporary work groups, decentralization, and emphasis on interpersonal processes appeared to work best for nonroutine operations. A raft of studies appeared and are still appearing, all trying to show how the nature of the task affects the structure of the organization.

This severely complicated things for the human relations school, since it suggested that openness and trust, while good things in themselves, did not have much impact, or perhaps were not even possible in some kinds of work situations. The prescriptions that were being handed out would have to be drastically qualified. What might work for nonroutine, high-status, interesting, and challenging jobs performed by highly educated people might not be relevant or even beneficial for the vast majority of jobs and people.

It also forced the upholders of the revised bureaucratic theory to qualify their recommendations, since research and development units should obviously be run differently from mass-production units, and the difference between both of these and highly programmed and highly sophisticated continuous-process firms was obscure in terms of bureaucratic theory. But the bureaucratic school perhaps came out on top, because the forces of evil—authority, structure, division of labor, etc.—no longer looked evil, even if they were not applicable to a minority of industrial units.

The emphasis on technology raised other questions, however. A can company might be quite routine, and a plastics division nonroutine, but there were both routine and nonroutine units within each. How should they be integrated if the prescription were followed that, say, production should be bureaucratized and R&D not? James Thompson began spelling out different forms of interdependence among units in organizations, and Paul Lawrence and Jay Lorsch looked closely at the nature of integrating mechanisms. Lawrence and Lorsch found that firms performed best when the differences between units were *maximized* (in contrast to both the human relations and the bureaucratic school), as long as the integrating mechanisms stood half-way between the two—being neither strongly bu-reaucratic nor nonroutine. They also noted that attempts at participative management in routine situations were counterproductive, that the environments of some kinds of organizations were far from tubulent and customers did not want innovations and changes, that cost reduction, price and efficiency were trivial considerations in some firms, and so on. The technical insight was demolishing our comfortable truths right and left. They were also being questioned from another quarter.

ENTER GOALS, ENVIRONMENTS, AND SYSTEMS

The final seam was being mined by the sociologists while all this went on. This was the concern with organizational goals and the environment. Borrowing from the political scientists to some extent, but pushing ahead on their own, this "institutional school" came to see that goals were not fixed; conflicting goals could be pursued simultaneously, if there were enough slack resources, or sequentially (growth for the next four years, then cost-cutting and profit-taking for the next four); that goals were up for grabs in organizations, and units fought over them. Goals were, of course, not what they seemed to be, the important ones were quite un-official; history played a big role; and assuming profit as the preeminent goal explained almost nothing about a firm's behavior.

They also did case studies that linked the organization to the web of influence of the environment; that showed how unique organizations were in many respects (so that, once again, there was no one best way to do things for all organizations); how organizations were embedded in their own history, making change difficult. Most striking of all, perhaps, the case studies revealed that the stated goals usually were not the real ones; the official leaders usually were not the real ones; the official leaders usually were not the powerful ones; claims of effectiveness and efficiency were deceptive or even untrue; the public interest was not being served; political influences were pervasive; favoritism, discrimination, and sheer corruption were commonplace. The accumulation of these studies presented quite a pill for either the forces of light or darkness to swallow, since it was hard to see how training sessions or interpersonal skills were relevant to these problems, and it was also clear that the vaunted efficiency of bureaucracy was hardly in evidence. What could they make of this wad of case studies?

We are still sorting it out. In one sense, the Weberian model is upheld because organizations are not, *by nature*, cooperative systems; top managers must exercise a great deal of effort to control them. But if organizations are tools in the hands of leaders, they may be very recalcitrant ones. Like the broom in the story of the sorcerer's apprentice, they occasionally get out of hand. If conflicting goals, bargaining, and unofficial leadership exists, where is the structure of Weberian bones and Simonian muscle? To what extent are organizations tools, and to what extent are they products of the varied interests and group strivings of their members? Does it vary by organization, in terms of some typological alchemy we have not discovered? We don't know. But at any rate, the bureaucratic model suffers again; it simply has not reckoned on the role of the environment. There are enormous sources of variations that the neat, though by now quite complex, neo-Weberian model could not account for.

The human relations model has also been badly-shaken by the findings of the institutional school, for it was wont to assume that goals were given and unproblematical, and that anything that promoted harmony and efficiency for an organization also was good for society. Human relationists assumed that the problems created by organizations were largely limited to the psychological consequences of poor interpersonal relations within them, rather than their impact on the environment. Could the organization really promote the psychological health of its members when by necessity it had to define psychological health in terms of the goals of the organization itself? The neo-Weberian model at least called manipulation "manipulation" and was skeptical of claims about autonomy and self-realization.

But on one thing all the varied schools of organizational analysis now seemed to be agreed: organizations are systems—indeed, they are open systems. As the growth of the field has forced ever more variables into our consciousness, flat claims of predictive power are beginning to decrease and research has become bewilderingly complex. Even consulting groups need more than one or two tools in their kit-bag as the software multiplies.

The systems view is intuitively simple. Everything is related to everything else, though in uneven degrees of tension and reciprocity. Every unit, organization, department, or work group takes in resources, transforms them, and sends them out, and thus interacts with the larger system. The psychological, sociological, and cultural aspects of units interact. The systems view was explicit in the institutional work, since they tried to study whole organizations; it became explicit in the human relations school, because they were so concerned with the interactions of people. The political science and technology viewpoints also had to come to this realization, since they deal with parts affecting each other (sales affecting production; technology affecting structure).

But as intuitively simple as it is, the systems view has been difficult to put into practical use. We still find ourselves ignoring the tenets of the open-systems view, possibly because of the cognitive limits on our rationality. General systems theory itself had not lived up to its heady predictions; it remains rather nebulous. But at least there is a model for calling us to account and for stretching our minds, our research tools, and our troubled nostrums.

SOME CONCLUSIONS

Where does all this leave us? We might summarize the prescriptions and proscriptions for management very roughly as follows:

1. A great deal of the "variance" in a firm's behavior depends on the environment. We have become more realistic about the limited range of change that can be induced through internal efforts. The goals of organizations, including those of profit and efficiency, vary greatly among industries and vary systematically by industries. This suggests that the impact of better management by itself will be limited, since so much will depend on market forces, competition, legislation, nature of the work force, available technologies and innovations, and so on. Another source of variation is, obviously, the history of the firm and its industry and its traditions.

2. A fair amount of variation in both firms and industries is due to the type of work done in the organization—the technology. We are now fairly confident in recommending that if work is predictable and routine, the necessary arrangement for getting the work done can be highly structured, and one can use a good deal of bureaucratic theory in accomplishing this. If it is not predictable, if it is nonroutine and there is a good deal of uncertainty as to how to do a job, then one had better utilize the theories that emphasize autonomy, temporary groups, multiple lines of authority and communications, and so on. We also know that this distinction is important when organizing different parts of an organization.

We are also getting a grasp on the question of what is the most critical function in different types of organizations. For some organizations, it is production; for others, marketing; for still others, development. Furthermore, firms go through phases whereby the initial development of a market or a product or manufacturing process or accounting scheme may require a nonbureaucratic structure, but once it comes on stream, the structure should change to reflect the changed character of the work.

3. In keeping with this, management should be advised that the attempt to produce change in an organization through managerial grids, sensitivity training, and even job enrichment and job enlargement is likely to be fairly ineffective for all but a few organizations. The critical reviews of research in all these fields show that there is no scientific evidence to support the claims of the proponents of these various methods; that research has told us a great deal about social psychology, but little about how to apply the highly complex findings to actual situations. The key word is *selectivity:* We have no broad-spectrum antibiotics for interpersonal relations. Of course, managers should be sensitive, decent, kind, courteous, and cour-

ageous, but we have known that for some time now, and beyond a minimal threshold level, the payoff is hard to measure. The various attempts to make work and interpersonal relations more humane and stimulating should be applauded, but we should not confuse this with solving problems of structure, or as the equivalent of decentralization or participatory democracy.

4. The burning cry in all organizations is for "good leadership," but we have learned that beyond a threshold level of adequacy it is extremely difficult to know what good leadership is. The hundreds of scientific studies of this phenomenon come to one general conclusion: Leadership is highly variable or "contingent" upon a large variety of important variables such as nature of task, size of the group, length of time the group has existed, type of personnel within the group and their relationships with each other, and amount of pressure the group is under. It does not seem likely that we'll be able to devise a way to select the best leader for a particular situation. Even if we could, that situation would probably change in a short time and thus would require a somewhat different type of leader.

Furthermore, we are beginning to realize that leadership involves more than smoothing the paths of human interaction. What has rarely been studied in this area is the wisdom or even the technical adequacy of a leader's decision. A leader does more than lead people; he also makes decisions about the allocation of resources, type of technology to be used, the nature of the market, and so on. This aspect of leadership remains very obscure, but it is obviously crucial.

5. If we cannot solve our problems through good human relations or through good leadership, what are we then left with? The literature suggests that changing the structures of organizations might be the most effective and certainly the quickest and cheapest method. However, we are now sophisticated enough to know that changing the formal structure by itself is not likely to produce the desired changes. In addition, one must be aware of a large range of subtle, unobtrusive, and even covert processes and change devices that exist. If inspection procedures are not working, we are now unlikely to rush in with sensitivity training, nor would we send down authoritative communications telling people to do a better job. We are more likely to find out where the authority really lies, whether the degree of specialization is adequate, what the rules and regulations are, and so on, but even this very likely will not be enough.

According to the neo-Weberian bureaucratic model, it has been influenced by work on decision making and behavioral psychology, we should find out how to manipulate the reward structure, change the premises of the decision makers through finer controls on the information received and the expectations generated, search for interdepartmental conflicts that prevent better inspection procedures from being followed, and after manipulating these variables, sit back and wait for two or three months for them to take hold. This is complicated and hardly as dramatic as many of the solutions currently being peddled, but I think the weight of organizational theory is in its favor.

We have probably learned more, over several decades of research and theory, about the things that do *not* work (even though some of them obviously *should* have worked) than we have about things that do work. On balance, this is an important gain and should not discourage us. As you know, organizations are extremely complicated. To have as much knowledge as we do have in a fledgling discipline that has had to borrow from the diverse tools and concepts of psychology, sociology, economics, engineering, biology, history, and even anthropology is not really so bad.

REFERENCES

This paper is an adaptation of the discussion to be found in Charles Perrow, *Complex Organizations: A Critical Essay*, Scott, Foresman, Glenview, Ill., 1972. All the points made in this paper are discussed thoroughly in that volume.

The best overview and discussion of classical management theory, and its changes over time is by Joseph Massie, 'Management Theory" in the *Handbook of Organizations* edited by James March, Rand McNally, Chicago, 1965, pp. 387–422.

The best discussion of the changing justifications for managerial rule and worker obedience as they are related to changes in technology, etc., can be found in Reinhard Bendix's *Work and Authority in Industry*, Wiley, New York, 1956. See especially the chapter on the American experience.

Some of the leading lights of the classical view—F. W. Taylor, Col. Urwick, and Henry Fayol—are briefly discussed in *Writers on Organizations* by D. S. Pugh, D. J. Hickson, and C. R. Hinings, Penguin, Baltimore, 1971. This brief, readable, and useful book also contains selections from many other schools that I discuss, including Weber, Woodward, Cyert and March, Simon, the Hawthorne Investigations, and the Human Relations Movement as represented by Argyris, Herzberg, Likert, McGregor, and Blake and Mouton.

As good a place as any to start examining the human relations tradition is Rensis Likert, *The Human Organization*, McGraw-Hill, New York, 1967. See also his *New Patterns of Management*, McGraw-Hill, 1961.

The Buck Rogers school of organizational theory is best represented by Warren Bennis. See his *Changing Orgnaizations*, McGraw-Hill, 1966, and his book with Philip Slater, *The Temporary Society*, Harper & Row, New York, 1968. Much of this work is linked into more general studies, e.g., Alvin Toffler's very popular paperback *Future Shock*, Random House, New York, 1970, and Bantam Paperbacks; or Zibigniew Brzezinsky's *Between Two Ages: America's Role in the Technitronic Era*, Viking Press, New York, 1970. One of the first intimations of the new type of environment and firm and still perhaps the most perceptive is to be found in the volume by Tom Burns and G. Stalker, *The Management of*

Innovation, Tavistock, London, 1961, where they distinguished between "organic" and "mechanistic" systems. The introduction, which is not very long, is an excellent and very tight summary of the book.

The political-science tradition came in through three important works. First, Herbert Simon's *Administrative Behavior,* Macmillan, New York, 1948, followed by the second half of James March and Herbert Simon's *Organizations,* Wiley, New York, 1958, then Richard M. Cyert and James March's *A Behavioral Theory of the Firm,* Prentice-Hall, Englewood Cliffs, N.J., 1963. All three of these books are fairly rough going, though chapters 1, 2, 3, and 6 of the last volume are fairly short and accessible. A quite interesting book in this tradition, though somewhat heavy-going, is Michael Crozier's *The Bureaucratic Phenomenon,* University of Chicago, and Tavistock Publications, 1964. This is a striking description of power in organizations, though there is a somewhat dubious attempt to link organization processes in France to the cultural traits of the French people.

The book by Joan Woodward, *Industrial Organisation: Theory and Practice,* Oxford University Press, London, 1965, is still very much worth reading. A fairly popular attempt to discuss the implications for this for management can be found in my own book *Organizational Analysis: A Sociological View,* Tavistock, 1970, chapters 2 and 3. The impact of technology on structure is still fairly controversial. A number of technical studies have found both support and nonsupport, largely because the concept is defined so differently, but there is general agreement that different structures and leadership techniques are needed for different situations. For studies that support and document this viewpoint see James Thompson, *Organizations in Action,* McGraw-Hill, 1967, and Paul Lawrence and Jay Lorsch, *Organizations and Environment,* Harvard University Press, Cambridge, Mass., 1967.

The best single work on the relation between the organization and the environment and one of the most readable books is the field is Philip Selznick's short volume *Leadership in Administration,* Row, Peterson, Evanston, Ill., 1957. But the large number of these studies are scattered about. I have summarized several in my *Complex Organizations: A Critical Essay.*

Lastly, the most elaborate and persuasive argument for a systems view of organizations is found in the first 100 pages of the book by Daniel Katz and Robert Kahn, *The Social Psychology of Organizations,* Wiley, 1966. It is not easy reading, however.

2

When Is an Organization Effective? A Process Approach to Understanding Effectiveness*

RICHARD M. STEERS

WHILE most organizational analysts agree that the pursuit of effectiveness is a basic managerial responsibility, there is a notable lack of consensus on what the concept itself means. The economist or financial analyst usually equates organizational effectiveness with high profits or return on investment. For a line manager, however, effectiveness is often measured by the amount and quality of goods or services generated. The R&D scientist may define effectiveness in terms of the number of patents, new inventions, or new products developed by an organization. And last, many labor union leaders conceive of effectiveness in terms of job security, wage levels, job satisfaction, and the quality of working life. In short, while there is general agreement that effectiveness is something all organizations should strive for, the criteria for assessment remain unclear.

In view of the many different ways in which managers and researchers conceptualize organizational effectiveness, it comes as no surprise that there is equal disagreement over the best strategy for attaining effectiveness. A principal reason for this lack of agreement stems from the parochial views that many people harbor about the effectiveness construct. As mentioned, many define effectiveness in terms of a single evaluation criterion (profit or productivity, for example). But it is difficult to conceive of an organization that would survive for long if it pursued profits to the ex-

* Reprinted by permission from *Organizational Dynamics* (Autumn 1976), pp. 50–63. Copyright 1976 by AMACOM, a division of American Management Associations. All rights reserved.

19

clusion of its employees' needs and goals or those of society at large. Organizations typically pursue multiple (and often conflicting) goals—and these goals tend to differ from organization to organization according to the nature of the enterprise and its environment.

Another explanation for the general absence of agreement on the nature of effectiveness arises from the ambiguity of the concept itself. Organizational analysts often assume, incorrectly, that it's relatively easy to identify the various criteria for evaluating effectiveness. In point of fact, such criteria tend to be somewhat intangible; indeed, they depend largely on who is doing the evaluating and within what specific frame of reference.

A number of organizational analysts have tried to identify relevant facets of effectiveness that could serve as useful evaluating criteria. I recently reviewed 17 different approaches to assessing organizational effectiveness and found a general absence of agreement among them. Figure 1 summarizes the criteria used in the 17 models and notes the frequency with which each is mentioned. As this table reveals, only one criterion (adaptability-flexibility) was mentioned in more than half of the models. This criterion was followed rather distantly by productivity, job satisfaction, profitability, and acquisition of scarce and valued resources. Thus there is little agreement among analysts concerning what criteria should be used to assess current levels of effectiveness.

PROBLEMS IN ASSESSMENT

This absence of convergence among competing assessment techniques poses a serious problem for both managers and organizational analysts. If appropriate assessment criteria cannot be agreed upon, it would be manifestly impossible to agree completely on an evaluation of an organization's success or failure. This inability to identify meaningful criteria to be used across organizations results in part from ignoring several questions (or problems) that must be resolved if we are to derive more meaningful approaches to assessing organizational effectiveness. Eight such issues are:

1. *Is there any such thing as organizational effectiveness?* It is only logical to ask whether there is indeed empirical justification for any such construct. In the absence of any tangible evidence, it may be that organizational effectiveness exists only on an abstract level, with little applicability to the workplace and its problems. But if effectiveness is indeed a viable concept from a managerial standpoint, its definition and characteristics must be made more explicit.

2. *How stable—consistently valid—are the assessment criteria?* A second problem encountered in attempts to assess effectiveness is that many of the assessment criteria change over time. In a growth economy, for example, the effectiveness of a business firm may be related to level of capi-

Figure 1
Frequency of Occurrence of Evaluation Criteria in 17 Models of Organizational Effectiveness

Evaluation Criteria	No. of Times Mentioned (N = 17)	Percent of Total
Adaptability-flexibility	10	59
Productivity	6	35
Job satisfaction	5	29
Profitability	3	18
Acquisition of scarce and valued resources	3	18
Absence of organizational strain	2	12
Control over external environment	2	12
Employee development	2	12
Efficiency	2	12
Employee retention	2	12
Growth	2	12
Integration of individual goals with organizational goals	2	12
Open communication	2	12
Survival	2	12
All other criteria	1	6

Source: R. M. Steers, "Problems in the Measurement of Organizational Effectiveness," *Administrative Science Quarterly*, 1975, vol. 20, pp. 546–558.

tal investment; during a recession or depression, however, capital liquidity may emerge as a more useful criterion, and high fixed investment may shift from being an asset to being a liability. Clearly, such criteria do not represent permanent indicators of organizational success. In fact, it is probably this transitory nature of many effectiveness criteria that has led some investigators to suggest that adaptability or flexibility represents the key variable in any model of effectiveness.

3. *Which time perspective is most appropriate in assessment?* Contributing to the problem of criterion instability is the question of which time perspective to take in assessing effectiveness. For example, if current production (a short-run criterion) consumes so much of an organization's resources that little is left over for investment in R&D, the organization may ultimately find itself with its products outmoded and its very survival (a long-term criterion) threatened. Thus the problem for the manager is how best to allocate available resources between short- and long-term considerations so that both receive sufficient support for their respective purposes.

4. *Are the assessment criteria related positively to each other?* Most approaches to assessing effectiveness rely on a series of relatively discrete criteria (for example, productivity, job satisfaction, profitability). The use of such multiple measures, however, often leads to situations in which these criteria are in conflict. Consider, for instance, an organization that uses productivity and job satisfaction as two of its criteria. Productivity

can often be increased (at least in the short run) by pressuring employees to exert greater energy and turn out more goods in the same period of time. Such managerial efforts are likely, however, to result in reduced job satisfaction. On the other hand, it's possible to increase job satisfaction by yielding to employee demands for increased leisure time and reduced production pressures—but at the price of lower productivity. Thus, while the use of multiple evaluation criteria adds breadth to any assessment attempt, it simultaneously opens the door to conflicting demands that management may not be able to satisfy.

5. *How accurate are the assessment criteria?* A further problem in assessing organizational effectiveness is how to secure accurate measures for assessment purposes. How does an organization accurately measure managerial performance or job satisfaction, if these are to be used as effectiveness criteria? And how consistent are such measures over time? In point of fact, we tend to measure the performance of the individual manager loosely in terms of an overall rating by his superior and to measure job satisfaction frequently in terms of turnover and absenteeism rates. Such operational definitions have their obvious limitations. Performance ratings, for example, may be skewed by personality factors, and a low turnover rate may indicate low performance standards born of a complacent or indifferent management.

6. *How widely can the criteria be applied?* A major problem with many of the criteria suggested for assessing effectiveness is the belief that they apply equally in a variety of organizations. Such is often not the case. While profitability and market share may be relevant criteria for most business firms, they have little applicability for organizations like a library or a police department. Thus, when considering appropriate criteria for purposes of assessment, we should take care to ensure that the criteria are consistent with the goals and purposes of a particular organization.

7. *How do such criteria help us understand organizational dynamics?* The organizational analyst of necessity is concerned with the utility of the effectiveness construct. What purposes are served by the existence of evaluation criteria for assessing effectiveness? Do they provide insight into the dynamics of ongoing organizations? Do they help us make predictions concerning the future actions of organizations? Unless such models facilitate a better understanding of organizational structures, processes, or behavior, they are of little value from an analytical or operational standpoint.

8. *At which level should effectiveness be assessed?* Finally, managers face the problem of the level at which to assess effectiveness. Logic suggests evaluating organizational effectiveness on an organizationwide basis. Such an approach, however, ignores the dynamic relationships between an organization and its various parts. We must bear in mind that the individual employee ultimately determines the degree of organizational success. If we are to increase our understanding of organizational processes, we must develop models of effectiveness that enable us, to the greatest

extent possible, to identify the nature of the relationships between individual processes and organizational behavior. Moreover, a comparison of the relative effectiveness of various departments or divisions is also useful. It is highly likely that certain of these subunits (for example, sales) may be more successful than others within the same organization. The existence of such differences complicates even further any attempts to draw firm conclusions concerning the effectiveness of a given organization.

Even a cursory examination of these problems reveals the magnitude and complexity of the subject. If managers are to reduce their dependence on simplistic criteria for evaluating effectiveness, we must provide them with a framework for analysis that surmounts these problems.

One solution that at least minimizes many of the obstacles to assessing effectiveness is to view effectiveness in terms of a process instead of an end state. Most of the earlier models of effectiveness place a heavy emphasis on identifying the criteria themselves (that is, the end state). Although such criteria may be useful, they tell us little about the ingredients that facilitate effectiveness. Nor do they help the manager better understand how effectiveness results. Hence it appears that we need to re-examine our notions about the concept of organizational effectiveness and about the kinds of analytical models managers require to help them make their own organizations effective.

EFFECTIVE AND INEFFECTIVE ORGANIZATIONS

Perhaps one of the best ways to understand the notion of organizational effectiveness is to examine several instances of *in*effectiveness. Consider the following three examples:

1. *Farm tractors.* There are many examples of organizations that correctly identify the nature of the problem and set relevant goals but then select a less than optimal strategy for attaining those goals.

One such example can be seen in the activities of the first Henry Ford as he tried to maintain the profitability of Ford Motor Company during the depression of the 1930s—when, of course, the demand for new cars had declined. Alfred Chandler reports in his book *Strategy and Structure* that Ford decided to enter the farm tractor market in order to employ some of his unused plant capacity. Within a relatively short period of time, his engineers had designed and built a versatile yet inexpensive tractor. Unfortunately, however, Ford selected an inappropriate marketing and distribution strategy for the new product. He tried to market the tractors through his existing automobile distribution system, which was largely concentrated in major cities and was not attuned to the needs of farms. Hence his product (however good it may have been) never really reached its intended market. The venture failed commercially until Ford realized his mistake and created a supplementary distribution system that reflected market realities and communicated with the farming audience in its own terms.

2. *Slide rules.*   Whereas Example 1 represents an attempt to apply the wrong strategy to the right goal, Example 2 we may describe as an attempt to apply the right strategy to the wrong goal—a goal that became wrong because of a technological advance that created a shift in market demand.

This example involves a company that manufactures slide rules. For many years, the organization had a reputation for producing and selling high-quality slide rules for a variety of applications. With the advent of relatively inexpensive electronic pocket calculators, however, sophisticated computations could be completed quickly and accurately. Almost overnight, demand shifted from slide rules to calculators. Within two years, sales dropped by 75 percent. The company either failed to predict environmental changes accurately or was unable to adapt to them in order to achieve its profit goal.

3. *Regulatory agencies.*   A third type of problem exists when an organization chooses an inappropriate strategy to achieve a suboptimal goal. Typically, we find examples of this type of situation in public bureaucracies (perhaps because of a lack of competitive pressure).

Consider the example of the Interstate Commerce Commission, an agency of the U.S. Government charged with facilitating and regulating commerce between the states. Purportedly, its primary goal is to achieve an effective level of operation in such commerce. In actual practice, however, many complain that its operative (or real) goals are just the opposite. For example, in order to ensure "equity" between the various trucking lines, the ICC for many years required certain firms to drive from point A to point B not directly, but through some out-of-the-way point C. The rationale for such a policy was based inn part on the belief that smaller firms, which often had less efficient routes, needed to be protected from the larger firms, which had more resources at their disposal. As a result, costs increased for both the trucking firms and the customers, and delivery times lengthened for all concerned.

In each of these cases, we have a clear example of ineffectiveness. The nature of the problem in each case, however, is quite different. Moreover, the strategies chosen by the organizations to achieve their stated objectives are also quite different. It is this lack of convergence in most approaches to organizational effectiveness that has led to so much confusion—not only over how organizations achieve effectiveness, but indeed over what we mean by the notion of effectiveness itself.

What Is Organizational Effectiveness?

The term *organizational effectiveness* has been used (and misused) in a variety of contexts. As noted above, some equate the term with profit or productivity, while others view it in terms of job satisfaction. While many analysts view these criteria as definitions of organizational effectiveness, a few investigators suggest that such variables actually constitute intervening variables that enhance the likelihood that effectiveness will result.

If we accept the notion that organizations are unique and pursue divergent goals (as the three examples suggest), then such definitions are too situation-specific and value-laden to be of much use. Instead, it appears more useful initially to follow the lead to Talcott Parsons and Amitai Etzioni and define organizational effectiveness in terms of an organization's ability to acquire and efficiently use available resources to achieve their goals. Viewed from this perspective, all three examples cited previously represent a case of goal failure.

Such a definition requires elaboration. First, we are focusing on operative goals as opposed to official goals. It seems more appropriate to assess the relative level of effectiveness against the real intended objectives of an organization rather than a static list of objectives meant principally for public consumption. For example, we often see public advertisements by corporations claiming that "progress is our most important product" or "the things we do improve the way we live." Such statements (or official goals) often give the impression that the company's primary objective is progress, while in fact other goals (for example, profit, growth, or an acceptable rate of return on investment) probably represent more accurate statements of intent (that is, operative goals). Thus whatever objectives the organization truly intends pursuing, it is against these criteria that effectiveness is best judged. Such an approach has the added advantage of minimizing the influence of the analyst's value judgments in the assessment process. While many would argue, for example, that job satisfaction is a desirable end, it remains for the organization, not an outside analyst, to set such a goal.

Inherent in such a definition, moreover, is the notion that effectiveness is best judged against an organization's ability to compete in a turbulent environment and successfully acquire and use its resources. This suggests that managers must deal effectively with their external environments to secure needed resources. Finally, this approach recognizes the concept of efficiency as a necessary yet insufficient ingredient (or facilitator) of effectiveness.

A Note on Efficiency

People often discuss efficiency and effectiveness as being interchangerationale for such a policy was based in part on the belief that smaller the importance of and interrelation between them. While we define effectiveness as the extent to which operative goals can be attained, we define efficiency as the cost/benefit ratio involved in the pursuit of those goals. An example should clarify this distinction. Shortly after World War II, a ranking German officer observed that the Allies had not "beaten" Germany but had instead "smothered" her. In other words, the officer was suggesting that while the Allies had been effective in the pursuit of their objectives, they had not been particularly efficient.

At some point, however, we would expect that increased inefficiency would have a detrimental effect on subsequent effectiveness. When this notion is applied to a business environment, it appears that the more costly goal effort becomes, the less likely the business is to be effective. As an example of this efficiency-effectiveness relationship, consider some of the current experiments in job redesign, such as the Volvo and Saab-Scania experiments in Sweden. Several prominent investigators have noted recently that, while job enrichment may have desirable social consequences, the costs associated with such efforts may be so high that they increase the price of the product beyond what customers are willing to pay. Hence the notion of efficiency emerges as an important element of organizational effectiveness.

A PROCESS MODEL FOR ANALYZING EFFECTIVENESS

From a static viewpoint, it may be enough to define effectiveness in terms of attaining operative goals. However, if we are to understand more fully the processes involved in bringing about an effective level of operations, it is necessary to take a more dynamic approach to the topic. The approach suggested here is essentially a "process model" of effectiveness. Its aim is to provide managers with a framework for analysis of the major *processes* involved in effectiveness. This approach contrasts sharply with earlier models that merely listed the requisite criteria for assessing organizational success.

The process model that is proposed here consists of three related components: (1) the notion of goal optimization; (2) a systems perspective; and (3) an emphasis on human behavior in organizational settings. I believe that these three components, taken together, provide a useful vehicle for the analysis of effectiveness-related processes in organizations. This multidimensional approach has several advantages over earlier models—in particular, the advantage of increasing the comprehensiveness of analysis aimed at a better understanding of a highly complex topic.

Goal Optimization

If we examine the various approaches currently used to assess organizational effectiveness, it becomes apparent that most ultimately rest on the notion of goal attainment. A primary advantage of using the operative goal concept for assessing levels of effectiveness is that organizational success is evaluated in the light of an organization's behavioral intentions. In view of the fact that different organizations pursue widely divergent goals, it is only logical to recognize this uniqueness in any assessment technique.

While many variations on the goal approach to evaluating effectiveness exist, the most fruitful approach is to view effectiveness in terms of goal *optimization.* Instead of evaluating success in terms of the extent to which "desired" goals have been maximized, we recognize a series of identifiable and irreducible constraints (for example, money, technology, personnel, other goals, and so on) that serve to inhibit goal maximization. Managers are seen as setting and pursuing "optimized" goals (that is, desired goals within the constraints dictated by the resources available). A company may, for example, feel that a 10 percent return on investment is a realistic goal in view of resource availability, the existing market environment, and so forth. We would argue that it is against this *feasible* goal set, not against an ultimate goal set, that effectiveness be judged. (Note: Goal optimization should not be confused with suboptimization, where less than optimal goals are intentionally pursued. Under suboptimized conditions, a company may intentionally set a 5 percent return-on-investment goal even though 10 percent may be feasible, given the situation.)

The goal optimization approach has several advantages over conventional approaches: First, it suggests that goal maximization is probably not possible and that, even if it were, it might be detrimental to an organization's well-being and survival. In most situations, for example, there appears to be little chance for a company to maximize productivity and job satisfaction at the same time. Instead, compromises must be made —compromises that provide for an optimal level of attainment of both objectives. We can observe such compromises in the ICC case mentioned previously; ideally, such a regulatory agency would try to meet the conflicting needs and demands of the trucking firms, the customers, the public at large, and so forth. Thus the use of a goal optimization approach permits the explicit recognition of multiple and often conflicting goals.

Second, goal optimization models recognize the existence of differential weights that managers place on the various goals in the feasible set. For instance, a company may place on the pursuit of its profit goal five times the weight, and resources, that it puts on its affirmative-action employment goal or its job satisfaction goal. While real-life examples would obviously be far more complex, this simple example emphasizes the differential weighting aspect inherent in any assessment of organizational effectiveness.

Third, the model also recognizes the existence of a series of constraints that can impede progress toward goal attainment. Many of these constraints (for example, limited finances, people, technology, and so on) may be impossible to alleviate, at least in the short run. Consider the case of the slide rule manufacturer. The production of slide rules requires a radically different technology than that required by the production of electronic calculators. Thus this firm, which had a competitive advantage using one technology, lost its edge when market demand shifted. Of course, if this company had anticipated environmental changes, accurately and far enough in advance, it might have developed new applications for existing technology—assuming the infeasibility of changing it. The firm might, for instance, have devoted its energies to developing new precision-measurement instruments not based on electronics. Thus it is important to recognize such constraints—and how a company reacts to them—in any final assessment of success or failure.

Fourth, this approach has the added advantage of allowing for increased flexibility of evaluation criteria. As the goals pursued by an organization change, or as the constraints associated with them change, a new optimal solution will emerge that could represent new evaluation criteria. Hence the means of assessment would remain current and would reflect the changing needs and goals of the organization.

Last, from the standpoint of long-range planning, weighted goals and their relevant constraints could be modeled by using computer simulations to derive optimal solutions for purposes of allocating future resources and effort.

The use of computer-simulation models in long-range planning has become commonplace among larger organizations. The same technique could be applied to examining organizational effectiveness. Major organizational and environmental variables could be systematically manipulated to analyze the impact of such changes on resulting facets of effectiveness (for example, profits, market share, adaptation, and productivity). From such manipulations, optimal solutions could be derived that would help managers direct the future of the enterprise.

Systems Perspective

The second important aspect of a process model of organizational effectiveness is the employment of an open-systems perspective for purposes of analysis. Such a perspective emphasizes interrelationships between the various parts of an organization and its environment as they jointly influence effectiveness.

If we take a systems perspective, we can identify the four major categories of influences on effectiveness (see Figure 2): (1) organizational characteristics, such as structure and technology; (2) environmental characteristics, such as economic and market conditions; (3) employee characteristics, such as level of job performance and job attachment; and (4) managerial policies and practices. While the precise manner in which these variables influence effectiveness goes beyond the scope of this

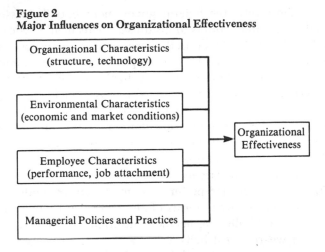

Figure 2
Major Influences on Organizational Effectiveness

article, it is suggested that these four sets of variables must be relatively consonant if effectiveness is to be achieved. The negative outcomes that result when these characteristics do not fit we saw in the example of the Ford tractor. While the product itself was good, the failure to recognize environmental variations and to adapt the marketing structure accordingly led to ineffectiveness.

Thus managers have a responsibility to understand the nature of their environment and to set realistic goals that accommodate and/or exploit that environment. Given these goals, the more effective organizations will tend to be those that successfully adapt structure, technology, work effort, policies, and so on to facilitate goal attainment.

Behavioral Emphasis

A final aspect of the process approach to understanding and analyzing effectiveness is the emphasis on the role of individual behavior as it affects organizational success or failure. The position taken here is in opposition to the stand taken by many that effectiveness is best examined exclusively on a "macro" (or organizationwide) basis. Instead, it appears that greater insight can result if analyses include consideration of how the behavior of individual employees impacts upon organizational goal attainment. If an organization's employees largely agree with the objectives of their employer, we would expect them to exert a relatively high level of effort toward achieving those goals. If, on the other hand, organizational goals largely conflict with employees' personal goals, there is little reason to believe that employees would exert their maximum effort.

As an interesting example of the importance of individuals in goal attainment, consider the controversy over automobile seat belts. In an effort to improve traffic safety, the federal government initially passed a law that required auto manufacturers to install seat belts in all new cars. When this action failed to have the desired consequences (many people simply did not use them), additional laws were passed requiring manufacturers to install warning lights, buzzers, and so forth to remind drivers to use seat belts. Finally, when these measures also proved ineffective, laws were passed requiring manufacturers to install devices that made it mandatory to use seat belts before the ignition could be activated—although even these devices could be circumvented with a degree of ingenuity. While the initial goal was laudatory, the processes (means) used to achieve this goal were largely ineffective because they ignored the predispositions and behavior patterns of most drivers. Perhaps a more effective strategy (certainly in terms of time and cost) would have been simply to pass a law nullifying accident insurance claims for drivers injured while not wearing seat belts.

Hence when we examine organizational effectiveness, it is important to recognize and account for the people who ultimately determine the quality and quantity of an organization's response to environmental demands.

CONCLUSION

Most contemporary organizations exist in turbulent environments in which threats to survival and growth are relatively commonplace. Within such environments, managers must try to secure and properly utilize resources in an effort to attain the operative goals set forth by the organization. The process by which they do so—or fail to do so—is at the heart of the concept of organizational effectiveness.

In the above discussion, I have tried to review the various approaches that have been taken to evaluating organizational effectiveness. Little homogeneity exists between the various approaches. This lack of consensus, in turn, results from the existence of at least eight problems inherent in the existing models. In an effort to overcome many of these problems, I have proposed a process model of organizational effectiveness.

The model described differs from the earlier models. Instead of specifying the criteria for effectiveness (for example, when is an organization effective?), this model focuses on the process of becoming effective (for example, what conditions are most conducive to effectiveness?). It is argued that the actual criteria for evaluation vary depending on the particular operative goals of the organization. Because of this, it appears appropriate to place greater emphasis on understanding the dynamics associated with effectiveness-oriented behavior.

It is further recommended that one way to conceptualize organizational effectiveness *as a process* is to examine three related factors. First, optimized goals (that is, what an organization is capable of attaining) can provide realistic parameters for the assessment process. Given an organization's operative goals, we can ask intelligent questions about the appropriateness of managerial resource-allocation decisions. In other words, is there a better way for managers to expend their limited resources?

Important questions to consider in connection with this first factor include the following:

To what extent are we applying our limited resources toward the attainment of our various goals? In point of fact, organizations often make resource-allocation decisions independent of goal decisions, resulting in "unfunded" goals and "funded" nongoals. This behavior is perhaps most clearly exemplified in the practice by various state and federal legislatures of passing authorization bills and appropriation bills separately. Thus it is possible (and, in fact, it often happens) that a bill (goal) becomes law without the appropriation of resources to implement it.

Is there a clear relationship between the amount of resources we spend on the various goals and the importance of each goal? If, for example, an organization truly believes it places equal weight on making a profit and on improving quality of working life, are such beliefs reflected in the allocation of resources? This does not suggest that equivalent amounts of resources must be spent on each goal. Instead, it implies that sufficient resources be spent to bring about the attainment of both goals.

What kind of return on investment, per goal, are we getting on our resources? If organizations pursue multiple goals, it would seem logical to examine the efficiency of effort invested in each goal. It may be that an organization is highly efficient in realizing its less important goals and relatively inefficient in realizing its more important goals. Where such inefficiencies are noted, decisions must be made concerning the desirability of continuing the pursuit of a goal. Where a goal is viewed as worthwhile (for example, hiring the hard-core unemployed), companies may pursue the goal despite a low return on investment.

Is the entire organization working together for goal attainment? As shown in the Ford tractor example, there are instances in which an organization's existing marketing channels are not suited to newer products —a "bad fit" that leads to suboptimal results. Moreover, a fairly common complaint against research and development departments is that scientists stress basic research projects at the expense of applied projects that generally have more immediate and more certain payoffs.

Is the "fit" between the organization and its environment changing? Organizations should continually raise questions concerning their place in the external environment. We saw in the example of the slide rule manufacturer how a company can lose a major share of its market by failing to adjust to changes in market demand. Under such circumstances, and without the necessary technology to compete with manufacturers of electronic calculators, this firm may find it desirable to establish its niche in the market by specializing in drafting equipment or other instruments not based on electronics. A relatively successful example of such organization-environment fit can be seen in American Motors Corporation (AMC), which for many years has specialized in small cars and jeeps while the "Big Three" stressed medium- and large-sized cars. As the other auto makers shift their focus toward smaller cars, however, AMC (with fewer resources) may find it necessary to adjust its efforts toward newer markets. Hence flexibility in the face of environmental change remains an important area of concern for effective organizations.

Second, it has been stressed throughout our discussion that the use of a systems perspective allows for the explicit recognition of the ways in which various organizational factors blend together to facilitate or inhibit effectiveness-related activities. This approach forces managers to employ more comprehensive analytical models when they ask questions about why the organization achieved or failed to achieve a particular goal. It facilitates a broader perspective both on the nature of the problem and on its possible solutions.

Third, it is highly desirable to recognize the important link between individual behavior and organizationwide performance. That is, any consideration of how organizations become effective (or more effective) must account for the primary determinant of ultimate organizational performance: the employees of the organization. Recent efforts to institute management-by-objectives programs in organizations represent one such attempt to coordinate efforts of various employees toward specific organizational objectives. Taken together, these three related factors should help managers and organizational analysts understand the various ways in which organizations move toward or away from goal attainment and organizational effectiveness.

Two general conclusions (with important implications for managers) emerge from our analysis of organizational effectiveness. First, the concept of organizational effectiveness is best understood in terms of a continuous process rather than an end state. Marshaling resources for goal-directed effort is an unceasing task for most managers. In view of the changing nature of the goals pursued in most organizations, managers have a continuing responsibility to recognize environmental changes, to restructure available resources, to modify technologies, to develop employees, and so forth in order to use the talents at their disposal to attain goals that are themselves in perpetual flux.

Second, our analysis also has emphasized the central role of contingencies in any discussion of effectiveness. Thus it is incumbent upon managers to recognize the unique qualities that define their own organization—its goals, structures, technologies, people, environments, and so on—and to respond in a manner consistent with this uniqueness. Our conclusion cautions against the arbitrary use of "rules" or "principles" for achieving success. Such rules and principles are of little use viewed against the background of organizational diversity. Instead, responsibility must fall to the organization and its management to develop employees so that they can better recognize and understand the nature of a particular situation and respond appropriately. When viewed in this manner, organizational effectiveness becomes largely a function of the extent to which managers and employees can pool their efforts and overcome the obstacles that inhibit goal attainment.

SELECTED BIBLIOGRAPHY

Several interesting pieces exist on the subject of organizational effectiveness. For a review of some early formulations of effectiveness that have greatly influenced our current thinking, the reader is referred to Basil S. Georgopoulos and Arnold S. Tannenbaum's "A Study of Organizational Effectiveness," *American Sociological Review*, vol. 22, pp. 534–540, 1957; Ephraim Yuchtman and Stanley E. Seashore's "A System Resource Approach to Organizational Effectiveness," *American Sociological Review*, vol. 32, pp. 891–903, 1967; and Thomas A. Mahoney and Peter J. Frost's "The Role of Technology in Models of Organizational Effectiveness," *Organizational Behavior and Human Performance*, vol. 11, pp. 127–138, 1974. Also of importance is James Price's *Organizational Effectiveness: An Inventory of Propositions* (Homewood, Ill.: Richard D. Irwin, 1968).

A systematic review and analysis of the major problems encountered in attempts to assess effectiveness can be found in a recent article by the author, "Problems in the Measurement of Organizational Effectiveness," *Administrative Science Quarterly*, vol. 20, pp. 546–558, 1975. A more complete description of the process model of organizational effectiveness, along with a review of the major determinants of effectiveness, is presented in a forthcoming book by the author entitled *Organizational Effectiveness: A Behavioral View* (Goodyear, in press).

Several excellent books on organizations are available that are consistent with the process view of effectiveness. In particular, Alfred D. Chandler's *Strategy and Structure* (Garden City, N.Y.: Anchor, 1964) reviews in detail the growth and adaptation of several major corporations. Chandler's basic hypothesis is that successful organizations structure themselves in accordance with their chosen strategy (goals) for responding to the environment. Paul R. Lawrence and Jay Lorsch's book, *Organization and Environment* (Cambridge, Mass.: Harvard Business School, 1967), takes a similar stand.

For a somewhat more theoretical treatment of a process model, the reader is referred to Daniel Katz and Robert L. Kahn's *The Social Psychology of Organizations* (New York: Wiley, 1966) and Richard Hall's *Organizations: Structure and Process* (Englewood Cliffs, N.J.: Prentice-Hall, Inc., 1972).

Managerial Work:
Analysis from Observation*

HENRY MINTZBERG

W HAT do managers do? Ask this question and you will likely be told
that managers plan, organize coordinate, and control. Since Henri
Fayol [9][1] first proposed these words in 1916, they have dominated
the vocabulary of management. (See, for example, [8], [12], [17].) How
valuable are they in describing managerial work? Consider one morning's work of the president of a large organization:

As he enters his office at 8:23, the manager's secretary motions for
him to pick up the telephone. "Jerry, there was a bad fire in the plant
last night, about $30,000 damage. We should be back in operation by
Wednesday. Thought you should know."

At 8:45 a Mr. Jamison is ushered into the manager's office. They discuss Mr. Jamison's retirement plans and his cottage in New Hampshire.
Then the manager presents a plaque to him commemorating his thirty-
two years with the organization.

Mail processing follows: An innocent-looking letter, signed by a Detroit
lawyer, reads: "A group of us in Detroit has decided not to buy any of
your products because you used that anti-flag, anti-American pinko, Bill
Lindell, upon your Thursday night TV show." The manager dictates a
restrained reply.

The 10:00 meeting is scheduled by a professional staffer. He claims that
his superior, a high-ranking vice-president of the organization, mistreats
his staff, and that if the man is not fired, they will all walk out. As soon as

---

* Reprinted by permission Henry Mintzberg, "Managerial Work: Analysis from
Observation," *Management Science*, October 1971. B 97–B 110.

[1] Numbers refer to References at the end of the article.

the meeting ends, the manager rearranges his schedule to investigate the claim and to react to this crisis.

Which of these activities may be called planning, and which may be called organizing, coordinating, and controlling? Indeed, what do words such as "coordinating" and "planning" mean in the context of real activity? In fact, these four words do not describe the actual work of managers at all; they describe certain vague objectives of managerial work. ". . . they are just ways of indicating what we need to explain." [1, p. 537]

Other approaches to the study of managerial work have developed, one dealing with managerial decision-making and policy-making processes, another with the manager's interpersonal activities. (See, for example, [2] and [10].) And some empirical researchers, using the "diary" method, have studied, what might be called, managerial "media"—by what means, with whom, how long, and where managers spend their time.[2] But in no part of this literature is the actual content of managerial work systematically and meaningfully described.[3] Thus, the question posed at the start—what do managers do?—remains essentially unanswered in the literature of management.

This is indeed an odd situation. We claim to teach management in schools of both business and public administration; we undertake major research programs in management; we find a growing segment of the management science community concerned with the problems of senior management. Most of these people—the planners, information and control theorists, systems analysts, etc.—are attempting to analyze and change working habits that they themselves do not understand. Thus, at a conference called at M.I.T. to assess the impact of the computer on the manager, and attended by a number of America's foremost management scientists, a participant found it necessary to comment after lengthy discussion [20, p. 198]:

> I'd like to return to an earlier point. It seems to me that until we get into the question of what the top manager does or what the functions are that define the top management job, we're not going to get out of the kind of difficulty that keeps cropping up. What I'm really doing is leading up to my earlier question which no one really answered. And that is: Is it possible to arrive at a specification of what constitutes the job of a top manager?

His question was not answered.

---

[2] Carlson [6] carried out the classic study just after World War II. He asked nine Swedish managing directors to record on diary pads details of each activity in which they engaged. His method was used by a group of other researchers, many of them working in the U.K. (See [4], [5], [15], [25].)

[3] One major project, involving numerous publications, took place at Ohio State University and spanned three decades. Some of the vocabulary used followed Fayol. The results have generated little interest in this area. (See, for example, [13].)

RESEARCH STUDY ON MANAGERIAL WORK

In late 1966, I began research on this question, seeking to replace Fayol's words by a set that would more accurately describe what managers do. In essence, I sought to develop by the process of induction a statement of managerial work that would have empirical validity. Using a method called "structured observation," I observed for one-week periods the chief executives of five medium to large organizations (a consulting firm, a school system, a technology firm, a consumer goods manufacturer, and a hospital).

Structured as well as unstructured (i.e., anecdotal) data were collected in three "records." In the *chronology record*, activity patterns throughout the working day were recorded. In the *mail record*, for each of 890 pieces of mail processed during the five weeks, were recorded its purpose, format and sender, the attention it received and the action it elicited. And, recorded in the *contact record*, for each of 368 verbal interactions, were the purpose, the medium (telephone call, scheduled or unscheduled meeting, tour), the participants, the form of initiation, and the location. It should be noted that all categorizing was done during and after observation so as to ensure that the categories reflected only the work under observation. [Mintzberg's study] [19] contains a fuller description of this methodology and a tabulation of the results of the study.

Two sets of conclusions are presented below. The first deals with certain characteristics of managerial work, as they appeared from analysis of the numerical data (e.g., How much time is spent with peers? What is the average duration of meetings? What proportion of contacts are initiated by the manager himself?) The second describes the basic content of managerial work in terms of ten roles. This description derives from an analysis of the data on the recorded *purpose* of each contact and piece of mail.

The liberty is taken of referring to these findings as descriptive of managerial, as opposed to chief executive, work. This is done because many of the findings are supported by studies of other types of managers. Specifically, most of the conclusions on work characteristics are to be found in the combined results of a group of studies of foremen [11], [16], middle managers [4], [5], [15], [25], and chief executives [6]. And although there is little useful material on managerial roles, three studies do provide some evidence of the applicability of the role set. Most important, Sayles' empirical study of production managers [24] suggests that at least five of the ten roles are performed at the lower end of the managerial hierarchy. And some further evidence is provided by comments in Whyte's study of leadership in a street gang [26] and Neustadt's study of three U.S. presidents [21]. (Reference is made to these findings where appropriate.) Thus, although most of the illustrations are drawn from my study of chief executives, there is some justification in asking the reader to consider when he sees the terms "manager" and his "organization" not only "presidents" and their "companies," but also "foremen" and their "shops," "directors" and their "branches," "vice-presidents" and their "divisions." The term *manager* shall be used with reference to all those people in charge of formal organizations or their subunits.

SOME CHARACTERISTICS OF MANAGERIAL WORK

Six sets of characteristics of managerial work derive from analysis of the data of this study. Each has a significant bearing on the manager's ability to administer a complex organization.

Characteristic 1.   The Manager Performs a Great Quantity of Work at an Unrelenting Pace

Despite a semblance of normal working hours, in truth managerial work appears to be very taxing. The five men in this study processed an average of 36 pieces of mail each day, participated in eight meetings (half of which were scheduled), engaged in five telephone calls, and took one tour. In his study of foremen, Guest [11] found that the number of activities per day averaged 583, with no real break in the pace.

Free time appears to be very rare. If by chance a manager has caught up with the mail, satisfied the callers, dealt with all the disturbances, and avoided scheduled meetings, a subordinate will likely show up to usurp the available time. It seems that the manager cannot expect to have much time for leisurely reflection during office hours. During "off" hours, our chief executives spent much time on work-related reading. High-level managers appear to be able to escape neither from an environment which recognizes the power and status of their positions nor from their own minds which have been trained to search continually for new information.

Characteristic 2.   Managerial Activity Is Characterized by Variety, Fragmentation, and Brevity

There seems to be no pattern to managerial activity. Rather, variety and fragmentation appear to be characteristic, as successive activities deal with issues that differ greatly both in type and in content. In effect the manager must be prepared to shift moods quickly and frequently.

A typical chief executive day may begin with a telephone call from a director who asks a favor (a "status request"); then a subordinate calls to tell of a strike at one of the facilities (fast movement of information, termed "instant communication"); this is followed by a relaxed scheduled event at which the manager speaks to a group of visiting dignitaries (ceremony); the manager returns to find a message from a major customer who is demanding the renegotiation of a contract (pressure); and so on. Throughout the day, the managers of our study encountered this great variety of activity. Most surprisingly, the significant activities were interspersed with the trivial in no particular pattern.

Furthermore, these manageral activities were characterized by their brevity. Half of all the activities studied lasted less than 9 minutes and only 10 percent exceeded one hour's duration. Guest's foremen averaged 48 seconds per activity, and Carlson [6] stressed that his chief executives were unable to work without frequent interruption.

In my own study of chief executives, I felt that the managers demonstrated a preference for tasks of short duration and encouraged interruption. Perhaps the manager becomes accustomed to variety, or perhaps the flow of "instant communication" cannot be delayed. A more plausible explanation might be that the manager becomes conditioned by his workload. He develops a sensitive appreciation for the opportunity cost of his own time. Also, he is aware of the ever present assortment of obligations associated with his job—accumulations of mail that cannot be delayed, the callers that must be attended to, the meetings that require his participation. In other words, no matter what he is doing, the manager is plagued by what he must do and what he might do. Thus, the manager is forced to treat issues in an abrupt and superficial way.

Characteristic 3.   Managers Prefer Issues That Are Current, Specific, and Ad Hoc

Ad hoc operating reports received more attention than did routine ones; current, uncertain information—gossip, speculation, hearsay—which flows quickly was preferred to historical, certain information; "instant communication" received first consideration; few contacts were held on a routine or "clocked" basis; almost all contacts concerned well-defined issues. The managerial environment is clearly one of stimulus-response. It breeds, not reflective planners, but adaptable information manipulators who prefer the live, concrete situation, men who demonstrate a marked action-orientation.

Characteristic 4.   The Manager Sits between His Organization and a Network of Contacts

In virtually every empirical study of managerial time allocation, it was reported that managers spent a surprisingly large amount of time in horizontal or lateral (nonline) communication. It is clear from this study and from that of Sayles [24] that the manager is surrounded by a diverse and complex web of contacts which serves as his self-designed external information system. Included in this web can be clients, associates and suppliers, outside staff experts, peers (managers of related or similar organizations), trade organizations, government officials, independents (those with no relevant organizational affiliation), and directors or superiors. (Among these, directors in this study and superiors in other studies did *not* stand out as particularly active individuals.)

The managers in this study received far more information than they emitted, much of it coming from contacts, and more from subordinates who acted as filters. Figuratively, the manager appears as the neck of an hour-glass, sifting information into his own organization from its environment.

Characteristic 5.   The Manager Demonstrates a Strong Preference for the Verbal Media

The manager has five media at his command—mail (documented), telephone (purely verbal), unscheduled meeting (informal face-to-face), scheduled meeting (formal face-to-face), and tour (observational). Along with all the other empirical studies of work characteristics, I found a strong predominance of verbal forms of communication.

Mail.   By all indications, managers dislike the documented form of communication. In this study, they gave cursory attention to such items as operating reports and periodicals. It was estimated that only 13 percent of the input mail was of specific and immediate use to the managers. Much of the rest dealt with formalities and provided general reference data. The managers studied initiated very little mail, only 25 pieces in the five weeks. The rest of the outgoing mail was sent in reaction to mail received—a reply to a request, an acknowledgment, some information forwarded to a part of the organization. The managers appeared to dislike this form of communication, perhaps because the mail is a relatively slow and tedious medium to use.

Telephone and Unscheduled Meetings.   The less formal means of verbal communication—the telephone, a purely verbal form, and the unscheduled meeting, a face-to-face form—were used frequently (two-thirds of the contacts in the study) but for brief encounters (average duration of 6 and 12 minutes, respectively). They were used primarily to deliver requests and to transmit pressing information to those outsiders and subordinates who had informal relationships with the manager.

Scheduled Meetings.   These tended to be of long duration, averaging 68 minutes in this study, and absorbing over half the managers' time. Such meetings provided the managers with their main opportunities to interact with large groups and to leave the confines of their own offices. Scheduled meetings were used when the participants were unfamiliar to the manager (e.g., students who request that he speak at a university), when a large quantity of information had to be transmitted (e.g., presentation of a report), when ceremony had to take place, and when complex strategy-making or negotiation had to be undertaken. An important feature of the scheduled meeting was the incidental, but by no means irrelevant, information that flowed at the start and end of such meetings.

Tours. Although the walking tour would appear to be a powerful tool for gaining information in an informal way, in this study tours accounted for only 3 percent of the managers' time.

In general, it can be concluded that the manager uses each medium for particular purposes. Nevertheless, where possible, he appears to gravitate to verbal media since these provide greater flexibility, require less effort, and bring faster response. It should be noted here that the manager does not leave the telephone or the meeting to get back to work. Rather, communication is his work, and these media are his tools. The operating work of the organization—producing a product, doing research, purchasing a part—appears to be undertaken infrequently by the senior manager. The manager's productive output must be measured in terms of information, a great part of which is transmitted verbally.

Characteristic 6. Despite the Preponderance of Obligations, the Manager Appears to Be Able to Control His Own Affairs

Carlson suggested in his study of Swedish chief executives that these men were puppets, with little control over their own affairs. A cursory examination of our data indicates that this is true. Our managers were responsible for the initiation of only 32 percent of their verbal contacts and a smaller proportion of their mail. Activities were also classified as to the nature of the managers' participation, and the active ones were outnumbered by the passive ones (e.g., making requests vs. receiving requests). On the surface, the manager is indeed a puppet, answering requests in the mail, returning telephone calls, attending meetings initiated by others, yielding to subordinates' requests for time, reacting to crises.

However, such a view is misleading. There is evidence that the senior manager can exert control over his own affairs in two significant ways: (1) It is he who defines many of his own long-term commitments by developing appropriate information channels which later feed him information, by initiating projects which later demand his time, by joining committees or outside boards which provide contacts in return for his services, and so on. (2) The manager can exploit situations that appear as obligations. He can lobby at ceremonial speeches; he can impose his values on his organization when his authorization is requested; he can motivate his subordinates whenever he interacts with them; he can use the crisis situation as an opportunity to innovate.

Perhaps these are two points that help distinguish successful and unsuccessful managers. All managers appear to be puppets. Some decide who will pull the strings and how, and they then take advantage of each move that they are forced to make. Others, unable to exploit this high-tension environment, are swallowed up by this most demanding of jobs.

THE MANAGER'S WORK ROLES

In describing the essential content of managerial work, one should aim to model managerial activity, that is, to describe it as a set of programs. But an undertaking as complex as this must be preceded by the development of a useful typological description of managerial work. In other words, we must first understand the distinct components of managerial work. At the present time we do not.

In this study, 890 pieces of mail and 368 verbal contacts were categorized as to purpose. The incoming mail was found to carry acknowledgements, requests and solicitations of various kinds, reference data, news, analytical reports, reports on events and on operations, advice on various situations, and statements of problems, pressures, and ideas. In reacting to mail, the managers acknowledged some, replied to the requests (e.g., by sending information), and forwarded much to subordinates (usually for their information). Verbal contacts involved a variety of purposes. In 15 percent of them activities were scheduled, in 6 percent ceremonial events took place, and a few involved external board work. About 34 percent involved requests of various kinds, some insignificant, some for information, some for authorization of proposed actions. Another 36 percent essentially involved the flow of information to and from the manager, while the remainder dealt specifically with issues of strategy and with negotiations. (For details, see [19].)

In this study, each piece of mail and verbal contact categorized in this way was subjected to one question: Why did the manager do this? The answers were collected and grouped and regrouped in various ways (over the course of three years) until a typology emerged that was felt to be satisfactory. While an example, presented below, will partially explain this process to the reader, it must be remembered that (in the words of Bronowski [3, p. 62]): "Every induction is a speculation and it guesses at a unity which the facts present but do not strictly imply."

Consider the following sequence of two episodes: A chief executive attends a meeting of an external board on which he sits. Upon his return to his organization, he immediately goes to the office of a subordinate, tells of a conversation he had with a fellow board member, and concludes with the statement: "It looks like we shall get the contract."

The purposes of these two contacts are clear—to attend an external board meeting, and to give current information (instant communication) to a subordinate. But why did the manager attend the meeting? Indeed, why does he belong to the board? And why did he give this particular information to his subordinate?

Basing analysis on this incident, one can argue as follows: The manager belongs to the board in part so that he can be exposed to special information which is of use to his organization. The subordinate needs the information but has not the status which would give him access to it. The chief executive does. Board memberships bring chief executives in contact with one another for the purpose of trading information.

Two aspects of managerial work emerge from this brief analysis. The manager serves in a "liaison" capacity because of the status of his office, and what he learns here enables him to act as "disseminator" of information into his organization. We refer to these as *roles*—organized sets of behaviors belonging to identifiable offices or positions [23]. Ten roles were chosen to capture all the activities observed during his study.

All activities were found to involve one or more of three basic behaviors —interpersonal contact, the processing of information, and the making of decisions. As a result, our ten roles are divided into three corresponding groups. Three roles—labelled *figurehead, liaison,* and *leader*—deal with behavior that is essentially interpersonal in nature. Three others—*nerve center, disseminator,* and *spokesman*—deal with information-processing activities performed by the manager. And the remaining four—*entrepreneur, disturbance handler, resource allocator,* and *negotiator*—cover the decision-making activities of the manager. We describe each of these roles in turn, asking the reader to note that they form a *gestalt,* a unified whole whose parts cannot be considered in isolation.

The Interpersonal Roles

Three roles relate to the manager's behavior that focuses on interpersonal contact. These roles dervie directly from the authority and status associated with holding managerial office.

Figurehead. As legal authority in his organization, the manager is a symbol, obliged to perform a number of duties. He must preside at ceremonial events, sign legal documents, receive visitors, make himself available to many of those who feel, in the words of one of the men studied, "that the only way to get something done is to get to the top." There is evidence that this role applies at other levels as well. Davis [7, pp. 43–44] cites the case of the field sales manager who must deal with those customers who believe that their accounts deserve his attention.

Leader. Leadership is the most widely recognized of managerial roles. It describes the manager's relationship with his subordinates—his attempts to motivate them and his development of the milieu in which they work. Leadership actions pervade all activity—in contrast to most roles, it is possible to designate only a few activities as dealing exclusively with leadership (these mostly related to staffing duties). Each time a manager encourages a subordinate, or meddles in his affairs, or replies to one of his requests, he is playing the *leader* role. Subordinates seek out and react to the leadership clues, and, as a result, they impart significant power to the manager.

Liaison.   As noted earlier, the empirical studies have emphasized the importance of lateral or horizontal communication in the work of managers at all levels. It is clear from our study that this is explained largely in terms of the *liaison* role. The manager establishes his network of contacts essentially to bring information and favors to his organization. As Sayles notes in his study of production supervisors [24, p. 258], "The one enduring objective [of the manager] is the effort to build and maintain a predictable, reciprocating system of relationships. . . ."

Making use of his status, the manager interacts with a variety of peers and other people outside his organization. He provides time, information, and favors in return for the same from others. Foremen deal with staff groups and other foremen; chief executives join boards of directors, and maintain extensive networks of individual relationships. Neustadt notes this behavior in analyzing the work of President Roosevelt [21, p. 150]:

> His personal sources were the product of a sociability and curiosity that reached back to the other Roosevelt's time. He had an enormous acquaintance in various phases of national life and at various levels of government; he also had his wife and her variety of contacts. He extended his acquaintanceships abroad; in the war years Winston Churchill, among others, become a "personal source." Roosevelt quite deliberately exploited these relationships and mixed them up to widen his own range of information. He changed his sources as his interests changed, but no one who had ever interested him was quite forgotten or immune to sudden use.

The Informational Roles

A second set of managerial activities relates primarily to the processing of information. Together they suggest three significant managerial roles, one describing the manager as a focal point for a certain kind of organizational information, the other two describing relatively simple transmission of this information.

Nerve Center.   There is indication, both from this study and from those by Neustadt and Whyte, that the manager serves as the focal point in his organization for the movement of nonroutine information. Homans, who analyzed Whyte's study, draws the following conclusions [14, p. 187]:

> Since interaction flowed toward [the leaders], they were better informed about the problems and desires of group members than were any of the followers and therefore better able to decide on an appropriate course of action. Since they were in close touch with other gang leaders, they were also better informed than their followers about conditions in Cornerville at large. Moreover, in their positions at the focus of the chains of interaction, they were better able than any follower to pass on to the group decisions that had been reached.

The term *nerve center* is chosen to encompass those many activities in which the manager receives information.

Within his own organization, the manager has legal authority that formally connects him—and only him— to *every* member. Hence, the manager emerges as *nerve center* of internal information. He may not know as much about any one function as the subordinate who specializes in it, but he comes to know more about his total organization than any other member. He is the information generalist. Furthermore, because of the manager's status and its manifestation in the *liaison* role, the manager gains unique access to a variety of knowledgeable outsiders including peers who are themselves *nerve centers* of their own organizations. Hence, the manager emerges as his organization's *nerve center* of external information as well.

As noted earlier, the manager's nerve center information is of a special kind. He appears to find it most important to get his information quickly and informally. As a result, he will not hesitate to bypass formal information channels to get it, and he is prepared to deal with a large amount of gossip, hearsay, and opinion which has not yet become substantial fact.

Disseminator.   Much of the manager's information must be transmitted to subordinates. Some of this is of a *factual* nature, received from outside the organization or from other subordinates. And some is of a *value* nature. Here, the manager acts as the mechanism by which organizational influencers (owners, governments, employee groups, the general public, etc., or simply the "boss") makes their preferences known to the organization. It is the manager's duty to integrate these value positions, and to express general organizational preferences as a guide to decisions made by subordinates. One of the men studied commented: "One of the principal functions of this position is to integrate the hospital interests with the public interests." Papandreou describes his duty in a paper published in 1952, referring to management as the "peak coordinator" [22].

Spokesman.   In his *spokesman* role, the manager is obliged to transmit his information to outsiders. He informs influencers and other interested parties about his organization's performance, its policies, and its plans. Furthermore, he is expected to serve outside his organization as an expert in its industry. Hospital administrators are expected to spend some time serving outside as public experts on health, and corporation presidents, perhaps as chamber of commerce executives.

The Decisional Roles

The manager's legal authority requires that he assume responsibility for all of his organization's important actions. The *nerve center* role suggests that only he can fully understand complex decisions, particularly those involving difficult value tradeoffs. As a result, the manager emerges as the key figure in the making and interrelating of all significant decisions in his organization, a process that can be referred to as *strategy-making*. Four roles describe the manager's control over the strategy-making system in his organization.

Entrepreneur. The *entrepreneur* role describes the manager as initiator and designer of much of the controlled change in his organization. The manager looks for opportunities and potential problems which may cause him to initiate action. Action takes the form of *improvement projects* —the marketing of a new product, the strengthening of a weak department, the purchasing of new equipment, the reorganization of formal structure, and so on.

The manager can involve himself in each improvement project in one of three ways: (1) He may *delegate* all responsibility for its design and approval, implicitly retaining the right to replace that subordinate who takes charge of it. (2) He may delegate the design work to a subordinate, but retain the right to *approve* it before implementation. (3) He may actively *supervise* the design work himself.

Improvement projects exhibit a number of interesting characteristics. They appear to involve a number of subdecisions, consciously sequenced over long periods of time and separated by delays of various kinds. Furthermore, the manager appears to supervise a great many of these at any one time—perhaps 50 to 100 in the case of chief executives. In fact, in his handling of improvement projects, the manager may be likened to a juggler. At any one point, he maintains a number of balls in the air. Periodically, one comes down, receives a short burst of energy, and goes up again. Meanwhile, an inventory of new balls waits on the sidelines and, at random intervals, old balls are discarded and new ones added. Both Lindblom [2] and Marples [18] touch on these aspects of strategy-making, the former stressing the disjointed and incremental nature of the decisions, and the latter depicting the sequential episodes in terms of a stranded rope made up of fibres of different lengths each of which surfaces periodically.

Disturbance Handler. While the *entrepreneur* role focuses on voluntary change, the *disturbance handler* role deals with corrections which the manager is forced to make. We may describe this role as follows: The organization consists basically of specialist operating programs. From time to time, it experiences a stimulus that cannot be handled routinely, either because an operating program has broken down or because the stimulus is new and it is not clear which operating program should handle it. These situations constitute disturbances. As generalist, the manager is obliged to assume responsibility for dealing with the stimulus. Thus, the handling of disturbances is an essential duty of the manager.

There is clear evidence for this role both in our study of chief executives and in Sayles study of production supervisors [24, p. 162]:

The achievement of this stability, which is the manager's objective, is a never-to-be-attained ideal. He is like a symphony orchestra conductor, endeavoring to maintain a melodious performance in which contributions of the various instruments are coordinated and sequenced, patterned and paced, while the orchestra members are having various personal difficulties, stage hands are moving music stands, alternating excessive heat and cold are creating audience and instrument problems, and the sponsor of the concert is insisting on irrational changes in the program.

Sayles goes further to point out the very important balance that the manager must maintain between change and stability. To Sayles, the manager seeks "a dynamic type of stability" (p. 162). Most disturbances elicit short-term adjustments which bring back equilibrium; persistent ones require the introduction of long-term structural change.

Resource Allocator. The manager maintains ultimate authority over his organization's strategy-making system by controlling the allocation of its resources. By deciding who will get what (and who will do what), the manager directs the course of his organization. He does this in three ways:

1. *In selecting his own time,* the manager allocates his most precious resource and thereby determines organizational priorities. Issues that receive low priority do not reach the *nerve center* of the organization and are blocked for want of resources.

2. In designing the organizational structure and in carrying out many improvement projects, the manager *programs the work of his subordinates.* In other words, he allocates their time by deciding what will be done and who will do it.

3. Most significantly, the manager maintains control over resource allocation by the requirement that he *authorize all significant decisions* before they are implemented. By retaining this power, the manager ensures that different decisions are interrelated—that conflicts are avoided, that resource constraints are respected, and that decisions complement one another.

Decisions appear to be authorized in one of two ways. Where the costs and benefits of a proposal can be quantified, where it is competing for specified resources with other known proposals, and where it can wait for a certain time of year, approval for a proposal is sought in the context of a formal *budgeting* procedure. But these conditions are most often not met—timing may be crucial, nonmonetary costs may predominate, and so on. In these cases, approval is sought in terms of an *ad hoc request for authorization.* Subordinate and manager meet (perhaps informally) to discuss one proposal alone.

Authorization choices are enormously complex ones for the manager. A myriad of factors must be considered (resource constraints, influencer preferences, consistency with other decisions, feasibility, payoff, timing, subordinate feelings, etc.). But the fact that the manager is authorizing the decision rather than supervising its design suggests that he has little time to give to it. To alleviate this difficulty, it appears that managers use special kinds of *models* and *plans* in their decision-making. These exist only in their minds and are loose, but they serve to guide behavior. Models may answer questions such as, "Does this proposal make sense in terms of the trends that I see in tariff legislation?" or "Will the EDP department be able to get along with marketing on this?" Plans exist in the sense that, on questioning, managers reveal images (in terms of proposed improvement projects) of where they would like their organizations to go: "Well, once I get these foreign operations fully developed, I would like to begin to look into a reorganization," said one subject of this study.

Negotiator. The final role describes the manager as participant in negotiation activity. To some students of the management process [8, p. 343], this is not truly part of the job of managing. But such distinctions are arbitrary. Negotiation is an integral part of managerial work, as this study notes for chief executives and as that of Sayles made very clear for production supervisors [24, p. 131]: "Sophisticated managers place great stress on negotiations as a way of life. They negotiate with groups who are setting standards for their work, who are performing support activity for them, and to whom they wish to 'sell' their services."

The manager must participate in important negotiation sessions because he is his organization's legal authority, its *spokesman* and its *resource allocator*. Negotiation is resource trading in real time. If the resource commitments are to be large, the legal authority must be present.

These ten roles suggest that the manager of an organization bears a great burden of responsibility. He must oversee his organization's status system; he must serve as a crucial informational link between it and its environment; he must interpret and reflect its basic values; he must maintain the stability of its operations; and he must adapt it in a controlled and balanced way to a changing environment.

MANAGEMENT AS A PROFESSION AND AS A SCIENCE

Is management a profession? To the extent that different managers perform one set of basic roles, management satisfies one criterion for becoming a profession. But a profession must require, in the words of the *Random House Dictionary*, "knowledge of some department of learning or science." Which of the ten roles now requires specialized learning? Indeed, what school of business or public administration teaches its students how to disseminate information, allocate resources, perform as figurehead, make contacts, or handle disturbances? We simply know very little about teaching these things. The reason is that we have never tried to document and describe in a meaningful way the procedures (or programs) that managers use.

The evidence of this research suggests that there is as yet no science in managerial work—that managers do not work according to procedures that have been prescribed by scientific analysis. Indeed, except for his use of the telephone, the airplane, and the dictating machine, it would appear that the manager of today is indistinguishable from his predecessors. He may seek different information, but he gets much of it in the same way— from word-of-mouth. He may make decisions dealing with modern technology but he uses the same intuitive (that is, nonexplicit) procedures in making them. Even the computer, which has had such a great impact on other kinds of organizational work, has apparently done little to alter the working methods of the general manager.

How do we develop a scientific base to understand the work of the manager? The description of roles is a first and necessary step. But tighter forms of research are necessary. Specifically, we must attempt to model managerial work—to describe it as a system of programs. First, it will be necessary to decide what programs managers actually use. Among a great number of programs in the manager's repertoire, we might expect to find a time-scheduling program, an information-disseminating program, and a disturbance-handling program. Then, researchers will have to devote a considerable amount of effort to studying and accurately describing the content of each of these programs—the information and heuristics used. Finally, it will be necessary to describe the interrelationships among all of these programs so that they may be combined into an integrated descriptive model of managerial work.

When the management scientist begins to understand the programs that managers use, he can begin to design meaningful systems and provide help for the manager. He may ask: Which managerial activities can be fully reprogrammed (i.e., automated)? Which cannot be reprogrammed because they require human responses? Which can be partially reprogrammed to operate in a man-machine system? Perhaps scheduling, information collecting, and resource-allocating activities lead themselves to varying degrees of reprogramming. Management will emerge as a science to the extent that such efforts are successful.

IMPROVING THE MANAGER'S EFFECTIVENESS

Fayol's 50-year-old description of managerial work is no longer of use to us. And we shall not disentangle the complexity of managerial work if we insist on viewing the manager simply as a decision-maker or simply as a motivator of subordinates. In fact, we are unlikely to overestimate the complexity of the manager's work, and we shall make little headway if we take over simple or narrow points of view in our research.

A major problem faces today's manager. Despite the growing size of modern organizations and the growing complexity of their problems (particularly those in the public sector), the manager can expect little help. He must design his own information system, and he must take full charge of his organization's strategy-making system. Furthermore, the manager faces what might be called the *dilemma of delegation*. He has unique access to much important information but he lacks a formal means of disseminating it. As much of it is verbal, he cannot spread it around in an efficient manner. How can he delegate a task with confidence when he has neither the time nor the means to send the necessary information along with it?

Thus, the manager is usually forced to carry a great burden of responsibility in his organization. As organizations become increasingly large and complex, this burden increases. Unfortunately, the man cannot significantly increase his available time or significantly improve his abilities to manage. Hence, in the large, complex bureaucracy, the top manager's time assumes an enormous opportunity cost and he faces the real danger of becoming a major obstruction in the flow of decisions and information.

Because of this, as we have seen, managerial work assumes a number of distinctive characteristics. The quantity of work is great; the pace is unrelenting; there is great variety, fragmentation, and brevity in the work activities; the manager must concentrate on issues that are current, specific, and ad hoc, and to do so, he finds that he must rely on verbal forms of communications. Yet it is on this man that the burden lies for designing and operating strategy-making and information-processing systems that are to solve his organization's (and society's) problems.

The manager can do something to alleviate these problems. He can learn more about his own roles in his organization, and he can use this information to schedule his time in a more efficient manner. He can recognize that only he has much of the information needed by his organization. Then, he can seek to find better means of disseminating it into the organization. Finally, he can turn to the skills of his management scientists to help reduce his workload and to improve his ability to make decisions.

The management scientist can learn to help the manager to the extent he can develop an understanding of the manager's work and the manager's information. To date, strategic planners, operations researchers, and information system designers have provided little help for the senior manager. They simply have had no framework available by which to understand the work of the men who employed them, and they have had poor access to the information which has never been documented. It is folly to believe that a man with poor access to the organization's true *nerve center* can design a formal management information system. Similarly, how can the long-range planner, a man usually uninformed about many of the *current* events that take place in and around his organization, design meaningful strategic plans? For good reason, the literature documents many manager complaints of naïve planning and many planner complaints of disinterested managers. In my view, our lack of understanding of managerial work has been the greatest block to the progress of management science.

The ultimate solution to the problem—to the overburdened manager seeking meaningful help—must derive from research. We must observe, describe, and understand the real work of managing; then and only then shall we significantly improve it.

REFERENCES

1. Braybrooke, David. "The Mystery of Executive Success Re-examined," *Administrative Science Quarterly,* vol. 8 (1964), pp. 533–60.

2. Braybrooke, David, and Lindblom, Charles E. *A Strategy of Decision.* New York: Free Press, 1963.

3. Bronowski, J. "The Creative Process," *Scientific American,* vol. 199 (September 1958), pp. 59–65.

4. Burns, Tom. "The Directions of Activity and Communications in a Departmental Executive Group," *Human Relations,* vol. 7 (1954), pp. 73–97.

5. Burns, Tom. "Management in Action," *Operational Research Quarterly,* vol. 8 (1957), pp. 45–60.

6. Carlson, Sune. *Executive Behavior.* Stockholm: Strömbergs, 1951.

7. Davis, Robert T. *Performance and Development of Field Sales Managers.* Boston: Division of Research, Graduate School of Business Administration, Harvard University, 1957.

8. Drucker, Peter F. *The Practice of Management.* New York: Harper and Row, 1954.

9. Fayol, Henri. *Administration industrielle et générale.* Paris: Dunods, 1950 (first published 1916).

10. Gibb, Cecil A. "Leadership," Chapter 31 in Gardner Lindzey and Elliott A. Aronson, eds. *The Handbook of Social Psychology.* 2d ed. Reading, Mass.: Addison-Wesley, 1969, vol. 4.

11. Guest, Robert H. "Of Time and the Foreman," *Personnel,* vol. 32 (1955–56), pp. 478–86.

12. Gulick, Luther H. "Notes on the Theory of Organization," in Luther Gulick and Lyndall Urwick, eds. *Papers on the Science of Administration.* New York: Columbia University Press, 1937.

13. Hemphill, John K. *Dimensions of Executive Positions.* Columbus, Ohio: Bureau of Business Research Monograph on Number 98, The Ohio State University, 1960.

14. Homans, George C. *The Human Group.* New York: Harcourt, Brace, 1950.

15. Horne, J. H., and Lupton, Tom. "The Work Activities of Middle Man-

agers—An Exploratory Study," *The Journal of Management Studies,* vol. 2 (February 1965), pp. 14–33.

16. Kelly, Joe. "The Study of Executive Behavior by Activity Sampling," *Human Relations,* vol. 17 (August 1964), pp. 277–87.

17. Mackenzie, R. Alex. "The Management Process in 3D" *Harvard Business Review,* November–December 1969, pp. 80–87.

18. Marples, D. L. "Studies of Managers—A Fresh Start?" *The Journal of Management Studies,* vol. 4 (October 1967), pp. 282–99.

19. Mintzberg, Henry. "Structured Observation as a Method to Study Managerial Work," *The Journal of Management Studies,* vol. 7 (February 1970), pp. 87–104.

20. Myers, Charles A., ed. *The Impact of Computers on Management.* Cambridge, Mass.: The M.I.T. Press, 1967.

21. Neustadt, Richard E. *Presidential Power: The Politics of Leadership.* New York: The New American Library, 1964.

22. Papandreou, Andreas G. "Some Basic Problems in the Theory of the Firm," in Bernard F. Haley, ed., *A Survey of Contemporary Economics,* Vol. II, Homewood, Ill.: Irwin, 1952, pp. 183–219.

23. Sarbin, T. R. and Allen, V. L. "Role Theory," in Gardner Lindzey and Elliott A. Aronson, eds., *The Handbook of Social Psychology,* Vol. I, 2d ed. Reading, Mass.: Addison-Wesley, 1968, pp. 488–567.

24. Sayles, Leonard R. *Managerial Behavior: Administration in Complex Enterprises.* New York: McGraw-Hill, 1964.

25. Stewart, Rosemary. *Managers and Their Jobs,* London: Macmillan, 1967.

26. Whyte, William F. *Street Corner Society.* 2d ed. Chicago: University of Chicago Press, 1955.

4

Work with Dignity*

FRANKLIN WALLICK

Humanization of work means many things to many people. To some it means giving workers a variety of jobs to do to break dull routine. To others, humanization means job enlargement, increased responsibility, no more time-clocks, an opportunity to air and settle grievances, a living wage, a battery of fringe benefits, and a workplace environment free of noise, dust, bad ventilation, and other health hazards.

Boredom on the job has become a media catch-phrase, and there are numerous worldwide experiments being made to find ways to make workers happier on the job. We are told that a generation of younger workers is in revolt against the traditional work ethic, a claim dramatized by the Lordstown strike of a few years ago when young, longhaired workers spat out their resentment against the drudgery of the faceless assembly line. A strike lasting 170 days at Norwood, Ohio, which involved less articulate, less flamboyant middle-aged workers occurred over the same issues which erupted at Lordstown; but this wasn't considered hot news, and few newspaper and television reporters paid much attention.

There are other symptoms indicating that all is not well in American industry or commerce. Absenteeism rates are high. Labor turnover confounds bosses. Drug addiction is common. There are even rumblings of trouble in Japan, where workers cheerfully sing the company song at the beginning of each workday.

Some excellent experiments in work enlargement and enrichment are occurring in Norway, Sweden, Yugoslavia, and right here in the United States. But how much of this is somebody's hobbyhorse and how much is for real? Many union officials are profoundly skeptical of the whole hu-

---

* This article first appeared in *The Humanist*, September–October 1973, pp. 16–18, and is reprinted by permission.

manization trend. To some, it seems to be a way to get more out of the workers without paying them more. Some experiments are conducted in non-unionized settings, often in an effort to prevent unionization. Naturally this alienates union people even more from the so-called humanizers.

Are we talking about a significantly youthful revolt? Is it a generational problem? Considerable research suggests that today's younger workers are less authoritarian, more acute in their perceptions, and less willing to take the conventional wear and tear of work than those in the past. My own union's president, Leonard Woodcock, thinks that the symptoms we see are more a result of a worldwide malaise than any unique characteristic of young workers. Certainly the Norwood strike bears this out.

One indication that a serious problem exists has been pointed out by Douglas Fraser, a UAW vice president and the union's chief negotiator with the Chrysler Corporation. Fraser reports that in a recent year Chrysler was forced to hire 44,000 workers in order to maintain a workforce of 100,000. This large turnover cut across age groups, reflecting a deep malady which begs for a cure. For this reason, auto management is as eager to find answers as are the workers and the union.

Malcolm Denise, a Ford Motor Company vice president, has been very candid in discussing the discontent problem with some of his fellow Ford executives. In 1969, Denise observed:

> Our new workforce has had a costly and unsettling impact on our operations. More money, time, and effort than ever before must now be expended in recruiting and acclimating hourly employees: quality-control programs have been put to severe tests; large numbers of employees remain unmoved by all attempts to motivate them; and order in the plants is maintained with rising difficulty.

At a recent seminar, an official of a large corporation said: "The enemy is Frederick Taylor." I found that statement fascinating because Frederick Taylor for many years was the epitome of efficient management—time study and the whole efficiency craze—which finally drove our union and many others into the training of time-study stewards so that we would be able to fight back. Mr. Taylor's method was to break one job into tiny pieces, and then assign workers and machines so that a single worker would do a single piece. This same management official, who deemed Taylor the enemy, told how his company had been plagued with faulty production, worker chaos, and heavy turnover because they would assign more than 20 people to work on one local telephone directory for some small towns in Indiana. Under his direction, the entire setup was changed. A single person was assigned to do the whole directory, and it became "his" or "her" directory. Mistakes were minimized, job satisfaction soared, and turnover declined. This was a white collar operation substantiating my original thesis that we are talking not only about the "blue collar blues" on the traditional assembly line but about work in any place with any kind of collar, blue or white.

Some of the experimental projects used as showcases in the U.S. are clearly designed to keep unions out. They are not overtly anti-union, but management thinks that a neat little dash of work-humanization will forestall any bid for unionization. Although we can learn from these experiments, healthy labor-management relations cannot develop in enterprises without unions or where unions are subverted.

Too many in management still think that unionization of their business represents some failure on their part. I would argue quite to the contrary: only through a trade-union relationship can a company establish the kind of non-manipulative and democratic work to its workers that is both civilized and equitable. The most enlightened management will provide less than a full voice for workers unless it has the benefit of a union relationship.

That brings me to the general trade-union attitude toward what we call "humanization of work." If you were to take a poll today, you would find most union officials turning thumbs down on humanization of work as a prime bargaining issue. A number of articles in the labor press poke fun at the boredom syndrome which so fascinates contemporary thinkers. I don't happen to agree with them, but that's the way they look at it.

Merely redesigning jobs, without raising incomes or improving the quality of the work environment, would be resisted vigorously by the unions. "Nobody is approaching me," said Doug Fraser, "and asking to humanize my job. But they are trying to clean up and make safer the places where people work. And, in the auto industry, they are asking for a pension they can live on after 30 years of service."

Today, more than 60 percent of American working families have incomes less than the Department of Labor's standard for an intermediate family budget. Therefore, income is, and will remain, a prime goal for most unions.

Working people have a canny knack for knowing what is possible; and, if there is skepticism today by workers and their leaders, it may simply be that no worker wants to take a leap which may not improve the current situation. The fact is, however, that many of the humanization experiments, in little fragmentary ways, are yielding valuable insights into better ways of organizing work.

Possibly because no one has found a magic formula for taking boredom out of work, "30 years and out," elimination of compulsory overtime, and health and safety on the job are the big issues in our industry. *These* are the issues raised again and again at special conventions by both skilled and unskilled workers in recent years. This does not mean that we should turn our backs to the boredom issue. Far from it. We are merely saying, if I read worker sentiment correctly, that we must keep our eyes on new job design experimentation. We insist that the union become a full partner in anything that management proposes, and we won't settle for less than the best. What irks us in the UAW is the unilateral method of imposing new techniques upon workers. This can be a sinister manipulation in the absence of union consultation and planning.

"Historically," writes Irving Bluestone, "the slogan has been to let management manage, and the workers will react to what they don't like. Yet, at some point, workers will want to and should participate in broader areas of decision-making (product, product design, etc.), and not merely some of the tinkering which the job-enlargement people are talking about these days." Any union or management which moves in the direction which Mr. Bluestone suggests is not reshuffling jobs to make people happier in superficial ways. It is, instead, fundamentally changing its direction toward democracy at the workplace. Some management people who delve into these arcane matters of humanization think this way, too, but it often comes out differently in print and in practice.

Humanization of work is not a fit subject for crisis bargaining. Management has as much of a stake in getting some answers as does the union and the workers. If Chrysler has to hire 44,000 workers in a single year to maintain a workforce of 100,000, then something is drastically wrong at Chrysler; and both the company and the workers have an equal stake in discovering what it is. We do not want to raise false hopes. We do not believe we can usher in an industrial utopia overnight. Nevertheless, we are going to keep the pressure on for something better, and we are keeping close watch on everything industry is doing. They often do more than meets the eye!

My own special concern is occupational health. I worked as a UAW lobbyist in Washington to help enact the Occupational Safety and Health Act of 1970. In the 10 years I have lived in Washington and worked for the UAW, there has been no other single legislative accomplishment which has more potential for good among working people and nothing of which I am prouder. The implementation of this Act leaves much to be desired; but this law, even with an unsympathetic administration, has done a great deal to lower noise levels, clean up workplace air, and monitor hazardous substances. Still, the federal government estimates that 400 American workers die every day from health hazards on the job. Assuming a 2,000 hour work-year, this is 50 deaths an hour. Such an insidious threat to life and limb represents a great challenge to the industrialized world.

A number of landmark workmen's compensation cases have been settled recently, such as over $1 million for lung damage to 32 workers in Wisconsin and a large payment for lung damage to a coke-oven worker in Pennsylvania. We have black-lung compensation in federal law, and a new move is underway to pay workers' compensation for any lung disease acquired on the job. One expert estimates that over $2 billion in compensation could be paid under present state law for occupational loss of hearing if workers knew their rights and sought to use them.

The disease and carnage of the workplace presents a great challenge to labor, management, government, and the world of science. The UAW has led a number of health and safety strikes. In a lead-batter plant in Delaware, one of our unions called a strike in order to improve health standards for protecting workers from the ravages of lead poisoning. There are close to a million workers exposed to dangerous levels of lead in the U.S. and the strike in Delaware is a harbinger of more to come.

I am dwelling on my pet subject, occupational health, because I am bothered by the great attention that academic circles and the public press give to humanization of work, while it is difficult to arouse scholarly and media concern over the safety and health hazards which are a daily problem for millions of the people I represent. It is easier to worry about boredom and forget noise, to write about monotony and ignore dusts, to fret about dull jobs and not mention fumes on the job. I submit that all of these ought to be the concerns of academics and the media, as well as labor and management. Certainly the credibility of those who worry about humanizing work would be stronger if they pushed for occupational safety and health with the same vigor with which they now espouse the cause of job enrichment.

Working people are demanding more pay, but they are also demanding better working conditions; our technological capability for attaining a fail-safe, pollution-free workplace environment is at hand.

In 1971, an Upjohn Institute survey showed some interesting findings when a cluster of questions were put to company presidents, union stewards, and both blue- and white-collar workers. Blue-collar workers (who were questioned in personal interviews, while the others were questioned by mail) all said that "good health and safety practices" ranked as their number-one priority; "opportunity for the individual worker to achieve and grow on the job" and "contingency protections like workmen's compensation" came next; "adequate income" ranked last.

It can be argued that these were well-paid workers and that they therefore didn't see money as a big goal and, further, that it is only one man's survey. I think, quite to the contrary, that non-economic problems loom big in workers' lives, and it behooves labor bureaucrats like myself to listen and do something.

The world does not stand still, and the world of working people is not an endless quest for more money. The environmental movement has made all of us, in office buildings, in our homes, and in factories, sniff the air with greater vigilance. It is not uncommon today for union stewards to carry noise meters to work in order to measure the level of noise pollution on their jobs. Millions of workers are simply no longer fatalistic about the grubbiness of work. There *is* a danger, I fear, that the humanization craze can become merely cosmetic and, thus, hide low pay and health hazards on the job.

What we need is a wholesale attack on all working-class problems: the quality of neighborhoods and schools (workers are often trapped in ugly urban situations from which upper-middle-class families can escape by moving to the suburbs); extra-heavy tax burdens (a working husband and wife pay more than their fair share of Social Security taxes, and the federal tax structure is not fair to workers); better outdoor transportation (getting to and from work is often a major problem for working people); outdoor recreational opportunities (workers have more leisure time, but there are increasingly fewer places in which to spend that time); better air and water (worker homes are often downwind from the city's worst polluters).

The American worker has been catered to, put down, caricatured, and even worshipped. Both political parties pay lip service to the hardworking American. Humanization of work, using insights gained from the dozens of experiments occurring here as well as overseas can be part of a new strategy to honor hard work, to give it dignity, and to enrich the lives of working Americans with more than a new round of superficial panaceas.

PART II

BEHAVIOR WITHIN ORGANIZATIONS: INDIVIDUALS, GROUP, MANAGERIAL

ATTEMPTS are continually being made by psychologists, social psychologists, sociologists, and anthropologists to understand human behavior. Administrators and entrepreneurs want to know what caused a person to behave in a particular way. Theory and research have provided managers with some general knowledge about behavior that can be used in real-world situations.

It is generally agreed that behavior is the product of two things: the nature of the individual who behaves and the nature of the situation in which individuals find themselves. The nature of an individual depends on heredity, group affiliations, culture, and the situations that a person has faced throughout life. These different background factors cause differences in perceptions, attitudes, motivations, and personalities.

The psychologist advances the premise that there is a casual sequence of behavior that a manager should understand. This sequence is briefly presented in Figure 1.

The double-headed arrows in Figure 1 indicate that the individual interacts with the environment and interprets the various stimuli. Thus, in order to explain behavior, one must be concerned with the stimuli as well as the individual.

Figure 1
Psychological View of a Causal Sequence of Behavior

Stimulus ⟷	Individual ⟶	Behavioral ⟶ Pattern	Goal Achievement
a. Action of managers or informal leaders	a. Heredity	a. Talking	a. Productivity
b. Climate of the unit	b. Cultural background	b. Expressions	b. Absenteeism
c. Group pressures	c. Situation	c. Thinking	c. Quitting
d. Working conditions	d. Group membership		

This part concentrates upon the stimulus-individual interaction, as well as the behavior and goal achievement which results from this interaction. Specifically, three major organizational concepts are analyzed in the selected readings—motivation, groups, and leadership. These three facets or organizational life in businesses, hospitals, schools, and government agencies are stimuli that definitely interact wih individuals and result in various levels of goal achievement.

The first article examines individual differences. In the article "The Individual Organization: Problems and Promise," Edward E. Lawler III, examines the notion of individual differences and how organizations respond to them. The differences among people are viewed in terms of pay systems, leadership, training, selection, and structuring jobs. It is Lawler's contention that the research on individual differences indicates that the shaping of organizations to people should be developed and tested.

The description of a person involved intrinsically with the job is presented in the "Woodworker" by Craig Mosher. The joys, feelings, and challenge of a person using self-developed skills are captured in this article. The sense of achievement, contribution, and what psychologists label self-actualization is actually presented in the author's vivid description.

Donald F. Roy in "Banana Time: Job Satisfaction and Informal Interaction" describes the social interaction which took place in a small work group in a factory. Some of the mysteries about the influence of the small group are presented in an interesting fashion.

An article by John M. Ivancevich and Michael T. Matteson discusses "Organizations and Coronary Heart Disease: The Stress Connection." The authors present a clear framework for examining stressors and outcomes associated with coronary heart disease. In addition, the stress and job performance relationship is considered. Various methods of reducing negative forms of stress which can be initiated by individuals and organizations are introduced.

Fred L. Fry in "Operant Conditioning in Organizational Settings: Of Mice or Men?" criticizes what is called organizational behavior modification. He claims that organizations are more complex than Skinner Boxes. Workers are considered to be more intelligent than mice. Fry sarcastically calls O.B. Mod. another form of behavioral Taylorism.

An article entitled "Group Norms: Key to Building a Winning Team" by P. C. André de la Porte emphasizes the importance of group norms in achieving effectiveness. He states that there is a direct correlation between group norms and corporate profitability. The power of group norms is illustrated by citing an example of how they can obstruct managerial actions.

In "The Abilene Paradox: The Management of Agreement" by Jerry B. Harvey presents an interesting description of negative consequences faced in organizations. He calls his description the Abilene Paradox. He defines the paradox as organizations taking actions in contradiction to what they really want to do and therefore defeat the very purposes they are trying to achieve. Harvey outlines the systems of the paradox, methods of diagnosing and coping with it.

James Owens discusses "The Uses of Leadership Theory." He attempts to blend research theory and managerial experience in helping a manager evaluate his or her leadership skills. The article also reports managerial opinions about leadership practices and summarizes the advantages and disadvantages of various leadership styles.

An article "Managers and Leaders: Are They Different?" by Abraham Zaleznik discusses the issue of whether managers and leaders are reasonably one and the same. The discussion focuses on the leader versus managerial personality concept. He presents comparisons on attitudes, on goals, conceptions of work, relation with others, and senses of self. He closes the article by presenting his view of whether organizations develop leaders.

The Individual Organization: Problems and Promise*

EDWARD E. LAWLER III

Two easily identified and distinctly different approaches to the study of behavior in organizations have dominated the organizational behavior literature for the past half century. One emphasizes the differences among people, the other the similarities.

The first and least dominant approach has its foundation in differential psychology and is concerned with the study of individual differences. The basic assumptions underlying this approach are that people differ in their needs, skills, and abilities; that these differences can be measured; that valid data about people's competence and motivation can be obtained by organizations; and that these data can be used to make organizations more effective.

When behavioral scientists who take this approach look at organizations, they tend to see selection and placement. Their concern is with selecting those people who are right for a given job by measuring the characteristics of both the people and jobs and then trying to achieve the best fit. Their paradigm of the ideal organization would seem to be one where everyone has the ability and motivation to do the job to which he is assigned. Rarely do behavioral scientists with this orientation try to change the design of jobs or of organizations. Jobs are taken as a given and the focus is on finding the right people for them. Where efforts at job redesign have been made, they typically are instituted in the tradition of human engineering. That is, jobs have been made simpler so that more people can do them.

---

* Copyright 1974 by the Regents of the University of California. Reprinted from *California Management Review* vol. 16, no. 4, pp. 31–39.

What is needed if this approach is to work?

1. People must differ in meaningful ways.
2. Valid data about the characteristics of people must exist.
3. People who are suited for the jobs must apply.
4. A favorable selection ratio must exist (a large number of qualified applicants must apply for the job).

The second approach has generally assumed that all employees in an organization are similar in many ways and that certain general rules or principles can and should be developed for the design of organizations. It is universalistic, propounding that there is a right way to deal with all people in organizations. This type of thinking is present in the work of such traditional organization theorists as Urwick and Taylor. It is also present in the writings of the human relations theorists such as Mayo and in the work of the human resource theorists such as McGregor and Likert. As John Morse notes, all these approaches contain either implicitly or explicitly the assumption that there is a right way to manage people.[1]

Douglas McGregor's discussion of Theory X and Theory Y points out that, although scientific management and the more modern theories make different assumptions about the nature of man, both emphasize the similarities among people rather than the differences.[2] Based upon the Theory Y view of the nature of people, McGregor develops a normative organization theory that, like Theory X, stresses universal principles of management. For any of the universality theories to be generally valid, a certain type of person must populate society: one that fits its assumptions about the nature of people. In the case of the human resource theorists, this universal person will respond favorably to such things as enriched jobs, participative leadership, and interpersonal relationships characterized by openness, trust, and leveling. For the scientific management theorists, the universal type responds well to the use of financial rewards and the simplification of work. Thus, the validity of all these theories rests upon the correctness of the assumptions about the nature of people.

The work of those behavioral scientists who are concerned with individual differences suggests that the assumptions of all the universal theorists are dangerous over-simplifications for one very important reason: they fail to acknowledge the significant differences (in needs, personalities, and abilities) that cause individuals to react differently to organization practices concerned with job design, pay systems, leadership, training, and

---

[1] John J. Morse, "A Contingency Look at Job Design," *California Management Review* (Fall 1973), pp. 67–75.

[2] Douglas McGregor, *The Human Side of Enterprise* (New York: McGraw-Hill, 1960).

selection. Although many studies of individual behavior in organizations have not looked for individual differences, there are some that have found significant diversities. They are worth reviewing briefly since they clearly illustrate what is wrong with all organization theories which make universal assumptions about the nature of people.

JOB DESIGN

Job enrichment is one of the key ideas in most of the recent human resource theories of organization. According to the argument presented by Frederick Herzberg and others, job enrichment can lead to appreciable increases in employee motivation, performance, and satisfaction.[3] In fact, there is a fairly large body of evidence to support this view.[4]

There is, however, also a considerable amount of evidence that all individuals do not respond to job enrichment with higher satisfaction, productivity, and quality. In many studies the researchers have not been concerned with explaining these individual differences and have treated them as error variance. In others, however, attempts have been made to find out what distinguishes those people who respond positively to job enrichment. It has been pointed out that the type of background a person comes from may be related to how he or she responds to an enriched job.[5] According to some analyses, employees from rural backgrounds are more likely to respond positively to enrichment than are workers from urban environments.

More recent findings have shown that individual differences in need strength determine how people respond to jobs; the reason previous researchers have found urban-rural differences to be important lies in the kind of needs that people from these backgrounds have.[6] Rural background people have stronger higher-order needs (self-actualization, competence, self-esteem), and people with these needs respond positively to job enrichment, while those who don't fail to respond. It is argued that job enrichment creates conditions under which people can experience growth and self-esteem, motivating them to perform well. Clearly, for those employees who do not want to experience competence and growth,

---

[3] Frederick Herzberg, *Work and the Nature of Man* (Cleveland: World, 1966).

[4] Robert Blauner, *Alienation and Freedom* (Chicago: University of Chicago, 1964); and Edward E. Lawler, "Job Design and Employee Motivation," *Personnel Psychology*, vol. 22 (1969), pp. 426–35.

[5] Arthur Turner and Paul R. Lawrence, *Industrial Jobs and the Worker* (Boston: Division of Research, Harvard Business School, 1965); and Charles L. Hulin and Milton R. Blood, "Job Enlargement, Individual Differences, and Worker Responses," *Psychological Bulletin*, vol. 69 (1968), pp. 41–55.

[6] J. Richard Hackman and Edward E. Lawler, "Employee Reactions to Job Characteristics," *Journal of Applied Psychology*, vol. 55 (1971), pp. 259–86.

the opportunity to experience them will not be motivating, and not everyone should be expected to respond well to enriched jobs.[7]

PAY SYSTEMS

The scientific management philosophy strongly emphasizes the potential usefulness of pay as a motivator as in many piece rate, bonus, profit sharing, and other pay incentive plans. There is abundant evidence to support the point that, when pay is tied to performance, motivation and performance are increased.[8] However, there is also evidence to indicate that not everyone responds to pay incentive plans by performing better. In one study, certain types of employees responded to a piece rate incentive system while others did not.[9] Who responded? Workers from rural backgrounds who owned their homes, were Protestants, and social isolates—workers who, in short, saw money as a way of getting what they wanted and for whom social relations were not highly important.

There are many different kinds of pay incentive systems; and the kind of pay system that will motivate one person often does not motivate others. For example, group plans apparently work best with people who have strong social needs.[10] This suggests that not only do the members of an organization have to be treated differently according to whether they will or will not respond to a pay incentive, but that those who will respond to pay systems may have to be subdivided according to the type of system to which they will respond.

There is abundant evidence that individuals differ in their responses to the fringe benefits they receive. Large differences, determined by such things as age, marital status, education, and so on, exist among individuals in the kind of benefits they want and need.[11] Most organizations ignore this and give everyone the same benefits, thereby often giving high cost benefits to people who do not want them. Maximizing individual satisfaction with fringe benefits would require a unique plan for each employee.

LEADERSHIP

Research on leadership style during the past two decades has stressed the advantages that can be gained from the use of the various forms of

---

[7] John J. Morse, "A Contingency Look at Job Design."

[8] Edward E. Lawler, *Pay and Organizational Effectiveness: A Psychological View* (New York: McGraw-Hill, 1971).

[9] William F. Whyte, *Money and Motivation* (New York: Harper, 1955).

[10] Edward E. Lawler, *Pay and Organizational Effectiveness.*

[11] Stanley Nealy, "Pay and Benefit Preferences," *Industrial Relations,* vol. 3 (1963), pp. 17–28.

power equalization. Participation, flat organizations, decentralization, and group decision-making are all power equalization approaches to motivating and satisfying employees. There is a considerable body of evidence to suggest that power equalization can lead to higher subordinate satisfaction, greater subordinate motivation, and better decision-making.[12] Unfortunately, much of this literature has only given brief mention to the fact that not all subordinates respond in the same way to power equalization and the fact that not all superiors can practice power equalization.

Victor Vroom was one of the first to point out that at least one type of subordinate does not respond positively to participative management.[13] His data show that subordinates who are high on the F-scale (a measure of authoritarianism) do not respond well when they are subordinates to a boss who is oriented toward participative management. Later studies have shown that at times the majority of the membership of a work group may not respond positively to power equalization efforts on the part of superiors.[14]

Many superiors cannot manage in a democratic manner.[15] This, combined with the poor responses of many employees to democratic management styles, raises the question of whether it is advisable even to think of encouraging most managers to lead in a democratic manner. Many superiors probably *cannot* adopt a democratic leadership style, and because of the likely responses of some of their subordinates they *shouldn't*—regardless of task and situational considerations.

TRAINING

To most modern organization theorists, training is an important element of organization design. It is particularly helpful in resolving individual differences. T-groups, managerial grid seminars, and leadership courses are some examples of the kinds of human relations training that organizations use. These training approaches help assure that most people in the organization have certain basic skills and abilities and that some valid assumptions about the capacity of the people in the organization can be made.

---

[12] Chris Argyris, "Personality and Organization Revisited," *Administrative Science Quarterly*, vol. 18 (1973), pp. 141–67.

[13] Victor H. Vroom, *Some Personality Determinants of the Effects of Participation* (Englewood Cliffs, N.J.: Prentice-Hall, 1960).

[14] John R. P. French, J. Israel, and Dagfin As, "An Experiment on Participation in a Norwegian Factory," *Human Relations*, vol. 13 (1960), pp. 3–19; and George Strauss, "Some Notes on Power-Equalization," in H. J. Leavitt (ed.), *The Social Science of Organizations* (Englewood Cliffs, N.J.: Prentice-Hall, 1963).

[15] Frederick E. Fiedler, "Predicting the Effects of Leadership Training and Experience from the Contingency Model," *Journal of Applied Psychology*, vol. 56 (1972), pp. 114–19.

Once again, the problem is that the very individual employee differences greatly affect the ability to learn from things such as T-groups and managerial grid seminars; this type of training is simply wasted on many people.[16] In fact, the training may end up increasing the range of individual differences in an organization rather than reducing it. It is also likely that while one type of human relations training may not affect a person, another type could have a significant impact. The same point can be made with respect to training people in the area of occupational skills. One person may learn best from a teaching machine while another learns the same material best from a lecture format.

SELECTION

In the work on selection the assumption has typically been made that people are sufficiently similar so that the same selection instruments can be used for everyone. Thus, all applicants for a job are often given the same battery of selection criteria—overlooking the fact that different instruments might work better as predictors for some groups than for others. This would not be a serious problem if individual difference factors were not related to the ability of the selection instruments to predict performance; but recent evidence suggests that they are. Certain kinds of tests work better for some segments of the population than for others.[17] However, this uniformity in selection testing is not the only reason for poor job performance prediction.

Differential psychologists have developed numerous valid tests of people's ability to perform jobs, but they have failed to develop tests that measure how employees will fit into particular organizational climates and how motivated they will be in particular organizations. All too often they have tried to predict individual behavior in organizations without measuring the characteristics of the organization. Trying to predict behavior by looking only at personal characteristics must inevitably lead to predictions whose validity is questionable.

All this is beginning to change, but it is doubtful if highly accurate predictions will ever be obtained. The measurement problems are too great, and both organizations and people change too much. The research evidence also shows that people sometimes don't give valid data in selection situations and that some important determinants of individual behavior in organizations are difficult to measure.[18]

---

[16] John P. Campbell and Marvin D. Dunnette, "Effectiveness of T-Group Experiences in Managerial Training and Development," *Psychological Bulletin*, vol. 70 (1968), pp. 73–104.

[17] Edwin E. Ghiselli, "Moderating Effects and Differential Reliability and Validity," *Journal of Applied Psychology*, vol. 47 (1963), pp. 81–86.

[18] Robert M. Guion, *Personnel Testing* (New York: McGraw-Hill, 1965).

INDIVIDUAL DIFFERENCES

One clear implication of the research on individual differences is that for any of the universalistic theories to operate effectively in a given organization or situation, one of two things must occur: either the organization must deal with the individuals it hires so that they will change to meet the assumptions of the theory, or it must hire only those individuals who fit the kind of system that the organization employs. Unfortunately, there is no solid evidence that individuals can be trained or dealt with in ways that will increase the degree to which they respond to such things as enriched jobs and democratic supervision. Proponents of job enrichment often stress that people will come to like it once they have tried it, but this point remains to be proven.

The validity of most selection instruments is so low that organizations should not count on finding instruments that will allow them to select only those who fit whatever system they use. There is always the prospect that the differential psychologist can develop appropriate measures and that this will lead to organizations being able to select more homogenous work forces. This, in turn, would allow approaches such as the human resources approach to be effectively utilized in some situations. However, it seems unlikely that they could ever be used in large complex organizations. Even if measures are developed, it may not be possible for large homogenous populations of workers to be selected by organizations. Effective selection depends on favorable selection ratios, which are rare, and on the legal ability of organizations to run selection programs. It is also obvious that there has been and will continue to be a large influx into the labor market and into organizations of people from different socio-economic backgrounds. This has and will continue to create more diversity rather than homogeneity in the work forces of most organizations, decreasing the likelihood that large organizations can ever be completely staffed by people who fit the assumptions of scientific management, Theory X, Theory Y, or any other organization theory that is based upon the view that people are similar in important ways.

Further, it soon may not be legally possible for organizations to conduct the kind of selection programs that will by themselves produce good individual-organization fits. The federal government restrictions on testing for selection purposes soon could create conditions under which testing will no longer be practical. Organizations may find themselves in a situation where they must randomly select from among the "qualified applicants" for a job. Thus, even if valid tests were developed, work forces probably could not be selected that would contain only people that fit either the human resources or the scientific management assumptions about people.

There is evidence in the literature that some organization theorists are moving away from the view that one style of management or one organization design is right for most organizations.[19] However, the focus so far has been on environmental variables, such as degree of uncertainty and stability, and production variables, such as whether the task is predictable and whether the product can be mass, process, or unit produced. The researchers point out that different structures and different management styles are appropriate under different conditions. Some of the evidence they present is persuasive: products and environmental factors need to be considered when organizations are being designed. However, they often fail to point out that the nature of the work force also needs to be considered and they fail to suggest organization structures that allow for the fact that the people in any organization will vary in their response to such things as tight controls, job enrichment, and so on.

What seems to be needed is an organization theory based upon assumptions like the following, which recognize the existence of differences among individuals:

1. Most individuals are goal-oriented in their behavior, but there are large differences in the goals people pursue.
2. Individuals differ both in what they enjoy doing and in what they can do.
3. Some individuals need to be closely supervised while others can exercise high levels of self-control.

In order to design an organization based on these assumptions, it is necessary to utilize various normative theories as guides to how different members of the same organization should be treated. In addition measures of individual needs and abilities, like those developed by differential psychologists, are needed. As will become apparent, it probably also is necessary to depend on the ability of individuals to help make decisions about where and how they will work. In short, it requires a synthesis of the individual differences approach and the work of the organization theorists into a new paradigm of how organizations should be designed—a new paradigm that emphasizes structuring organizations so that they can better adapt themselves to the needs, desires, and abilities of their members.

STRUCTURING THE INDIVIDUALIZED ORGANIZATION

The research on job design, training, reward systems, and leadership provides a number of suggestions about what an organization designed on

---

[19] Joan Woodward, *Industrial Organization: Theory and Practice* (London: Oxford University Press, 1965); Paul R. Lawrence and Jay W. Lorsch, *Organization and Environment* (Boston: Division of Research, Harvard Business School, 1967); Chris Argyris, *Integrating the Individual and the Organization* (New York: John Wiley, 1964); and Tom Burns and G. M. Stalker, *The Management of Innovation* (London: Tavistock Publications Limited, 1961).

the basis of individual differences assumptions would look like. A brief review will help to illustrate how an individualized organization might operate and identify some of the practical problems of the approach.

The research on job design shows that jobs can be fit to people if organizations can tolerate having a wide range of jobs and tasks. One plant in Florida has done this by having an assembly line operating next to a bench assembly of the same product. Employees are given a choice of which kind of job they want. The fact that some want to work on each kind is impressive evidence of the existence of individual differences. Robert Kahn has suggested that the fit process can be facilitated by allowing individuals to choose among different groups of tasks or modules that would be several hours long.[20] In his system, workers would bid for those tasks which they would like to do. For this system to work, all individuals would, of course, have to know a considerable amount about the nature of the different modules, and the approach would probably have to take place in conjunction with some job enrichment activities. Otherwise, the employee might be faced with choosing among modules made up of simple, repetitive tasks, thus giving them no real choice. As Kahn notes, the work module concept is also intriguing because it should make it easier for individuals to choose not to work a standard 40-hour work week. This is important because of the difference in people's preferences with respect to hours of work. The whole module approach rests on the ability of individuals to make valid choices about when and where they should work.

The leadership research shows that people respond to different types of leadership. This could be handled by fitting the superior's style to the personality of subordinates—the superior who can only behave in an authoritarian manner will be given subordinates who perform well under that type of supervision; the superior who can only behave participatively could be given only people who respond to that style; and the superior who is capable of varying his style could be given either people who respond to different styles in different conditions or a mix of people with which he or she would be encouraged to behave differently.

The research shows that training needs to be individualized so that it will fit the needs and abilities of the employee. Implementation requires careful assessment of the individual's abilities and motivation, and good career counseling. Once it has been accepted that not everyone in the organization can profit from a given kind of training, then training becomes a matter of trying to develop people as much as possible with the kind of training to which they will respond. It requires accepting the fact that people may develop quite different leadership styles or ways of behaving in general and trying to capitalize on these by fitting the job the person holds and the groups he supervises to his style.

---

[20] Robert Kahn, "The Work Module—A Tonic for Lunchpail Lassitude," *Psychology Today*, vol. 6 (1973), pp. 94–95.

The research shows that pay systems need to be fit to the person. Fringe benefit packages are a good example of this; several companies have already developed cafeteria-style fringe benefit packages that allow employees to select the benefits they want. The research also suggests that those individuals whose desire for money is strong should be placed on jobs that lend themselves to pay incentive plans.

In summary, an organization based on individual differences assumptions would have a job environment for each person which fits his or her unique skills and abilities. It would accomplish this by a combination of good selection and self-placement choices in the areas of fringe benefits, job design, hours of work, style of supervision, and training programs. But creating truly individualized job situations presents many practical problems in organization design—it is difficult to create gratifying jobs for both the person who responds to an enriched job and the person who responds to a routinized job. One way of accomplishing this could be by creating relatively autonomous subunits that vary widely in climate, job design, leadership style, and so on. For example, within the same organization the same product might be produced by mass production in one unit and by unit production using enriched jobs in another. One subunit might have a warm, supportive climate while another might have a cold, demanding one. The size of the subunit would also vary depending upon the type of climate that is desired and the type of production it uses. This variation is desirable as long as the placement process is able to help people find the modules that fit them.

An organization would have to have an immense number of subunits if it were to try to have one to represent each of the possible combinations of climate, leadership style, incentive systems, and job design. Since such a large number is not practical, a selection should be made based on a study of the labor market, attention to the principles of motivation and satisfaction, and the nature of the product and market. A study of the labor market to see what type of people the organization is likely to attract should help determine what combinations will be needed to fit the characteristics of most of the workers. In most homogenous labor markets, this may be only a few of the many possible combinations. Traditional selection instruments can help the organization decide who will fit into the subunits; and, if individuals are given information about the nature of the subunits, they can often make valid decisions themselves.

Motivation theory argues that when important rewards are tied to performance, it is possible to have both high satisfaction and high performance.[21] This suggests that all new work modules must meet one crucial condition: some rewards that are valued by members of that part of the organization must be tied to performance. This rules out many situations.

---

[21] Victor Vroom, *Work and Motivation* (New York: Wiley, 1964).

For example, a situation in which no extrinsic rewards such as pay and promotion are tied to performance and which has authoritarian management and repetitive jobs should not exist. Finally, the research on job design and organization structures shows that the type of product and type of market limit the kind of subunit which can be successful. For example, authoritarian management, routine jobs, and tall organization structures are not effective when the product is technically sophisticated and must be marketed in a rapidly changing environment.

Creating subunits with distinctly different climates and practices is one way, but not the only way, to create an individualized organization. In small organizations this probably is not possible; thus, it is important to encourage differences within the same unit. This may mean training supervisors to deal differently with subordinates who have distinctly different personal characteristics. It may also mean designing jobs that can be done in various ways. For example, in one group a product might be built by a team and passed from one member to another while in another group everyone might build the entire product without help. Obviously, this approach generally will not allow for as much variation as does the approach of building distinctive subunits, but it permits some degree of individualization.

It is not yet entirely clear how such divergent organization practices as work modules, cafeteria-style pay plans, and job enrichment that is guided by individual difference measures can be integrated in practice. Research on how organizations can be individualized and on how individual differences affect behavior in organizations is sorely needed.

RESEARCH ON INDIVIDUAL DIFFERENCES

The work on measurng individual differences that has been done so far has focused largely on measuring the "can do" aspects of behavior for the purpose of selection. The effective individualization of organizations depends on the development of measures which tap the "will do" aspects of behavior, such as measures of motivation and reactions to different organizational climates, and measures that can be used for placing people in positions that best fit their needs.

This is not to say that selection should be ignored; the kinds of individual differences that exist in an organization should be kept at a manageable number, and those who clearly cannot do the job should be excluded. But it is important that, in selection, measures of such things as motivation, reactions to different leadership styles, and preferred organization climate be collected and evaluated in relationship to the climate of the organization, the psychological characteristics of the jobs in the organizations, and the leadership style of various managers. The same measures are obviously relevant when consideration is given to placing new employees in different parts of the organization or in different jobs. The difficulty in doing this kind of selection and placement is that there are few measures of the relevant individual differences, of the organization climate, and of the psychological characteristics of jobs. In many cases, it is not even known what the relevant individual difference variables are when consideration is being given to predicting how people will react to different administrative practices, policies, and to different organization climates. This is where the differential psychologist can make a major contribution.

Also needed is research on selection that is responsive to the new demands that society is placing on organizations and which recognizes that individuals can contribute to better selection decisions. Since organizations are rapidly losing the ability to select who their members will be, research is needed on how the selection situation can be turned into more of a counseling situation so that enlightened self-selection will operate. There is evidence that when job applicants are given valid information about the job, they will make better choices. Joseph Weitz showed this long ago with insurance agents, and more recently it has been illustrated with West Point cadets and telephone operators.[22] In the future the most effective selection programs will have to emphasize providing individuals with valid data about themselves and about the nature of the organization. After this information is presented to the applicants, they will make the decision of whether to join the organization. Before this kind of "selection" system can be put into effect, however, much research is needed to determine how this process can be handled. We need to know, for example, what kind of information should be presented to individuals and how it should be presented. However, the problems involved in the approach are solvable, and given the current trends in society, this approach represents the most viable selection approach in many situations.

CONCLUSIONS

The research on reward systems, job design, leadership, selection, and training shows that significant individual differences exist in how individuals respond to organizational policies and practices. Because of this, an effective normative organization theory has to suggest an organization design that will treat individuals differently. Existing normative theories usually fail to emphasize this point. There are, however, a number of things that organizations can do now to deal with individual differences. These include cafeteria-style pay plans and selective job enrichment. Unfortu-

---

[22] Joseph Weitz, "Job Expectancy and Survival," *Journal of Applied Psychology*, vol. 40 (1956), pp. 245–47; and John P. Wanous, "Effect of a Realistic Job Preview on Job Acceptance, Job Survival and Job Attitudes," *Journal of Applied Psychology*, vol. 58 (1973), pp. 327–32.

nately, a fully developed practical organization theory based upon an individual difference approach can not be yet stated. Still, it is important to note that approaches to shaping organizations to individuals are developing. It seems logical, therefore, to identify these and other similar efforts as attempts to individualize organizations. It is hoped that the identification of these efforts and the establishment of the concept of individualization will lead to two very important developments: the generation of more practices that will individualize organizations and work on how these different practices can simultaneously be made operational in organizations. Only if these developments take place will individualized organizations ever be created.

Woodworker*

CRAIG MOSHER

As my hands press the plane forward, a smooth shaving curls up from the keen edge, filling the air with the tangy scent of fresh-cut pine.

There is a soothing rhythm to the strokes of the plane and a delightful uniqueness in each spiraled shaving.

My chisel and mallet seek some more-organic form hidden within a block of Hawaiian koa wood. The power saw that cut the block is no respecter of the flowing lines of light and dark that mark the pattern of growth. Sometimes, when my efforts at seeking the life-lines in the wood succeed, the form seems to take on a liveliness reminiscent of the forces that shaped the once tall and supple tree.

Now, as I seek to shape my life in more flexible, natural ways, the schools and offices that claimed so many of my years seem like a buzz saw that cut me into blocks irrespective of the life forms hidden within.

There are so many joys in my new vocation I wonder that I did not find it sooner. Perhaps, my life had to be cut into blocks in order for me to know that was not the form I sought. Yet, there are connections, too. The enjoyment I once got from organizing ideas and programs and peace matches I now find in planning the sequence of tasks and gathering materials to build a table. It is satisfying to see my hands transforming boards and glue into functional and even beautiful objects.

Working for myself I have a flexibility and a discipline that is rarely found in offices that structure work into eight-hour days and fifty-week years. I find freedom within my work, not just during my "time off." Even when I choose to discipline myself to eight-hour days, I feel more free knowing that I am choosing that schedule, either as self-discipline or so I

---

* This article first appeared in *The Humanist,* January–February 1975, pp. 36–37, and is reprinted by permission.

can conveniently work with others. I struggle, when working for myself, to find a balance between demanding regular eight-hour days of myself in order to earn money, learn new skills, and do quality work, on the one hand, and taking time to play with my family, on the other.

I have time between jobs for other activities. I can take a day off each week to build projects for my own pleasure. In fact, the line between work and play blurs because I have such fun at my work. Tools become toys when I go to play in the shop.

As a free-lance woodworker I work for myself or for a client with whom I have some personal contact. The client knows that it is I and not some impersonal factory or machine creating the product. Both praise and criticism come directly to me. Expectations for the form and quality of the job are set by me, alone or in dialogue with the client. In either case I participate directly in setting expectations for my work, and thereby find myself committed to them. This brings pleasure when the product meets the standard and anguish when I sometimes fall short. As in any demanding personal endeavor, part of myself becomes invested in my work, so that I am happy when it is going well and sometimes depressed when I do poorly.

I am also learning more about my relationship to authority. I find it easier to use external authority—like a foreman's or client's expecting me on the job at 8 A.M. each morning—to motivate myself to work. Yet, I find greater satisfaction when I can internalize the authority and muster the self-discipline to go to work regularly in my own shop when only I know how many hours I work. I learned such self-discipline as a student, but then it was under the external threat of grades and disapproving teachers, which I came to internalize as guilt. The wide range of available jobs, from wood carving in my own shop to framing houses on a crew or even working in a factory, provides many levels of internal and external authority, so I have some flexibility to choose the level at which I feel comfortable at any given time.

There is clarity and concreteness in the woodworking craft. I work with materials rather than ideas or personalities. Most of my work is sequential, orderly, and structured. Work proceeds step by step. Foundations must be built before walls, wood cut before being finished. Progress is easily seen as walls are raised and rafters set. Sometimes work goes fast and sometimes slow, but at the end of every day I can see what I have done. I find this continually rewarding.

These rewards are immediate and "self-bestowed." I need not wait for a teacher or boss to tell me whether a cabinet is square or a floor level. Once I have learned the standards of high quality for a particular type of work, I decide for myself whether the job is properly done. I enjoy the freedom to judge my own work and also the challenge to my integrity that is implicit in every decision I make about quality.

I find satisfaction in discovering the direct link between the form and the function of the things I build. There is pleasure in erecting a house that will warmly shelter a family and provide spaces that facilitate their particular living patterns. The same is true of a child's pull toy, which both evokes laughter and withstands considerable knocking about. When I understand and observe the direct relation between the form and the function of a project, I get a sense of clarity that makes the work flow more smoothly.

Every job seems to pose new challenges to my growing skills. There is such variety in the types of work available that when I get bored I simply choose a different area for my next job. When I tire of framing houses, I build furniture. When I get lonely in the shop, I seek bigger jobs with other workers. The range of skills that can be developed is so broad that I know I will spend many years as an active learner, enduring the frustrations and cherishing the joys of that process.

The many different woodworking skills can be generalized and transferred, so I rarely feel completely at a loss about how to solve a new problem. Relevant past experience is usually available to guide new learning. This range of transferable skills also gives me the secure feeling that I will likely be able to find work in almost any place at almost any time. The work is not always steady. There are seasonal fluctuations and changes dependent upon the state of the economy, but there are so many kinds of work that something is almost always available.

The key to finding plenty of work seems to be developing a reputation for quality and efficiency (that is, reasonable cost). I am encouraged by an increasing demand in the nation for quality hand craftsmanship. Perhaps it is a passing fashion, or perhaps it is a real trend away from the dreary uniformity of mass-produced goods, large factories, anonymous, alienated employees, and concentrations of power and wealth in the hands of a few capitalists.

A client once told me that he felt guilty asking me to remodel his garage for him while he sat in his office, since he was capable of doing the job himself. I realized that I was very happy it was he and not I going to his office every day in a suit and tie and that I was glad he had the money to pay me to do work I enjoy.

Most of the skills I have were learned on the job—what John Dewey and his followers called "learning by doing." Sometimes I learn slowly by my own trials and errors. I learn more quickly when I work with someone more skilled than I who can offer advice and answer questions. Apprenticeship is one of the oldest and most effective teaching-learning strategies. This teacher-apprentice relationship has, in my experience, also been an opportunity for forming friendships that make the work flow more smoothly. My woodworking teachers shared their skills and knowledge so that together we could do the work more quickly and accurately

—quite unlike some authoritarian teaching styles I experienced in classrooms.

I am intrigued by the possibilities for cooperation inherent in the crafts and trades. Their variety, flexibility, and lack of officially determined credentials make for fewer barriers caused by specialization and less emphasis on hierarchical measures of status, all of which should make it easier for people to form cooperative work groups in which they can share their tools and skills, as well as themselves. The friendships and group cohesion that can develop in such a cooperative endeavor make the work all that much more enjoyable.

I now find myself with a set of useful skills that contribute to a sense of identity based on concrete work and achievements. These skills and the work I can produce give meaning to my life, meaning that is tangible, self-renewing, and growing—and very personal. To the extent that my craft becomes art my individuality is expressed through work that others can use and enjoy.

It is, after all, more healthy, both personally and socially, for me to gain pleasure and self-esteem through the quality of my craftsmanship and the beauty and functionality of my work than through struggling for a position of wealth, authority, and power over other people. And it is certainly more fun.

Banana Time: Job Satisfaction and Informal Interaction*

DONALD F. ROY

T HIS paper undertakes description and exploratory analysis of the social interaction which took place within a small work group of factory machine operatives during a two-month period of participant observation. The factual and ideational materials which it presents lie at an intersection of two lines of research interest and should, in their dual bearing, contribute to both. Since the operatives were engaged in work which involved the repetition of very simple operations over an extra-long workday, six days a week, they were faced with the problem of dealing with a formidable "beast of monotony." Revelation of how the group utilized its resources to combat the "beast" should merit the attention of those who are seeking solution to the practical problem of job satisfaction, or employee morale. It should also provide insights for those who are trying to penetrate the mysteries of the small group.

Convergence of these two lines of interest is, of course, no new thing. Among the host of writers and researchers who have suggested connections between "group" and "joy in work" are Walker and Guest, observers of social interaction on the automobile assembly line.[1] They quote assembly-line workers as saying, "We have a lot of fun and talk all the time,"[2] and, "If it weren't for talking and fooling, you'd go nuts."[3]

My account of how one group of machine operators kept from "going

---

* Reproduced by permission of the Society for Applied Anthropology from *Human Organization,* vol. 18, no. 4 (1960).

[1] Charles R. Walker and Robert H. Guest, *The Man on the Assembly Line* (Cambridge, Mass.: Harvard University Press, 1952).

[2] Ibid., p. 77.

[3] Ibid., p. 68.

nuts" in a situation of monotonous work activity attempts to lay bare the tissues of interaction which made up the content of their adjustment. The talking, fun, and fooling which provided solution to the elemental problem of "psychological survival" will be described according to their embodiment in intra-group relations. In addition, an unusual opportunity for close observation of behavior involved in the maintenance of group equilibrium was afforded by the fortuitous introduction of a "natural experiment." My unwitting injection of explosive materials into the stream of interaction resulted in sudden, but temporary, loss of group interaction.

My fellow operatives and I spent our long days of simple repetitive work in relative isolation from other employees of the factory. Our line of machines was sealed off from other work areas of the plant by the four walls of the clicking room. The one door of this room was usually closed. Even when it was kept open, during periods of hot weather, the consequences were not social; it opened on an uninhabited storage room of the shipping department. Not even the sound of work activity going on elsewhere in the factory carried to this isolated work place. There were occasional contacts with "outside" employees, usually on matters connected with the work; but, with the exception of the daily calls of one fellow who came to pick up finished materials for the next step in processing, such visits were sporadic and infrequent.

Moreover, face-to-face contact with members of the managerial hierarchy were few and far between. No one bearing the title of foreman ever came around. The only company official who showed himself more than once during the two-month observation period was the plant superintendent. Evidently overloaded with supervisory duties and production problems which kept him busy elsewhere, he managed to pay his respects every week or two. His visits were in the nature of short, businesslike, but friendly exchanges. Otherwise he confined his observable communications with the group to occasional utilization of a public address system. During the two-month period, the company president and the chief chemist paid one friendly call apiece. One man, who may or may not have been of managerial status, was seen on various occasions lurking about in a manner which excited suspicion. Although no observable consequences accrued from the peculiar visitations of this silent fellow, it was assumed that he was some sort of efficiency expert, and he was referred to as "The Snooper."

As far as our work group was concerned, this was truly a situation of laissez-faire management. There was no interference from staff experts, no hounding by time-study engineers or personnel men hot on the scent of efficiency or good human relations. Nor were there any signs of industrial democracy in the form of safety, recreational, or production committees. There was an international union, and there was a highly publicized union-management cooperation program; but actual interactional processes of cooperation were carried on somewhere beyond my range of observation and without participation of members of my work group. Furthermore, these union-management get-togethers had no determinable connection with the problem of "toughing out" a twelve-hour day at monotonous work.

Our work group was thus not only abandoned to its own resources for creating job satisfaction, but left without that basic reservoir of ill-will toward management which can sometimes be counted on to stimulate the development of interesting activities to occupy hand and brain. Lacking was the challenge of intergroup conflict, that perennial source of creative experience to fill the otherwise empty hours of meaningless work routine.[4]

The clicking machines were housed in a room approximately thirty by twenty-four feet. They were four in number, set in a row, and so arranged along one wall that the busy operator could, merely by raising his head from his work, freshen his reveries with a glance through one of three large barred windows. To the rear of one of the end machines sat a long cutting table; here the operators cut up rolls of plastic materials into small sheets manageable for further processing at the clickers. Behind the machine at the opposite end of the line sat another table which was intermittently the work station of a female employee who performed sundry scissors operations of a more intricate nature on raincoat parts. Boxed in on all sides by shelves and stocks of materials, this latter locus of work appeared a cell within a cell.

The clickers were of the genus punching machines; of mechanical construction similar to that of the better-known punch presses, their leading features were hammer and block. The hammer, or punching head, was approximately eight inches by twelve inches at its flat striking surface. The descent upon the block was initially forced by the operator, who exerted pressure on a handle attached to the side of the hammer head. A few inches of traved downward established electrical connection for a sharp, power-driven blow. The hammer also traveled, by manual guidance, in a horizontal plane to and from, and in an arc around, the central column of the machine. Thus the operator, up to the point of establishing electrical connections for the sudden and irrevocable downward thrust, had flexibility in maneuvering his instrument over the larger surface of the block. The latter, approximately twenty-four inches wide, eighteen inches deep, and ten inches thick, was made, like a butcher's block, of inlaid hardwood; it was set in the machine at a convenient waist height. On it the operator placed his materials, one sheet at a time if leather, stacks of sheets if plastic to be cut with steel dies of assorted sizes and shapes. The particular die in use would be moved, by hand, from spot to spot over the material each

---

[4] Donald F. Roy, "Work Satisfaction and Social Reward in Quota Achievement: An Analysis of Piecework Incentive." *American Sociological Review*, vol. 18 (October 1953), pp. 507–14.

time a cut was made; less frequently, materials would be shifted on the block as the operator saw need for such adjustment.

Introduction to the new job, with its relatively simple machine skills and work routines, was accomplished with what proved to be, in my experience, an all-time minimum of job training. The clicking machine assigned to me was situated at one end of the row. Here the superintendent and one of the operators gave a few brief demonstrations, accompanied by bits of advice which included a warning to keep hands clear of the descending hammer. After a short practice period, at the end of which the super-intendent expressed satisfaction with progress and potentialities, I was left to develop my learning curve with no other supervision than that afforded by members of the work group. Further advise and assistance did come, from time to time, from my fellow operatives, sometimes upon request, sometimes unsolicited.

THE WORK GROUP

Absorbed at first in three related goals of improving my clicking skill, increasing my rate of output, and keeping my left hand unclicked, I paid little attention to my fellow operatives save to observe that they were friendly, middle-aged, foreign-born, full of advice, and very talkative. Their names, according to the way they addressed each other, were George, Ike, and Sammy.[5] George, a stocky fellow in his late fifties, operated the machine at the opposite end of the line; he, I later discovered, had emigrated in early youth from a country in Southeastern Europe. Ike, stationed at George's left, was tall, slender, in his early fifties, and Jewish; he had come from Eastern Europe in his youth. Sammy, number three man in the line, and my neighbor, was heavy set, in his late fifties, and Jewish; he had escaped from a country in Eastern Europe just before Hitler's legions had moved in. All three men had been downwardly mobile as to occupation in recent years. George and Sammy had been proprietors of small businesses; the former had been "wiped out" when his uninsured establishment burned down; the latter had been entrepreneuring on a small scale before he left all behind him to flee the Germans. According to his account, Ike had left a highly skilled trade which he had practiced for years in Chicago.

I discovered also that the clicker line represented a ranking system in descending order from George to myself. George not only had top seniority for the group, but functioned as a sort of lead man. His superior status was marked in the fact that he received five cents more per hour than the other clickermen, put in the longest workday, made daily contact, outside the workroom, with the superintendent on work matters which concerned the entire line, and communicated to the rest of us the directives which he

---

[5] All names used are fictitious.

received. The narrow margin of superordination was seen in the fact that directives were always relayed in the superintendent's name; they were on the order of, "You'd better let that go now, and get on the green. Joe says they're running low on the fifth floor," or "Joe says he wants two boxes of the 3-1 die today." The narrow margin was also seen in the fact that the superintendent would communicate directly with his operatives over the public address system; and, on occasion, Ike or Sammy would leave the workroom to confer with him for decisions or advice in regard to work orders.

Ike was next to George in seniority, then Sammy. I was, of course, low man on the totem pole. Other indices to status differentiation lay in informal interaction, to be described later.

With one exception, job status tended to be matched by length of workday. George worked a thirteen-hour day, from 7 A.M. to 8:30 P.M. Ike worked eleven hours, from 7 A.M. to 6:30 P.M.; occasionally he worked until 7 or 7:30 for an eleven and a half- or a twelve-hour day. Sammy put in a nine-hour day, from 8 A.M. to 5:30 P.M. My twelve hours spanned from 8 A.M. to 8:30 P.M. We had a half hour for lunch, from 12 to 12:30.

The female who worked at the secluded table behind George's machine put in a regular plant-wide eight-hour shift from 8 to 4:30. Two women held this job during the period of my employment: Mable was succeeded by Baby. Both were Negroes, and in their late twenties.

A fifth clicker operator, an Arabian emigré called Boo, worked a night shift by himself. He usually arrived about 7 P.M. to take over Ike's machine.

THE WORK

It was evident to me, before my first workday drew to a weary close, that my clicking career was going to be a grim process of fighting the clock, the particular timepiece in this situation being an old-fashioned alarm clock which ticked away on a shelf near George's machine. I had struggled through many dreary rounds with the minutes and hours during the various phases of my industrial experience, but never had I been confronted with such a dismal combination of working conditions as the extra-long workday, the infinitesimal cerebral excitation, and the extreme limitation of physical movement. The contrast with a recent stint in the California oil fields was striking. This was no eight-hour day of racing hither and yon over desert and foothills with a rollicking crew of "roustabouts" on a variety of repair missions at oil wells, pipe lines, and storage tanks. Here there was no afternoon dallying to search the sands for horned toads, tarantulas, and rattlesnakes, or to climb old wooden derricks for raven's nests, with an eye out, of course, for the tell-tale streak of dust in the distance which gave ample warning of the approach of the boss. This was standing all day in one spot beside three old codgers in a dingy room looking out through barred windows at the bare walls of a brick warehouse, leg movements largely restricted to the shifting of body weight from one foot to the other, hand and arm movement confined, for the most part, to a simple repetitive sequence of place the die, —— punch the clicker, —— place the die, —— punch the clicker, and intellectual activity reduced to computing the hours to quitting time. It is true that from time to time a fresh stack of sheets would have to be substituted for the clicked-out old one; but the stack would have been prepared by someone else, and the exchange would be only a minute or two in the making. Now and then a box of finished work would have to be moved back out of the way, and an empty box brought up; but the moving back and the bringing up involved only a step or two. And there was the half hour for lunch, and occasional trips to the lavatory or the drinking fountain to break up the day into digestible parts. But after each momentary respite, hammer and die were moving again: click, —— move die, —— click, —— move die.

Before the end of the first day, Monotony was joined by his twin brother, Fatigue. I got tired. My legs ached, and my feet hurt. Early in the afternoon I discovered a tall stool and moved it up to my machine to "take the load off my feet." But the superintendent dropped in to see how I was "doing" and promptly informed me that "we don't sit down on this job." My reverie toyed with the idea of quitting the job and looking for other work.

The next day was the same: the monotony of the work, the tired legs and sore feet and thoughts of quitting.

THE GAME OF WORK

In discussing the factory operative's struggle to "cling to the remnants of joy in work," Henri de Man makes the general observations that "it is psychologically impossible to deprive any kind of work of all its positive emotional elements," that the worker will find some meaning in any activity assigned to him, a "certain scope for initiative which can satisfy after a fashion the instinct for play and the creative impulse," that "even in the Taylor system there is found luxury of self-determination."[6] De Man cites the case of one worker who wrapped 13,000 incandescent bulbs a day; she found her outlet for creative impulse, her self-determination, her meaning in work by varying her wrapping movements a little from time to time.[7]

So did I search for some meaning in my continuous mincing of plastic sheets into small ovals, fingers, and trapezoids. The richness of possibility for creative expression previously discovered in my experience with the

---

[6] Henri de Man, *The Psychology of Socialism* (New York: Henry Holt and Company, 1927), pp. 80–81.

[7] Ibid., p. 81.

"Taylor system"[8] did not reveal itself here. There was no piecework, so on piecework game. There was no conflict with management, so no war game. But, like the light bulb wrapper, I did find a "certain scope for initiative," and out of this slight freedom to vary activity, I developed a game of work.

The game developed was quite simple, so elementary in fact, that its playing was reminiscent of rainy-day preoccupations in childhood, when attention could be centered by the hour on colored bits of things of assorted sizes and shapes. But this adult activity was not mere pottering and piddling; what it lacked in the earlier imaginative content, it made up for in clean-cut structure. Fundamentally involved were: (a) variation in color of the materials cut (b) variation in shape of the dies used, and (c) a process called "scraping the block." The basic procedure which ordered the particular combination of components employed could be stated in the form: "As soon as I do so many of these, I'll get to do those." If, for example, production scheduled for the day featured small, rectangular strips in three colors, the game might go: "As soon as I finish a thousand of the green ones, I'll click some brown ones." And, with success in attaining the objective of working with brown materials, a new goal of "I'll get to do the white ones" might be set. Or the new goal might involve switching dies.

Scraping the block made the game more interesting by adding to the number of possible variations in its playing; and what was perhaps more important, provided the only substantial reward, save for going to the lavatory or getting a drink of water, on days when work with one die and one color of material was scheduled. As a physical operation, scraping the block was fairly simple; it involved application of a coarse file to the upper surface of the block to remove roughness and unevenness resulting from the wear and tear of die penetration. But, as part of the intellectual and emotional content of the game of work, it could be in itself a source of variation in activity. The upper left-hand corner of the block could be chewed up in the clicking of 1,000 white trapezoid pieces, then scraped. Next, the upper right-hand corner, and so on until the entire block had been worked over. Then, on the next round of scraping by quadrants, there yas the possibility of a change of color or die to green trapezoid or white oval pieces.

Thus the game of work might be described as a continuous sequence of short-range production goals with achievement rewards in the form of activity change. The superiority of this relatively complex and self-determined system over the technically simple and outside-controlled job satisfaction injections experienced by Milner at the beginner's table in a shop of the feather industry should be immediately apparent: "Twice a day our work was completely changed to break the monotony. First Jennie would

---

[8] Roy, *op. cit.*

give us feathers of a brilliant green, then bright orange or a light blue or black. The "ohs" and "ahs" that came from the girls at each change was proof enough that this was an effective way of breaking the monotony of the tedious work."[9]

But a hasty conclusion that I was having lots of fun playing my clicking game should be avoided. These games were not as interesting in the experiencing as they might seem to be from the telling. Emotional tone of the activity was low, and intellectual currents weak. Such rewards as scraping the block or "getting to do the blue ones" were not very exciting, and the stretches of repetitive movement involved in achieving them were long enough to permit lapses into obsessive reverie. Henri de Man speaks of "clinging to the remnants of joy in work," and this situation represented just that. How tenacious the clinging was, how long I could have "stuck it out" with my remnants, was never determined. Before the first week was out this adjustment to the work situation was complicated by other developments. The game of work continued, but in a different context. Its influence became decidedly subordinated to, if not completely overshadowed by, another source of job satisfaction.

INFORMAL SOCIAL ACTIVITY OF THE WORK GROUP: TIMES AND THEMES

The change came about when I began to take serious note of the social activity going on around me; my attentiveness to this activity came with growing involvement in it. What I heard at first, before I started to listen, was a stream of disconnected bits of communication which did not make much sense. Foreign accents were strong and referents were not joined to coherent contexts of meaning. It was just "jabbering." What I saw at first, before I began to observe, was occasional flurries of horseplay so simple and unvarying in pattern and so childish in quality that they made no strong bid for attention. For example, Ike would regularly switch off the power at Sammy's machine whenever Sammy made a trip to the lavatory or the drinking fountain. Correlatively, Sammy invariably fell victim to the plot by making an attempt to operate his clicking hammer after returning to the shop. And, as the simple pattern went, this blind stumbling into the trap was always followed by indignation and reproach from Sammy, smirking satisfaction from Ike, and mild paternal scolding from George. My interest in this procedure was at first confined to wondering when Ike would weary of his tedious joke or when Sammy would learn to check his power switch before trying the hammer.

But, as I began to pay closer attention, as I began to develop familiarity

---

[9] Lucille Milner, *Education of An American Liberal* (New York: Horizon Press, 1954), p. 97.

with the communication system, the disconnected became connected, the nonsense made sense, the obscure became clear, and the silly actually funny. And, as the content of the interaction took on more meaning, the interaction began to reveal structure. There were "times" and "themes," and roles to serve their enaction. The interaction had subtleties, and I began to savor and appreciate them. I started to record what hitherto had seemed unimportant.

Times

This emerging awareness of structure and meaning included recognition that the long day's grind was broken by interruptions of a kind other than the formally instituted or idiosyncratically developed disjunctions in work routine previously described. These additional interruptions appeared in daily repetition in an ordered series of informal interactions. They were, in part, but only in part and in very rough comparison, similar to those common fractures of the production process known as the coffee break, the coke break, and the cigarette break. Their distinction lay in frequency of occurrence and in brevity. As phases of the daily series, they occurred almost hourly, and so short were they in duration that they disrupted work activity only slightly. Their significance lay not so much in their function as rest pauses, although it cannot be denied that physical refreshment was involved. Nor did their chief importance lie in the accentuation of progress points in the passage of time, although they could perform that function far more strikingly than the hour hand on the dull face of George's alarm clock. If the daily series of interruptions be likened to a clock, then the comparison might best be made with a special kind of cuckoo clock, one with a cuckoo which can provide variation in its announcements and can create such an interest in them that the intervening minutes become filled with intellectual content. The major significance of the interactional inter-ruptions lay in such a carryover of interest. The physical interplay which momentarily halted work activity would initiate verbal exchanges and thought processes to occupy group members until the next interruption. The group interactions thus not only marked off the time; they gave it content and hurried it along.

Most of the breaks in the daily series were designated as "times" in the parlance of the clicker operators, and they featured the consumption of food or drink of one sort or another. There was coffee time, peach time, banana time, fish time, coke time, and, of course, lunch time. Other inter-ruptions, which formed part of the series but were not verbally recog-nized as times, were window time, pickup time, and the staggered quitting times of Sammy and Ike. These latter unnamed times did not involve the partaking of refreshments.

My attention was first drawn to this times business during my first week of employment when I was encouraged to join in the sharing of two peaches. It was Sammy who provided the peaches; he drew them from his lunch box after making the announcement, "Peach time!" On this first occasion I refused the proffered fruit, but thereafter regularly consumed my half peach. Sammy continued to provide the peaches and to make the "Peach time!" announcement, although there were days when Ike would remind him that it was peach time, urging him to hurry up with the mid-morning snack. Ike invariably complained about the quality of the fruit, and his complaints fed the fires of continued banter between peach donor and critical recipient. I did find the fruit a bit on the scrubby side but felt, before I achieved insight into the function of peach time, that Ike was showing poor manners by looking a gift horse in the mouth. I wondered why Sammy continued to share his peaches with such an ingrate.

Banana time followed peach time by approximately an hour. Sammy again provided the refreshments, namely, one banana. There was, however, no four-way sharing of Sammy's banana. Ike would gulp it down by himself after surreptitiously extracting it from Sammy's lunch box, kept on a shelf behind Sammy's work station. Each morning, after making the snatch, Ike would call out, "Banana time!" and proceed to down his prize while Sammy made futile protests and denunciations. George would join in with mild remonstrances, sometimes scolding Sammy for making so much fuss. The banana was one which Sammy brought for his own consumption at lunch time; he never did get to eat his banana, but kept bringing one for his lunch. At first this daily theft startled and amazed me. Then I grew to look forward to the daily seizure and the verbal interaction which followed.

Window time came next. It followed banana time as a regular consequence of Ike's castigation by the indignant Sammy. After "taking" repeated references to himself as a person badly lacking in morality and character, Ike would "finally" retaliate by opening the window which faced Sammy's machine, to let the "cold air" blow in on Sammy. The slandering which would, in its echolalic repetition, wear down Ike's patience and forbearance usually took the form of the invidious comparison. "George is a good daddy! Ike is a bad man! A very bad man!" Opening the window would take a little time to accomplish and would involve a great deal of verbal interplay between Ike and Sammy, both before and after the event. Ike would threaten, make feints toward the window, then finally open it. Sammy would protest, argue, and make claims that the air blowing in on him would give him a cold; he would eventually have to leave his machine to close the window. Sometimes the weather was slightly chilly, and the draft from the window unpleasant; but cool or hot, windy or still, window time arrived each day. (I assume that it was originally a cold season development.) George's part in this interplay, in spite of the "good daddy" laudations, was to encourage Ike in his window work. He would stress the tonic values of fresh air and chide Sammy for his unappreciativeness.

Following window time came lunch time, a formally designated half-hour for the midday repast and rest break. At this time, informal interaction would feature exchanges between Ike and George. The former would start eating his lunch a few minutes before noon, and the latter, in his role as straw boss, would censure him for malobservance of the rules. Ike's off-beat luncheon usually involved a previous tampering with George's alarm clock. Ike would set the clock ahead a few minutes in order to maintain his eating schedule without detection, and George would discover these small daylight saving changes.

The first "time" interruption of the day I did not share. It occurred soon after I arrived on the job, at eight o'clock. George and Ike would share a small pot of coffee brewed on George's hot plate.

Pickup time, fish time, and coke time came in the afternoon. I name it pickup time to represent the official visit of the man who made daily calls to cart away boxes of clicked materials. The arrival of the pickup man, a Negro, was always a noisy one, like the arrival of a daily passenger train in an isolated small town. Interaction attained a quick peak of intensity to crowd into a few minutes all communications, necessary and otherwise. Exchanges invariably included loud depreciations by the pickup man of the amount of work accomplished in the clicking department during the preceding twenty-four hours. Such scoffing would be on the order of "Is that all you've got done? What do you boys do all day?" These devaluations would be countered with allusions to the "soft job" enjoyed by the pickup man. During the course of the exchanges news items would be dropped, some of serious import, such as reports of accomplished or impending layoffs in the various plants of the company, or of gains or losses in orders for company products. Most of the news items, however, involved bits of information on plant employees told in a light vein. Information relayed by the clicker operators was usually told about each other, mainly in the form of summaries of the most recent kidding sequences. Some of this material was repetitive, carried over from day to day. Sammy would be the butt of most of this newscasting, although he would make occasional counter-reports on Ike and George. An invariable part of the interactional content of pickup time was Ike's introduction of the pickup man to George. "Meet Mr. Papeatis!" Ike would say in mock solemnity and dignity. Each day the pickup man "met" Mr. Papeatis, to the obvious irritation of the latter. Another pickup time invariably would bring Baby (or Mable) into the interaction. George would always issue the loud warning to the pickup man: "Now I want you to stay away from Baby! She's Henry's girl!" Henry was a burly Negro with a booming bass voice who made infrequent trips to the clicking room with lift-truck loads of materials. He was reputedly quite a ladies' man among the colored population of the factory. George's warning to "Stay away from Baby!" was issued to every Negro who entered the shop. Baby's only part in this was to laugh at the horseplay.

About mid-afternoon came fish time. George and Ike would stop work for a few minutes to consume some sort of pickled fish which Ike provided. Neither Sammy nor I partook of this nourishment, nor were we invited. For this omission I was grateful; the fish, brought in a newspaper and with the head and tail intact, produced a reverse effect on my appetite. George and Ike seemed to share a great liking for fish. Each Friday night, as a regular ritual, they would enjoy a fish dinner together at a nearby restaurant. On these nights Ike would work until 8:30 and leave the plant with George.

Coke time came late in the afternoon, and was an occasion for total participation. The four of us took turns in buying the drinks and in making the trip for them to a fourth floor vending machine. Through George's manipulation of the situation, it eventually became my daily chore to go after the cokes; the straw boss had noted that I made a much faster trip to the fourth floor and back than Sammy or Ike.

Sammy left the plant at 5:30, and Ike ordinarily retired from the scene an hour and a half later. These quitting times were not marked by any distinctive interaction save the one regular exchange between Sammy and George over the former's "early washup." Sammy's tendency was to crowd his washing up toward five o'clock, and it was George's concern to keep it from further creeping advance. After Ike's departure came Boo's arrival. Boo's was a striking personality productive of a change in topics of conversation to fill in the last hour of the long workday.

Themes

To put flesh, so to speak, on this interactional frame of "times," my work group had developed various "themes" of verbal interplay which had become standardized in their repetition. These topics of conversation ranged in quality from an extreme of nonsensical chatter to another extreme of serious discourse. Unlike the times, these themes flowed one into the other in no particular sequence of predictability. Serious conversation could suddenly melt into horseplay, and vice versa. In the middle of a serious discussion on the high cost of living, Ike might drop a weight behind the easily startled Sammy, who hit him over the head with a dusty paper sack. Interaction would immediately drop to a low comedy exchange of slaps, threats, guffaws, and disapprobations which would invariably include a ten-minute echolalia of "Ike is a bad man, a very bad man! George is a good daddy, a very fine man!" Or, on the other hand, a stream of such invidious comparisons as followed a surreptitious switching-off of Sammy's machine by the playful Ike might merge suddenly into a discussion of the pros and cons of saving for one's funeral.

"Kidding themes" were usually started by George or Ike, and Sammy was usually the butt of the joke. Sometimes Ike would have to "take it," seldom George. One favorite kidding theme involved Sammy's alleged receipt of $100 a month from his son. The points stressed were that Sammy did not have to work long hours, or did not have to work at all, because he had a son to support him. George would always point out that he sent money to his daughter; she did not send money to him. Sammy received occasional calls from his wife, and his claim that these calls were requests to shop for groceries on the way home were greeted with feigned disbelief. Sammy was ribbed for being closely watched, bossed, and henpecked by his wife, and the expression "Are you a man or mouse?" became an echolalic utterance, used both in and out of the original context.

Ike, who shared his machine and the work scheduled for it with Boo, the night operator, came in for constant invidious comparison on the subject of output. The socially isolated Boo, who chose work rather than sleep on his lonely night shift, kept up a high level of performance, and George never tired of pointing this out to Ike. It so happened that Boo, an Arabian Moslem from Palestine, had no use for Jews in general; and Ike, who was Jewish, had no use for Boo in particular. Whenever George would extol Boo's previous night's production, Ike would try to turn the conversation into a general discussion on the need for educating the Arabs. George, never permitting the development of serious discussion on the topic, would repeat a smirking warning, "You watch out for Boo! He's got a long knife!"

The "poom poom" theme was one that caused no sting. It would come up several times a day to be enjoyed as unbarbed fun by the three older clicker operators. Ike was usually the one to raise the question, "How many times you go poom poom last night?" The person questioned usually replied with claims of being "too old for poom poom." If this theme did develop a goat, it was I. When it was pointed out that I was a younger man, this provided further grist for the poom poom mill. I soon grew weary of this poom poom business, so dear to the hearts of the three old satyrs, and, knowing where the conversation would inevitably lead, winced whenever Ike brought up the subject. . . .

Serious themes included the relating of major misfortunes suffered in the past by group members. George referred again and again to the loss, by fire, of his business establishment. Ike's chief complaints centered around a chronically ill wife who had undergone various operations and periods of hospital care. Ike spoke with discouragement of the expenses attendant upon hiring a housekeeper for himself and his children; he referred with disappointment and disgust to a teen-age son, an inept lad who "couldn't even fix his own lunch. He couldn't even make himself a sandwich!" Sammy's reminiscences centered on the loss of a flourishing business when he had to flee Europe ahead of Nazi invasion.

But all serious topics were not tales of woe. One favorite serious theme which was optimistic in tone could be called either "Danelly's future" or "getting Danelly a better job." It was known that I had been attending "college," the magic door to opportunity, although my specific course of study remained somewhat obscure. Suggestions poured forth on good lines of work to get into, and these suggestions were backed with accounts of friends, and friends of friends, who had made good via the academic route. My answer to the expected question, "Why are you working here?" always stressed the "lots of overtime" feature, and this explanation seemed to suffice for short-range goals.

There was one theme of especially solemn import, the "professor theme." This theme might also be termed "George's daughter's marriage theme"; for the recent marriage of George's only child was inextricably bound up with George's connection with higher learning. The daughter had married the son of a professor who instructed in one of the local colleges. This professor theme was not in the strictest sense a conversation piece; when the subject came up, George did all the talking. The two Jewish operatives remained silent as they listened with deep respect, if not actual awe, to George's accounts of the Big Wedding which, including the wedding pictures, entailed an expense of $1,000. It was monologue, but there was listening, there was communication, the sacred communication of a temple, when George told of going for Sunday afternoon walks on the Midway with the professor, or of joining the professor for a Sunday dinner. Whenever he spoke of the professor, his daughter, the wedding, or even of the new son-in-law, who remained for the most part in the background, a sort of incidental like the wedding cake, George was complete master of the interaction. His manner, in speaking to the rank-and-file of clicker operators, was indeed that of master deigning to notice his underlings. I came to the conclusion that it was the professor connection, not the straw-boss-ship or the extra nickel an hour, which provided the fount of George's superior status in the group.

If the professor theme may be regarded as the cream of verbal interaction, the "chatter themes" should be classed as the dregs. The chatter themes were hardly themes at all; perhaps they should be labelled "verbal states," or "oral autisms." Some were of doubtful status as communication; they were like the howl or cry of an animal responding to its own physiological state. They were exclamations, ejaculations, snatches of song or doggerel, talkings-to-oneself, mutterings. Their classification as themes would rest on their repetitive character. They were echolalic utterances, repeated over and over. An already mentioned example would be Sammy's repetition of "George is a good daddy, a very fine man! Ike is a bad man,

a very bad man!" Also, Sammy's repetition of "Don't bother me! Can't you
see I'm busy? I'm a very busy man!" for ten minutes after Ike had dropped
a weight behind him would fit the classification. Ike would shout "Ma-
mariba!" at intervals between repetition of bits of verse, such as

Mama on the bed,
Papa on the floor,
Baby in the crib
Says giver some more!

Sometimes the three operators would pick up one of these simple chatter-
ings in a sort of chorus. "Are you man or mouse? I ask you, are you man or
mouse?" was a favorite of this type.

So initial discouragement with the meagerness of social interaction I
now recognized as due to lack of observation. The interaction was there,
in constant flow. It captured attention and held interest to make the long
day pass. The twelve hours of "click, ———— move die, ———— click, ————
move die" became as easy to endure as eight hours of varied activity
in the oil fields or eight hours of playing the piece-work game in a machine shop. The "beast of boredom" was gentled to the harmlessness of a
kitten.

BLACK FRIDAY: DISINTEGRATION OF
THE GROUP

But all this was before "Black Friday." Events of that dark day shattered
the edifice of interaction, its framework of times and mosaic of themes,
and reduced the work situation to a state of social atomization and machine-
tending drudgery. The explosive element was introduced deliberately,
but without prevision of its consequences.

On Black Friday, Sammy was not present; he was on vacation. There
was no peach time that morning, of course, and no banana time. But
George and Ike held their coffee time, as usual, and a steady flow of
themes was filling the morning quite adequately. It seemed like a normal
day in the making, at least one which was going to meet the somewhat
reduced expectations created by Sammy's absence

Suddenly I was possessed of an inspiration for modification of the professor theme. When the idea struck, I was working at Sammy's machine,
clicking out leather parts for billfolds. It was not difficult to get the attention of close neighbor Ike to suggest sotto voice, "Why don't you tell him
you saw the professor teaching in a barber college on Madison Street? . . .
Make it near Halsted Street."

Ike thought this one over for a few minutes, and caught the vision of
its possibilities. After an interval of steady application to his clicking, he
informed the unsuspecting George of his near West Side discovery; he

had seen the professor busy at his instructing in a barber college in the lower reaches of Hobohemia.

George reacted to this announcement with stony silence. The burden of questioning Ike for further details on his discovery fell upon me. Ike had not elaborated his story very much before we realized that the show was not going over. George kept getting redder in the face, and more tight-lipped; he slammed into his clicking with increased vigor. I made one last weak attempt to keep the play on the road by remarking that barber colleges paid pretty well. George turned to hiss at me, "You'll have to go to Kankakee with Ike!" I dropped the subject. Ike whispered to me, "George is sore!"

George was indeed sore. He didn't say another word the rest of the morning. There was no conversation at lunchtime, nor was there any after lunch. A pall of silence had fallen over the clicker room. Fish time fell a casualty. George did not touch the coke I brought for him. A very long, very dreary afternoon dragged on. Finally, after Ike left for home, George broke the silence to reveal his feelings to me: "Ike acts like a five-year-old, not a man! He doesn't even have the respect of the niggers. But he's got to act like a man around here! He's always fooling around! I'm going to stop that! I'm going to show him his place! . . . Jews will ruin you, if you let them. I don't care if he sings, but the first time he mentions my name, I'm going to shut him up! It's always 'Meet Mr. Papeatis! George is a good daddy!" And all that. He's paid to work! If he doesn't work, I'm going to tell Joe!"

Then came a succession of dismal workdays devoid of times and barren of themes. Ike did not sing, nor did he recite bawdy verse. The shop songbird was caught in the grip of icy winter. What meager communication there was took a sequence of patterns which proved interesting only in retrospect.

For three days, George would not speak to Ike. Ike made several weak attempts to break the wall of silence which George had put between them, but George did not respond; it was as if he did not hear. George would speak to me, on infrequent occasions, and so would Ike. They did not speak to each other.

On the third day George advised me of his new communication policy, designed for dealing with Ike, and for Sammy, too. when the latter returned to work. Interaction was now on a "strictly business" basis, with emphasis to be placed on raising the level of shop output. The effect of this new policy on production remained indeterminate. Before the fourth day had ended, George got carried away by his narrowed interests to the point of making sarcastic remarks about the poor work performances of the absent Sammy. Although addressed to me, these caustic depreciations were obviously for the benefit of Ike. Later in the day Ike spoke to me, for George's benefit, of Sammy's outstanding ability to run out billfold parts.

For the next four days, the prevailing silence of the shop was occasionally broken by either harsh criticism or fulsome praise of Sammy's outstanding workmanship. I did not risk replying to either impeachment or panegyric for fear of involvement in further situational deteriorations.

Twelve-hour days were creeping again at snails' pace. The strictly business communications were of no help, and the sporadic bursts of distaste or enthusiasm for Sammy's clicking ability helped very little. With the return of boredom, came a return of fatigue. My legs tired as the afternoons dragged on, and I became engaged in conscious efforts to rest one by shifting my weight to the other. I would pause in my work to stare through the barred windows at the grimy brick wall across the alley; and, turning my head, I would notice that Ike was staring at the wall too. George would do very little work after Ike left the shop at night. He would sit in a chair and complain of weariness and sore feet.

In desperation, I fell back on my game of work, my blues and greens and whites, my ovals and trapezoids, and my scraping the block. I came to surpass Boo, the energetic night worker, in volume of output. George referred to me as a "day Boo" (dayshift Boo) and suggested that I "keep" Sammy's machine. I managed to avoid this promotion, and consequent estrangement with Sammy, by pleading attachment to my own machine.

When Sammy returned to work, discovery of the cleavage between George and Ike left him stunned. "They were the best of friends!" he said to me in bewilderment.

George now offered Sammy direct, savage criticisms of his work. For several days the good-natured Sammy endured these verbal aggressions without losing his temper, but when George shouted at him "You work like a preacher!" Sammy became very angry, indeed. I had a few anxious moments when I thought that the two old friends were going to come to blows.

Then, thirteen days after Black Friday, came an abrupt change in the pattern of interaction. George and Ike spoke to each other again, in friendly conversation: I noticed Ike talking to George after lunch. The two had newspapers of fish at George's cabinet. Ike was excited; he said, "I'll pull up a chair!" The two ate for ten minutes. . . . It seems that they went up to the 22nd Street Exchange together during lunch period to cash pay checks.

That afternoon Ike and Sammy started to play again, and Ike burst once more into song. Old themes reappeared as suddenly as the desert flowers in spring. At first, George managed to maintain some show of the dignity of superordination. When Ike started to sing snatches of "You Are My Sunshine," George suggested that he get "more production." Then Ike backed up George in pressuring Sammy for more production. Sammy turned this exhortation into low comedy by calling Ike a "slave driver" and by shouting over and over again, "Don't bother me! I'm a busy man!" On one occasion, as if almost overcome with joy and excitement, Sammy cried out, "Don't bother me! I'll tell Rothman! [the company president] I'll tell the union! Don't mention my name! I hate you!"

I knew that George was definitely back into the spirit of the thing when he called to Sammy, "Are you man or mouse?" He kept up the "man or mouse" chatter for some time.

George was for a time reluctant to accept fruit when it was offered to him, and he did not make a final capitulation to coke time until five days after renewal of the fun and fooling. Strictly speaking, there never was a return to banana time, peach time, or window time. However, the sharing and snitching of fruit did go on once more, and the window in front of Sammy's machine played a more prominent part than ever in the renaissance of horseplay in the clicker room. In fact, the "rush to the window" became an integral part of increasingly complex themes and repeated sequences of interaction. This window rushing became especially bound up with new developments which featured what may be termed the "anal gesture."[10] Introduced by Ike, and given backing by an enthusiastic, very playful George, the anal gesture became a key component of fun and fooling during the remaining weeks of my stay in the shop: Ike broke wind, and put his head in his hand on the block as Sammy grabbed a rod and made a mock rush to open the window. He beat Ike on the head, and George threw some water on him, playfully. In came the Negro head of the Leather Department; he remarked jokingly that we should take out the machines and make a playroom out of the shop.

Of course, George's demand for greater production was metamorphized into horseplay. His shout of "Production please!" became a chatter theme to accompany the varied antics of Ike and Sammy.

The professor theme was dropped completely. George never again mentioned his Sunday walks on the Midway with the professor.

CONCLUSIONS

Speculative assessment of the possible significance of my observations on informal interaction in the clicking room may be set forth in a series of general statements.

Practical Application

First, in regard to possible practical application to problems of industrial management, these observations seem to support the generally accepted

---

[10] I have been puzzled to note widespread appreciation of this gesture in the "consumatory" communication of the working men of this nation. For the present I leave it to clinical psychologists to account for the nature and pervasiveness of this social bond.

notion that one key source of job satisfaction lies in the informal interaction shared by members of a work group. In the clicking-room situation the spontaneous development of a pattern combination of horseplay, serious conversation, and frequent sharing of food and drink reduced the monotony of simple, repetitive operations to the point where a regular schedule of long work days became livable. This kind of group interplay may be termed "consumatory" in the sense indicated by Dewey, when he makes a basic distinction between "instrumental" and "consumatory" communication.[11] The enjoyment of communication "for its own sake" as "mere sociabilities," as "free, aimless social intercourse," brings job satisfaction, at least job endurance, to work situations largely bereft of creative experience.

In regard to another managerial concern, employee productivity, any appraisal of the influence of group interaction upon clicking-room output could be no more than roughly impressionistic. I obtained no evidence to warrant a claim that banana time, or any of its accompaniments in consumatory interaction, boosted production. To the contrary, my diary recordings express an occasional perplexity in the form of "How does this company manage to stay in business?" However, I did not obtain sufficient evidence to indicate that, under the prevailing conditions of laissez-faire management, the output of our group would have been more impressive if the playful cavorting of three middle-aged gentlemen about the barred windows had never been. As far as achievement of managerial goals is concerned, the most that could be suggested is that leavening the deadly boredom of individualized work routines with a concurrent flow of group festivities had a negative effect on turnover. I left the group, with sad reluctance, under the pressure of strong urgings to accept a research fellowship which would involve no factory toil. My fellow clickers stayed with their machines to carry on their labors in the spirit of banana time.

Theoretical Considerations

Secondly, possible contribution to ongoing sociological inquiry into the behavior of small groups, in general, and factory work groups, in particular, may lie in one or more of the following ideational products of my clicking-room experience.

1. In their day-long confinement together in a small room spatially and socially isolated from other work areas of the factory the Clicking Department employees found themselves ecologically situated for development of a "natural" group. Such a development did take place; from worker intercommunications did emerge the full-blown sociocultural system of consumatory interactions which I came to share, observe, and record in the process of my socialization.

---

[11] John Dewey, *Experience and Nature* (Chicago: Open Court Publishing Co., 1925), pp. 202–06.

2.   These interactions had a content which could be abstracted from the total existential flow of observable doings and sayings for labelling and objective consideration. That is, they represented a distinctive subculture, with its recurring patterns of reciprocal influencings which I have described as times and themes.

3.   From these interactions may also be abstracted a social structure of statuses and roles. This structure may be discerned in the carrying out of the various informal activities which provide the content of the subculture of the group. The times and themes were performed with a system of roles which formed a sort of pecking hierarchy. Horseplay had its initiators and its victims, its amplifiers and its chorus; kidding had its attackers and attacked, its least attacked and its most attacked, its ready acceptors of attack and its strong resistors to attack. The fun went on with the participation of all, but within the controlling frame of status, a matter of who can say or do what to whom and get away with it.

4.   In both the cultural content and the social structure of clicker group interaction could be seen the permeation of influences which flowed from the various multiple group memberships of the participants. Past and present "other-group" experiences or anticipated "outside" social connections provided significant materials for the building of themes and for the establishment and maintenance of status and role relationships. The impact of reference group affiliations on clicking-room interaction was notably revealed in the sacred, status-conferring expression of the professor theme. This impact was brought into very sharp focus in developments which followed my attempt to degrade the topic, and correlatively, to demote George.

5.   Stability of the clicking-room social system was never threatened by immediate outside pressures. Ours was not an instrumental group, subject to disintegration in a losing struggle against environmental obstacles or oppositions. It was not striving for corporate goals; nor was it faced with the enmity of other groups. It was strictly a consumatory group, devoted to the maintenance of patterns of self-entertainment. Under existing conditions, disruption of unity could come only from within.

Potentials for breakdown were endemic in the interpersonal interactions involved in conducting the group's activities. Patterns of fun and fooling had developed within a matrix of frustration. Tensions born of long hours of relatively meaningless work were released in the mock aggressions of horseplay. In the recurrent attack, defense, and counterattack there continually lurked the possibility that words or gestures harmless in conscious intent might cross the subtle boundary of accepted, playful aggression to be perceived as real assault. While such an occurrence might incur displeasure no more lasting than necessary for the quick clarification or creation of kidding norms, it might also spark a charge of hostility sufficient to disorganize the group.

A contributory potential for breakdown from within lay in the dissimilar "other group" experiences of the operators. These other-group affiliations and identifications could provide differences in tastes and sensitivities, including appreciation of humor, differences which could make maintenance of consensus in regard to kidding norms a hazardous process of trial and error adjustments.

6. The risk involved in this trial and error determination of consensus on fun and fooling in a touchy situation of frustration—mock aggression—was made evident when I attempted to introduce alterations in the professor theme. The group disintegrated, *instanter*. That is, there was an abrupt cessation of the interactions which constituted our groupness. Although both George and I were solidly linked in other-group affiliations with the higher learning, there was not enough agreement in our attitudes toward university professors to prevent the interactional development which shattered our factory play group. George perceived my offered alterations as a real attack, and he responded with strong hostility directed against Ike, the perceived assailant, and Sammy, a fellow traveler.

My innovations, if accepted, would have lowered the tone of the sacred professor theme, if not to "Stay Away From Baby" ribaldry, then at least to the verbal slapstick level of "finding Danelly an apartment." Such a downgrading of George's reference group would, in turn, have downgraded George. His status in the shop group hinged largely upon his claimed relations with the professor.

7. Integration of our group was fully restored after a series of changes in the patterning and quality in clicking-room interaction. It might be said that reintegration took place in these changes, that the series was a progressive one of step-by-step improvement in relations, that re-equilibration was in process during the three weeks that passed between initial communication collapse and complete return to "normal" interaction.

The cycle of loss and recovery of equilibrium may be crudely charted according to the following sequence of phases: *(a)* the stony silence of "not speaking"; *(b)* the confining of communication to formal matters connected with work routines; *(c)* the return of informal give-and-take in the form of harshly sarcastic kidding, mainly on the subject of work performance, addressed to a neutral go-between for the "benefit" of the object of aggression; *(d)* highly emotional direct attack, and counter-attack, in the form of criticism and defense of work performance; *(e)* a sudden rapprochement expressed in serious, dignified, but friendly conversation; *(f)* return to informal interaction in the form of mutually enjoyed mock aggression; *(g)* return to informal interaction in the form of regular patterns of sharing food and drink.

The group had disintegrated when George withdraw from participation; and, since the rest of us were at all times ready for rapprochement, reintegration was dependent upon his "return." Therefore, each change of phase in interaction on the road to recovery could be said to represent an increment of return on George's part. Or, conversely, each phase could represent an increment of reacceptance of punished deviants. Perhaps more generally applicable to description of a variety of reunion situations would be conceptualization of the phase changes as increments of reassociation without an atomistic differentiation of the "movements" of individuals.

8.   To point out that George played a key role in this particular case of re-equilibration is not to suggest that the homeostatic controls of a social system may be located in a type of role or in a patterning of role relationships. Such controls could be but partially described in terms of human interaction; they would be functional to the total configuration of conditions within the field of influence. The automatic controls of a mechanical system operate a such only under certain achieved and controlled conditions. The human body recovers from disease when conditions for such homeostasis are "right." The clicking-room group regained equilibrium under certain undetermined conditions. One of a number of other possible outcomes could have developed had conditions not been favorable for recovery.

For purposes of illustration, and from reflections on the case, I would consider the following as possibly necessary conditions for reintegration of our group: (a) Continued monotony of work operations; (b) Continued lack of a comparatively adequate substitute for the fun and fooling release from work tensions; (c) Inability of the operatives to escape from the work situation or from each other, within the work situation. George could not fire Ike or Sammy to remove them from his presence, and it would have been difficult for the three middle-aged men to find other jobs if they were to quit the shop. Shop space was small, and the machines close together. Like a submarine crew, they had to "live together"; (d) Lack of conflicting definitions of the situation after Ike's perception of George's reaction to the "barber college" attack. George's anger and his punishment of the offenders were perceived as justified; (e) Lack of introduction of new issues or causes which might have carried justification for new attacks and counter-attacks, thus leading interaction into a spiral of conflict and crystallization of conflict norms. For instance, had George reported his offenders to the superintendent for their poor work performance; had he, in his anger, committed some offense which would have led to reporting of a grievance to local union officials; had he made his anti-Semitic remarks in the presence of Ike or Sammy, or had I relayed these remarks to them; had I tried to "take over" Sammy's machine, as George had urged; then the interactional outcome might have been permanent disintegration of the group.

9.   Whether or not the particular patterning of interactional change previously noted is somehow typical of a "re-equilibration process" is not a major question here. My purpose in discriminating the seven changes is primarily to suggest that re-equilibration, when it does occur, may be de-

scribed in observable phases and that the emergence of each succeeding phase should be dependent upon the configuration of conditions of the preceding one. Alternative eventual outcomes may change in their probabilities, as the phases succeed each other, just as prognosis for recovery in sickness may change as the disease situation changes.

10.   Finally, discrimination of phase changes in social process may have practical as well as scientific value. Trained and skillful administrators might follow the practice in medicine of introducing aids to re-equilibration when diagnosis shows that they are needed.

Organizations and Coronary Heart Disease: The Stress Connection*

JOHN M. IVANCEVICH and
MICHAEL T. MATTESON

WITHIN a year, at least 425 readers of this issue of *Management Review* will die as a result of cardiovascular disease. Such is the pervasive nature of this killer. Each year in the United States alone, approximately 1 million people die from various forms of cardiovascular disease; about 600,000 to 700,000 of these die from heart attacks or coronary heart disease (CHD). Since approximately 1920, there has been a steady and significant increase in the recorded death rate from heart attacks in the Western world. While the precise causes of this phenomenon remain poorly understood, one partial explanation growing in popularity points to the increasing complexity and stress of modern life as a contributing factor. A not insignificant portion of this stress may have its genesis in organizational related forces which are called "stressors." Stressors are present anytime individuals are confronted by situations where their usual behaviors are inappropriate or insufficient and where there are negative consequences associated with not properly dealing with the situation.

It has been suggested by at least one medical practitioner that if such things as blood pressure, cholesterol, and smoking could be completely controlled, no more than 25 percent of heart disease would be eliminated. In the same article the doctor concludes that there is strong evidence that *organizational stress plays an important role in the development of the remaining 75 percent of the instances of heart disease.*

It has not been easy for management to accept the proposition that for some individuals organizational related stress can be a contributor to coronary and other diseases. In recent years, however, medical journals have devoted increased space to studies dealing with the relationship between life and organizational stress and CHD. From these studies, one stream of findings tends to show up again and again: organizational stressors can and do cause changes in the physiological and psychological makeup of some individuals. Further, these changes can be contributors to CHD as well as other ailments such as peptic ulcers, migraine headaches, certain types of asthma, sexual dysfunctions, and alcoholism.

In this article we will present a framework for sorting out some of the stressors and outcomes associated with organizational life and their possible linkage to CHD. The framework serves as a model for systematically attempting to identify not only stressors and the reactions to them exhibited by employees, but also the combative programs that can be individually and organizationally initiated to minimize potentially harmful stress effects.

The Stress Puzzle

The notion of stress is a popular topic of conversation. A young doctor named Hans Selye (pronounced sell-yea), who emigrated from Central Europe to Canada in the 1930s, first borrowed the English word from physics to describe the body's responses to everything from flu viruses and cold temperatures to emotions such as fear and anger. Today *stress* is often broadly defined as a consequence of any action, situation, or force that places special physical and/or psychological demands upon a person. Stress creates a condition of imbalance within a person. This imbalance is the precipitor of many common stress symptoms such as insomnia, sweating, nervousness, and irritability. However, stress symptoms can also be positive such as an increased state of self-motivation and more commitment to finish a job. What makes the pieces of the stress puzzle so difficult to fit together, however, is that negative and positive stress symptoms are not the same for every individual.

All of us vary in our capacity to cope with stress. Personality characteristics, emotional balance, physical condition and health, and past experiences are major factors that operate to determine our individual response to stress. Some amount of stress is good and has positive, productive consequences. Unfortunately, generalizations about how much organizational stress is optimal or is needed to contribute to high job performance from an individual are impossible to reach. Some organizational stressors such as a demotion, losing a job, or receiving conflicting demands from more than one superior, have negative consequences for most employees. On the other hand, some stressors such as being passed over for promotion or not participating in decision-making, produce no negative or harmful stress reactions in some individuals. There are even some stressors such as a difficult job or numerous job assignments that have positive consequences for some people.

One striking theme of Hans Selye's research is that some individuals enjoy stress, and are only happy with a vigorous, fast-paced lifestyle. These individuals he calls "racehorses." On the other hand, some individuals want a peaceful, quiet, and tranquil environment. These individuals are referred to as "turtles." It is Selye's contention that both categories of people—"racehorses" and "turtles"—require a certain amount of stress. But the degree and the sources will differ. And even for the racehorses the same stress which is so important to them and motivates them to high levels of performance may be brewing subtle internal transformations that will increase the likelihood that some of these individuals will "unexpectedly" become CHD statistics.

Stress and Job Performance: The Critical Curve

The main question here is, How much stress is enough? An optimum level of organizational stress can improve job performance, whereas excessive stress can retard performance and ruin health. When stress has positive consequences for an individual, job performance will in most cases improve, at least in the short run. Being overburdened by stress-producing forces or situations however can have negative consequences for performance. Figure 1 provides a visual picture of the relationship between organizational stress and individual performance.

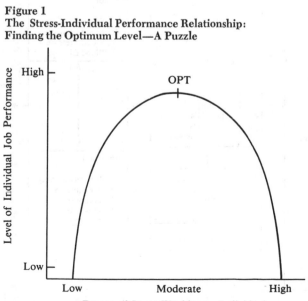

Figure 1
The Stress-Individual Performance Relationship:
Finding the Optimum Level—A Puzzle

What is shown in Figure 1 is a performance curve. The curve points out that from a performance standpoint some stress is good, but excessive stress is bad. As organizational stress increases, so does individual performance—up to the optimum point (OPT). Beyond this level, stress causes a rapid decrease in individual performance.

The Stress Connection

A framework may be helpful to you as a manager in identifying individual stress problems and taking necessary corrective action. At a minimum, the following elements should be part of such a framework: major organizational *stressors;* the manner in which stressors are *perceived;* the *responses* or *outcomes* to the perception of stressors; and important *results* or *consequences.*

The variables in the Figure 2 model have been identified by medical and behavioral researchers as potentially significant for understanding the stressor and CHD link. They are however, not exhaustive. A variety of other stressors may operate to bring about the same outcomes and consequences as the ones identified in this figure.

Figure 2
A Managerial-Based Perspective of the Relationship between Organizational Stressors and Coronary Heart Disease

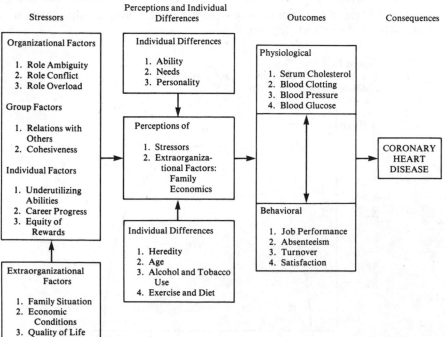

The framework illustrates a number of organizational stressor categories. Conflicting and too many work demands can create role ambiguity, conflict, and overload. Cohesiveness and relations with others are group factors which may serve either as stressors or stress reducers. For example, while low cohesion in a work group may create stress, high cohesion may serve to offset the effects of other stressors by providing the employee with a great deal of psychological support.

With respect to individual factors, a potential major and widespread stressor is being underutilized. Lack of management attention to the underutilization issue may further compound the situation by adversely affecting employee satisfaction levels, creating even greater stress. A perceived lack of career progress and inequity in reward systems are two other powerful stressors for some people.

As individuals we carry "psychological baggage" into an organization just as we export our job problems into our homes and personal life. The impact of extra organizational stressors should never be underestimated. About the best any manager can do about extra organizational stressors is to be aware of their potential significance, alert to their presence, and show compassion, interest, and understanding. Attempting to intrude on such stress filled situations as marital problems or child-rearing practices is definitely not recommended. Well-meaning managers who attempt to play amateur psychiatrists may find that the only thing they have accomplished is elevating their own stress levels!

The framework presented points out that individual perceptions are important in understanding outcomes and consequences. Whether or not a stressor is stress provoking depends a great deal on the perception of the employee experiencing the stressor. That perception is influenced in turn by a variety of individual differences. From these perceptions flow both the physiological and behavioral outcomes.

Figure 2 is not meant to be interpreted as stating that organizational stressors invariably result in coronary heart disease. This is most assuredly not the case. Research clearly indicates that organizational stressors can in some cases result in positive consequences such as improved performance, increased motivation to work harder, and more creativity. In many other cases their physiological impact is of no real significance. Instead, the framework introduces the notion that individual differences may play a major part in unraveling the mysteries of how organizational stressors contribute to an increased incidence of CHD for *some* individuals.

How We Respond to Stress

Employees may react to stress conditions in three ways: emotionally, behaviorally, and physiologically. The emotional reactions are the ones many people associate with being under stress. These range from anger and fear to anxiety and hostility. In some cases the employee suffering from severe stress may act irresponsibly and irrationally.

The behavioral reactions to stress can be either positive or negative. As shown in Figure 1, moderate stress can result in improved or high levels of job performance. However, people suffering from excessive organizationally related stress tend to be absent more, frequently quit their jobs, and often make more errors in carrying out job tasks. They may also increase cigarette and/or alcohol consumption, turn to ill-advised medications, and in severe cases exhibit paranoid behavior.

Underlying all reactions to stress are physiological responses within the body. These responses can lead to a wide variety of physical ailments including: migraine headaches, peptic ulcers, hypertension, and heart attack. Stressors such as role overload, poor relations with others, a deadline to complete a project, or a family argument stimulate our glands and nervous system to produce hormones that equip us to combat the stress.

These physiological reactions of the body prepare it to "fight" or "flee." When either route is taken, eventually the system restores itself to a position of balance. A problem within organizational settings and one which managers need to be aware of is that the stressors build up rather slowly and most people do not take a total fight or flight stance. *Therefore, stress reactions tend to accumulate and persist for long periods of time.* This is where organic problems such as coronary heart disease enter the picture. Frequently, CHD gives few obvious early warning signals. Unless the best physiological predictors of coronary heart disease are monitored, there is little hope in reducing the widespread tragedy of a heart attack.

Stress and Occupations

Everyone has heard of the story of the person who boasted, "I'm a top-level executive and I've got an ulcer to prove it." Unfortunately, there is abundant evidence in the medical literature to indicate that people in some occupations have a higher incidence of physical ailments such as ulcers, heart disease, and high blood pressure. Since human resources must be regarded as an irreplaceable asset of any company, the relationship between occupational stressors and heart disease can provide important information for developing action programs. Examples of organizational stressors related to three occupational groups may serve to illustrate this point.

Business Executives. Successful executives are generally described as driving, ambitious, intense, task-oriented individuals. They are company oriented and job-centered and are therefore more prone to coronary problems, especially if all their personal interests are narrowly based. Friedman and Rosenman, two cardiologists, have correlated the traits of some hard driving executives to produce a coronary prone profile. The profiles are called Type A and Type B personality. The Type A personality fits an executive with intense ambition, competitive drive, a sense of urgency, and restlessness. The research of Friedman and Rosenman suggests that the Type A executive has a higher probability of developing coronary heart disease or suffering a fatal heart attack.

Despite the pioneering work of Friedman and Rosenman, there is concern about labeling the Type A personality as coronary prone. In fact, some Type A business executives appear to be very healthy and thrive on fact paced challenges. It seems more feasible to consider executives individually to establish their personal stress condition and their ability to cope with stressors. Evidence suggests that it is the executives who have not attained their goals or ambitions who report the highest degree of stress. It is the young 35-year-old comer who's still in the same position at 40 who feels high stress. Less stress is reported by top-level executives who have worked hard and long and have achieved their career goals. The executive who has risen to the top appears to be able to channel new pressures and challenges into productive stress.

Accountants. Much medical research has suggested that cholesterol is a factor in coronary heart disease. Cholesterol levels appear to be a valid indicator of stress among accountants. In one study of accountants the effects of occupational stress upon levels of serum cholesterol was monitored. The accountants involved had fairly routine work schedules except during urgent tax deadlines! Each accountant's highest level of cholesterol occurred during the points of highest stress or right before the deadlines. That is, cholesterol levels rose as tax deadlines approached. (One might question whether that phenomenon is restricted to accountants!) The lowest level of serum cholesterol occurred at times of minimal stress. This study suggests that cholesterol is extremely sensitive to stress associated with job conditions such as overload, urgency, and task completion.

Operating Employees. A number of research reports indicate that job pressures at the operating employee level affect job satisfaction and consequently, various physiological factors such as blood pressure and cholesterol. *In fact, job satisfaction has been found to be inversely related to the frequency of heart attacks for telephone operators, manufacturing employees, sales personnel, and other occupational groups.* Job pressures are caused by such factors as unclear requests from supervisors, emphasis on completing job tasks in unrealistic amounts of time, misunderstanding of the reward system being used, inability to accomplish challenging goals, and underutilization of abilities.

PRESCRIPTIONS FOR REDUCING STRESS

Since potentially harmful stressors exist in every organization, at all levels and for every occupation from the chief operating officer to the window washer, it is important to understand stress, reactions to it, and methods of reducing the negative forms of stress. Fortunately, there are numerous techniques ranging from psychotherapy to transcendental meditation which are available for reducing negative stress reactions. One way of looking at these methods is to classify them as involving either *individual* or *organization* initiated programs.

Individual Methods of Stress Reduction

Ultimately employees must assume the responsibility for their health. *Awareness* and then *action* are the steps needed for an individual to reduce potentially harmful stress. As part of the awareness step a doctor should be consulted for a physical examination. Typically, the doctor will evaluate such things as your blood pressure, cholesterol level, smoking and drinking habits, coronary history and heredity, electrocardiogram, weight, physical activity record, and cardiorespiratory fitness index. (A suggestion here: A growing number of medical practitioners are recommending that in addition to the customary resting electrocardiogram, individuals should undergo a stress ECG as well, usually involving strenuous levels of performance on a treadmill. Stress electrocardiograms are detecting coronary abnormalities in about 15 percent of patients with normal resting ECGs.) The results of this type of examination will provide you with specific information on current and projected health. While the medical exam is discussed here under individual methods, organizational resources can most definitely be utilized to promote and facilitate this activity. Special programs set up with the company's medical department or an outside preventive medicine clinic can encourage employees to take the important awareness step.

Beyond the physical exam, becoming intimately acquainted with yourself and the organizational and life stressors that make you tense or uncomfortable is a necessary antecedent to any individually initiated action. It is essentially a task of introspection, the importance of which cannot be underestimated. Medical records indicate that many heart attack survivors report becoming more introspective and personally reflective *after* their attacks. An unknown number of these may have averted their heart attacks altogether had they shown the same degree of insight into their activities much earlier.

Once the awareness program of your physical condition and organizational life is underway, then *action* steps are appropriate. A full gamut of techniques are available. Some action may involve nothing more than a decision to repattern certain activities such as various interpersonal relationships within the company, or a resolve to seek clarification of ambiguous aspects of your organizational role. There is some research that indicates that diet and exercise programs supervised by qualified medical professionals can be beneficial in reducing some amount of stress. The National Jogging Association, a nonprofit organization of some 20,000 members dedicated to fitness, reports that many joggers indicate their running activities release mental tension and depression and seem to add to their ability to react to stressors in more positive ways.

More exotic individual stress control techniques include such practices as yoga, transcendental meditation, and biofeedback. While the scientific evidence of the benefit of such practices is scant, indications are that some individuals definitely are able to alter both psychological and physiological factors through such activities. Perhaps the day will soon come when the coffee break will be replaced by the exercise break or the meditation break!

Organizational Methods of Reducing Stress

The issue of responsibility of the organization in the health and fitness of employees is somewhat controversial. There are opinions that health is a personal matter and therefore the responsibility of the individual. However, other opinions state that work, life, and health are so interrelated that the management of any organization must be concerned. Whether viewed from the pragmatic standpoint of productivity or simply the humane interest in general welfare it would seem that since employees at all levels are the human resource core of any organization, management has a responsibility to minimize potentially harmful stress. Thus, the preservation of health by managerial action can serve not only to protect the human assets of the organization, but also bring about a worthy social and personal outcome as well.

As stated earlier stressors such as role ambiguity, role conflict, role overload, underutilizing abilities, and poor working relations with others appear to be potentially bad for both individual health and also organizational effectiveness. Managers, through clear communication, the establishment of unambiguous job demands, and properly planned division of labor can reduce some of these job stressors. Discussions between each subordinate and supervisor about the job and its range and depth could reduce ambiguity and conflict.

It is possible to change the overall climate of the organization by managerial action focusing on stressor reduction. A chief contributor to the type of climate prevailing in a company is the day-to-day practices and philosophy of its managers. Better managerial practices would include methods of early identification of stress related problems so that employees who are under high amounts of stress can be helped. If the manager is viewed as an important resource for seeking help, employees may be more likely to recognize their own stress problems and be more willing to ask for help. The authors are currently working on the development of a Stress Diagnostic Survey (SDS) which is designed to provide an index of stressor producing conditions. This index could be used by managers to assess stressors and also to develop appropriate training programs to improve management awareness of stress conditions.

An important awareness requirement exists for managers in that they must understand that organizational stressors can endanger their health and the health of their employees. Therefore, working at changing organizational climate conditions that can contribute to increased physical ailments is an important, sound and worthy managerial practice. Being aware of the different reactions to stress and following up when signs of stressful response are picked up are part of the awareness program. *Asking, listening,* and *observing* are three actions that will improve a manager's understanding of subordinate stress factors.

Another managerial action with some potential for reducing stress effects for some employees involves the use of increased participation in decision making (PDM). Some research indicates that low PDM is related to excessive job stress. Attempts to decrease stress by PDM should be legitimate and requires an analysis of important decision situations. Participation in routine and trivial decisions is quite transparent and liable to result in even more stress. Additionally, allowing employees to participate should be considered a long-term endeavor. Research clearly demonstrates that involving employees in PDM and then suddenly stopping participation after a short period can create negative emotional, behavioral, and physiological reactions.

Job enrichment is another potential strategy for reducing job stress. Through enriching the job, an employee may feel more important and satisfied with the activities he or she must perform. Job enrichment may also solve or minimize underutilization problems. Of course, not all jobs can be enriched, nor do all employees want enriched jobs. There is also the problem of continual enrichment or later efforts to redesign jobs. How many times can a job be enriched? After the initial stimulation of an enriched job wears off, employees may again feel bored, dissatisfied or underutilized.

To Sum It up

Individuals at different times react differently to stress. For this and other reasons the precise relationship between stress and heart disease and other health ailments is not—and may not ever be known. However, it is equally clear that stress is taking its toll in organizational effectiveness, efficiency, productivity, and most importantly, in human lives. Some of the things we do know about stress and have tried to emphasize are:

1. Stress is inevitable in organizations and it can have positive or negative consequences.

2. Individuals create stress by not accomplishing career goals.
3. Organizations create stress by making ambiguous and conflicting requests or overloading employees with work.
4. Reactions to stress can be emotional, behavioral, or physiological. Managers need to become more astute at detecting emotional and behavioral reactions both in themselves and in others.
5. Many of the popular stress reduction techniques have not been rigorously evaluated to determine their effectiveness. A technique that is an effective stress reducer for one employee may not work for another employee.
6. Methods to reduce stress can be individually and/or organizationally initiated. The correct sequence for a manager combating excessive organizational stress is to first become aware of it and then to select the best action for the situation and subordinates.
7. Increased attention to organizational stress may be the most important step a manager can take to ensure both organizational effectiveness and employee health.

Operant Conditioning in Organizational Settings: Of Mice or Men?*

FRED L. FRY

THE relatively old theoretical concept of operant conditioning has become a relatively new management technique. Operant conditioning, basically a product of Skinnerian psychology, suggests that individuals will emit responses that are rewarded, and will not emit responses that are either not rewarded or are punished. Recent authors have attempted to introduce—or re-introduce—the concept into the organizational setting. A current series of studies introduces the terminology organizational behavior modification, or O.B. Mod. . . .

It cannot be argued that operant conditioning is an invalid psychological concept. Work done over several years demonstrated that animals can be "taught" to respond in certain ways in order to obtain food or avoid shock. Similarly, work has been done in mental hospitals and with individuals who cannot function normally. Research has shown that autistic and deaf children and certain others can benefit from operant conditioning methods. The recent work, however, has focused on operant conditioning as a viable technique for management of workers in an organizational setting. Although conceding that operant conditioning, in general, is indeed a viable concept and can influence behavior in certain cases, this author maintains that it is far overrated as a management technique. Operant conditioning in organizations, or O.B. Mod., can explain why many management problems exist; but it does not provide an acceptable alternative.

O.B. Mod. is criticized here on the following points: Organizations are more complex than Skinner Boxes; men are more intelligent than mice; O.B. Mod. is simply behavioral Taylorism; O.B. Mod. requires continuing reinforcement; and most of the effects supposedly the result of successful O.B. Mod. can be explained as a "Hawthorne effect."

ORGANIZATIONS VS. CONTROL BOXES

A classic statement is that "the biggest thing wrong with psychology is that experiments were made using either white rats or college sophomores. White rats aren't human and college sophomores are questionable." Control boxes are univariate tests of the stimulus/response relationships. Organizations are open systems with multivariate, multiple-cue, multiple-response situations. Expectancy theorists suggest that a single act may result in many different outcomes, each with its own valence. In operant conditioning terminology, this is saying that any response will elicit many rewards and punishments. We might consider, for example, the sources of rewards. The individual may be rewarded by the formal system, a variety of subgroups within the formal system, various informal groups in and out of the organization, and his own family. In essence, we can say that every social system to which an individual belongs is a potential provider of rewards. Thus, we can say that people will respond in ways that are rewarded, but management is only one of many sources of rewards. Stated formally, a person's "reward set," the totality of all possible rewards for a given response, contains a large number of elements, many of which are beyond the control of the organization.

Somewhat separate from the multiple-reward problem is the complexity of the reward problem. A given reward may be highly valued by one individual but not valued at all by others. In fact, what is perceived as reward by one worker may be perceived as punishment by another. Suppose, for example, that two managers are "rewarded" for their favorable responses with a $1,000 bonus. One manager may consider this a significant reward and will continue his favorable responses. The second manager may see the bonus as punishment, rather than reward, perhaps because of perceived inequities or unfulfilled expectations of a larger bonus. The supervisor has a tough enough task to reward workers appropriately, but in addition, under O.B. Mod., he faces the problem of not knowing in advance how a given reward will be perceived. To complicate things, the consequence that the supervisor may see as punishment (or lack of reward) may be interpreted as a reward by the worker. ([Some authors] assert that punishment is not punishment unless the act is extinguished. There is, in their view, no such thing as punishment that did not work. Although this may be a semantics problem, the concept is important. The question will be avoided here by using the phrase "perceived punishment.")

Coupled with the problem of the complex organization is the problem of lack of control over rewards by the organization. Luthans and Lyman suggest that "there are many reinforcers available to any supervisor," yet they themselves suggest that neither the pat on the back nor monetary rewards can be effectively used over time, and suggest that the supervisor should "make better use of the reinforcers that are already at hand on the job." But in considering this we are forced to ask just what reinforcers are "already at hand" for the supervisor. Certainly, one of the biggest problems in organizations is that pay, promotion, and fringe benefits are, in most cases, tied to seniority, not performance. They are almost totally beyond the control of the supervisor. When one ponders possible long-term reinforcers, he may discover that there really are very few reinforcers readily available to the supervisor. Only a small portion of an individual's reward set is controllable by the organization.

MEN MORE INTELLIGENT THAN MICE

In this writer's opinion, O.B. Mod. insults the intelligence of all but the most ignorant worker. Throughout the literature on O.B. Mod. the case is made that workers and supervisors should understand the importance of being contingent—the reinforcement should come as soon after the act as possible. Although this may be important for animals, man has developed an ability to remember the past and to expect from the future. The absurdity of this emphasis on immediacy to underscore contingency of rewards is illustrated by an example used by Luthans and Kreitner. To impress upon a worker the relationship between being late for work and docked pay, they suggest we "walk him to the pay section, where he observes the clerk calculate and subtract the pay adjustment." Presumably, the worker will better understand the relationship and therefore will repent.

If we consider the example, however, we see not only absurdity but a fallacy of O.B. Mod. First, we can assume that most workers are already aware of the relationship between lateness and docked pay. Thus, walking the individual to the pay section will do little if anything to increase the awareness of the relationship. The only punishment that might be derived from the exercise is the embarrassment of "being walked to the pay section," somewhat reminiscent of the gradeschooler being walked to the principal's office for a minor infraction. Second, many of us who underwent that "punishment" in our younger days will recall a certain amount of status associated with the act—enough in some cases to outweigh any punishment meted out. In the example given, rewards might include the chance to make acquaintance with the payroll clerk, not to mention the additional time off the job while making the trek. The example shows clearly, then, not how O.B. Mod. can be used effectively, but how it can backfire.

In the introductory sentences of this paper, I pointed out that operant conditioning has worked well with animals, mental patients, autistic children, and others. Here, I have said that the approach insults the intelligence of the average worker. The human subjects with whom it has worked well have had in common some impairment in their ability to fully utilize their intelligence. Even the literature dealing with the hard-core unemployables suggests that, because of environmental, cultural, or educational deficiencies, they cannot function properly. From these experiences I infer that operant conditioning may be a very valuable aid in working with those who either have a low intelligence or cannot properly use their intelligence. It is a logical extension of this observation to conclude that operant conditioning works best for those whose level of functional intelligence allows them to see only very short-run, lowest-order needs, as described by Maslow. These individuals may have the capability of perceiving only the close relationship between an act and an immediate reward. The general run of workers, we hope, are beyond that stage and, if so, O.B. Mod. cannot be expected to have the pervasive results claimed for it.

BEHAVIORAL TAYLORISM—AN OLD CONCEPT REVISITED?

Frederick Taylor is best remembered as the proponent of breaking jobs into minute parts, possibly recombining them into more efficient groupings of actions, and rewarding workers on the basis of their completion of these subparts. O.B. Mod. does essentially the same thing, if the theory is to be optimally effective. To an extent, then, it is nothing new, but simply an old concept revisited. Craig Schneier gives an example of O.B. Mod. in action (*Personnel*, May–June 1973). In this case, hard-core workers were originally given short on-the-job training in the overall procedures involved in packing a product. Turnover and dissatisfaction were severe. Then the jobs were studied and broken down, and training was given in each step of the process. Better results were achieved and credit was given to behavior modification, but couldn't credit have been given just as well to scientific management? Couldn't we say that the improved learning was the result of better, more efficient training and analysis of the tasks? I do not mean to disparage operant conditioning, but I do mean to suggest that the approach should not be considered a new and innovative management technique.

Since O.B. Mod. is very close to Taylorism, one of the criticisms of Taylorism also applies to it—that both are inherently autocratic methods of management. In both situations, the individual responds strictly because of the incentives (or avoidance of punishment). Responses are made without cognitive acceptance of the task. Most modern management theory, however, holds that higher levels of performance should be gained through rational acceptance of tasks, rather than through use of rewards and punishment.

THE PROBLEM OF CONTINUING REINFORCEMENT

If we accept the operant conditioning view that individuals will not emit responses unless rewarded, we then see the need for some type of continuing reinforcement. Psychologists tell us that intermittent reinforcement is preferable to fixed-interval reinforcement, but if we do not reward undesirable behavior and only intermittently reward desirable behavior, the worker on the job may have a very low level of total reward, especially if the reward is monetary. Proponents of O.B. Mod. might suggest we make the reward larger, but that is not practicable in an organization that sets a fixed monetary total for workers. We have, then, not the ability to control total rewards, but only the ability to divide it up. Further, if the supervisor is to be able to administer these rewards appropriately, we must assume that he is closely monitoring performance in order to know how to reinforce the response. Few supervisors have that much time available, and research has shown that, by and large, workers do not want close supervision anyway. If we don't monitor the operations closely, however, our intermittent reinforcing interval may become too spaced, and unintentionally the result will be extinction of the desired response. If we try to convince ourselves otherwise—that the worker will continue the response even if we forget or do not have time to adequately reinforce the behavior—we are violating the basic premise of operant conditioning, which is that only rewarded behavior will be emitted.

Related to the need for continuing reinforcement is the rewarding of approximations of the desired response. According to the theorists, we should reward responses that are successively closer to the desired response, yet, again, if we reward the approximations, it is those approximations that will be repeated, and the desired response will not be forthcoming. Nor do we have any real assurance that the next response will be closer to the desired response. Moreover, the intermittent reinforcement technique may complicate the problem. If, by chance, a response is exactly the desired but happens not to be reinforced, the subject should logically conclude that the response was *not* the desired one, and he will then focus more precisely on an earlier approximation. Thus, we have reinforced error.

DO EXTERNAL REWARDS EXTINGUISH INTRINSIC REWARDS?

A side effect of the problem associated with the need for continued reinforcement has recently been reported. O.B. Mod. theorists imply that, over time, the intrinsic rewards associated with work may surface and the need for externally provided rewards will be reduced. In effect, the job itself becomes a reinforcer. Edward Deci found, in an experimental situation, that utilizing external rewards actually *decreases,* not increases, the intrinsic motivation to do the task (*Human Resource Management,* Summer 1973). He suggests that relating tasks either to punishment or reward reduces the intrinsic pleasure of the task to such an extent that the task, rather than becoming a reinforcer per se, becomes dependent upon the reward.

For example, many professors do research in addition to teaching, and find it intrinsically rewarding. In many cases the external rewards are few, but through the research we feel we are "self-actualizing." In schools that typify the "publish or perish syndrome," however, teachers are under pressure to produce (or leave because of the pressure). Here we have people who no longer see research as intrinsically satisfying, because external rewards are explicitly tied to it. And to make matters worse, the university or department may find itself tied to the external rewards because it can no longer keep the active researcher *unless* he is paid for it. If the worker becomes dependent upon external reward, the organization is similarly dependent upon external rewards.

A last criticism of O.B. Mod. in the area of continuing reinforcement has to do with what can be called the diminishing marginal utility of rewards. As the total amount of rewards increases, the incremental utility of those rewards decreases. We see this in very well-paid workers who no longer value salary increases highly. We see it in the individual who continually receives the "pats on the back" for whom those pats on the back no longer mean much. We also see it in the worker who is frequently threatened with being fired, and for whom those threats are no longer threatening. People tend to become immune to the level of rewards or punishments they receive. If good performance is to be achieved, the reward set must take on successively higher values. If rewards are not increased, the propensity to perform well decreases.

HAWTHORNE EFFECTS MISINTERPRETED AS O.B. MOD. RESULTS

The Schneier example cited earlier suggested that hard-core workers improved performance when O.B. Mod. was used. This may have been the case, however, a more likely explanation, in addition to the one suggested earlier, is that performance improved because of the attention given to the workers. The process of breaking the tasks into subparts and rewarding completion of each forced the supervisors to give more attention to the workers. And since the work had to be checked to see if a reward was merited or not, the interaction by itself cannot be considered as a reward in the O.B. Mod. sense. Any theorists, and particularly the O.B. Mod. advocates, should be very careful about construing the Hawthorne effect as support for their theory.

To summarize, operant conditioning, or O.B. Mod., can be a useful tool, but it has been overrated as a management technique. The empirical evidence has shown primarily that operant conditioning can work with animals and those humans who, for one reason or another, cannot make full use of their intelligence. When it comes to management, operant conditioning is basically a univariate method applied to a multivariate organization and to individuals whose "reward set" contains elements not controlled by the formal organization. O.B. Mod. is in actuality a revival of Tayloristic management and has some of the same problems as scientific management. To be effective, O.B. Mod. requires continued reinforcement, a need that in turn causes other problems, including the possible reduction of intrinsic motivation. Last, many of the results attributed to O.B. Mod. could be the result of Hawthorne effects.

Group Norms: Key to Building a Winning Team*

P. C. ANDRÉ de la PORTE

CORPORATE viability and success, management experts agree, rest on (among others) three essential human factors: commonness of purpose; adaptability to change in the business environment and operating conditions; and the qualitative excellence of each individual's work contribution. So far, so good, but attaining this state of effectiveness is not all that easy, chiefly because of the second factor—or absence of it. There seems always to be that hard wall of resistance to change.

Some ascribe this to general apathy in an increasingly impersonal world, others to waning senses of responsibility. Managers who give the problem deeper thought, however, are struck by the fact that traditional motivational and other approaches work well enough when the climate is receptive; they just fail to produce results when it is not—and that is most of the time in problem-ridden companies. Many personnel and top managers have long suspected this to be the crux of the problem. But no one seemed to have the answer. Attitude surveys, for instance, do little more than point to the existence of a poor climate, without indicating what must be done to improve it. Other approaches, too, in most cases proved unsatisfactory.

This impasse persisted until the late 1960s, when research into group norms—a theory developed by the American organizational psychologist Dr. Saul Pilnick—began to be applied successfully to actual corporate problems. Simply put, group norms are man's attempt at resolving a potentially explosive conflict of interests. At stake are two universal, related

* Reprinted by permission of the publisher from *Personnel* (September–October 1974). Copyright © 1974 by AMACOM, a division of American Management Associations.

phenomena; on one hand, our eternal quest for the company and recognition of our peers, those people we like to identify with, and on the other, natural tendency toward exclusivity that established groups display. The solution: A "price" is set for admission and recognition, in the form of certain values and modes of behavior to be respected by group members at all times. These rules are formalized only rarely, when the group itself is or becomes formal, for example, in the bylaws of a club. More often, they are established informally, by group leaders or by tradition, and obeyed tacitly.

Norms are as varied and plentiful as there are groups. They come in three grades—positive, negative, neutral—as viewed from the standpoint of the group's ultimate aims—that is, they can support, obstruct, or have no effect on those aims. And members switch from one group's norms to another's with ease. For example, a soldier will casually use obscene language (his fellow-conscripts' norm) in the barracks, but when attending a meeting of his parent-teacher association, will put on his best behavior quite effortlessly.

THE SPECIAL NORMS OF A CORPORATE CLIMATE

How and why does all this relate to companies and their resistance-to-change problem? Systematic study of the phenomenon has verified the existence of a direct correlation between group norms and corporate profitability. Here are the elements behind this correlation:

Man seeks to belong to peer groups wherever he congregates, including corporate surroundings. (The contrary would be surprising, since man spends about a third of his waking hours in this environment.)

The tendency toward exclusivity exists even in open-ended situations, such as corporate ones, where people come and go. In fact, it does so there with a twist, because the formation of groups is influenced by the fact that fellow-workers have been thrown together from the start in unnatural mixes. At a large cocktail party, say, groups will drift together and apart without constraint, but in a company, people with different backgrounds and views are forced to work together and form groups. The bigger the company and the wider the range in social (and other) attributes of individuals, the better the chances are that there will be numerous groups with tight-knit and defensive norms.

When both formal and informal norms coexist, as they do in companies, the informal norms transcend the formal. This leads to what has been called "shadow organization," in which the apparent management structure is actually superseded in importance by the mesh of group-norm dictates.

Individuals will go to extreme lengths to live up to their peers' expectations, even doing things that in other circumstances they recognize as going counter to their *own* best interests. They can persevere in this behavior, however, with the easy rationalization that "Everybody around here does it."

Norms-imposed habits are lasting. Even when the original members of a group have disappeared and/or when the norms themselves have lost their original purpose, there will be strong norm remnants, unthinkingly respected by new members.

Negative norms cannot be changed unless the norm-follower is made aware of their existence, because most—if not all—people respect and go along with norms quite unconsciously.

All these powerful forces can, and do, obstruct managers' best efforts to change given situations. Here is a simple illustration:

Most managers have heard at least once an employee righteously protest that the reason he failed to do something was that "It's not my department!" Almost always, that employee is obeying a norm—unthinkingly, without bothering to question the norm's validity. This norm may originally have come about because some employee realized that there was no particular reward—if not downright criticism—for carrying out other departments' activities. He recounted the incident to his fellowworkers—his peer-group from 9 to 5—and his conclusion may have been something to the effect that "there's no use breaking your back for *this* company. Just do what you're told and draw your salary." A new norm was born there and then, if his group agreed with the conclusion.

And, as we have pointed out, the norm will have a long life. This explains, for instance, why promising newcomers often turn out the same sort of performance as less-than-satisfactory department colleagues within a few weeks of their arrival. They've put membership in the group above management-approved performance. And the most frustrating aspect for a manager is that, however convincingly he talks to an employee, tries to make him see the light and mend his ways, and however much the employee seems to agree, there will be no change in his attitude, because the power of the group norms is stronger than that of any pep talk by his superior.

Still, this is not to say that there is no hope. Students of normative analysis have had successes—and lasting ones with this change-oriented technique. Here are some examples:

Quality defects in a manufacturing company were reduced by 55 percent.

The management committee of an international corporation found its decisions being made twice as fast (and just as accurately), with a tangible improvement in participant commitment.

Product breakage and pilferage in a retail chain was cut by 70 percent.

Average productivity of sales calls in a food service company was boosted by 60 percent.

A medium-size airline eradicated what it called the "bored ticket-puncher" mentality of its check-in hostesses.

Absenteeism in a manufacturing plant was halved, and turnover considerably reduced.

Less easily measured than these, mostly profit-focused improvements, but of paramount importance nevertheless, are the gains in effectiveness, opportunity-catching mobility, and morale that the companies experienced by adopting normative system programs.

NORMATIVE ANALYSIS: IDENTIFYING THE NORMS

Bringing about change entails following three steps:

1. Detecting norms and getting their followers to recognize their existence and influence.
2. Scientifically measuring the norms and establishing the company's normative profile.
3. Bringing about normative change.

To find out what norms exist within an organization, the investigators observe behavior patterns. This may or may not be combined with preliminary interviews; most people will tell of their behavior patterns if given a chance (though they are more likely to reveal them if an indirect approach is adopted, for example, if they are asked what other people do in certain circumstances).

From the start, identification of norms gives a strong push toward freeing members from behavior patterns that have until then been by and large beyond their control. People who have tacitly agreed to go along with negative norms will usually find, when these are brought to light, that they never wanted to behave according to them in the first place. And identifying the norm for them (or, better still, letting them identify it themselves) will also have the effect of suggesting alternative modes of behavior.

NORMATIVE ANALYSIS: THE NORMATIVE PROFILE

The formal identification of norms is followed by a process of charting them in order to arrive at the normative profile of the group under consideration. Corporate norms fall within one or another of ten norm clusters: (1) organizational pride; (2) performance; (3) profitability/cost effectiveness; (4) teamwork/communication; (5) planning (6) supervision; (7) training and development; (8) innovation/change; (9) customer relations; and (10) honesty and security.

All norms have an ideal excellence point. The difference between that and their actual score on the profile is the normative gap (see Figure 1). Usually, a company will have a zig-zag profile, with certain norms more accentuated than others. The idea then, is to improve the mediocre norms, and keep the better-performing ones alive and healthy.

NORMATIVE ANALYSIS: THE CHANGE PROCESS

To perform this amelioration, we have worked out a systematic change process. Flexible enough to authorize shortcuts in times of urgency, yet rigid enough that its users will not unwittingly skip one or more important phases, this system involves eight interrelated steps:

Creating understanding and appreciation of the significance of norms, how they influence organizational effectiveness, and how they contribute to both the creation and the solution of key organizational problems. Group members are taught to think in normative terms and to identify and state norms. The process starts at the top of the company and permeates downward as each organizational level becomes involved in change.

Establishing positive norm goals through cooperative action. A group can establish acceptable norm goals just as it would establish functional goals.

Determining the excellence point of norms for the company concerned, and therefore the improvement distance to be covered.

Establishing normative change priorities. The size of the normative gap is only one factor. More important is the relationship of the norm area to the effectiveness and profitability (or other problems) of the organization. This leads to weighting—and giving more urgent attention to—those norm clusters that have more direct impact than others on the given problem, even though the gap may be narrower than average.

Developing systematic change strategies by examining and modifying ten specific (and crucial) areas, among which are management commitment to change; information, communication and feedback on and about results; recognition and reward of consistent employee behavior; and recruitment and selection of new employees. Inclusion of the last recognizes the fact that newcomers can introduce new negative norms, just as they can be trained to conform to positive norms.

Implementing the change strategy. Here, the essential point is to begin at the top of the organization and move downward, with the assurance of top management commitment, support, and modeling behavior.

Providing follow-through and maintenance on a continuous basis. The emphasis here is on assigning responsibilities for change programs (often best accomplished by setting up a task force or change committee).

Providing for continuous evaluation of the effectiveness of change strategies, and standing ready to modify plans, by reviewing change strategies, if and when they fall short of expectations.

One of the major built-in advantages of the normative change process is that it does not hurt anyone's feelings—no one is singled out. The existence

Figure 1

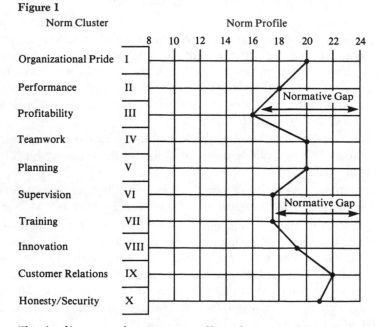

This (real) company's normative profile is characterized by a not unusual number of inconsistencies. Thus, a high level of organizational pride and good customer relations are more than offset by employees' lack of concern for profitability. What actually happened was that employees liked to work for this customer-oriented company, but placed customer desires so much in the forefront of their working priorities that they were eating into profits at a rate which stunned them when they discovered the underlying normative mechanism. The other gap relates to the low level of supervision and training, which left employees free to form close-knit, supervision-resenting groups, a common enough vicious circle.

of a negative norm, explained in terms of the norm concept, is freely admitted. The impersonal "we" of the group is substituted for the accusatory "you" and defensive "I." Moreover, since norm followers participate fully in the change process, bringing to light the negative effects of their own behavior and suggesting alternatives, the new course of action is enforced by the ex-offenders themselves—just as the old, negative norm was enforced by the group. Repeating the change process as often as negative norms are observed results in weaving a new norm fabric for the organization. Into it will go norms emphasizing teamwork, commonness of purpose, individual effort and achievement—norms will become part and parcel of the corporate makeup.

The Abilene Paradox:
The Management of Agreement*

JERRY B. HARVEY

THE July afternoon in Coleman, Texas (population 5,607) was particularly hot—104 degrees as measured by the Walgreen's Rexall Ex-Lax temperature gauge. In addition, the wind was blowing fine-grained West Texas topsoil through the house. But the afternoon was still tolerable —even potentially enjoyable. There was a fan going on the back porch; there was cold lemonade; and finally, there was entertainment. Dominoes. Perfect for the conditions. The game required little more physical exertion than an occasional mumbled comment, "Shuffle 'em," and an unhurried movement of the arm to place the spots in the appropriate perspective on the table. All in all, it had the makings of an agreeable Sunday afternoon in Coleman—that is, it was until my father-in-law suddenly said, "Let's get in the car and go to Abilene and have dinner at the cafeteria."

I thought, "What, go to Abilene? Fifty-three miles? In this dust storm and heat? And in an unairconditioned 1958 Buick?"

But my wife chimed in with, "Sounds like a great idea. I'd like to go. How about you, Jerry?" Since my own preferences were obviously out of step with the rest I replied, "Sounds good to me," and added, "I just hope your mother wants to go."

"Of course I want to go," said my mother-in-law. "I haven't been to Abilene in a long time."

So into the car and off to Abilene we went. My predictions were fulfilled. The heat was brutal. We were coated with a fine layer of dust that was cemented with perspiration by the time we arrived. The food at the

---

* Reprinted by permission of the publisher from *Organizational Dynamics* (Summer 1974). Copyright © 1974 by AMACOM, a division of American Management Associations. All rights reserved.

cafeteria provided first-rate testimonial material for antacid commercials.

Some four hours and 106 miles later we returned to Coleman, hot and exhausted. We sat in front of the fan for a long time in silence. Then, both to be sociable and to break the silence, I said, "It was a great trip, wasn't it?"

No one spoke.

Finally my mother-in-law said, with some irritation, "Well, to tell the truth, I really didn't enjoy it much and would rather have stayed here. I just went along because the three of you were so enthusiastic about going. I wouldn't have gone if you all hadn't pressured me into it."

I couldn't believe it. "What do you mean 'you all'?" I said. "Don't put me in the 'you all' group. I was delighted to be doing what we were doing. I didn't want to go. I only went to satisfy the rest of you. You're the culprits."

My wife looked shocked. "Don't call me a culprit. You and Daddy and Mama were the ones who wanted to go. I just went along to be sociable and to keep you happy. I would have had to be crazy to want to go out in heat like that."

Her father entered the conversation abruptly. "Hell!" he said.

He proceeded to expand on what was already absolutely clear. "Listen, I never wanted to go to Abilene. I just thought you might be bored. You visit so seldom I wanted to be sure you enjoyed it. I would have preferred to play another game of dominoes and eat the leftovers in the ice box."

After the outburst of recrimination we all sat back in silence. Here we were, four reasonably sensible people who, of our own volition, had just taken a 106-mile trip across a godforsaken desert in a furnace-like temperature through a cloud-like dust storm to eat unpalatable food at a hole-in-the-wall cafeteria in Abilene, when none of us had really wanted to go. In fact, to be more accurate, we'd done just the opposite of what we wanted to do. The whole situation simply didn't make sense.

At least it didn't make sense at the time. But since that day in Coleman, I have observed, consulted with, and been a part of more than one organization that has been caught in the same situation. As a result, they have either taken a side-trip, or, occasionally, a terminal journey to Abilene, when Dallas or Houston or Tokyo was where they really wanted to go. And for most of those organizations, the negative consequences of such trips, measured in terms of both human misery and economic loss, have been much greater than for our little Abilene group.

This article is concerned with that paradox—the Abilene Paradox. Stated simply, it is as follows: Organizations frequently take actions in contradiction to what they really want to do and therefore defeat the very purposes they are trying to achieve. It also deals with a major corollary of the paradox, which is that *the inability to manage agreement is a major source of organization dysfunction.* Last, the article is designed to help members of organizations cope more effectively with the paradox's pernicious influence.

As a means of accomplishing the above, I shall: (1) describe the symptoms exhibited by organizations caught in the paradox; (2) describe, in summarized case-study examples, how they occur in a variety of organizations; (3) discuss the underlying causal dynamics; (4) indicate some of the implications of accepting this model for describing organizational behavior; (5) make recommendations for coping with the paradox; and, in conclusion, (6) relate the paradox to a broader existential issue.

SYMPTOMS OF THE PARADOX

The inability to manage agreement, not the inability to manage conflict, is the essential symptom that defines organizations caught in the web of the Abilene Paradox. That inability effectively to manage agreement is expressed by six specific subsymptoms, all of which were present in our family Abilene group.

1.   Organization members agree privately, as individuals, as to the nature of the situation or problem facing the organization. For example, members of the Abilene group agreed that they were enjoying themselves sitting in front of the fan, sipping lemonade, and playing dominoes.

2.   Organization members agree privately, as individuals, as to the steps that would be required to cope with the situation or problem they face. For members of the Abilene group "more of the same" was a solution that would have adequately satisfied their individual and collective desires.

3.   Organization members fail to accurately communicate their desires and/or beliefs to one another. In fact, they do just the opposite and thereby lead one another into misperceiving the collective reality. Each member of the Abilene group, for example, communicated inaccurate data to other members of the organization. The data, in effect, said, "Yeah, it's a great idea. Let's go to Abilene," when in reality members of the organization individually and collectively preferred to stay in Coleman.

4.   With such invalid and inaccurate information, organization members make collective decisions that lead them to take actions contrary to what they want to do, and thereby arrive at results that are counterproductive to the organization's intent and purposes. Thus, the Abilene group went to Abilene when it preferred to do something else.

5.   As a result of taking actions that are counterproductive, organization members experience frustration, anger, irritation, and dissatisfaction with their organization. Consequently, they form subgroups with trusted acquaintances and blame other subgroups for the organization's dilemma. Frequently, they also blame authority figures and one another. Such phenomena were illustrated in the Abilene group by the "culprit" argument that occurred when we had returned to the comfort of the fan.

6.   Finally, if organization members do not deal with the generic issue —the inability to manage agreement—the cycle repeats itself with greater intensity. The Abilene group, for a variety of reasons, the most important of which was that it became conscious of the process, did not reach that point.

To repeat, the Abilene Paradox reflects a failure to manage agreement. In fact, it is my contention that the inability to cope with (manage) agreement, rather than the inability to cope with (manage) conflict is the single most pressing issue of modern organizations.

OTHER TRIPS TO ABILENE

The Abilene Paradox is no respecter of individuals, organizations, or institutions. Following are descriptions of two other trips to Abilene that illustrate both the pervasiveness of the paradox and its underlying dynamics.

Case 1: The Boardroom.   The Ozyx Corporation is a relatively small industrial company that has embarked on a trip to Abilene. The president of Ozyx has hired a consultant to help discover the reasons for the poor profit picture of the company in general and the low morale and productivity of the R&D division in particular. During the process of investigation, the consultant becomes interested in a research project in which the company has invested a sizable proportion of its R&D budget.

When asked about the project by the consultant in the privacy of their offices, the president, the vice president for research, and the research manager each describes it as an idea that looked great on paper but will ultimately fail because of the unavailability of the technology required to make it work. Each of them also acknowledges that continued support of the project will create cash flow problems that will jeopardize the very existence of the total organization.

Furthermore, each individual indicates he has not told the others about his reservations. When asked why, the president says he can't reveal his "true" feelings because abandoning the project, which has been widely publicized, would make the company look bad in the press and, in addition, would probably cause his vice president's ulcer to kick up or perhaps even cause him to quit, "because he has staked his professional reputation on the project's success."

Similarly, the vice president for research says he can't let the president or the research manager know his reservations because the president is so committed to it that "I would probably get fired for insubordination if I questioned the project."

Finally, the research manager says he can't let the president or vice president know of his doubts about the project because of their extreme commitment to the project's success.

All indicate that, in meetings with one another, they try to maintain an optimistic facade so the others won't worry unduly about the project. The research director, in particular, admits to writing ambiguous progress reports so the president and the vice president can "interpret them to suit themselves." In fact, he says he tends to slant them to the "positive" side, "given how committed the brass are."

The scent of the Abilene trail wafts from a paneled conference room where the project research budget is being considered for the following fiscal year. In the meeting itself, praises are heaped on the questionable project and a unanimous decision is made to continue it for yet another year. Symbolically, the organization has boarded a bus to Abilene.

In fact, although the real issue of agreement was confronted approximately eight months after the bus departed, it was nearly too late. The organization failed to meet a payroll and underwent a two-year period of personnel cutbacks, retrenchments, and austerity. Morale suffered, the most competent technical personnel resigned, and the organization's prestige in the industry declined.

Case 2: The Watergate.

Apart from the grave question of who did what, Watergate presents America with the profound puzzle of why. What is it that led such a wide assortment of men, many of them high public officials, possibly including the President himself, either to instigate or to go along with and later try to hide a pattern of behavior that by now appears not only reprehensible, but stupid? (*The Washington Star and Daily News*, editorial, May 27, 1973.)

One possible answer to the editorial writer's question can be found by probing into the dynamics of the Abilene paradox. I shall let the reader reach his own conclusions, though, on the basis of the following excerpts from testimony before the Senate investigating committee on "The Watergate Affair."

In one exchange, Senator Howard Baker asked Herbert Porter, then a member of the White House staff, why he (Porter) found himself "in charge of or deeply involved in a dirty tricks operation of the campaign." In response, Porter indicated that he had had qualms about what he was doing, but that he ". . . was not one to stand up in a meeting and say that this should be stopped. . . . I kind of drifted along."

And when asked by Baker why he had "drifted along," Porter replied, "In all honesty, because of the fear of the group pressure that would ensue, of not being a team player," and ". . . I felt a deep sense of loyalty to him [the President] or was appealed to on that basis." (*The Washington Post*, June 8, 1973, p. 20.)

Jeb Magruder gave a similar response to a question posed by committee counsel Dash. Specifically, when asked about his, Mr. Dean's, and Mr. Mitchell's reactions to Mr. Liddy's proposal, which included bugging the

Watergate, Mr. Magruder replied, "I think all three of us were appalled. The scope and size of the project were something that at least in my mind were not envisioned. I do not think it was in Mr. Mitchell's mind or Mr. Dean's, although I can't comment on their states of mind at that time."

Mr. Mitchell, in an understated way, which was his way of dealing with difficult problems like this, indicated that this was not an "acceptable project." (*The Washington Post,* June 15, 1973, p. A14.)

Later in his testimony, Mr. Magruder said, ". . . I think I can honestly say that no one was particularly overwhelmed with the project. But I think we felt that this information could be useful, and Mr. Mitchell agreed to approve the project, and I then notified the parties of Mr. Mitchell's approval." (*The Washington Post,* June 15, 1973, p. A14.)

Although I obviously was not privy to the private conversations of the principal characters, the data seem to reflect the essential elements of the Abilene Paradox. First, they indicate agreement. Evidently, Mitchell, Porter, Dean, and Magruder agreed that the plan was inappropriate. ("I think I can honestly say that no one was particularly overwhelmed with the project.") Second, the data indicate that the principal figures then proceeded to implement the plan in contradiction to their shared agreement. Third, the data surrounding the case clearly indicate that the plan multiplied the organization's problems rather than solved them. And finally, the organization broke into subgroups with the various principals, such as the President, Mitchell, Porter, Dean, and Magruder, blaming one another for the dilemma in which they found themselves, and internecine warfare ensued.

In summary, it is possible that because of the inability of White House staff members to cope with the fact that they agreed, the organization took a trip to Abilene.

ANALYZING THE PARADOX

The Abilene Paradox can be stated succinctly as follows: Organizations frequently take actions in contradiction to the data they have for dealing with problems and, as a result, compound their problems rather than solve them. Like all paradoxes, the Abilene Paradox deals with absurdity. On the surface, it makes little sense for organizations, whether they are couples or companies, bureaucracies or governments, to take actions that are diametrically opposed to the data they possess for solving crucial organizational problems. Such actions are particularly absurd since they tend to compound the very problems they are designed to solve and thereby defeat the purposes the organization is trying to achieve. However, as Robert Rapaport and others have so cogently expressed it, paradoxes are generally paradoxes only because they are based on a logic or rationale different from what we understand or expect.

Discovering that different logic not only destroys the paradoxical quality but also offers alternative ways for coping with similar situations. Therefore, part of the dilemma facing an Abilene-bound organization may be the lack of a map—a theory or model—that provides rationality to the paradox. The purpose of the following discussion is to provide such a map.

The map will be developed by examining the underlying psychological themes of the profit-making organization and the bureaucracy and it will include the following landmarks: (1) Action Anxiety; (2) Negative Fantasies; (3) Real Risk; (4) Separation Anxiety; and (5) the Psychological Reversal of Risk and Certainty. I hope that the discussion of such landmarks will provide harried organization travelers with a new map that will assist them in arriving at where they really want to go and, in addition, will help them in assessing the risks that are an inevitable part of the journey.

ACTION ANXIETY

Action anxiety provides the first landmark for locating roadways that bypass Abilene. The concept of action anxiety says that the reason organization members take actions in contradiction to their understanding of the organization's problems lies in the intense anxiety that is created as they think about acting in accordance with what they believe needs to be done. As a result, they opt to endure the professional and economic degradation of pursuing an unworkable research project or the consequence of participating in an illegal activity rather than act in a manner congruent with their beliefs. It is not that organization members do not know what needs to be done—they do know. For example, the various principals in the research organization cited *knew* they were working on a research project that had no real possibility of succeeding. And the central figures of the Watergate episode apparently *knew* that, for a variety of reasons, the plan to bug the Watergate did not make sense.

Such action anxiety experienced by the various protagonists may not make sense, but the dilemma is not a new one. In fact, it is very similar to the anxiety experienced by Hamlet, who expressed it most eloquently in the opening lines of his famous soliloquy:

> To be or not to be; that is the question:
> Whether 'tis nobler in the mind to suffer
> The slings and arrows of outrageous fortune
> Or to take arms against a sea of troubles
> And by opposing, end them? . . . (*Hamlet,* Act III, Scene II)

It is easy to translate Hamlet's anxious lament into that of the research manager of our R&D organization as he contemplates his report to the meeting of the budget committee. It might go something like this:

To maintain my sense of integrity and self-worth or compromise it, that is the question. Whether 'tis nobler in the mind to suffer the ignominy that comes from managing a nonsensical research project, or the fear and anxiety that comes from making a report the president and V.P. may not like to hear.

So, the anguish, procrastination, and counterproductive behavior of the research manager or members of the White House staff are not much different from those of Hamlet; all might ask with equal justification Hamlet's subsequent searching question of what it is that

makes us rather bear those ills we have than fly to others we know not of. (*Hamlet,* Act III, Scene II)

In short, like the various Abilene protagonists, we are faced with a deeper question: Why does action anxiety occur?

NEGATIVE FANTASIES

Part of the answer to that question may be found in the negative fantasies organization members have about acting in congruence with what they believe should be done.

Hamlet experienced such fantasies. Specifically, Hamlet's fantasies of the alternatives to current evils were more evils, and he didn't entertain the possibility that any action he might take could lead to an improvement in the situation. Hamlet's was not an unusual case, though. In fact, the "Hamlet syndrome" clearly occurred in both organizations previously described. All of the organization protagonists had negative fantasies about what would happen if they acted in accordance with what they believed needed to be done.

The various managers in the R&D organization foresaw loss of face, prestige, position, and even health as the outcome of confronting the issues about which they believed, incorrectly, that they disagreed. Similarly, members of the White House staff feared being made scapegoats, branded as disloyal, or ostracized as non-team players if they acted in accordance with their understanding of reality.

To sum up, action anxiety is supported by the negative fantasies that organization members have about what will happen as a consequence of their acting in accordance with their understanding of what is sensible. The negative fantasies, in turn, serve an important function for the persons who have them. Specifically, they provide the individual with an excuse that releases him psychologically, both in his own eyes and frequently in the eyes of others, from the responsibility of having to act to solve organization problems.

It is not sufficient, though, to stop with the explanation of negative fantasies as the basis for the inability of organizations to cope with agreement.

We must look deeper and ask still other questions: What is the source of the negative fantasies? Why do they occur?

REAL RISK

Risk is a reality of life, a condition of existence. John Kennedy articulated it in another way when he said at a news conference, "Life is unfair." By that I believe he meant we do not know, nor can we predict or control with certainty, either the events that impinge upon us or the outcomes of actions we undertake in response to those events.

Consequently, in the business environment, the research manager might find that confronting the president and the vice-president with the fact that the project was a "turkey" might result in his being fired. And Mr. Porter's saying that an illegal plan of surveillance should not be carried out could have caused his ostracism as a nonteam player. There are too many cases when confrontation of this sort has resulted in such consequences. The real question, though, is not, Are such fantasized consequences possible? but, Are such fantasized consequences likely?

Thus, real risk is an existential condition, and all actions do have consequences that, to paraphrase Hamlet, may be worse than the evils of the present. As a result of their unwillingness to accept existential risk as one of life's givens, however, people may opt to take their organizations to Abilene rather than run the risk, no matter how small, of ending up somewhere worse.

Again, though, one must ask, What is the real risk that underlies the decision to opt for Abilene? What is at the core of the paradox?

FEAR OF SEPARATION

One is tempted to say that the core of the paradox lies in the individual's fear of the unknown. Actually, we do not fear what is unknown, but we are afraid of things we do know about. What do we know about that frightens us into such apparently inexplicable organizational behavior?

Separation, alienation, and loneliness are things we do know about—and fear. Both research and experience indicate that ostracism is one of the most powerful punishments that can be devised. Solitary confinement does not draw its coercive strength from physical deprivation. The evidence is overwhelming that we have a fundamental need to be connected, engaged, and related and a reciprocal need not to be separated or alone. Everyone of us, though, has experienced aloneness. From the time the umbilical cord was cut, we have experienced the real anguish of separation—broken friendships, divorces, deaths, and exclusions. C. P. Snow vividly described the tragic interplay between loneliness and connection:

Each of us is alone; sometimes we escape from our solitariness, through love and affection or perhaps creative moments, but these triumphs of life are pools of light we make for ourselves while the edge of the road is black. Each of us dies alone.

That fear of taking risks that may result in our separation from others is at the core of the paradox. It finds expression in ways of which we may be unaware, and it is ultimately the cause of the self-defeating, collective deception that leads to self-destructive decisions within organizations.

Concretely, such fear of separation leads research committees to fund projects that none of its members want and, perhaps, White House staff members to engage in illegal activities that they don't really support.

THE PSYCHOLOGICAL RESEARCH OF RISK AND CERTAINTY

One piece of the map is still missing. It relates to the peculiar reversal that occurs in our thought processes as we try to cope with the Abilene Paradox. For example, we frequently fail to take action in an organizational setting because we fear that the actions we take may result in our separation from others, or, in the language of Mr. Porter, we are afraid of being tabbed as "disloyal" or are afraid of being ostracized as "non-team players." But therein lies a paradox within a paradox, because our very unwillingness to take such risks virtually ensures the separation and aloneness we so fear. In effect, we reverse "real existential risk" and "fantasied risk" and by doing so transform what is a probability statement into what, for all practical purposes, becomes a certainty.

Take the R&D organization described earlier. When the project fails, some people will get fired, demoted, or sentenced to the purgatory of a make-work job in an out-of-the-way office. For those who remain, the atmosphere of blame, distrust, suspicion, and backbiting that accompanies such failure will serve only to further alienate and separate those who remain.

The Watergate situation is similar. The principals evidently feared being ostracized as disloyal non-team players. When the illegality of the act surfaced, however, it was nearly inevitable that blaming, self-protective actions, and scapegoating would result in the very emotional separation from both the President and one another that the principals feared. Thus, by reversing real and fantasied risk, they had taken effective action to ensure the outcome they least desired.

One final question remains: Why do we make this peculiar reversal? I support the general thesis of Alvin Toffler and Philip Slater, who contend that our cultural emphasis on technology, competition, individualism, temporariness, and mobility has resulted in a population that has frequently experienced the terror of loneliness and seldom the satisfaction of engagement. Consequently, though we have learned of the reality of separation, we have not had the opportunity to learn the reciprocal skills of connection, with the result that, like the ancient dinosaurs, we are breeding organizations with self-destructive decision-making proclivities.

A POSSIBLE ABILENE BYPASS

Existential risk is inherent in living, so it is impossible to provide a map that meets the no-risk criterion, but it may be possible to describe the route in terms that make the landmarks understandable and that will clarify the risks involved. In order to do that, however, some commonly used terms such as victim, victimizer, collusion, responsibility, conflict, conformity, courage, confrontation, reality, and knowledge have to be redefined. In addition, we need to explore the relevance of the redefined concepts for bypassing or getting out of Abilene.

Victim and Victimizer. Blaming and fault-finding behavior is one of the basic symptoms of organizations that have found their way to Abilene, and the target of blame generally doesn't include the one who criticizes. Stated in different terms, executives begin to assign one another to roles of victims and victimizers. Ironic as it may seem, however, this assignment of roles is both irrelevant and dysfunctional, because once a business or a government fails to manage its agreement and arrives in Abilene, all its members are victims. Thus, arguments and accusations that identify victims and victimizers at best become symptoms of the paradox, and, at worst, drain energy from the problem-solving efforts required to redirect the organization along the route it really wants to take.

Collusion. A basic implication of the Abilene Paradox is that human problems of organization are reciprocal in nature. As Robert Tannenbaum has pointed out, you can't have an autocratic boss unless subordinates are willing to collude with his autocracy, and you can't have obsequious subordinates unless the boss is willing to collude with their obsequiousness.

Thus, in plain terms, each person in a self-defeating, Abilene-bound organization *colludes* with others, including peers, superiors, and subordinates, sometimes consciously and sometimes subconsciously, to create the dilemma in which the organization finds itself. To adopt a cliché of modern organization, "It takes a real team effort to go to Abilene." In that sense each person, in his own collusive manner, shares responsibility for the trip, so searching for a locus of blame outside oneself serves no useful purpose for either the organization or the individual. It neither helps the organization handle its dilemma of unrecognized agreement nor does it provide psychological relief for the individual, because focusing on conflict when agreement is the issue is devoid of reality. In fact, it does just the opposite, for it causes the organization to focus on managing conflict when it should be focusing on managing agreement.

Responsibility for Problem-Solving Action. A second question is, Who is responsible for getting us out of this place? To that question is frequently appended a third one, generally rhetorical in nature, with "should" over-tones, such as, Isn't it the boss (or the ranking government official) who is responsible for doing something about the situation?

The answer to that question is No.

The key to understanding the functionality of the No answer is the knowledge that, when the dynamics of the paradox are in operation, the authority figure—and others—are in unknowing agreement with one another concerning the organization's problems and the steps necessary to solve them. Consequently, the power to destroy the paradox's pernicious influence comes from confronting and speaking to the underlying reality of the situation, and not from one's hierarchical position within the orga-nization. Therefore, any organization member who chooses to risk con-fronting that reality possesses the necessary leverage to release the orga-nization from the paradox's grip.

In one situation, it may be a research director's saying, "I don't think this project can succeed." In another, it may be Jeb Magruder's response to this question by Senator Baker:

> If you were concerned because the action was known to you to be illegal, because you thought it improper or unethical, you thought the prospects for success were very meager, and you doubted the reliability of Mr. Liddy, what on earth would it have taken to decide against the plan?

Magruder's reply was brief and to the point:

> Not very much, sir. I am sure that if I had fought vigorously against it, I think any of us could have had the plan cancelled. (*Time*, June 25, 1973, p. 12.)

Reality, Knowledge, Confrontation. Accepting the paradox as a model describing certain kinds of organizational dilemmas also requires re-thinking the nature of reality and knowledge, as they are generally de-scribed in organizations. In brief, the underlying dynamics of the paradox clearly indicate that organization members generally know more about issues confronting the organization than they don't know. The various principals attending the research budget meeting, for example, knew the research project was doomed to failure. And Jeb Magruder spoke as a true Abilener when he said, "We knew it was illegal, probably, inappropriate." (*The Washington Post*, June 15, 1973, p. A16.)

Given this concept of reality and its relationship to knowledge, confron-tation becomes the process of facing issues squarely, openly, and directly in an effort to discover whether the nature of the underlying collective reality is agreement or conflict. Accepting such a definition of confrontation has an important implication for change agents interested in making organizations more effective. That is, organization change and effectiveness may be facilitated as much by confronting the organization with what it knows and agrees upon as by confronting it with what it doesn't know or disagrees about.

REAL CONFLICT AND PHONY CONFLICT

Conflict is a part of any organization. Couples, R&D divisions, and White House staffs all engage in it. However, analysis of the Abilene Paradox opens up the possibility of two kinds of conflict—real and phony. On the surface, they look alike, but, like headaches, have different causes and therefore require different treatment.

Real conflict occurs when people have real differences. ("My reading of the research printouts says that we can make the project profitable." "I come to the opposite conclusion.") ("I suggest we 'bug' the Watergate." "I'm not in favor of it.")

Phony conflict, on the other hand, occurs when people agree on the actions they want to take, and then do the opposite. The resulting anger, frustration, and blaming behavior generally termed "conflict" are not based on real differences. Rather, they stem from the protective reactions that occur when a decision that no one believed in or was committed to in the first place goes sour. In fact, as a paradox within a paradox, such conflict is symptomatic of agreement!

GROUP TYRANNY AND CONFORMITY

Understanding the dynamics of the Abilene Paradox also requires a "reorientation" in thinking about concepts such as "group tyranny"—the loss of the individual's distinctiveness in a group, and the impact of conformity pressures on individual behavior in organizations.

Group tyranny and its result, individual conformity, generally refer to the coercive effect of group pressures on individual behavior. Sometimes referred to as Group-think, it has been damned as the cause for everything from the lack of creativity in organizations ("A camel is a horse designed by a committee") to antisocial behavior in juveniles ("My Johnny is a good boy. He was just pressured into shoplifting by the kids he runs around with").

However, analysis of the dynamics underlying the Abilene Paradox opens up the possibility that individuals frequently perceive and feel as if they are experiencing the coercive organization conformity pressures when, in actuality, they are responding to the dynamics of mismanaged agreement.

Conceptualizing, experiencing, and responding to such experiences as reflecting the tyrannical pressures of a group again serves as important psychological use for the individual: As was previously said, it releases him from the responsibility of taking action and thus becomes a defense against action. Thus, much behavior within an organization that heretofore has been conceptualized as reflecting the tyranny of conformity pressures is really an expression of collective anxiety and therefore must be reconceptualized as a defense against acting.

A well-known example of such faulty conceptualization comes to mind. It involves the heroic sheriff in the classic Western movies who stands alone in the jailhouse door and singlehandedly protects a suspected (and usually innocent) horsethief or murderer from the irrational, tyrannical forces of group behavior—that is, an armed lynch mob. Generally, as a part of the ritual, he threatens to blow off the head of anyone who takes a step toward the door. Few ever take the challenge, and the reason is not the sheriff's six-shooter. What good would one pistol be against an armed mob of several hundred people who *really* want to hang somebody? Thus, the gun in fact serves as a face-saving measure for people who don't wish to participate in a hanging anyway. ("We had to back off. The sheriff threatened to blow our heads off.")

The situation is one involving agreement management, for a careful investigator canvassing the crowd under conditions in which the anonymity of the interviewees' responses could be guaranteed would probably find: (1) that few of the individuals in the crowd really wanted to take part in the hanging; (2) that each person's participation came about because he perceived, falsely, that others wanted to do so; and (3) that each person was afraid that others in the crowd would ostracize or in some other way punish him if he did not go along.

DIAGNOSING THE PARADOX

Most individuals like quick solutions, "clean" solutions, "no risk" solutions to organization problems. Furthermore, they tend to prefer solutions based on mechanics and technology, rather than on attitudes of "being." Unfortunately, the underlying reality of the paradox makes it impossible to provide either no-risk solutions or action technologies divorced from existential attitudes and realities. I do, however, have two sets of suggestions for dealing with these situations. One set of suggestions relates to diagnosing the situation, the other to confronting it.

When faced with the possibility that the paradox is operating, one must first make a diagnosis of the situation, and the key to diagnosis is an answer to the question, Is the organization involved in a conflict-management or an agreement-management situation? As an organization member, I have found it relatively easy to make a preliminary diagnosis as to whether an organization is on the way to Abilene or is involved in legitimate, substantive conflict by responding to the Diagnostic Survey shown in the accompanying figure. If the answer to the first question is "not characteristic," the organization is probably not in Abilene or conflict. If the answer is "characteristic," the organization has a problem of either real or phony conflict, and the answers to the succeeding questions help to determine which it is.

In brief, for reasons that should be apparent from the theory discussed here, the more times "characteristic" is checked, the more likely the organization is on its way to Abilene. In practical terms, a process for managing agreements is called for. And finally, if the answer to the first question falls into the "characteristic" category and most of the other answers fall into the category "not characteristic," one may be relatively sure the organization is in a real conflict situation and some sort of conflict management intervention is in order.

COPING WITH THE PARADOX

Assuming a preliminary diagnosis leads one to believe he and/or his organization is on the way to Abilene, the individual may choose to actively confront the situation to determine directly whether the underlying reality is one of agreement or conflict. Although there are, perhaps, a number of ways to do it, I have found one way in particular to be effective —confrontation in a group setting. The basic approach involves gathering organization members who are key figures in the problem and its solution into a group setting. Working within the context of a group is important, because the dynamics of the Abilene Paradox involve collusion among group members; therefore, to try to solve the dilemma by working with individuals and small subgroups would involve further collusion with the dynamics leading up to the paradox.

The first step in the meeting is for the individual who "calls" it (that is, the confronter) to own up to his position first and be open to the feedback he gets. The owning up process lets the others know that he is concerned lest the organization may be making a decision contrary to the desires of any of its members. A statement like this demonstrates the beginning of such an approach:

> I want to talk with you about the research project. Although I have previously said things to the contrary, I frankly don't think it will work, and I am very anxious about it. I suspect others may feel the same, but I don't know. Anyway, I am concerned that I may end up misleading you and that we may end up misleading one another, and if we aren't careful, we may continue to work on a problem that none of use wants and that might even bankrupt us. That's why I need to know where the rest of you stand. I would appreciate any of your thoughts about the project. Do you think it can succeed?

What kinds of results can one expect if he decides to undertake the process of confrontation? I have found that the results can be divided into *two* categories, at the technical level and at the level of existential experience. Of the two, I have found that for the person who undertakes to initiate the process of confrontation, the existential experience takes precedence in his ultimate evaluation of the outcome of the action he takes.

ORGANIZATION DIAGNOSTIC SURVEY

Instructions: For each of the following statements please indicate whether it *is* or *is not* characteristic of your organization.

1. There is conflict in the organization.
2. Organization members feel frustrated, impotent, and unhappy when trying to deal with it. Many are looking for ways to escape. They may avoid meetings at which the conflict is discussed, they may be looking for other jobs, or they may spend as much time away from the office as possible by taking unneeded trips or vacation or sick leave.
3. Organization members place much of the blame for the dilemma on the boss or other groups. In "back room" conversations among friends the boss is termed incompetent, ineffective, "out of touch," or a candidate for early retirement. To his face, nothing is said, or at best, only oblique references are made concerning his role in the organization's problems. If the boss isn't blamed, some other group, division, or unit is seen as the cause of the trouble: "We would do fine if it were not for the damn fools in Division X."
4. Small subgroups of trusted friends and associates meet informally over coffee, lunch, and so on to discuss organizational problems. There is a lot of agreement among the members of these subgroups as to the cause of the troubles and the solutions that would be effective in solving them. Such conversations are frequently punctuated with statements beginning with, "We should do . . ."
5. In meetings where those same people meet with members from other subgroups to discuss the problem they "soften their positions," state them in ambiguous language, or even reverse them to suit the apparent positions taken by others.
6. After such meetings, members complain to trusted associates that they really didn't say what they wanted to say, but also provide a list of convincing reasons why the comments, suggestions, and reactions they wanted to make would have been impossible. Trusted associates commiserate and say the same was true for them.
7. Attempts to solve the problem do not seem to work. In fact, such attempts seem to add to the problem or make it worse.
8. Outside the organization individuals seem to get along better, be happier, and operate more effectively than they do within it.

The Technical Level. If one is correct in diagnosing the presence of the paradox, I have found the solution to the technical problem may be almost absurdly quick and simple, nearly on the order of this:

"Do you mean that you and I and the rest of us have been dragging along with a research project that none of us has thought would work? It's crazy. I can't believe we would do it, but we did. Let's figure out how we can cancel it and get to doing something productive." In fact, the simplicity and quickness of the solution frequently don't seem possible to most of us, since we have been trained to believe that the solution to conflict requires a long, arduous process of debilitating problem solving.

Also, since existential risk is always present, it is possible that one's diagnosis is incorrect, and the process of confrontation lifts to the level of public examination real, substantive conflict, which may result in heated debate about technology, personalities, and/or administrative approaches. There is evidence that such debates, properly managed, can be the basis for creativity in organizational problem solving. There is also the possibility, however, that such debates cannot be managed, and, substantiating the concept of existential risk, the person who initiates the risk may get fired or ostracized. But that again leads to the necessity of evaluating the results of such confrontation at the existential level.

Existential Results. Evaluating the outcome of confrontation from an existential framework is quite different from evaluating it from a set of technical criteria. How do I reach this conclusion? Simply from interviewing a variety of people who have chosen to confront the paradox and listening to their responses. In short, for them, psychological success and failure apparently are divorced from what is traditionally accepted in organizations as criteria for success and failure.

For instance, some examples of success are described when people are asked, "What happened when you confronted the issue?" They may answer this way:

> I was told we had enough boat rockers in the organization, and I got fired. It hurt at first, but in retrospect it was the greatest day of my life. I've got another job and I'm delighted. I'm a free man.

Another description of success might be this:

> I said I don't think the research project can succeed and the others looked shocked and quickly agreed. The upshot of the whole deal is that I got a promotion and am now known as a "rising star." It was the high point of my career.

Similarly, those who fail to confront the paradox describe failure in terms divorced from technical results. For example, one may report:

> I didn't say anything and we rocked along until the whole thing exploded and Joe got fired. There is still a lot of tension in the organization, and we

are still in trouble, but I got a good performance review last time. I still feel lousy about the whole thing, though.

From a different viewpoint, an individual may describe his sense of failure in these words.

I knew I should have said something and I didn't. When the project failed, I was a convenient whipping boy. I got demoted; I still have a job, but my future here is definitely limited. In a way I deserve what I got, but it doesn't make it any easier to accept because of that.

Most important, the act of confrontation apparently provides intrinsic psychological satisfaction, regardless of the technological outcomes for those who attempt it. The real meaning of that existential experience, and its relevance to a wide variety of organizations, may lie, therefore, not in the scientific analysis of decision making but in the plight of Sisyphus. That is something the reader will have to decide for himself.

THE ABILENE PARADOX AND THE MYTH OF SISYPHUS

In essence, this paper proposes that there is an underlying organizational reality that includes both agreement and disagreement, cooperation and conflict. However, the decision to confront the possibility of organization agreement is all too difficult and rare, and its opposite, the decision to accept the evils of the present, is all too common. Yet those two decisions may reflect the essence of both our human potential and our human imperfectibility. Consequently, the choice to confront reality in the family, the church, the business, or the bureaucracy, though made only occasionally, may reflect those "peak experiences" that provide meaning to the valleys.

In many ways, they may reflect the experience of Sisyphus. As you may remember, Sisyphus was condemned by Pluto to a perpetuity of pushing a large stone to the top of a mountain, only to see it return to its original position when he released it. As Camus suggested in his revision of the myth, Sisyphus' task was absurd and totally devoid of meaning. For most of us, though, the lives we lead pushing papers or hubcaps are no less absurd, and in many ways we probably spend about as much time pushing rocks in our organizations as Sisyphus did in his.

Camus also points out, though, that on occasion as Sisyphus released his rock and watched it return to its resting place at the bottom of the hill, he was able to recognize the absurdity of his lot, and for brief periods of time, transcend it.

So it may be with confronting the Abilene Paradox. Confronting the absurd paradox of agreement may provide, through activity, what Sisyphus gained from his passive but conscious acceptance of his fate. Thus, through the process of active confrontation with reality, we may take respite from pushing our rocks on their endless journeys and, for brief moments, experience what C. P. Snow termed "the triumphs of life we make for ourselves" within those absurdities we call organizations.

SELECTED BIBLIOGRAPHY

Chris Argyris in *Intervention Theory and Method: A Behavioral Science View* (Reading, Mass.: Addison-Wesley, 1970) gives an excellent description of the process of "owning up" and being "open," both of which are major skills required if one is to assist his organization in avoiding or leaving Abilene.

Albert Camus in *The Myth of Sisyphus and Other Essays* (New York: Vintage Books, Random House, 1955) provides an existential viewpoint for coping with absurdity, of which the Abilene Paradox is a clear example.

Jerry B. Harvey and R. Albertson in "Neurotic Organizations: Symptoms, Causes and Treatment," Parts I and II, *Personnel Journal* (September and October 1971) provide a detailed example of a third-party intervention into an organization caught in a variety of agreement-management dilemmas.

Irving Janis in *Victims of Groupthink* (Boston: Houghton-Mifflin Co., 1972) offers an alternative viewpoint for understanding and dealing with many of the dilemmas described in "The Abilene Paradox." Specifically, many of the events that Janis describes as examples of conformity pressures (that is, group tyranny) I would conceptualize as mismanaged agreement.

In his *The Pursuit of Loneliness* (Boston: Beacon Press, 1970), Philip Slater contributes an in-depth description of the impact of the role of alienation, separation, and loneliness (a major contribution to the Abilene Paradox) in our culture.

Richard Walton in *Interpersonal Peacemaking: Confrontation and Third Party Consultation* (Reading, Mass.: Addison-Wesley, 1969) describes a variety of approaches for dealing with conflict when it is real, rather than phony.

The Uses of Leadership Theory*

JAMES OWENS

Carl L. was facing a crisis. A technician by background and now in his late 30s, he had recently become manager of a group of technicians and found himself in the midst of almost open rebellion. He knew the job well and was outstanding in his abilities to organize, handle detail, plan and control. His technicians were competent. But the group's morale had fallen to a point where all spirit and will seemed suctioned out of the group; the talent was there in abundance but simply not operating. What had gone wrong? And what should he do about it? His career depended on the answers.

Carl's managerial failure and variations of it are, unfortunately, commonplace incidents within organizations, despite the personal tragedy and organizational nightmares involved.

What had gone wrong in Carl's group? Probably leadership, that still mysterious and only vaguely understood ingredient which must be created and sustained daily by a manager, with it, other managerial skills and resources come to life and work; without it, managerial skills and group talents become paralyzed—and work results grind to a halt.

This article aims (1) to present a practical framework, consisting of essential leadership theory, which can serve to facilitate a manager's understanding, analysis and evaluation of his personal leadership skills; and (2) to report on a composite managerial opinion about leadership practices, drawn from the author's work with many practicing managers over the past seven years, summarizing the insights of these managers themselves based on their years of practical experience.

Thus, my intent is to present a blend of research theory and practical managerial experience *as hopefully, a rich information-base for any man-*

Reprinted by permission from the January 1973 issue of the *Michigan Business Review*, published by the Graduate School of Business Administration, The University of Michigan.

ager seriously intent on improving his own managerial performance and career growth.

TRAIT THEORY VERSUS BEHAVIOR THEORY

The earliest studies of leadership hypothesized that what makes a leader (manager) effective is his personality, what he is as a person. Proponents of this "trait theory" searched for some set of built-in traits which successful leaders possess and ineffective leaders lack such as "aggressiveness," "self-control," "independence," "friendliness," "religious orientation," "optimism," and many others. Decades of social science research, when finally tallied, added up disappointingly to very ambiguous results: effective leaders were found to be sometimes aggressive, self-disciplined, independent, friendly, religious, and optimistic—but often none or few of these things.

The mystery of leadership was not so easily or simplistically to be revealed and entered, definitively, into neat columns. Such research proved what most managers know intuitively, sometimes from bitter experience— such as Carl's—that effective leadership is one of the most complex phenomena in human relations and an ever-elusive riddle to those who must master it. (The obvious irony here is that the successful manager must master this phenomenon in practice, if not in theory and understanding, because—unlike social scientists—his very survival, as a career manager, depends on it!)

A "behavior theory" of leadership then came upon the scene: what makes a leader effective is (quite independently of his personality) simply what he does. Much less ambitious than trait theory, behavior theory tried to search out the right things that effective leaders do: such as how they communicate, give directions, motivate, delegate, plan, handle meetings, and so on. The value of the theory, to the extent it was valid, was its implication that "leaders need not be born to it but could be trained to do the right things," independently of their inner personality traits. Unfortunately, this approach, too, missed the essence of leadership and proved to be not only unambitious but too often degenerated into mechanical "techniques" and other superficial "gimmicks," which, on the job, emerged as robot-like counterfeits of genuine leadership—and thus failed.

The decades of work by both camps, however, were not wasted. It seems clear, today, that, on balance, there is truth—and valuable knowledge— to be gained from each theory.

THE USES OF TRAIT THEORY

Although trait theory advocates failed to build a comprehensive model of leadership, their work articulated and forced into sharp focus a practical truth: one's personality, what he fundamentally is as a person, is an ever-present and massive influence on how, and with what success, he functions as a manager.

The personality of a man is his inner life, including such inner elements as background, life history, beliefs, life experiences, attitudes, prejudices, self-image, fears, loves, hates, hopes and philosophy of life. In this sense, a man is like an iceberg: only a small fraction of what he is appears above the surface (his observable behavior, what he does); the rest is his inner life, the 7/8ths of the iceberg that lie, unobservable, below the surface.

However, the manager's inner personality causes—or "spills over" into—his behavior which, in turn, affects others with whom he works, eliciting from them either cooperative or resistance reactions. And, therein lies the manager's fate: cooperative reactions from his people spell success; resistance reactions, however irrational from the manager's viewpoint, usually assure his failure (as, probably, in the case of Carl above).

Any attempt to "formulize" this cause-effect process in the form of simple one-to-one correlations, such as trait "Z_1" causing invariably behavior "Z_2" causing invariably effect "Z_3" is doomed to failure—as the efforts of the trait-theorists proved. However, it is clear that there is an influential relationship between a manager's total personality and his success, as a manager, on the job. I have submitted this precise concept to several thousand practicing managers over the years and, based on their experience, virtually all acknowledge its validity. For example, most of these managers concluded that a manager who is naturally low in his ability to trust others, has little chance to succeed; despite his best efforts, he will be unable to delegate properly and thus becomes a "bottle-neck" as work piles up on his desk, and a source of frustration to people who want a chance to get involved and grow. Or, a manager whose personality requires a high degree of security in his life, is unable to take any risks, and thus fails because he decides and does nothing! Or, a manager who struggles within himself with a poor self-image and an inherent low level of self-confidence, avoids decisions and radiates, as a kind of "self-fulfilling prophecy," certain failure. Other examples include the effect on managerial success of personality characteristics like racial prejudice, intolerance for unfamiliar ideas, dislike or distrust of the young, respect for (or general cynicism about) other people because of their background, sex, intelligence, experience, or appearance, and so on.

The virtually unanimous opinion of these thousands of practical managers has been that any manager, who genuinely has ambitions for managerial growth and advancement, can achieve it only if he adds to his efforts a periodic evaluation of his total personality, especially his attitudes, and their effect on his people as well as the success (or failure) they produce for him. Such a manager, who is capable even of managing his own career, will find that most of his personality characteristics are assets; but, if he pursues the search objectively, he will find, too, that some are liabilities. These he must begin to change, if he can or wishes; and, if he cannot, then he must, as a mature person with mature judgment, assess himself carefully and find the kind of job that fits his personality.

In short, these managers believe—and I do too— that a manager can grow in his managerial career only if he grows as a total personality, which he is long before he begins to function as a manager. What a man is and brings to the office in the form of a total personality largely determines what and how he does and with what degree of success. What this means is that personal growth as a human being underlines and becomes, to a great extent, the real foundation upon which managerial and career growth can develop. Managerial success is not a peripheral set of "techniques"; it is a working-out of one's essential being in the form of action.

THE USES OF BEHAVIOR THEORY

What "behavior theory" has taught us, over the years, is that, within certain limits imposed by the inner personality of the individual, each person has the capability of cultivating habits of behavior (by act of will) which optimize his effects upon people. Many of us feel moody, but, by act of will, virtually never act moody. Constructive habits of courtesy, self-control, two-way communication, delegation and interest in the problems of others can be learned and practiced, by act of will.

The most important contribution of "behavior theory," however, is the development of a classification of leadership behaviors (styles) which provides a manager an analytical tool with which he can consciously and intelligently build a personally successful leadership style.

A MATRIX OF LEADERSHIP STYLES

Probably the most practical contribution of research to the day-to-day life of the manager is the analytic model of leadership styles—their description and properties. Virtually all of the managers to whom I have presented this classic model agree that it clarifies their options and serves well as a means for productive analysis and evaluation of their personal leadership styles as well as their relative success.

The exact form of the leadership matrix varies as do its details but the following version is standard. The brief descriptions of each style are, of course, stereotyped and over-simplified for purposes of clear identification and analysis. Also, they are defined in neutral language, avoiding, as much as possible, either favoring or disparaging overtones at this point. The five leadership styles, which comprise the matrix, are as follows:

1.   The Autocratic Leader

The autocrat has authority, from some source such as his position, knowledge, strength, or power to reward and punish, and he uses this authority as his principal, or only method of getting things done. He is frankly authoritarian, knows what he wants done, and how, "tells" people what their work-assignments are, and demands unquestioning obedience. The autocrat ranges from "tough" to "paternalistic" depending on how much he stresses, as motivation, threat and punishment in the former case or rewards in the latter. The "tough" autocart demands and gets compliance, "or else." The "paternalistic" autocrat demands and expects compliance but mainly on a "father-knows-best"—and often very personal—relationship, implying personal dependence, rewards, and security. The autocrat permits people little or no freedom.

2.   The Bureaucratic Leader

Like the autocrat, the bureaucrat "tells" people what to do, and how, but the basis for his orders is almost exclusively the organization's policies, procedures, and rules. For the bureaucrat, these rules are absolute. He manages entirely "by the book," and no exceptions are permitted. He treats rules and administers their force upon people as a judge might treat and permit no departure or exception from—laws, including their every technicality. Like the autocrat, the bureaucrat permits people little or no freedom.

3.   The Diplomatic Leader

The diplomat is an artist who, like the salesman, lives by the arts of personal persuasion. Although he has the same clear authority as the autocrat, the diplomat prefers to "sell" people and operate, as much as possible, by persuasion and broad-scale individual motivation of people. He will "revert," if necessary, to the autocratic style, but prefers to avoid this. Some term him a "sell-type" leader who uses a large variety and degree of persuasion-tactics, ranging from simple explanation of the reasons for an order to full-scale bargaining with people. He will usually relate his organizational goals to the personal individual needs and aspirations of his people. Such a leader retains his authority in that he knows and will insist on a particular course of action; but, he provides some—limited—freedom to his people in that he permits them to react, question, raise objections, discuss, and even argue their side of the issue.

4.   The Participative Leader

The participative leader openly invites his people to participate or share, to a greater or lesser extent, in decisions, policy-making and operation methods. He is either a "democratic" or a "consultative" leader.

The "democratic" leader "joins" his group and makes it clear, in advance, that he will abide by the group's decision whether arrived at by consensus or majority vote. (This style is sometimes seen in the operations of research and development groups.)

The "consultative" leader consults his people and invites frank involvement, discussion, pro and con argument, and recommendations from the group, but makes it clear that he alone is accountable and reserves the final decision to himself.

In both forms of the participative style of leadership people are given a high degree of freedom—as they are, too, in the Free-Rein style.

5. The Free-Rein Leader

The "free-rein" leader (the analogy, of course, is to a horseman who has left the reins free) does not literally abandon all control. He sets a goal for his subordinate as well as clear parameters such as policies, deadlines, and budget and then drops the "reins" and sets his subordinate free to operate without further direction or control, unless the subordinate himself requests it.

THE "BEST" LEADERSHIP STYLE

Despite certain implications in the literature that there is a "best" and ideal leadership style, the managers I surveyed categorically reject this simple solution suggested by some social scientists. Their virtually unanimous view was that the "best" leadership style depends on:

a. the individual personality of the manager himself ("Trait theory" revisited);
b. the individual followers, the kind of people they are and the kind of work they do;
c. and, the particular situation and circumstances on any given day or hour.

In short, no "cook-book" or formulized recipe for effective leadership "rang true" as realistic with these managers. The complexity and mystery of leadership does not permit simplistic approaches.

Only a manager, himself, examining, and exploring the varieties of leadership styles, their advantages and weaknesses, as well as the people and the situation with which he is dealing, can decide what is the "best" leadership style for him, and with them, and in this particular situation. It must be an act of individual judgment. A theoretical framework can assist, as can the opinions of thousands of managers, but the choice and practice of leadership style must always remain the act of judgment of the individual manager.

Some authors have coined the expression "tool-box approach" for this necessity that faces managers of choosing the "right style" at the "right time" in the "right situation" (as opposed to the easy and utopian formula of a single, predominant leadership style for all people and all situations).

A SUMMARY OF MANAGERS' VIEWS

Working closely over the years with many practicing managers, I have had the opportunity to learn much of what they learned about leadership—based, not on textbook abstractions, but realistically on years of hard experience. The essential results of this seven-year informal survey of these managers are organized below as telegraphic propositions expressed as either advantages or weaknesses of each classic leadership style. Each proposition is a kind of composite view representing a virtual consensus of the opinions of these managers. Naturally, they are general statements and, as such allow for exceptions in individual cases. Even so, these propositions are experience-based insights of managers themselves and should be helpful to any manager seriously intent on evaluating and improving his own leadership.

I.   The autocratic leadership style
  A.   Advantages
    1.   When appropriate, can increase efficiency, save time and get quick results, especially in a crisis or emergency situation.
    2.   The paternalistic form of this style of leadership works well with employees who have a low tolerance for ambiguity, feel insecure with freedom and even minor decision-making requirements, and thrive under clear, detailed, and achievable directives.
    3.   Chain of command and division of work (who is supposed to do what) are clear and fully understood by all.
  B.   Weaknesses
    1.   The apparent efficiency of one-way communication often becomes a false efficiency since one-way communication, without "feed-back," typically leads to misunderstandings, communication breakdowns and costly errors.
    2.   The autocratic manager must really be an expert, not just think he is, because he receives little, if any, information and ideas from his people as inputs into his decision-making. He is really alone in his decision-making and this is generally dangerous in today's environment of technological and organizational complexity.
    3.   The critical weakness, however, of the autocratic style is its effect on people. Many managers pine for the good old days when the boss gave orders and people obeyed meekly and

without question. These managers, however, agree that—like it or not—those days are gone forever. Today, most people resent authoritarian rule which excludes them from involvement and reduces them to machine-like cogs without human dignity or importance. They express their resentment in the form of massive resistance, low morale and low productivity (if not downright work stoppage or sabotage). This is especially true, today, with technical or educated people, youths entering the job market, and members of most minority groups.

II. The bureaucratic leadership style
    A. Advantages
        1. Insures consistency of policy and operations which can be critical in industries where legal parameters are common (banking, sales, etc.).
        2. Consistent application of personnel-related rules, for one and for all, contributes a sense of fairness and impartiality in the manager's many and complex dealings with people.
        3. People know where they stand. Most decisions concerning them are by known—and accepted—rule, predictable, objective (rather than by the whim or mood of a manager)—and there is security and a sense of fairness.
    B. Weaknesses
        1. Inflexibility in situations where exceptions to rules should be made or requested.
        2. Paralysis in situations not covered by rules or where rules are ambiguous (as is often the case: policies and rules represent legislation for the majority of situations but can never substitute for individual human judgment in a particular specific situation).
        3. The reaction of people working under a strongly bureaucratic manager is essentially the same as described above in the case of the autocratic manager: again, resentment, resistance, and low morale.

III. The diplomatic leadership style
    A. Advantages
        1. People cooperate and work more enthusiastically if managers take even a few minutes—and respect people enough—to give them the simple reasons and explanations of the reasons that make a particular task important—rather than just a blind chore.
        2. A manager's personal effort to explain to or persuade a subordinate is usually received as an important compliment and

show of respect—and usually appreciated and responded to with a high degree of cooperation and effort.

3. This style of leadership is indispensable for the legions of so-called "staff" people (and even "line" people who realize the inadequacy of their real authority). They must achieve the results, for which they are accountable, "unfairly" deprived of the clear-cut authority required and, therefore, are utterly dependent on the skills of persuasion to get the help and cooperation needed.

B. Weaknesses

1. Some people interpret efforts to persuade them, rather than order them, as a sign of weakness and, thus lose respect for a manager. The basic weakness, however, of the diplomatic style is the same as the pitfall always facing those who use consistently the "tool-box" approach to leadership; namely, hypocrisy. Unless handled with judgment, skill and sincerity, the diplomatic style—as well as any "tool box" approach with people—quickly degenerates and "comes through" to people as insincerity, frank manipulation and exploitation—and is, thus, deeply resented and resisted. And, naturally, a complete failure.

2. Anyone employing the diplomatic style must be a skilled and competent salesman, who usually "wins" the "sale." A salesman routinely expects and invites objections—a manager who operates this way must be able to convince and "sell" people, or he will be forced to "revert" (hypocritically) to a frank autocratic order. The effect of this on people is both obvious and disastrous.

IV. The participative leadership style

A. Advantages

1. When people participate in and help formulate a decision, they support it (instead of fighting or ignoring it) and work hard to make it work, because it's their idea and, now, part of their life and their "ego."

2. The manager consistently receives the benefit of the best information, ideas, suggestions, and talent—and operating experience—of his people. The rich information-source which they represent becomes his and a key input into his decision-making.

3. Group discussion, even though time-consuming, before a decision is made, can force critical information to the surface which, when considered, improves decision-making—or, in some cases, actually averts a disaster which would

have occurred if key operating-level information were not made available.

4. This style of leadership permits and encourages people to develop, grow and rise in the organization (both in terms of responsibility they can assume and service they can contribute).

5. Most people work better, more enthusiastically and at a high level of motivation when they are given a reasonable degree of freedom to act and contribute. They enjoy a sense of personal importance, value and achievement, unlike human cogs in machine-like organizational systems.

6. Most importantly, as already implied above, the participative manager establishes a work-climate which easily unleashes the enormous power of people who are motivated by—and will strive hard for—goals which they help create and in the accomplishment of which they gain deep personal satisfaction in the form of recognition, sense of accomplishment, sense of importance and personal value. In short, the participative manager has the critical factor of built-in personal motivation working for him.

B. Weaknesses

1. The participative style can take enormous amounts of time and, when used inappropriately, be simply inefficient.

2. Some managers "use" the democratic style as a way of avoiding (or abdicating) responsibility.

3. People resent the invitation to offer recommendations when such recommendations are consistently ignored and rejected. It follows that any manager, who must reject a recommendation, should quickly explain why such recommendations had to be rejected.

4. Use of the participative styles can easily, if not handled well, degenerate into a complete loss of managerial control.

V. The free-rein leadership style

A. Advantages

1. This style comprises the essence of full managerial delegation with its benefits of optimum utilization of time and resources.

2. Many people are motivated to full effort only if given this kind of free-rein.

B. Weaknesses

1. Very little managerial control and a high degree of risk.

2. This style can be a disaster if the manager does not know well the competence and integrity of his people and their ability to handle this kind of freedom.

CONCLUSION

Leadership is still an art despite the efforts of social science researchers to make it a science. The summaries, here, of essential leadership theory and managerial opinion (based on experience) are presented only as a help to (not a substitute for) the final individual judgment of the manager as he lives with his particular people in his particular situation.

Every such manager, however, must operate by some leadership style or styles and it is hoped that the ideas presented above will aid the manager in his analysis, evaluation and development of his own personal leadership style.

Managers and Leaders:
Are They Different?*

ABRAHAM ZALEZNIK

WHAT is the ideal way to develop leadership? Every society provides its own answer to this question, and each, in groping for answers, defines its deepest concerns about the purposes, distributions, and uses of power. Business has contributed its answer to the leadership question by evolving a new breed called the manager. Simultaneously, business has established a new power ethic that favors collective over individual leadership, the cult of the group over that of personality. While ensuring the competence, control, and the balance of power relations among groups with the potential for rivalry, managerial leadership unfortunately does not necessarily ensure imagination, creativity, or ethical behavior in guiding the destinies of corporate enterprises.

Leadership inevitably requires using power to influence the thoughts and actions of other people. Power in the hands of an individual entails human risks: first, the risk of equating power with the ability to get immediate results; second, the risk of ignoring the many different ways people can legitimately accumulate power; and third, the risk of losing self-control in the desire for power. The need to hedge these risks accounts in part for the development of collective leadership and the managerial ethic. Consequently, an inherent conservatism dominates the culture of large organizations. In *The Second American Revolution,* John D. Rockefeller III describes the conservatism of organizations:

> An organization is a system, with a logic of its own, and all the weight
> of tradition and inertia. The deck is stacked in favor of the tried and proven

way of doing things and against the taking of risks and striking out in new directions.[1]

Out of this conservatism and inertia organizations provide succession to power through the development of managers rather than individual leaders. And the irony of the managerial ethic is that it fosters a bureaucratic culture in business, supposedly the last bastion protecting us from the encroachments and controls of bureaucracy in government and education. Perhaps the risks associated with power in the hands of an individual may be necessary ones for business to take if organizations are to break free of their inertia and bureaucratic conservatism.

MANAGER VERSUS LEADER PERSONALITY

Theodore Levitt has described the essential features of a managerial culture with its emphasis on rationality and control:

> Management consists of the rational assessment of a situation and the systematic selection of goals and purposes (what is to be done?); the systematic development of strategies to achieve these goals; the marshalling of the required resources; the rational design, organization, direction, and control of the activities required to attain the selected purposes; and, finally, the motivating and rewarding of people to do the work.[2]

In other words, whether his or her energies are directed toward goals, resources, organization structures, or people, a manager is a problem solver. The manager asks himself, "What problems have to be solved, and what are the best ways to achieve results so that people will continue to contribute to this organization?" In this conception, leadership is a practical effort to direct affairs; and to fulfill his task, a manager requires that many people operate at different levels of status and responsibility. Our democratic society is, in fact, unique in having solved the problem of providing well-trained managers for business. The same solution stands ready to be applied to government, education, health care, and other institutions. It takes neither genius nor heroism to be a manager, but rather persistence, tough-mindedness, hard work, intelligence, analytical ability and, perhaps most important, tolerance and good will.

Another conception, however, attaches almost mystical beliefs to what leadership is and assumes that only great people are worthy of the drama of power and politics. Here, leadership is a psychodrama in which, as a precondition for control of a political structure, a lonely person must gain control of him or herself. Such an expectation of leadership contrasts

---

[1] John D. Rockefeller III, *The Second American Revolution* (New York: Harper-Row, 1973), p. 72.

[2] Theodore Levitt, "Management and the Post Industrial Society," *The Public Interest*, Summer 1976, p. 73.

sharply with the mundane, practical, and yet important conception that leadership is really managing work that other people do.

Two questions come to mind. Is this mystique of leadership merely a holdover from our collective childhood of dependency and our longing for good and heroic parents? Or, is there a basic truth lurking behind the need for leaders that no matter how competent managers are, their leadership stagnates because of their limitations in visualizing purposes and generating value in work? Without this imaginative capacity and the ability to communicate, managers, driven by their narrow purposes, perpetuate group conflicts instead of reforming them into broader desires and goals.

If indeed problems demand greatness, then, judging by past performance, the selection and development of leaders leave a great deal to chance. There are no known ways to train "great" leaders. Furthermore, beyond what we leave to chance, there is a deeper issue in the relationship between the need for competent managers and the longing for great leaders.

What it takes to ensure the supply of people who will assume practical responsibility may inhibit the development of great leaders. Conversely, the presence of great leaders may undermine the development of managers who become very anxious in the relative disorder that leaders seem to generate. The antagonism in aim (to have many competent managers as well as great leaders) often remains obscure in stable and well-developed societies. But the antagonism surfaces during periods of stress and change, as it did in the Western countries during both the Great Depression and World War II. The tension also appears in the struggle for power between theorists and professional managers in revolutionary societies.

It is easy enough to dismiss the dilemma I pose (of training managers while we may need new leaders, or leaders at the expense of managers) by saying that the need is for people who can be *both* managers and leaders. The truth of the matter as I see it, however, is that just as a managerial culture is different from the entrepreneurial culture that develops when leaders appear in organizations, managers and leaders are very different kinds of people. They differ in motivation, personal history, and in how they think and act.

A technologically oriented and economically successful society tends to depreciate the need for great leaders. Such societies hold a deep and abiding faith in rational methods of solving problems, including problems of value, economics, and justice. Once rational methods of solving problems are broken down into elements, organized, and taught as skills, then society's faith in technique over personal qualities in leadership remains the guiding conception for a democratic society contemplating its leadership requirements. But there are times when tinkering and trial and error prove inadequate to the emerging problems of selecting goals, allocating resources, and distributing wealth and opportunity. During such times, the democratic society needs to find leaders who use themselves as the instruments of learning and acting, instead of managers who use their accumulation of collective experience to get where they are going.

The most impressive spokesman, as well as exemplar of the managerial viewpoint, was Alfred P. Sloan, Jr. who, along with Pierre du Pont, designed the modern corporate structure. Reflecting on what makes one management successful while another fails, Sloan suggested that "good management rests on a reconciliation of centralization, or 'decentralization with coordinated control.' "[3]

Sloan's conception of management, as well as his practice, developed by trial and error, and by the accumulation of experience. Sloan wrote:

> There is no hard and fast rule for sorting out the various responsibilities and the best way to assign them. The balance which is struck . . . varies according to what is being decided, the circmstances of the time, past experience, and the temperaments and skills of the executive involved.[4]

In other words, in much the same way that the inventors of the late nineteenth century tried, failed, and fitted until they hit on a product or method, managers who innovate in developing organizations are "tinkerers." They do not have a grand design or experience the intuitive flash of insight that, borrowing from modern science, we have come to call the "breakthrough."

Managers and leaders differ fundamentally in their world views. The dimensions for assessing these differences include managers' and leaders' orientations toward their goals, their work, their human relations, and their selves.

Attitudes toward Goals

Managers tend to adopt impersonal, if not passive, attitudes toward goals. Managerial goals arise out of necessities rather than desires, and, therefore, are deeply embedded in the history and culture of the organization.

Frederic G. Donner, chairman and chief executive officer of General Motors from 1958 to 1967, expressed this impersonal and passive attitude toward goals in defining GM's position on product development:

> . . . To meet the challenge of the marketplace, we must recognize changes in customer needs and desires far enough ahead to have the right products in the right places at the right time and in the right quantity.
>
> We must balance trends in preference against the many compromises that are necessary to make a final product that is both reliable and good

---

[3] Alfred P. Sloan, Jr., *My Years with General Motors* (New York: Doubleday & Co. 1964), p. 429.

[4] Ibid., p. 429.

looking, that performs well and that sells at a competitive price in the necessary volume. We must design, not just the cars we would like to build, but more importantly, the cars that our customers want to buy.[5]

Nowhere in this formulation of how a product comes into being is there a notion that consumer tastes and preferences arise in part as a result of what manufacturers do. In reality, through product design, advertising, and promotion, consumers learn to like what they then say they need. Few would argue that people who enjoy taking snapshots *need* a camera that also develops pictures. But in response to novelty, convenience, a shorter interval between acting (taking the snap) and gaining pleasure (seeing the shot), the Polaroid camera succeeded in the marketplace. But it is inconceivable that Edwin Land responded to impressions of consumer need. Instead, he translated a technology (polarization of light) into a product, which proliferated and stimulated consumers' desires.

The example of Polaroid and Land suggests how leaders think about goals. They are active instead of reactive, shaping ideas instead of responding to them. Leaders adopt a personal and active attitude toward goals. The influence a leader exerts in altering moods, evoking images and expectations, and in establishing specific desires and objectives determines the direction a business takes. The net result of this influence is to change the way people think about what is desirable, possible, and necessary.

Conceptions of Work

What do managers and leaders do? What is the nature of their respective work?

Leaders and managers differ in their conceptions. Managers tend to view work as an enabling process involving some combination of people and ideas interacting to establish strategies and make decisions. Managers help the process along by a range of skills, including calculating the interests in opposition, staging and timing the surfacing of controversial issues, and reducing tensions. In this enabling process, managers appear flexible in the use of tactics: they negotiate and bargain, on the one hand, and use rewards and punishments, and other forms of coercion, on the other. Machiavelli wrote for managers and not necessarily for leaders.

Alfred Sloan illustrated how this enabling process works in situations of conflict. The time was the early 1920s when the Ford Motor Co. still dominated the automobile industry using, as did General Motors, the conventional water-cooled engine. With the full backing of Pierre du Pont, Charles Kettering dedicated himself to the design of an air-cooled engine, which, if successful, would have been a great technical and market

[5] Ibid., p. 440.

coup for GM. Kettering believed in his product, but the manufacturing division heads at GM remained skeptical and later opposed the new design on two grounds: first, that it was technically unreliable, and second, that the corporation was putting all its eggs in one basket by investing in a new product instead of attending to the current marketing situation.

In the summer of 1923 after a series of false starts and after its decision to recall the copper-cooled Chevrolets from dealers and customers, GM management reorganized and finally scrapped the project. When it dawned on Kettering that the company had rejected the engine, he was deeply discouraged and wrote to Sloan that without the "organized resistance" against the project it would succeed and that unless the project were saved, he would leave the company.

Alfred Sloan was all too aware of the fact that Kettering was unhappy and indeed intended to leave General Motors. Sloan was also aware of the fact that, while the manufacturing divisions strongly opposed the new engine, Pierre du Pont supported Kettering. Furthermore, Sloan had himself gone on record in a letter to Kettering less than two years earlier expressing full confidence in him. The problem Sloan now had was to make his decision stick, keep Kettering in the organization (he was much too valuable to lose), avoid alienating du Pont, and encourage the division heads to move speedily in developing product lines using conventional water-cooled engines.

The actions that Sloan took in the face of this conflict reveal much about how managers work. First, he tried to reassure Kettering by presenting the problem in a very ambiguous fashion, suggesting that he and the Executive Committee sided with Kettering, but that it would not be practical to force the divisions to do what they were opposed to. He presented the problem as being a question of the people, not the product. Second, he proposed to reorganize around the problem by consolidating all functions in a new division that would be responsible for the design, production, and marketing of the new car. This solution, however, appeared as ambiguous as his efforts to placate and keep Kettering in General Motors. Sloan wrote: "My plan was to create an independent pilot operation under the sole jurisdiction of Mr. Kettering, a kind of copper-cooled-car division. Mr. Kettering would designate his own chief engineer and his production staff to solve the technical problems of manufacture."[6]

While Sloan did not discuss the practical value of this solution, which included saddling an inventor with management responsibility, he in effect used this plan to limit his conflict with Pierre du Pont.

In effect, the managerial solution that Sloan arranged and pressed for adoption limited the options available to others. The structural solution narrowed choices, even limiting emotional reactions to the point where

---

[6] Ibid., p. 91.

the key people could do nothing but go along, and even allowed Sloan
to say in his memorandum to du Pont, "We have discussed the matter
with Mr. Kettering at some length this morning and he agrees with us
absolutely on every point we made. He appears to receive the suggestion
enthusiastically and has every confidence that it can be put across along
these lines."[7]

Having placated people who opposed his views by developing a structural solution that appeared to give something but in reality only limited
options, Sloan could then authorize the car division's general manager,
with whom he basically agreed, to move quickly in designing water-cooled
cars for the immediate market demand.

Years later Sloan wrote, evidently with tongue in cheek, "The copper-
cooled car never came up again in a big way. It just died out, I don't know
why."[8]

In order to get people to accept solutions to problems, managers need
to coordinate and balance continually. Interestingly enough, this managerial work has much in common with what diplomats and mediators
do, with Henry Kissinger apparently an outstanding practitioner. The
manager aims at shifting balances of power toward solutions acceptable as
a compromise among conflicting values.

What about leaders, what do they do? Where managers act to limit
choices, leaders work in the opposite direction, to develop fresh approaches
to long-standing problems and to open issues for new options. Stanley
and Inge Hoffmann, the political scientists, liken the leader's work to that
of the artist. But unlike most artists, the leader himself is an integral part
of the aesthetic product. One cannot look at a leader's art without looking
at the artist. On Charles de Gaulle as a political artist, they wrote: "And
each of his major political acts, however tortuous the means or the details,
has been whole, indivisible and unmistakably his own, like an artistic
act."[9]

The closest one can get to a product apart from the artist is the ideas
that occupy, indeed at times obsess the leader's mental life. To be effective,
however, the leader needs to project his ideas into images that excite people, and only then develop choices that give the projected images substance. Consequently, leaders create excitement in work.

John F. Kennedy's brief presidency shows both the strengths and weaknesses connected with the excitement leaders generate in their work. In
his inaugural address he said, "Let every nation know, whether it wishes
us well or ill, that we shall pay any price, bear any burden, meet any hard-

---

[7] Ibid., p. 91.

[8] Ibid., p. 93.

[9] Stanley and Inge Hoffmann, "The Will for Grandeur: de Gaulle as Political
Artist," *Daedalus*, Summer 1968, p. 849.

ship, support any friend, oppose any foe, in order to assure the survival and the success of liberty."

This much-quoted statement forced people to react beyond immediate concerns and to identify with Kennedy and with important shared ideals. But upon closer scrutiny the statement must be seen as absurd because it promises a position which if in fact adopted, as in the Viet Nam War, could produce disastrous results. Yet unless expectations are aroused and mobilized, with all the dangers of frustration inherent in heightened desire, new thinking and new choice can never come to light.

Leaders work from high-risk positions, indeed often are temperamentally disposed to seek out risk and danger, especially where opportunity and reward appear high. From my observations, why one individual seeks risks while another approaches problems conservatively depends more on his or her personality and less on conscious choice. For some, especially those who become managers, the instinct for survival dominates their need for risk, and their ability to tolerate mundane, practical work assists their survival. The same cannot be said for leaders who sometimes react to mundane work as to an affliction.

Relations with Others

Managers prefer to work with people; they avoid solitary activity because it makes them anxious. Several years ago, I directed studies on the psychological aspects of career. The need to seek out others with whom to work and collaborate seemed to stand out as important characteristics of managers. When asked, for example, to write imaginative stories in response to a picture showing a single figure (a boy contemplating a violin, or a man silhouetted in a state of reflection), managers populated their stories with people. The following is an example of a manager's imaginative story about the young boy contemplating a violin:

> Mom and Dad insisted that junior take music lessons so that someday he can become a concert musician. His instrument was ordered and had just arrived. Junior is weighing the alternatives of playing football with the other kids or playing with the squeak box. He can't understand how his parents could think a violin is better than a touchdown.
>
> After four months of practicing the violin, junior has had more than enough, Daddy is going out of his mind, and Mommy is willing to give in reluctantly to the men's wishes. Football season is now over, but a good third baseman will take the field next spring.[10]

This story illustrates two themes that clarify managerial attitudes toward human relations. The first, as I have suggested, is to seek out activ-

---

[10] Abraham Zaleznik, Gene W. Dalton, and Louis B. Barnes, *Orientation and Conflict in Career* (Boston: Division of Research, Harvard Business School, 1970), p. 316.

ity with other people (i.e., the football team), and the second is to maintain a low level of emotional involvement in these relationships. The low emotional involvement appears in the writer's use of conventional metaphors, even clichés, and in the depiction of the ready transformation of potential conflict into harmonious decisions. In this case, Junior, Mommy, and Daddy agree to give up the violin for manly sports.

These two themes may seem paradoxical, but their coexistence supports what a manager does, including reconciling differences, seeking compromises, and establishing a balance of power. A further idea demonstrated by how the manager wrote the story is that managers may lack empathy, or the capacity to sense intuitively the thoughts and feelings of others. To illustrate attempts to be empathic, here is another story written to the same stimulus picture by someone considered by his peers to be a leader:

> This little boy has the appearance of being a sincere artist, one who is deeply affected by the violin, and has an intense desire to master the instrument.
>
> He seems to have just completed his normal practice session and appears to be somewhat crestfallen at his inability to produce the sounds which he is sure lie within the violin.
>
> He appears to be in the process of making a vow to himself to expend the necessary time and effort to play this instrument until he satisfies himself that he is able to bring forth the qualities of music which he feels within himself.
>
> With this type of determination and carry through, this boy became one of the great violinists of his day.[11]

Empathy is not simply a matter of paying attention to other people. It is also the capacity to take in emotional signals and to make them mean something in a relationship with an individual. People who describe another person as "deeply affected" with "intense desire," as capable of feeling "crestfallen" and as one who can "vow to himself," would seem to have and inner perceptiveness that they can use in their relationships with others.

Managers relate to people according to the role they play in a sequence of events or in a decision-making *process*, while leaders, who are concerned with ideas, relate in more intuitive and empathic ways. The manager's orientation to people, as actors in a sequence of events, deflects his or her attention away from the substance of people's concerns and toward their roles in a process. The distinction is simply between a manager's attention to *how* things get done and a leader's to *what* the events and decisions mean to participants.

In recent years, managers have taken over from game theory the no-

---

[11] Ibid., p. 294.

tion that decision-making events can be one of two types: the win-lose situation (or zero-sum game) or the win-win situation in which everybody in the action comes out ahead. As part of the process of reconciling differences among people and maintaining balances of power, managers strive to convert win-lose into win-win situations.

At an illustration, take the decision of how to allocate capital resources among operating divisions in a large, decentralized organization. On the face of it, the dollars available for distribution are limited at any given time. Presumably, therefore, the more one division gets, the less is available for other divisions.

Managers tend to view this situation (as it affects human relations) as a conversion issue: how to make what seems like a win-lose problem into a win-win problem. Several solutions to this situation come to mind. First, the manager focuses others' attention on procedure and not on substance. Here the actors become engrossed in the bigger problem of *how* to make decisions, not *what* decisions to make. Once committed to the bigger problems, the actors have to support the outcome since they were involved in formulating decision rules. Because the actors believe in the rules they formulated, they will accept present losses in the expectation that next time they will win.

Second, the manager communicates to his subordinates indirectly, using "signals" instead of "messages." A signal has a number of possible implicit positions in it while a message clearly states a position. Signals are inconclusive and subject to reinterpretaton should people become upset and angry, while messages involve the direct consequence that some people will indeed not like what they hear. The nature of messages heightens emotional response, and, as I have indicated, emotionally makes managers anxious. With signals, the question of who wins and who loses often becomes obscured.

Third, the manager plays for time. Managers seem to recognize that with the passage of time and the delay of major decisions, compromises emerge that take the sting out of win-lose situations, and the original "game" will be superseded by additional ones. Therefore, compromises may mean that one wins and loses simultaneously, depending on which of the games one evaluates.

There are undoubtedly many other tactical moves managers use to change human situations from win-lose to win-win. But the point to be made is that such tactics focus on the decision-making process itself and interest managers rather than leaders. The interest in tactics involves costs as well as benefits, including making organizations fatter in bureaucratic and political intrigue and leaner in direct, hard activity and warm human relationships. Consequently, one often hears subordinates characterize managers as inscrutable, detached, and manipulative. These adjectives arise from the subordinates' perception that they are linked together in a process whose purpose, beyond simply making decisions, is to maintain a controlled as well as rational and equitable structure. These adjectives suggest that managers need order in the face of the potential chaos that many fear in human relationships.

In contrast, one often hears leaders referred to in adjectives rich in emotional content. Leaders attract strong feelings of identity and difference, or of love and hate. Human relations in leader-dominated structures often appear turbulent, intense, and at times even disorganized. Such an atmosphere intensifies individual motivation and often produces unanticipated outcomes. Does this intense motivation lead to innovation and high performance, or does it represent wasted energy?

Senses of Self

In *The Varieties of Religious Experience*, William James describes two basic personality types, "once-born" and "twice-born."[12] People of the former personality type are those for whom adjustments to life have been straightforward and whose lives have been more or less a peaceful flow from the moment of their births. The twice-borns, on the other hand, have not had an easy time of it. Their lives are marked by a continual struggle to attain some sense of order. Unlike the once-borns they cannot take things for granted. According to James, these personalities have equally different world views. For a once-born personality, the sense of self, as a guide to conduct and attitude, derives from a feeling of being at home and in harmony with one's environment. For a twice-born, the sense of self derives from a feeling of profound separateness.

A sense of belonging or of being separate has a practical significance for the kinds of investments managers and leaders make in their careers. Managers see themselves as conservators and regulators of an existing order of affairs with which they personally identify and from which they gain rewards. Perpetuating and strengthening existing institutions enhances a manager's sense of self-worth: he or she is performing in a role that harmonizes with the ideals of duty and responsibility. William James had this harmony in mind—this sense of self as flowing easily to and from the outer world—in defining a once-born personality. If one feels oneself as a member of institutions, contributing to their well-being, then one fulfills a mission in life and feels rewarded for having measured up to ideals. This reward transcends material gains and answers the more fundamental desire for personal integrity which is achieved by identifying with existing institutions.

Leaders tend to be twice-born personalities, people who feel separate from their environment, including other people. They may work in orga-

---

12 William James, *Varieties of Religious Experience* (New York: Mentor Books, 1958).

nizations, but they never belong to them. Their sense of who they are does not depend upon memberships, work roles, or other social indicators of identity. What seems to follow from this idea about separateness is some theoretical basis for explaining why certain individuals search out opportunities for change. The methods to bring about change may be technological, political, or ideological, but the object is the same: to profoundly alter human, economic, and political relationships.

Sociologists refer to the preparation individuals undergo to perform in roles as the socialization process. Where individuals experience themselves as an integral part of the social structure (their self-esteem gains strength through participation and conformity), social standards exert powerful effects in maintaining the individual's personal sense of continuity, even beyond the early years in the family. The line of development from the family to schools, then to career is cumulative and reinforcing. When the line of development is not reinforcing because of significant disruptions in relationships or other problems experienced in the family or other social institutions, the individual turns inward and struggles to establish self-esteem, identity, and order. Here the psychological dynamics center on the experience with loss and the efforts at recovery.

In considering the development of leadership, we have to examine two different courses of life history: (1) development through socialization, which prepares the individual to guide institutions and to maintain the existing balance of social relations; and (2) development through personal mastery, which impels an individual to struggle for psychological and social change. Society produces its managerial talent through the first line of development, while through the second leaders emerge.

DEVELOPMENT OF LEADERSHIP

The development of every person begins in the family. Each person experiences the traumas associated with separating from his or her parents, as well as the pain that follows such frustration. In the same vein, all individuals face the difficulties of achieving self-regulation and self-control. But for some, perhaps a majority, the fortunes of childhood provide adequate gratifications and sufficient opportunities to find substitutes for rewards no longer available. Such individuals, the "once-borns," make moderate identifications with parents and find a harmony between what they expect and what they are able to realize from life.

But suppose the pains of separation are amplified by a combination of parental demands and the individual's needs to the degree that a sense of isolation, of being special, and of wariness disrupts the bonds that attach children to parents and other authority figures? Under such conditions, and given a special aptitude, the origins of which remain mysterious, the person becomes deeply involved in his or her inner world at the expense of interest in the outer world. For such a person, self-esteem no longer depends solely upon positive attachments and real rewards. A form a self-reliance takes hold along with expectations of performance and achievement, and perhaps even the desire to do great works.

Such self-perceptions can come to nothing if the individual's talents are negligible. Even with strong talents, there are no guarantees that achievement will follow, let alone that the end result will be for good rather than evil. Other factors enter into development. For one thing, leaders are like artists and other gifted people who often struggle with neuroses; their ability to function varies considerably even over the short run, and some potential leaders may lose the struggle altogether. Also, beyond early childhood, the patterns of development that affect managers and leaders involve the selective influence of particular people. Just as they appear flexible and evenly distributed in the types of talents available for development, managers form moderate and widely distributed attachments. Leaders, on the other hand, establish, and also break off, intensive one-to-one relationships.

It is a common observation that people with great talents are often only indifferent students. No one, for example, could have predicted Einstein's great achievements on the basis of his mediocre record in school. The reason for mediocrity is obviously not the absence of ability. It may result, instead, from self-absorption and the inability to pay attention to the ordinary tasks at hand. The only sure way an individual can interrupt reverie-like preoccupation and self-absorption is to form a deep attachment to a great teacher or other benevolent person who understands and has the ability to communicate with the gifted individual.

Whether gifted individuals find what they need in one-to-one relationships depends on the availability of sensitive and intuitive mentors who have a vocation in cultivating talent. Fortunately, when the generations do meet and the self-selections occur, we learn more about how to develop leaders and how talented people of different generations influence each other.

While apparently destined for a mediocre career, people who form important one-to-one relationships are able to accelerate and intensify their development through an apprenticeship. The background for such apprenticeships, or the psychological readiness of an individual to benefit from an intensive relationship, depends upon some experience in life that forces the individual to turn inward. A case example will make this point clearer. This example comes from the life of Dwight David Eisenhower, and illustrates the transformation of a career from competent to outstanding.[13]

Dwight Eisenhower's early career in the Army foreshadowed very little

---

[13] This example is included in Abraham Zaleznik and Manfred F.R. Kets de Vries, *Power and the Corporate Mind* (Boston: Houghton Mifflin, 1975).

about his future development. During World War I, while some of his West
Point classmates were already experiencing the war first-hand in France,
Eisenhower felt "embedded in the monotony and unsought safety of the
Zone of the Interior . . . that was intolerable punishment."[14]

Shortly after World War I, Eisenhower, then a young officer somewhat
pessimistic about his career chances, asked for a transfer to Panama to
work under General Fox Connor, a senior officer whom Eisenhower ad-
mired. The army turned down Eisenhower's request. This setback was
very much on Eisenhower's mind when Ikey, his first-born son, succumbed
to influenza. By some sense of responsibility for its own, the army transferred Eisenhower to Panama, where he took up his duties under General
Connor with the shadow of his lost son very much upon him.

In a relationship with the kind of father he would have wanted to be,
Eisenhower reverted to being the son he lost. In this highly charged situation, Eisenhower began to learn from his mentor. General Connor offered,
and Eisenhower gladly took, a magnificent tutorial on the military. The
effects of this relationship on Eisenhower cannot be measured quantitatively, but, in Eisenhower's own reflections and the unfolding of his career,
one cannot overestimate its significance in the reintegration of a person
shattered by grief.

As Eisenhower wrote later about Connor, "Life with General Connor
was a sort of graduate school in military affairs and the humanities,
leavened by a man who was experienced in his knowledge of men and
their conduct. I can never adequately express my gratitude to this one
gentleman. . . . In a lifetime of association with great and good men, he
is the one more or less invisible figure to whom I owe an incalculable
debt."[15]

Some time after his tour of duty with General Connor, Eisenhower's
breakthrough occurred. He received orders to attend the Command and
General Staff School at Fort Leavenworth, one of the most competitive
schools in the army. It was a coveted appointment, and Eisenhower took
advantage of the opportunity. Unlike his performance in high school and
West Point, his work at the Command School was excellent; he was grad-
uated first in his class.

Psychological biographies of gifted people repeatedly demonstrate the
important part a mentor plays in developing an individual. Andrew
Carnegie owed much to his senior, Thomas A. Scott. As head of the Western Division of the Pennsylvania Railroad, Scott recognized talent and the
desire to learn in the young telegrapher assigned to him. By giving Carnegie increasing responsibility and by providing him with the opportunity

---

[14] Dwight D. Eisenhower, *At Ease: Stories I Tell to Friends* (New York: Doubleday, 1967), p. 136.

[15] Ibid., p. 187.

to learn through close personal observation, Scott added to Carnegie's self-confidence and sense of achievement. Because of his own personal strength and achievement, Scott did not fear Carnegie's aggressiveness. Rather, he gave it full play in encouraging Carnegie's initiative.

Mentors take risks with people. They bet initially on talent they perceive in younger people. Mentors also risk emotional involvement in working closely with their juniors. The risks do not always pay off, but the willingness to take them appears crucial in developing leaders.

CAN ORGANIZATIONS DEVELOP LEADERS?

The examples I have given of how leaders develop suggest the importance of personal influence and the one-to-one relationship. For organizations to encourage consciously the development of leaders as compared with managers would mean developing one-to-one relationships between junior and senior executives and, more important, fostering a culture of individualism and possibly elitism. The elitism arises out of the desire to identify talent and other qualities suggestve of the ability to lead and not simply to manage.

The Jewel Companies Inc. enjoy a reputation for developing talented people. The chairman and chief executive officer, Donald S. Perkins, is perhaps a good example of a person brought along through the mentor approach. Franklin J. Lunding, who was Perkins's mentor, expressed the philosophy of taking risks with young people this way.

> Young people today want in on the action. They don't want to sit around
> for six months trimming lettuce.[16]

This statement runs counter to the culture that attaches primary importance to slow progression based on experience and proved competence. It is a high-risk philosophy, one that requires time for the attachment between senior and junior people to grow and be meaningful, and one that is bound to produce more failures than successes.

The elitism is an especially sensitive issue. At Jewel the MBA degree symbolized the elite. Lunding attracted Perkins to Jewel at a time when business school graduates had little interest in retailing in general, and food distribution in particular. Yet the elitism seemed to pay off: not only did Perkins become the president at age 37, but also under the leadership of young executives recruited into Jewel with the promise of opportunity for growth and advancement, Jewel managed to diversify into discount and drug chains and still remain strong in food retailing. By assigning each recruit to a vice president who acted as sponsor, Jewel evidently tried to build a structure around the mentor approach to developing leaders.

---

[16] "Jewel Lets Young Men Make Mistakes," *Business Week*, January 17, 1970, p. 90.

To counteract the elitism implied in such an approach, the company also introduced an "equalizer" in what Perkins described as "the first assistant philosophy." Perkins stated:

> Being a good first assistant means that each management person thinks of himself not as the order-giving, domineering boss, but as the first assistant to those who "report" to him in a more typical organizational sense. Thus we mentally turn our organizational charts upside-down and challenge ourselves to seek ways in which we can lead . . . by helping . . . by teaching . . . by listening . . . and by managing in the true democratic sense . . . that is, with the consent of the managed. Thus the satisfactions of leadership come from helping others to get things done and changed—and not from getting credit for doing and changing things ourselves.[17]

While this statement would seem to be more egalitarian than elitist, it does reinforce a youth-oriented culture since it defines the senior officer's job as primarily helping the junior person.

A myth about how people learn and develop that seems to have taken hold in the American culture also dominates thinking in business. The myth is that people learn best from their peers. Supposedly, the threat of evaluation and even humiliation recedes in peer relations because of the tendency for mutual identification and the social restraints on authoritarian behavior among equals. Peer training in organizations occurs in various forms. The use, for example, of task forces made up of peers from several interested occupational groups (sales, production, research, and finance) supposedly removes the restraints of authority on the individual's willingness to assert and exchange ideas. As a result, so the theory goes, people interact more freely, listen more objectively to criticism and other points of view and, finally, learn from this healthy interchange.

Another application of peer training exists in some large corporations, such as Philips, N.V. in Holland, where organization structure is built on the principle of joint responsibility of two peers, one representing the commercial end of the business and the other the technical. Formally, both hold equal responsibility for geographic operations or product groups, as the case may be. As a practical matter, it may turn out that one or the other of the peers dominates the management. Nevertheless, the main interaction is between two or more equals.

The principal question I would raise about such arrangements is whether they perpetuate the managerial orientation, and preclude the formation of one-to-one relationships between senior people and potential leaders.

Aware of the possible stifling effects of peer relationships on aggressiveness and individual initiative, another company, much smaller than Philips, utilizes joint responsibility of peers for operating units, with one important

---

[17] "What Makes Jewel Shine so Bright," *Progressive Grocer*, September, 1973, p. 76.

difference. The chief executive of this company encourages competition and rivalry among peers, ultimately appointing the one who comes out on top for increased responsibility. These hybrid arrangements produce some unintended consequences that can be disastrous. There is no easy way to limit rivalry. Instead, it permeates all levels of the operation and opens the way for the formation of cliques in an atmosphere of intrigue.

A large, integrated oil company has accepted the importance of developing leaders through the direct influence of senior on junior executives. One chairman and chief executive officer regularly selected one talented university graduate whom he appointed his special assistant, and with whom he would work closely for a year. At the end of the year, the junior executive would become available for assignment to one of the operating divisions, where he would be assigned to a responsible post rather than a training position. The mentor relationship had acquainted the junior executive firsthand with the use of power, and with the important antidotes to the power disease called *hubris*—performance and integrity.

Working in one-to-one relationships, where there is a formal and recognized difference in the power of the actors, takes a great deal of tolerance for emotional interchange. This interchange, inevitable in close working arrangements, probably accounts for the reluctance of many executives to become involved in such relationships. *Fortune* carried an interesting story on the departure of a key executive, John W. Hanley, from the top management of Procter & Gamble, for the chief executive officer position at Monsanto.[18] According to this account, the chief executive and chairman of P&G passed over Hanley for appointment to the presidency and named another executive vice president to this post instead.

The chairman evidently felt he could not work well with Hanley who, by his own acknowledgement, was aggressive, eager to experiment and change practices, and constantly challenged his superior. A chief executive officer naturally has the right to select people with whom he feels congenial. But I wonder whether a greater capacity on the part of senior officers to tolerate the competitive impulses and behavior of their subordinates might not be healthy for corporations. At least a greater tolerance for interchange would not favor the managerial team player at the expense of the individual who might become a leader.

I am constantly surprised at the frequency with which chief executives feel threatened by open challenges to their ideas, as though the source of their authority, rather than their specific ideas, were at issue. In one case a chief executive officer, who was troubled by the aggressiveness and sometimes outright rudeness of one of his talented vice presidents, used various indirect methods such as group meetings and hints from outside directors to avoid dealing with his subordinate. I advised the executive

---

[18] "Jack Hanley Got There by Selling Harder," *Fortune*, November 1976.

to deal head-on with what irritated him. I suggested that by direct, face-to-face confrontation, both he and his subordinate would learn to validate the distinction between the authority to be preserved and the issues to be debated.

To confront is also to tolerate aggressive interchange, and has the net effect of stripping away the veils of ambiguity and signaling so characteristic of managerial cultures, as well as encouraging the emotional relationship leaders need if they are to survive.

PART III

STRUCTURE AND ORGANIZATIONAL BEHAVIOR

THE structure of an organization consists of relatively fixed relationships among jobs and groups of jobs. The formal structure is created by managerial decisions which (1) *define* jobs, (2) *group* jobs into departments, (3) *determine* size of groups reporting to a single manager, and (4) *delegate* authority to the manager. The resultant structure of jobs and authority determines to a considerable degree the behaviors of people who perform the jobs.

The decisions which managers must make in designing the structure relate to each of the four steps. The job definition subdecision must determine the extent to which jobs are highly specialized or highly generalized; the departmentalization subdecision determines the extent to which departments are highly homogeneous or highly heterogeneous; the size of the group must define whether a small or large number of subordinates reports to a manager; and the delegation subdecision must determine the extent to which authority is centralized or decentralized. If the range of alternatives for each of the four subdecisions is viewed as a continuum, then one can visualize an infinite variety of alternative organization structures.

Several general theories of organization structure appear in the literature. Important in this regard are the concepts of bureaucracy and System 4 organization. The bureaucratic theory argues that effective organization structures tend to be at one extreme of the continua—specialized jobs, homogeneous departments, narrow spans of managerial control, and centralized authority. System 4 organization proposes the opposite case—organizations characterized by generalized jobs, heterogeneous departments, wide spans, and decentralized authority. Contemporary theory is now advancing a situational, or contingency, point of view. According to situational theory, the most effective organization structure must be related to the situational factors, such as environmental demands and technological parameters.

Yet even with some generalized theory to guide the organizational design decision, management must still deal with specific problems of specialization, departmentalization, span of control, and delegation. Each of the six articles in this part discusses one or more of these problems. Moreover we shall see that these problems have their counterparts in academic departments and hospitals as well as in business firms.

The lead article in this section is "Should the Quality of Work Life Be Legislated?" by Edward E. Lawler III. It is his contention that unless the government acts, work life will not improve within organizations. Lawler's article is presented in this part of the reader because it has implications for those in charge of structuring the organization and its jobs. Those at the top of the structure are asked by the author to come up with a public report on the quality of work life within the organization.

One of the most publicized applications of motivational procedures is job enrichment. Mitchell Fein in "The Myth of Job Enrichment" in an insightful and challenging dialogue criticizes the behaviorists' enthusiasm about job enrichment. Fein emphatically claims that behaviorists are not speaking accurately for workers.

"Organization-Environment: Concepts and Issues" by Raymond E. Miles, Charles C. Snow, and Jeffrey Pfeffer claims that there is a need to examine the literature on environmental impact of organizations. They discuss organizational boundaries, dimensions of environment, technology, and managerial perceptions.

Charles G. Burck in "How G.M. Turned Itself Around" talks about the remodeled management at G.M. The story of G.M.'s reactions to marketplace changes in terms of structural rearrangements is presented. There is a historical tracing of recent changes in the organization which presents an interesting picture of how reorganization which involves project centers occurred.

"Problems of Matrix Organizations" by Stanley M. Davis and Paul R. Lawrence presents the advantages and some problems of the matrix form. The problems of matrix organizations such as power struggles and economic pressures are presented. The prevention and treatment for various ills of the matrix form are clearly presented.

Jay R. Galbraith in "Organization Design: An Information Processing View" presents a model. Organization design strategies are introduced and discussed. The author attempts to show why an organization must adopt one of the four strategies he discusses when faced with greater uncertainty.

14

Should the Quality of Work Life Be Legislated?*

EDWARD E. LAWLER III

WHY would we want the government to legislate a better quality of work life? I believe that unless the government acts, work life will not improve for many people. In many situations there is presently no clear motivation for organizations to provide employees with opportunities for personal growth and development, to see that employee needs are satisfied or to eliminate those working conditions that contribute to mental illness, alcoholism and drug abuse.

Little evidence exists to show that simply improving the quality of work will increase the profitability and economic soundness of most organizations. Given this situation, it is hardly surprising that many organizations are hesitant to undertake significant efforts to improve the quality of work life of their employees. Managers are held responsible for profitability; they cannot be expected to take actions which will endanger the economic soundness of their organization even though they might increase employee satisfaction. In my opinion, the only way this can be changed is by legislative action or by producing evidence that quality of work life improvement is good business from an economic point of view.

There are some situations in which improving the quality of work life may not, in fact, increase an organization's costs so as to put it at a competitive disadvantage. The research on job design, for example, suggests that job enrichment can, in some cases, reduce costs by bringing about higher quality products and lower turnover, while at the same time improving the quality of work life. In these situations there is economic pressure present toward improving the psychological quality of work life be-

* From the *Personnel Administrator,* January 1976, pp. 17–21. Copyright 1976. Reprinted with permission.

cause it promises higher profit. These situations will probably correct themselves without government intervention, although the government could speed change by financing experimentation and information dissemination programs.

On the other hand, where the psychological quality of work life needs to be changed and increased costs are involved, the government may have to intervene to alter the economics of the situation, thus providing a strong motivation for change on the part of the organization in question. Despite the work that has gone into job enrichment, it is not clear how to enrich some assembly line jobs without increasing production costs. It is clear however, that in many of these situations enrichment would increase the quality of many people's lives. To change the situation so that organizations can act to improve these conditions without finding themselves at a competitive disadvantage, two types of government intervention are possible.

First, the government could charge organizations for the negative social outcomes they produce. For example, if because of a poor quality of work life a company had an unusually high rate of turnover, alcoholism, drug addiction and mental illness among its employees, the government could increase its taxes proportionately. This is not dissimilar to present government practice in the area of unemployment insurance.

The second approach is to fine organizations not for the outcomes they produce (e.g., accidents, sick people) but for the practices in which they engage. In applying this approach to the area of the quality of work life, organizations could be fined or taxed on the basis of their management practices and policies and the nature of the jobs they have. For example, they might be taxed if they produce goods on an assembly line that had highly repetitive jobs. Such action could obviously serve to eliminate the economic advantages of producing goods on an assembly line.

It may seem far-fetched to envision the government taxing or fining an organization because it has a destructive human system that provides a poor quality of work life, but there are evidence and precedents available to suggest that these actions can and should happen. In the area of physical safety, for instance, there has been a long history of legislation regulating those organization practices and working conditions that can affect a person's physical health. Hours of work and equipment design are specified in considerable detail. Perhaps even more pertinent to problems of the psychological quality of work life, however, is the recent enactment of state and federal legislation controlling pollution.

A POSSIBLE PRECEDENT

Organizations that pollute the air, water and soil are now subject to fines and, in some cases, shutdown. Since it costs industry more to manufacture many products in ways that will not pollute, any organization that tries to produce a product without polluting is at a competitive disadvantage in the market because pollution control equipment is expensive and adds to the company's costs. In a real sense, when goods are produced in a way that pollutes, their actual price tends to be too low because their full production costs are not charged to the customer. They are borne by society as a whole because it is the society which bears the cost of pollution (e.g., rivers to clean up, air that increases illness, etc.).

Using this logic, legislation that fines organizations for causing pollution is very much justified; it simply involves charging organizations in the name of the public for the cost of the pollution they are causing. It is also fair if this raises the price to the customer; he or she thus bears the full cost of the product rather than sharing it with people who do not buy and benefit from the item in question.

A parallel exists between the economics of pollution and the economics of providing a poor quality of work life for employees. Providing employees with dissatisfying, meaningless work lives is a form of pollution, the cost of which is borne by the society and the individual harmed rather than by the organizations responsible. This type of pollution leads to increased costs in such areas as mental illness, alcoholism, shorter life expectancy and less involvement in the community. These are expensive outcomes and ones that are paid for by the government and private funds that support unemployment insurance, welfare payments, hospitals, mental health centers and civic programs. Because these costs are absorbed by society, some goods are underpriced relative to their real costs; and just as with environmental pollution, a case can be made for government intervention designed to correct this situation.

All this talk about government action is very heady stuff and is indeed the kind of issue the people concerned with personnel should be debating. But before we go too far off into the stratosphere, we need to look at how well we can measure the quality of work life. Measures of it or the consequences of it are necessary if any of the legislative approaches mentioned so far are to work.

POSSIBLE MEASUREMENT APPROACHES

The behavioral science research that has been done on how people react to their work environments suggests the model shown in Figure 1. It shows that people's affective and attitudinal reactions to jobs are caused by a combination of the characteristics the person brings to the job and the characteristics of the job situation. These affective reactions in turn cause certain observable behavioral reactions which lead to organizational performance. This approach suggests three different kinds of measures: job and organizational conditions, affective reactions and employee behavior. The problem is to determine which can and should be measured.

Figure 1

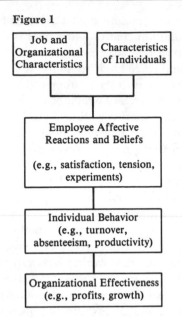

There are three characteristics desirable for any measure. First, the measure should be valid, in that it measures accurately all the important aspects of what needs to be measured. Secondly, it should have enough face validity so that it will be seen by all involved as a legitimate measure. Finally, it should be objective. This last point is important because objective measures are verifiable, can be audited by others and are therefore less subject to distortion.

The importance of these characteristics (and especially of the last) varies according to the purpose for which the information is to be used. It is always desirable to have objective measures, but in some instances it is less crucial. For example, it is often desirable to use self-report measures of the quality of work life and these are subjective. Despite their subjectivity, they do represent the most direct data available about the psychological state of an employee. Further, they allow us to account for individual differences better than do any of the other measures. The problem with measures of the working conditions to which individuals are exposed is that they cannot take into account individual differences in the way people respond to those conditions. This is not a serious problem when the issue is psychological.

Being exposed to extreme temperatures and noises of greater than 90 decibels is harmful to almost everyone; therefore, it makes sense to measure noise and temperature and to prohibit certain levels. It is not true, however, that repetitive assembly line jobs or authoritarian supervision are necessarily regarded as negative by all workers. Quite to the contrary, some see these factors as part of a high quality of work life. Others see them as very negative and as part of a low quality of work life.

Although self-reports of satisfaction do take into account individual differences, they are limited in their usefulness. They are satisfactory solutions only in those situations where there is little motivation present for the individual to report false data. In some instances the use for which the data are being gathered creates motivation for distortion as it probably would if government regulations were involved. In these cases, self-report measures would seem to be an unsatisfactory solution unless nonfakable measures are used and, at the moment, no such measures exist.

There have been some pioneering attempts in Europe to objectively define the conditions that are associated with the high quality of work life, but it is not clear that these efforts have been successful. One union in Germany, for example, has negotiated a contract that specifies the minimum repetitive cycle times for jobs. The assumption is that cycle time is a measure of job challenge and that by requiring "long" cycle times, jobs will be made more satisfying. Cycle times have the advantage of being objectively measureable, but it is not clear that they are the best thing to focus on in order to assure that workers have satisfying jobs.

The governments of several countries have tried to increase the quality of work by requiring that organizations have workers on their boards of directors (e.g., West Germany) and that they have profit sharing or joint ownership plans (e.g., Peru). Requiring administrative practices such as these makes some sense in that their presence or absence can be objectively measured. However, it remains to be established that these or similar practices will contribute to the quality of work life of most employees. Thus, as far as organizational conditions are concerned, we find ourselves in the position of being able to measure things that we are not sure contribute to a high quality of work life and not being able to specify or measure adequately what organizational conditions contribute to a high quality of work life.

One alternative to using the self-report and working condition measures mentioned earlier is to focus on the behavioral outcomes produced by working in an organization. Indicators such as turnover rates, absenteeism rates, mental illness rates, alcoholism rates and community service rates can be measured and costed in terms of their economic impact on the community. This approach has the advantage of focusing on more "objective" outcomes. However, before the costing aspects can be operationalized, more work will have to be done to determine the actual value of these outcomes and the degree to which they can be linked to the work situation. This approach also has the disadvantage that it identifies bad conditions only after they have done their damage. Work situations that do not fit individuals produce dissatisfaction and a psychologically poor work environment. These, in turn, seem to produce social costs such as mental illness and alcoholism. Where possible, it is important to identify poor work environments before they produce serious negative outcomes.

PUBLIC REPORTING

It seems quite clear that none of the measures we have considered are sufficiently well developed to use as a basis for fining or regulating organizations. Does this mean there is nothing the government can do to improve the quality of work at this time? I don't think so. There are some things (in addition to sponsoring research) that the government can do. It can, as it has done with pollution, require organizations to prepare quality of work life statements when they build new plants and facilities. If nothing else, this would force organizations to think about how their way of designing and administering a plant is going to affect their employees' lives. Presently this is often considered only after an organization begins to have personnel problems (e.g., turnover, absenteeism and strikes).

At the moment, companies are not required to inform stockholders about either the kind of life they provide for their employees or the kind of employee-organization relationship that exists. A case can be made for requiring organizations to furnish this kind of data. The quality of life a company affords can influence its financial success (turnover, absenteeism, etc., are expensive); thus it would seem that investors should have the right to know what it is, so that they can make intelligent decisions. This is the logic that underlies the government requirement that organizations report on their economic conditions. But perhaps the most important effect of collecting and reporting these data would be to focus the attention of managers on the way the human resources in the organization are being managed. It has often been shown that managers attend to those things which are being measured. It should also help acquaint potential employees with the kind of work situation the organization offers; there is evidence that this kind of information can help people make better job choices. Disclosure of quality of work life data could result in bringing public and stockholder pressure to bear on those organizations that engage in deleterious practices; we might even see consumers boycotting those organizations that provide a poor quality of work life. Stockholders have recently demanded information from companies as to whether they discriminate against blacks and as to whether they pollute. It follows that before too long they may ask for information about the kind of life "their" company provides for its employees. They may even demand practices that will reduce profits in order to increase the quality of the life of the people who work in the company. This has already happened to a limited extent in some companies. For example, stockholders have demanded that American companies pay equal wages to blacks in South Africa, even though such payment is not required by law and could put the company at a financial disadvantage.

What kind of quality of life data should stockholders receive? Some have suggested that Human Resource Accounting (HRA) data should be provided and this might prove to be useful. (The R. G. Barry Corporation has been doing this for several years.) However, such data indicate only the worth of each individual employee and ignore the value of the total human organization.

As a first step, organizations could provide their stockholders with data on turnover, absenteeism, tardiness, accident and grievance rates, as well as information on the rates of job-related physical and mental illness. Even though these measures may not be the kind that we would be willing to base fines and penalties on, they are sufficiently meaningful so that their release can be justified. Many of these measures can be costed so their financial impact could also be reported. They might be combined in a single "Quality of Life Index" that would provide some indication of what the consequences were of working for a particular company. If comparable data were collected from a number of companies, these could be reported in terms of the percentile standing of each company.

The difficult question to answer concerning any report to stockholders is whether it should include self-report data. This is information that investors should find very helpful since they are investing in the future of the company. However, if the employees are stockholders, they might be motivated to give invalid data. Since attitude data have never been gathered for distribution to stockholders, it is difficult to know how serious this problem would be. It is an area where some experimentation might be profitable.

The possibility of reporting to stockholders on the condition of the human aspects of organizations raises the question of who should prepare these reports. Just as with financial statements, it is not a job to be trusted to management; there simply would be too much pressure on them to give invalid data, since the reputation and value of the company are at stake. This suggests that people trained in behavioral science would be needed to audit the human system, just as accountants audit the financial system. They would have certain standard tests and procedures to use and they could eventually engage in direct observation of the management, leadership and decision-making practices that take place. As in financial accounting, they would have to develop over time a standardized set of procedures and measures so that comparable data could be obtained from different firms. Presumably they, like accountants, would have the power to certify statements. Admittedly, considerable work needs to be done before it will be practical to begin doing certified human system audits, but that time will come sooner if the government requires this kind of reporting. At present there is little incentive for organizations to develop these measures. Like accounting measures, they can only be developed by a trial and error method that allows for refinements and the development of new principles.

It appears that some sort of government action is required to improve quality of work of many individuals. However, legislative action involving standards or fines does not seem appropriate because the needed measures do not exist. There is something the government can do. It is possible for the government to focus attention on the quality of work life in organizations by legislating that organizations publicly report on the quality of work they provide. This should result in efforts to develop better measures and to improve the quality of work life. The precedents for this action exist already in the financial reporting requirements. Considerable work needs to be done on measurement development but now is the time to begin and government action is the stimulus that is needed.

The Myth of Job Enrichment*

MITCHELL FEIN

P RACTICALLY all writing that deals with worker boredom and frustration starts with the idea that the nature of work in industry and offices degrades the human spirit, is antithetical to workers' needs and damages their mental health, and that the redesign of work is socially desirable and beneficial to workers. Curiously, however, this view is not supported by workers or their unions. If workers faced the dire consequences of deprivation projected by the behaviorists, they should be conscious of the need to redesign and enrich their jobs. (The term "behaviorist" is used in this article to include psychologists, social scientists, and others who favor the redesign of work and job enrichment as a way to enhance the quality of working life. Many behaviorists, in fact, may not hold these views. Still, there is a sharp difference of opinion between what workers say they want and what behaviorists say workers want.)

WHO SPEAKS FOR WORKERS?

Workers' feelings about their work and what goes on at the workplace are expressed quite freely by workers themselves and their spokesmen in the unions. Since no union has yet raised the issue of work boredom and the redesign of jobs, is it not reasonable to assume that the question is not important to workers? Workers are not bashful in their demands, and worker representatives are quite vocal in championing workers' needs. One might argue that workers do not comprehend the harm that is done to them by their work and that they must be shown that many of their problems and troubles really stem from the nature of their jobs. But that assumes that workers are naive or stupid, which is not the case.

---

* This article first appeared in *The Humanist*, September–October 1973, pp. 71–77, and is reprinted by permission.

The judgments of those advocating job changes derive from people whom Abraham Maslow would characterize as "superior people (called self-actualizers) who are also superior perceivers, not only of facts but of values, . . . their ultimate values [are then used] as possibly the ultimate values for the whole species."[1] These advocates of change maintain that healthy progress for people is toward self-fulfillment through work, and they see most jobs as dull, repetitive, seemingly meaningless tasks, offering little challenge or autonomy. They view the nature of work as the main deterrent to more fulfilling lives for the workers and the redesign of jobs as the keystone of their plans for accomplishing the desired changes.

Paul Kurtz has stated: "Humanists today attack all those social forces which seek to destroy man: they deplore the dehumanization and alienation of man within the industrial and technological society. . . . and the failure of modern man to achieve the full measure of his potential excellence. The problem for the humanist is to create the conditions that would emancipate man from oppressive and corruptive social organization, and from the denigration and perversion of his human talents. . . ."[2] Humanists' goals and behaviorists' objectives appear similar. Both accept Maslow's self-actualization concepts as the preferred route to fulfillment. But by what divine right does one group assume that its values are superior to others and should be accepted as normal? Both the selection of goals and attitudes toward work are uniquely personal. The judges of human values have no moral right to press their normative concepts on others as preferable.

SATISFACTION AND ACHIEVEMENT

The fundamental question is whether or not the nature of work prevents people from achieving the full measure of their potential. When behaviorists view people at work, they see two main groups: those who are satisfied and those who are not. They examine the satisfied and like what they see. These are eager, energetic people, who are generally enthusiastic about their jobs and life in general. The behaviorists hold them up as ideal and prepare to convert the dissatisfied.

In contrasting the satisfied workers with the dissatisfied ones, behaviorists see the nature of the work performed as the main difference. So they propose to change the work of the dissatisfied to more closely resemble that performed by the satisfied. But there is a large "if" in this approach: What if the nature of the work is not the reason for the satisfaction?

---

[1] Abraham Maslow, *The Farther Reaches of Human Nature* (New York: Viking, 1971), p. 10.

[2] Paul Kurtz, "What Is Humanism?" in *Moral Problems in Contemporary Society: Essays in Humanistic Ethics*, ed. P. Kurtz (Buffalo: Prometheus Books, 1973), p. 11.

It could very well be that the satisfied have more drive, which creates greater material wants and higher goals, which in turn motivates them to make more-effective efforts in the workplace and to bid for more highly skilled jobs, and so on. Restructuring the work and creating new opportunities may make some people enthusiastic, but to what extent is the nature of the work the determinant of a person's drive?

There are no data that definitively show that restructuring and enriching jobs will increase the will to work or give workers greater satisfaction. Similarly, I have not seen any research data that show that a person with drive is deterred from reaching his potential by the nature of the work.

I believe that ethical considerations alone should keep behaviorists from setting up their values as the ideals for society. In addition, I will attempt to demonstrate that the behaviorists' views on redesigning jobs are misguided; they do not understand the work process in plants, and they misjudge workers' attitudes toward their jobs.

WORKERS' ATTITUDES TOWARD THEIR WORK

A 1972 Gallup Poll found that 80 to 90 percent of American workers are satisfied with their jobs. A 1973 poll by Thomas C. Sorenson found that from 82 to 91 percent of blue- and white-collar workers like their work. He asked, "If there were one thing you could change about your job, what would it be?" He found that "Astonishingly, very few mentioned making their jobs 'less boring' or 'more interesting.'"[3]

Behaviorists and humanists find it difficult to understand how workers can possibly say they like their work when it appears so barren to intellectuals. This view was recently expressed by the behavioral scientist David Sirota, after making a study in a garment plant. He was surprised to find that most sewing-machine operators found their work interesting. Since the work appeared highly repetitive to him, he had expected that they would say they were bored and that their talents were not fully utilized. These workers' views are supported in a study by Emanuel Weintraub of 2,535 female sewing-machine operators in seventeen plants from Massachusetts to Texas. He found that "most of the operators like the nature of their work."[4] What the behaviorists find so difficult to comprehend is really quite simply explained: Workers have similar attitudes toward their work because *they are not a cross-section of the population, but rather a select group.*

---

[3] Thomas C. Sorenson, "Do Americans Like Their Jobs?" *Parade,* June 3, 1973.

[4] Emanuel Weintraub, "Has Job Enrichment Been Oversold?" an address to the 25th annual convention of the American Institute of Industrial Engineers, May 1973, *Technical Papers,* p. 349.

There is greater choice in the selection of jobs by workers than is supposed. The selection process in factories and offices goes on without conscious direction by either workers or management. The data for white- and blue-collar jobs show that there is tremendous turnover in the initial employment period but that the turnover drops sharply with time on the job. What occurs is that a worker comes onto a new job, tries it out for several days or weeks, and decides whether or not the work suits his needs and desires. Impressions about a job are a composite of many factors: pay, proximity to home, nature of work, working conditions, attitude of supervision, congeniality of fellow workers, past employment history of the company, job security, physical demands, possibilities for advancement, and many others. Working conditions may be bad, but if the pay and job security are high, the job may be tolerable. To a married woman, the pay may be low, but if the job is close to home and working conditions are good, it may be desirable. There are numerous combinations of factors that influence a worker's disposition to stay on the job or not.

There is a dual screening process that sifts out many of those who will be dissatisfied with the work. The process operates as follows: The worker in the first instance decides whether or not to stay on the job; management then has the opportunity to determine whether or not to keep him beyond the trial period. The combination of the worker's choice to remain and management's decision regarding the worker's acceptability screens out many workers who might find the job unsatisfying.

Some workers find highly repetitive work in factories intolerable, so they become truck drivers, where they can be out on the road with no supervisor on their back all day. Others prefer to work in gas stations, warehouses, retail stores, and other such places. Increasingly workers are taking white-collar jobs that in many ways are similar to repetitive factory jobs but which have cleaner physical surroundings and better working conditions. In times of high unemployment, workers stay in safe jobs for continuity of income; but, as the job market improves, the rate of turnover increases and selection of jobs resumes.

There would undoubtedly be much greater dissatisfaction among workers if they were not free to make changes and selections in the work they do. Some prefer to remain in high repetitive, low-skilled work even when they have an opportunity to advance to more-highly skilled jobs through job bidding. A minority of workers strive to move into the more skilled jobs, such as machinists, maintenance mechanics, setup men, group leaders, and utility men, where work is discretionary and the workers have considerable autonomy in the tasks they perform.

The continued evaluation of workers by management and the mobility available to workers in the job market refine the selection process. A year or two after entering a plant, most workers are on jobs or job progressions that suit them or which they find tolerable.

However, the work force in the plant is not homogeneous. There are two main groups, the achievers and the nonachievers. Their attitudes toward work and their goals are vastly different. A minority of the work force, which I find to be 15 percent, have a drive for achievement and identify with their work. These workers' attitudes match the ideal projected by behaviorists. They dislike repetitive work and escape from it by moving into more-skilled jobs, which have the autonomy and interest they look for in their work. Only a minority of jobs in industry and offices are in the skilled category, and fortunately only a minority of workers aspire to these jobs. About 85 percent of workers do not identify with their work, do not prefer more complicated and restructured jobs, and simply work in order to eat. Yet they, too, like their work and find it interesting.[5]

For different reasons, both groups of workers find their work interesting and satisfying. The work of the 85 percent who are nonachievers is interesting to them though boring to the other 15 percent. And the 15 percent who are achievers find their work interesting, though it is not sufficiently appealing for the majority to covet it. The selection process does amazingly well in matching workers and jobs.

What blinds behaviorists to this process is their belief that the achievement drive is an intrinsic part of human nature, that fulfillment at work is essential to sound mental health, and that, given the opportunity, workers would choose to become more involved in their work and take on larger and more-complicated tasks. Once behaviorists take this view, they cannot understand what really happens on the plant floor or why workers do one thing rather than another.

WHY DO BEHAVIORISTS CLAIM TO SPEAK FOR WORKERS?

Behaviorists' insistence that they know more about what workers want than workers themselves is largely based on a number of job-enrichment case histories and studies of workers over the past decade. It is claimed that these studies show that workers really want job enrichment and benefit from it. But when these studies are examined closely, four things are found. (1) What actually occurred was quite different from what was reported by the behaviorists. (2) Most of the studies were conducted with hand-picked employees, usually working in areas or plants isolated from the main operation, and they do not reflect a cross-section of the working population. Practically all are in nonunion plants. (3) Only a handful of job-enrichment cases have been reported in the past ten years, despite

---

[5] A more complete discussion and supporting data for the 15/85 worker composition is contained in M. Fein's "Motivation for Work," in *Handbook of Work Organization and Society*, ed. Robert Dubin (Skokie, Ill.: Rand-McNally, 1973).

the behaviorists' claims of gains for employees and management obtained through job changes. (4) In all instances, the experiments were initiated by management, never by workers or unions.

The *Survey of Working Conditions,* conducted for the United States Department of Labor by the Survey Research Center of the University of Michigan, contained serious errors.[6] The General Foods-Topeka case reported by Richard E. Walton [7] omits important information that shows that the sixty-three workers for this plant were handpicked from seven hundred applicants. Texas Instruments, which conducted the longest and broadest experiments, only attracted 10 percent of its employees to the program.[8] The Texas Instruments cleaning-employees case, as well as others, was grossly misreported in HEW's *Work in America.*

There are no job-enrichment successes that bear out the predictions of the behaviorists, because the vast majority of workers reject the concept. A small proportion of workers who desire job changes are prevented from participating by the social climate in the plant. They find involvement by moving into skilled jobs. Perhaps behaviorists do not recognize the moral issues raised by their proposals to redesign work—for example: intrusion upon a person's right to personal decisions; exploitation of workers' job satisfaction for company gains; distortion of the truth.

The boundless wisdom of this country's founders in separating religion from government and public practices has been revealed in countless ways. But along comes a new faith that proclaims that people should derive satisfaction from their work. When up to 90 percent of workers are reported to be satisfied with their work, the behaviorists say that workers do not really know what satisfaction is and that they will lead them to a superior kind. This sounds oddly like the proselytizing of a missionary. If behaviorists called for making enriched work available for those who want it, I would support them because I believe a minority of workers do want it. But I oppose foisting these practices on workers who do not call for it. In any case, I believe the minority has all the enrichment they want.

Exploiting workers' job satisfaction for management's gain can backfire dangerously. Workers expect management to develop new approaches and production processes to increase productivity; they are prepared for continuous pressure for more output. But when these changes are designed primarily to create a more receptive worker attitude toward greater productivity, they may see that they have been "had." If management's gains

---

[6] *Survey of Working Conditions* (Washington, D.C.: U.S. Dept. of Labor, 1971). These errors were disclosed in my analysis in "The Real Needs and Goals of Blue Collar Workers," *The Conference Board Record,* February 1973.

[7] Richard E. Walton, "How to Counter Alienation in the Plant," *Harvard Business Review,* November–December 1972, pp. 70–81.

[8] Fein, "Motivation for Work."

are real, while workers' benefits are only in their minds, who has really benefited? The behaviorists now say that workers should also share in productivity gains. But these statements have come late and are couched in such vague terms as to be meaningless.

When a supposedly good thing must be put into fancy wrappings to enhance it, something is amiss. Why must the job-enrichment cases be distorted to make the final results appealing? Why must behaviorists use phrases such as "work humanization" to describe their proposals, as though work were now inhuman? Workers understand the meaning of money, job security, health benefits, and retirement without fancy explanations. If the enrichment and redesign of work is such a good thing, why is it rejected by those who would benefit from it? The so-called new industrial democracy is not really democracy but a new autocracy of "we know better than you what's good for you."

Organization-Environment: Concepts and Issues*

RAYMOND E. MILES, CHARLES C. SNOW, and JEFFREY PFEFFER

To what extent are organizations shaped by their environments, that is, by the network of individuals, groups, agencies, and organizations with whom they interact? Are there organizational characteristics—strategies, technologies, structures, processes—which are appropriate for one environment but which may lead to failure in another? More pointedly, are there linkages across these characteristics which determine organizational success—are there, for example, particular structures and processes which fit certain technologies or strategies but not others?

Over the past two decades, an increasing number of studies have been aimed at these and related questions. At best, however, these efforts have been only modestly successful—the clear stream of association discovered in one study is frequently muddied in the next.

In part, this confusion concerning what is and is not known about organizational responses to environmental demands and the linkages among technology, structure, and process can be attributed to the usual set of definitional and measurement problems which plague research in all areas of organizational behavior and which are exacerbated here by the extreme complexity of the variables being examined. However, we believe that a more basic problem exists: the theory-map which should help us locate where organization-environment research is and the direction it should take is incomplete and in many areas obscure.

The purpose of this article is to take stock of the organization-environ-

* Raymond E. Miles, Charles C. Snow, and Jeffrey Pfeffer, "Organization-Environment: Concepts and Issues," *Industrial Relations,* October 1974, pp. 244–66. Reprinted by permission.

ment literature to this point and to make some preliminary suggestions concerning future research on this topic. We will first briefly outline the route which research in this area appears to have taken to this point. Next we will describe the general requirements for a useful map or model of organization-environment relations by which we can measure progress and plan future research. Then, using this model as a conceptual framework, we will attempt to organize some of the salient contributions to theory and research in this area and, more importantly, to examine the points at which current theory and research fall short of the requirements of the complete model. Finally, these deficiencies will be used to plot out a tentative course for future theory building, data collection, and analysis.

AN OVERVIEW OF
ORGANIZATION-ENVIRONMENT RESEARCH

For the first half of this century, management and organization theorists tended to ignore the environment, or at least to hold it constant, as they sought universalistic principles of structure, planning, control, and the like. Weber, while aware of some of the dysfunctions of bureaucratic structures and processes, implied that these structures were appropriate for all organizational settings.[1] Similarly, Taylor viewed his principles of scientific management as universally applicable and treated environmental demands and organizational objectives as fixed in his search for the "one best way."[2] And, later developers of administrative principles gave little attention to environmental differences as they attempted to integrate experiences from the church, the military, and business into a common set of practical prescriptions.

Economists, of course, were concerned with organizational adjustments to the environment, but by and large these were treated simply as formal exercises in profit-maximizing logic. In their models, market forces set the prices for goods and services, and the entire organization was characterized as a production function whose blend of capital and labor was dictated by the quest for cost minimization. Entrepreneurial and marketing decisions were viewed as important, but little effort was made to specify the impact of these decisions on organizational structure and processes.[3]

Attacks on universalistic organization and management principles be-

---

[1] Max Weber, *The Theory of Social and Economic Organization,* trans. by A. M. Henderson and Talcott Parsons (New York: Free Press, 1947), p. 34.

[2] Frederick W. Taylor, *The Principles of Scientific Management* (New York: Harper & Brothers, 1911).

[3] For a criticism of the economic theory of the firm from a behavioral standpoint, see Richard Cyert and James G. March, *A Behavioral Theory of the Firm* (Englewood Cliffs, N.J.: Prentice-Hall, 1963).

gan in the thirties and forties and heated up in the fifties. The initial criticism concerned the alleged inability of bureaucracies to adapt to the needs of individuals and changes in the government. Gouldner provided case study evidence suggesting that bureaucratization could be efficacious in one setting (an office) but damaging in another (a mine).[4] Burns and Stalker extended this notion of contingent organizational responses by noting that successful firms in a stable environment tended to have "mechanistic" or highly bureaucratized structures and processes while successful firms in changing and uncertain environments tended to have "organic" or flexible structures and processes.[5] The impact of Burns and Stalker's work was augmented by the growing acceptance of the "systems" view of organizations which portrayed them as socio-technical mechanisms drawing resources from the environment at one end and exporting goods and services into the environment at the other.

Through the late fifties and the sixties, a series of increasingly elaborate models portraying the linkages among environment, technology, structure, and process were developed. Most of these, however, dealt with only a limited aspect of the full adjustment sequence (e.g., tying particular technologies to specific products or markets or relating types of production processes to organization structure and staffing), and most were content to describe the expected relationships without specifying how they were achieved—that is, the role of managerial choice in the adjustment process was seldom treated. Finally, most of these descriptive models failed to deal with the adjustment process over time, and, therefore, we have little understanding of how today's managerial decisions affect the ability of the organization to adjust to changing environmental demands in the future.

The deficiencies noted in this overview are, we feel, largely the result of misdirection. As suggested earlier, a clearer model of the crucial elements of the organization-environment relationship is needed. In the following section, we outline the dimensions of an improved "map."

A "DECISION-POINTS" MAP

In our view, the study of organizational adaptation to environmental demands should be focused on a series of intertwined "decision points";

1. The decisions by which the organization selects a portion of the total environment as its particular arena of activity (i.e., its *domain*) and chooses a basic strategy for managing the domain;

---

[4] Alvin W. Gouldner, *Patterns of Industrial Bureaucracy* (New York: Free Press, 1954).

[5] Tom Burns and G. M. Stalker, *The Management of Innovation* (London: Tavistock, 1961).

2. The decisions by which the organization establishes an appropriate *technology* for implementing its basic operating strategy;
3. The decisions by which the organization creates a *structure* of roles and relationships to control and coordinate technology and strategy; and
4. The decisions made to assure organizational *continuity*—the capacity to survive, adjust, and grow.

Focused specifically on these decision points, research should highlight those aspects of organization-environment relations which are "determined" or "fixed" either by the environment or by preceding decisions and those which allow for the exercise of managerial judgment. The examination of the demands and constraints which alternative choices at each decision point place on those which follow should provide evidence concerning the "feasible set" of choices available and the costs and benefits among these alternatives. Research directed to these decision points would both highlight the role of managerial judgment in the organization-environment adjustment process and provide guidance to managers faced with crucial choices in these areas.

Obviously by specifying these decision points we do not intend to imply that a particular individual or group in the organization makes *a* definitive decision or consciously chooses *a* specific course of action in each of the four areas listed here. Instead, we are saying that these broad categories provide a convenient way of grouping together numerous decisions and actions which, in the aggregate, define the organization's relationship to its environment.

In the following sections, we will examine some of the more important contributions to the existing organization-environment literature, structuring our selective review around the decision-point framework described above and noting the extent to which its requirements have been met by previous research.

THE ORGANIZATION AND ENVIRONMENT LITERATURE

Before we review the literature on organization and environment, following the decision-points map outlined above, it may be helpful to first consider the concept of environment itself—is there such a thing, and, if so, how has it been and how can it be described?

Organizational Boundaries

It is usually taken for granted that there is some boundary separating the organization from its environment, environment potentially being everything which is outside of the organization. Starbuck has compared the problem of finding the organization's boundary to that of finding the boundary of a cloud.[6] In defining a cloud, we can measure the density of its moisture and, by selecting some specific level of density, determine what properly "belongs" to the cloud and what "belongs" to its environment. But what organizations, as opposed to clouds, the boundary problem is more difficult. If, for example, we wish to measure the density of member interaction and involvement, we must specify the decisions or issues which concern us. Clearly, interaction patterns and degree of involvement of various individuals and groups, e.g., stockholders, unions, suppliers, etc., vary depending upon whether our concern is with long-range planning, wage and salary issues, or the imminent bankruptcy of the firm. Thus, while the density of interaction and involvement can be measured, it changes over time and across decision areas, thereby changing the determination of what is "in" the organization and what is "in" the environment.

Because organizations are open social systems, they are constantly changing, and their boundaries fluctuate accordingly. At a minimum—indeed perhaps it is the best that can be hoped for—the definition of the organization's boundary should be consistent with the problem under investigation.

Dimensions of Environment

Assuming that we can distinguish between the organization and its environment, how can the environment be described in a way that is analytically useful? Emery and Trist developed a typology of environments based on the degree of interconnectedness and the extent of change in the environment.[7] Other authors (e.g., Dill, Burns and Stalker, Thompson, Lawrence and Lorsch, Duncan, Osborn and Hunt) have also focused on change as an important environmental dimension, the general argument being that bureaucratic structures inhibit the organization's ability to perceive and adjust to rapid environmental change.[8]

---

[6] William H. Starbuck, "Organizations and Their Environments," in Marvin D. Dunnette, ed., *Handbook of Industrial and Organizational Psychology* (Chicago: Rand McNally, 1975).

[7] Fred E. Emery and Eric L. Trist, "The Causal Texture of Organizational Environments," *Human Relations*, vol. 18 (February 1965), pp. 21–32. The four types of environments are placid-randomized, placid-clustered, disturbed-reactive, and the turbulent field. These are arranged in ascending order of change and uncertainty, and Emery and Trist argue that each type of environment requires a different form of organization structure.

[8] William R. Dill, "Environment as an Influence on Managerial Autonomy," *Administrative Science Quarterly*, vol. 2 (March 1958), pp. 404–43; Burns and Stalker, op. cit.; James D. Thompson, *Organizations in Action* (New York: McGraw-Hill,

Some authors, however, have not distinguished between rate of environmental change and degree of uncertainty (unpredictable change) and have, therefore, implicitly equated the two. It is possible to have rapid but largely predictable change in the environment, and, in such a situation, the organization does not really confront uncertainty, as it knows reasonably well what environmental conditions it will face in the future. A related problem involves treating the environment and the organization as global entities, as if somehow a monolithic environment produces uniform responses across the entire organization. However, it is quite plausible to think of a flexible technology with stable customer demands, changing credit and money market conditions with a stable technology, relatively constant patterns of external dependence with a flexible organization structure, etc. The failure to distinguish between change and uncertainty, and the failure to specifically address less global aspects of the environment and organization, have confounded attempts to link environmental dimensions to organizational characteristics.

Finally, theorists (particularly Thompson, Perrow, and Duncan) have stressed the heterogeneity of the environment.[9] Here it is argued that complex, differentiated environments are likely to require different organizational structures than do environments which are simple and homogeneous. Once again, however, some confusion develops. Thompson treats the dimensions of heterogeneity and change as independent, while Duncan views both as components of environmental uncertainty.[10]

The Enacted Environment

Regardless of the analytical dimensions used to describe the environment, there remains the issue of how the environment becomes known to the organization (i.e., its managers). Weick has argued that the important organizational environments are those which are *enacted* or created

---

1967); Paul R. Lawrence and Jay W. Lorsch, *Organization and Environment* (Boston: Harvard Graduate School of Business Administration, 1967); Robert B. Duncan, "Characteristics of Organizational Environments and Perceived Environmental Uncertainty," *Administrative Science Quarterly*, vol. 17 (September 1972), pp. 313–27; Richard N. Osborn and James G. Hunt, "Environment and Organizational Effectiveness," *Administrative Science Quarterly*, vol. 19 (June 1974), pp. 231–46.

[9] Thompson, op. cit.; Charles Perrow, "A Framework for the Comparative Analysis of Organizations," *American Sociological Review*, vol. 32 (April 1967), pp. 195–208; *Organizational Analysis: A Sociological View* (Belmont, Calif.: Wadsworth, 1970); and *Complex Organizations: A Critical Essay* (Glenview, Ill.: Scott, Foresman, 1972); Duncan, op. cit.

[10] Other dimensions of the environment which have been investigated are: (1) concentrated-dispersed, (2) environmental capacity (rich-lean), (3) domain consensus-dissensus, and (4) mutability-immutability. See Howard Aldrich, "An Organization-Environment Perspective on Cooperation and Conflict between Organizations in the Manpower Training System," New York State School of Industrial and Labor Relations Reprint Series, 1972.

through a process of attention.[11] The organization responds only to what it perceives; those things that are not noticed do not affect the organization's decisions and actions. This focus on the process of attention means that the same "objective" environment may appear differently to different organizations, and this may be the main reason why previous research using so-called "objective" or "hard" (i.e., nonperceptual) measures of environmental variables has largely failed to predict organizational responses. Clearly, the organization will ultimately be victimized by perceptions which ignore or distort crucial environmental elements, but a wide range of "perceived environments" may be tolerable for lengthy periods in many real circumstances.

The emphasis on enactment also means that organizational information-processing systems are critical in determining how the organization adjusts to its environment. How organizations attend to various aspects of their environment and how this information is collected and processed are issues that are both unexplored and critical to our understanding of organizational adaptation. It is entirely conceivable that organization structure itself conditions the enactment process. Thus, one could argue that complex, differentiated organization structures will be more likely to produce complex, differentiated managerial perceptions of the environment. Therefore, structure may not only be a consequence of the environment but may also influence the environment through its effect on managerial attention processes.

DOMAIN DEFINITION AND STRATEGIC RESPONSE

In enacting its environment, the organization has, in part, defined its domain. An organization's domain consists of those activities it intends to pursue, and, in choosing a domain of activity, the organization simultaneously determines its pattern of interdependence with elements of the environment (suppliers, customers, unions, etc.). For example, if the organization decides to be a general hospital, it defines a pattern of interdependence with environmental elements that may be distinctly different from a hospital specializing in only a few major ailments. Unfortunately, there is little descriptive literature concerning the organization's strategic choice of a domain of activity—why, for example, within the same general environment some organizations choose to specialize while others diversify.[12]

---

11 Karl E. Weick, *The Social Psychology of Organizing* (Reading, Mass.: Addison-Wesley, 1969).

12 Drucker has offered perhaps the best discussions of how organizations define a domain of activity, but he does not go deeply into the effects of domain definition on organizational structure and process. See Peter F. Drucker, *The Practice of Manage-*

Also, as Thompson has pointed out, the organization cannot unilaterally choose its domain. There must be some degree of consensus among those with whom the organization comes into contact—either resource providers or critics of the organization's proposed activities—regarding the desired arena of activity, and this process of attaining domain consensus frequently constrains what activities the organization undertakes.[13]

The patterns of interdependence established by the organization's choice of domain subsequently affect its behavior. Randall investigated the willingness of state employment offices in Wisconsin to undertake human-resources development activities.[14] He found that such activities were more likely to occur when the office had a community-action agency in its domain acting as a source of pressure. Pfeffer, in a study of Israeli managers' attitudes, found that managers were more willing to undertake activities favored by the government to the extent that their firms were (1) more dependent on the government for financial assistance; (2) sold a relatively greater proportion of their output to the government; and (3) had a higher proportion of foreign ownership.[15] He also found that managers in firms which were in poor financial condition claimed that their decisions were more influenced by bankers.

Managing the Environment

While organizations are clearly influenced by forces in their domain, they also have a wealth of available means for altering their environments to make them conform more closely to what the organization can manage. One strategy for dealing with environmental interdependence involves working directly with the groups or organizations concerned, using such means as long-term contracts, joint ventures, cooptation, or merger.[16] An-

---

ment (New York: Harper & Brothers, 1954) and *Management: Tasks, Responsibilities and Practices* (New York: Harper & Row, 1974). For an excellent study of the effects of organizational strategy on structure, see Alfred D. Chandler, Jr., *Strategy and Structure* (Garden City, N.Y.: Doubleday, 1962).

[13] See Thompson, op. cit., pp. 28–29. For two examples of research using the concept of domain consensus, see Sol Levine and Paul E. White, "Exchange as a Conceptual Framework for the Study of Interorganizational Relationships," *Administrative Science Quarterly*, vol. 5 (March 1961), pp. 583–601; and Burton R. Clark, *The Open Door College* (New York: McGraw-Hill, 1960).

[14] Ronald Randall, "Influence of Environmental Support and Policy Space on Organizational Behavior," *Administrative Science Quarterly*, vol. 18 (June 1973), pp. 236–47.

[15] Jeffrey Pfeffer, "Interorganizational Influence and Managerial Attitudes," *Academy of Management Journal*, vol. 15 (September 1972), pp. 317–30.

[16] Long-term contracts as a means of stabilizing the environment have been discussed by Harold Guetzkow, "Relations among Organizations," in Raymond V. Bowers, ed., *Studies on Behavior in Organizations* (Athens, Ga.: University of Georgia Press, 1966), pp. 13–44. For joint ventures, see Michael Aiken and Jerald Hage, "Organi-

other strategy works indirectly to influence or regulate interdependence, using third parties such as trade associations, coordinating groups, or government agencies (which may provide, for example, direct cash subsidies to the organization or legislation to restrict competition).[17] A third strategy is less clear-cut than the previous ones. Phillips has argued that in oligopolistic industries, firms behave as if they were in a small group, conforming to group norms and implicitly or explicitly coordinating their activities.[18] Perrow has described instances where corporations "willingly suspended" competition in the short run because of strong industrial norms of how business relations ought to be conducted.[19] Finally, if environmental factors prove difficult to "manage," the organization has the option of choosing another domain, avoiding uncertainty or dependence by getting into a new line of activity; consequently, diversification is another way of coping with the environment.

ESTABLISHING AN ORGANIZATIONAL TECHNOLOGY

Having determined a domain, or sphere of activity, the organization next requires a technology to produce the goods or services that it has decided to provide. Broadly defined, technology is the combination of skills, equipment, and relevant technical knowledge needed to bring about desired transformations in materials, information, or people.[20]

It should be emphasized that, as with domain definition, there is a good deal of choice involved in the selection of a technology, depending on how

---

zational Interdependence and Intraorganizational Structure," *American Sociological Review*, vol. 33 (December 1968), pp. 912–30. For cooptation, see Philip Selznick, *TVA and the Grass Roots: A Study in the Sociology of Formal Organization* (Berkeley and Los Angeles: University of California Press, 1949). Merger activity has been investigated by, among others, Jeffrey Pfeffer, "Merger as a Response to Organizational Interdependence," *Administrative Science Quarterly*, vol. 17 (September 1972), pp. 382–94.

[17] On coordinating agencies, see Eugene Litwak and Lydia F. Hylton, "Interorganizational Analysis: A Hypothesis on Co-ordinating Agencies," *Administrative Science Quarterly*, vol. 6 (March 1962), pp. 395–420. Among the many sources on attempts to influence government agencies, see George J. Stigler, "The Theory of Economic Regulation," *Bell Journal of Economics and Management Science*, vol. 2 (Spring 1971), pp. 3–21; Raymond A. Bauer, Ithiel de Sola Pool, and Lewis A. Dexter, *American Business and Public Policy* (New York: Atherton, 1964); Donald R. Hall, *Cooperative Lobbying: The Power of Pressure* (Tucson: University of Arizona Press, 1969).

[18] Almarin Phillips, "A Theory of Interfirm Organization," *Quarterly Journal of Economics*, vol. 74 (November 1960), pp. 602–13.

[19] Perrow, *Organizational Analysis*, chap. 4.

[20] This definition comes from Louis E. Davis, "Job Satisfaction Research: The Post-Industrial View," *Industrial Relations*, vol. 10 (May 1971), p. 180.

the organization perceives the environment and how it defines its activities. Perrow, for example, described two correctional institutions dealing with delinquent youths.[21] One was operated as if its primary goal were custody, and to simply confine people required only a very "routine" technology—a small custodial staff, centralized decision making, and generally uniform treatment of the raw materials (i.e., the youths). The other institution operated as if it were pursuing more therapeutic goals, with a "nonroutine" technology that permitted much more flexibility in dealing with the youths. Similarly, there is not much in common between the technology used by a large military kitchen and a fine gourmet restaurant, though in broad terms both have established a domain which involves providing meals.

Thus, depending on the organization's strategy for dealing with the domain, one type of technology may appear to be more appropriate than another, while others are disregarded as totally infeasible. Thus, within the feasible range of technologies, managers are free to choose some particular mix of skills, equipment, etc., and may have even greater discretion in deciding how this technology is to be operated.

Types of Technology

Several typologies of technology have been advanced. Woodward, the first to introduce technology as an important organizational variable, constructed a technological scale ranging from unit or prototype production, through small-batch, mass, and finally continous-process production.[22] Each of these technologies differs in the degree to which it is labor or capital intensive and particularly in the extent to which it permits specialized handling. Other typologies have been offered (e.g., Perrow, Thompson, Hickson, et al.),[23] but Woodward's scheme allows us to make some broad comparisons across different types.

Comparisons among Technologies

The unit or small-batch production technology is labor intensive and highly flexible. Thus, it is not well suited to strategies involving standardized products and long production runs but rather to customized products. This type of technology can operate at low output levels or where there

---

[21] Perrow, *Organizational Analysis*, pp. 28–37.

[22] Joan Woodward, *Industrial Organization: Theory and Practice* (Oxford: Oxford University Press, 1965).

[23] Perrow, "A Framework"; Thompson, op. cit.; David J. Hickson, D. S. Pugh, and Diana C. Pheysey, "Operations Technology and Structure: An Empirical Reappraisal," *Administrative Science Quarterly*, vol. 14 (September 1969), pp. 378–97.

is considerable fluctuation in output. A unit technology is usually accompanied by an organization structure which utilizes general as opposed to specialized employee skills, and this technology may be relatively easily adjusted in order to experiment with new developments and work processes.

Mass-production technologies also tend to be labor intensive, although their more rigid forms, such as the automobile assembly line, are capital intensive. A mass-production technology, because it typically employs expensive limited-purpose equipment, is much less flexible than a unit technology and requires a very high volume of output in order to be economical. And, because of its rigid scheduling requirements, even small fluctuations in output are costly to this type of system. In contrast to unit production, the organization structure appropriate for a mass-production technology includes numerous standardized procedures and employees with limited and specialized skills who may be relatively interchangeable within the system but cannot be easily converted to new methods and processes.

Finally, continuous-process technology is highly capital intensive and requires a large output volume. Although this type of technology usually allows a diverse range of related products to be manufactured, the technology itself is quite inflexible—it can be adapted to produce other products only at great cost. Continuous-process technology requires relatively few individuals to monitor the machinery, but such employees frequently must have high levels of judgmental and technical skill.

Sealing off the Technical Core

Because of the variety in these technologies, each requires different means of protecting it from costly environmental disturbances. Woodward found different sequences of production (manufacturing cycles) for each type of system. In unit production, the organization first obtains a customer order and then develops and manufactures the product. In mass production, the organization spends a great deal of time developing and producing the product, then engages in extensive marketing efforts in order to sell it. Lastly, in continuous-process production, the most critical function is to continually develop and market new products amenable to the existing technology, while producing the present product mix.

The time span of managerial decision making also varies with each type of technology. Whereas in unit production, the time span of decisions is short, it is considerably longer in mass production, and in continuous-process production, the large capital investments involved mean that many decisions require ten to twenty years and more to implement. Put another way, each technology places a unique set of demands on the organization structure to maintain control and coordination.

DEVELOPMENT OF AN ORGANIZATION STRUCTURE

Organization structure refers to the decomposition of the entire organization into subunits and to the relatively enduring relationships among them, and, therefore, structure includes such major organizational (as opposed to individual) variables as complexity, formalization, centralization, and administrative intensity (the ratio of clerical and managerial employees to all other employees). As mentioned earlier, the organization's structure exists to control and coordinate the technology and serves as a buffer between the technical core and the environment. However, the relationship between technology and structure is more complicated than was once believed.

Relationship between Technology and Structure

Studies of technology and structure appear to have had two overriding concerns. First, there have been several attempts to determine whether or not there is a direct relationship between the organization's technology and its structure. Second, and more recently, there has been a research interest in determining whether technology or organization size has the greater impact on structure. Two reviews of the technology, size, and structure literature have summarized the research as follows: (1) the definition and measurement of both technology and structure have not been consistent across studies, and, therefore, these studies are not strictly comparable; (2) studies across several types of organizations may reflect interindustry differences and their impact on structure rather than the specific influence of technology; (3) a single organization may operate more than one technology, making the "dominant" technological influence on structure difficult to ascertain; (4) organization size appears to be a somewhat stronger determinant of structure than does technology—only in small organizations does technology appear to have a clear and consistent impact on structure; and (5) because technology and size together explain such a small amount of the variance in organization structure, other predictors of structure (e.g., measures of the environment and managerial ideologies) need to be investigated.[24]

Some recent research, however, has suggested that structure may not respond directly to technology per se but rather to the different demands for control and coordination associated with each type of technology. For example, Woodward found that as technology moves from unit to mass

---

[24] Lawrence B. Mohr, "Organizational Technology and Organizational Structure," *Administrative Science Quarterly,* vol. 16 (December 1971), pp. 444–59; John Child and Roger Mansfield, "Technology, Size, and Organization Structure," *Sociology,* vol. 6 (September 1972), pp. 369–93.

production and then to continuous process, there is an increase in mechanical over personal forms of control.[25] At the same time, as one moves through the technology classification, control systems tend to be unitary (i.e., applied throughout the organization) in unit technologies, fragmented (i.e., different control standards and mechanisms for each major organizational subunit) in mass-production technologies, and unitary once again in continuous-process technologies. Thus, Woodward argued, the different technologies require different forms of control, and these in turn place some demands on, but do not precisely determine, a particular organization structure (e.g., unitary control can be achieved by formalized rules or by centralized decision making).

Similarly, each type of technology must be coordinated differently, and these different coordination demands must be accommodated by the organization's structure. Although definitive empirical research remains to be done in this area, it is generally true that as the organization's technology becomes more routine, coordination tends to become more formalized. Thus, with a unit or small-batch technology, coordination by mutual adjustment—where the technological process is modified on an ad hoc basis to meet the transformation needs of the inputs—seems to be most appropriate. With mass and continuous-process technologies, however, it is possible to coordinate these production processes by standardized procedures and longer-range plans (a variety of which may be accommodated within particular organization structures).

DEFICIENCIES IN CURRENT THEORY AND RESEARCH

As indicated in the review above, several of the decision points in our map of organization-environment relations have not been adequately researched. However, we should hasten to add that the areas which remain incomplete are obviously the most difficult ones, so the limitations of previous research are more often those of omission rather than commission. Three areas in particular need special attention in future research. First, although we frequently talk about managerial perceptions of the environment, we have no convenient way of describing or categorizing these perceptions, and we therefore tend to speak of managerial perceptions in global terms or ignore them completely. Secondly, previous research has primarily attempted to discover associations between environmental variables and particular *types* of organization structure, but we believe that this search for precise relationships is likely to prove futile. Instead we feel that future research should focus on the *demands* made by each decision

---

[25] Joan Woodward, ed., *Industrial Organization: Behaviour and Control* (Oxford, England: Oxford University Press, 1970).

point on the next decision point—the extent to which managerial choice is constrained—rather than on the ultimate adjustment(s) to these demands. Such a focus would permit us to account for the frequent observation that organizations adopt a variety of forms in response to apparently similar environmental demands. And, finally, by far the vast majority of previous organization-environment research has treated the organization as a static entity, leaving us with little understanding of how organizations adjust to their environments over time.

MANAGERIAL PERCEPTIONS

Child has argued that managerial perceptions and actions have a strong influence on organizational responses to the environment.[26] His concept of *strategic choice* corresponds closely to our concept of a decision point—at each stage of the adjustment process, managers have more or less discretion in guiding their organizations along different courses.

In a very preliminary way, Snow and Miles have attempted to categorize managerial perceptions of the environment and to describe how these perceptions are transformed into organizational responses.[27] From interviews with top managers in 16 college textbook publishing firms, these authors have developed four relatively distinct types of environmental enactment. Although the typology is crude, subsuming a number of variables in addition to managerial perceptions, each of the four types portrays a distinct pattern of organization-environment interaction. The four types of enactment are:

1. *Domain Defenders*, organizations whose top managers perceive some or no change and uncertainty in the environment and who have little inclination to make anything other than minor adjustments in organization structure and processes.
2. *Reluctant Reactors*, organizations where top managers perceive some change and uncertainty in the environment but who are not likely to make any substantial organizational adjustments until forced to do so by environmental pressures.
3. *Anxious Analyzers*, organizations where top managers perceive a good deal of change and uncertainty in the environment but who wait until competing organizations develop a viable response and then quickly adopt it.
4. *Enthusiastic Prospectors*, organizations whose top managers continually perceive (almost create) change and uncertainty in the environ-

[26] John Child, "Organizational Structure, Environment and Performance—The Role of Strategic Choice," *Sociology*, vol. 6 (January 1972), pp. 1–22.

[27] Charles C. Snow and Raymond E. Miles, "Managerial Perceptions and Organizational Adjustment Processes," unpublished working paper.

ment and who regularly experiment with potential responses to new environmental trends.

Subsequent decisions concerning strategy, technology, and structure appear to be quite consistent with each of these respective types (e.g., Domain Defenders, as opposed to Enthusiastic Prospectors, were more likely to have mass-production than unit technologies and to have "mechanistic" rather than "organic" organization structures). Moreover, the findings of this study suggest that the actions an organization takes in responding to its environment are much more likely to be consistent with top management perceptions of the environment than any "objective" indicator of environmental conditions is likely to predict.[28] We do not, however, mean to imply that the search for objective environmental measures be abandoned. Quite the contrary. Actual environmental conditions, as suggested earlier, clearly do influence organizational behavior, at least in the longer run. Moreover, measures of these characteristics are needed as a validity check for measures of managerial perceptions. We are arguing, as does Child, that perceptions guide the strategic choices managers make to achieve a better fit between their organizations and the environment and that these perceptions must be included in any model of organizational adaptation.

ADJUSTMENTS TO THE DEMANDS OF EACH DECISION POINT

A second major deficiency in the previous research concerns what we believe to be a somewhat misdirected research emphasis. As noted earlier, the typical study in this area attempts to correlate measures of predetermined environmental and organizational variables in the hope of discovering significant relationships among aspects of the environment and various forms of organization structure. Such a procedure, however, does not usually allow for the possibility that, across a particular set of organizations, a wide range of responses to similar environmental demands may be observed. For example, in the college textbook publishing study, two organizations whose top managements perceived a great deal of change and uncertainty in their environments nevertheless made substantially differ-

---

[28] In a criticism of Lawrence and Lorsch's Environmental Uncertainty Questionnaire, Tosi, et al. show that different objective measures of environmental uncertainty produce different results when they are correlated with organizational variables. Henry Tosi, Ramon Aldag, and Ronald Storey, "On the Measurement of the Environment: An Assessment of the Lawrence and Lorsch Environmental Uncertainty Questionnaire," *Administrative Science Quarterly*, vol. 18 (March 1973), 27–36. (It should also be noted that different perceptual measures of environmental uncertainty might also produce results similar to those of Tosi et al. The concept of environmental uncertainty is badly in need of both theoretical and operational refinement.)

ent adjustments to this environmental turbulence. One firm went through a major effort to restructure the organization while simultaneously creating a program to financially underwrite a small number of free-lance professionals who were to experiment with new publishing techniques. The other organization, by contrast, retained its current overall organization structure but set up several cross-functional project teams to develop publishing programs to deal with changing environmental demands. Conventional measures of organization structure might easily misrepresent what was occurring in either or both of these organizations and might show little relationship between uncertainty and structure. In fact, however, both organizations were responding, albeit differently, to the same set of environmental demands and with the same intended outcomes.

Two points are worth noting about this example. The first is that future research needs to investigate the *demands* which the choice of a domain makes on a basic operating strategy, the demands which strategy makes on technology, which technology makes on structure, etc. Once the demands which each decision point makes on the next are understood, then we can investigate the various responses which are made to each of these demands. Following the decision points map offered here, it is not necessary to demonstrate, for example, a specific set of structural features flowing from a given set of technological demands. Rather, it is important only to show that adjustments are or are not being made and to determine whether these appear to fall within some feasible set of responses. Secondly, we need more longitudinal studies of organizational adaptation. The management of the second publishing firm in the above example was, at the time of the study, tentatively considering some structural reorganizations, and its experimentation with cross-functional project teams may have been only the first step in a larger move resembling the changes made in the first publishing company. Cross-sectional studies utilizing static models cannot possibly capture the richness of the responses which organizations make to ensure their survival and foster growth.

A DEFICIENCY IN DYNAMICS

Despite the fact that the bulk of the theory and research discussed here deals with a dynamic process—the alignment of organizational strategy, structure, and process with environmental demands—surprisingly little specific attention has been given to the impact of current adjustment decisions on those which will (or should) follow as the environment changes and as the organization commits itself to a particular way of functioning. There is a body of literature on organizational growth, but to this point there has been little effort to integrate growth theories and research with the more recent flow of concepts and models attempting to link environmental demands with specific types of organizational technology and structure.[29] Dynamic models are, of course, far more difficult to build and test than static models, but it is our belief that such attempts must be made.

Original Strategy and Structural Decisions

Stinchcombe has shown that organizations are "imprinted" by the conditions existing in the industry to which they belong at the time the industry is "born."[30] He suggests that environmental conditions at any point in time not only specify the needs for particular goods and services but also determine many of the characteristics of the organizations created to provide them. Stinchcombe believes, for example, that the "railroad age" could occur only after society had developed the institutions, expertise, and means of legitimizing the organizational structures and processes necessary to develop and implement already existing technology.

More importantly, Stinchcombe argues that organizational structures, processes, and norms of behavior born (imprinted) in a given era tend to persist even though environmental conditions, including perhaps both the demands for different types of goods and services and the capacities for different forms of organizations to meet these, may have changed dramatically. He notes that this "imprinting" process appears to affect not only "first-born" firms but also those created as the industry expands—newer organizations imitate those already in existence. He further asserts that the "liability of newness" tends to restrict the adoption of new structures and processes unless the changes in environmental conditions are especially stark and dramatic. Thus, well into the twentieth century most railroad companies had structures, staffing patterns, managerial views of the market, etc., which may have been far more appropriate to the environmental conditions in the period of their birth.

"Nonrational" Adjustment Process

How then do organizations adapt to changing environmental conditions? Alchian has suggested that the process can be envisioned as essentially one of natural selection.[31] That is, given that imitation is never perfect, some organizations, by chance alone, will have characteristics more amenable to newly arising conditions than will their counterparts. Success-

---

[29] For a review of the literature on organizational growth (up to 1965), see William H. Starbuck, "Organizational Growth and Development," in James G. March, ed., *Handbook of Organizations* (Chicago: Rand McNally, 1965), pp. 451–533.

[30] Arthur Stinchcombe, "Social Structure and Organizations," in March, op. cit., pp. 142–93.

[31] Armen A. Alchian, "Uncertainty, Evolution, and Economic Theory," *Journal of Political Economy*, vol. 58 (June 1960), pp. 211–21.

ful chance adaptations will be imitated as less fortunate organizations feel the pressure of their improper alignment with the environment, and a new cycle will begin. Alchian does not argue against the possibility of rationality in the adjustment process; he simply points out that it is not necessary to assume rationality in order to explain organizational growth and survival. In other words, one could build a model which, in effect, holds organizations constant and shifts the environment so that some organizations in a given group are more "favored" than others.

Taken together, the arguments of Stinchcombe and Alchian may appear to discourage efforts to describe relationships between organizations and their environments. That is, if as Stinchcombe argues, organizational structures and processes are natural products of cultural norms and capabilities, then initial choices of domain, strategy, technology, etc., among organizations in older industries are greatly constrained. Moreover, if one adopts Alchian's view, chance variation in initial organizational form and process may well be the key to future success or failure. Thus, neither the original set of decisions nor subsequent adjustments would appear to turn on the correctness of managerial choice—in fact, what might first appear to be a poor adjustment could later prove to be a triumph of unintended foresight!

However well these notions fit reality, managers are not likely to be satisfied with theories which ignore or diminish the requirements of organizational rationality in the process of diagnosing environmental demands and choosing appropriate structures and processes to meet them. The image of various species of organizations originating simply by the grace of a benevolent environment and then growing by extending their existing forms and processes (to the limits of technological capacity), with certain of the species benefiting at random from environmental changes, may be accurate—but it is also discomforting.

Growth and Adjustment through Excess Managerial Capacity

A more palatable line of reasoning, but one difficult both to specify completely and to test, is offered by Penrose.[32] She argues that ignoring managerial decision making as an important factor in organizational growth and survival is as much at odds with observable behavior as is the economic assumption of perfect profit-maximizing decisions in response to environmental change. She urges the incorporation of managerial capability as a determinant of growth and survival—in fact, she offers a theory of organizational growth with excess managerial capacity as a prime in-

---

[32] Edith T. Penrose, *The Theory of the Growth of the Firm* (New York: Wiley, 1959). See, particularly, pp. 46–54 and 200–201.

gradient. That is, Penrose believes that the organization whose managerial talent is fully employed in the operation of the existing technology and process is unlikely to perceive new environmental threats or opportunities, or, if they are perceived, to be able to respond beyond the simple extension of existing practices. She further contends that the organization with excess managerial capacity is not only able to take advantage of uncertainty but will be under strong internal pressure from this underemployed cadre of managerial talent to seek out and confront environmental uncertainty.

Penrose's model appears to fit nicely with our earlier characterizations of the types of environmental enactment and response among publishing companies. Those organizations and their top managerial groups characterized as Domain Defenders tend, by and large, to fully employ their existing managerial resources in the administration and improvement of their current operations. Managers in such organizations are typically greatly knowledgeable about the processes in their particular firm, but the demands of their jobs—highly standardized procedures and centralized decision making—offer little opportunity or incentive for search or innovation other than that linked closely to cost-cutting and other attempts to make existing practices more efficient. At the other extreme, the Enthusiastic Prospectors deliberately attempt to both develop and import managerial talent specifically for the purpose of searching out and responding to new environmental opportunities. It would appear to follow that while both types of organizations may succeed, there are more limits placed on the growth possibilities of the Domain Defenders than on the Enthusiastic Prospectors, and the latter have more insurance against the threat of disaster (or at least the requirement for some major adjustments) as the result of environmental changes than do their perhaps presently more efficient counterparts. This last point requires elaboration.

Adjustment Costs and Benefits

We have suggested, based on our research, that within the same "objective" environment both Domain Defenders and Enthusiastic Prospectors can apparently survive and even flourish, at least in the short run. Domain Defenders survive by working more intensively in a narrow segment of the environment, perhaps offsetting the loss of some potential gains in new areas by servicing their known area with increasing cost efficiency. Enthusiastic Prospectors, on the other hand, are less likely to invest their key talent in improving existing products or procedures and more likely to invest them in exploring new opportunities. They may thus operate on a higher cost curve but offset this by frequent successes in new areas. Note that, at a given point in time, both Domain Defenders and

Enthusiastic Prospectors feel that the strategies, structures, and processes of their organizations fit the demands of their environment as it has been perceived and enacted by their managements.

What happens, however, if the environment becomes more or less turbulent? If the environment moves toward greater stability, the Domain Defenders would appear to be favored. Given their stable goals, they can build on their existing capabilities to improve efficiency and reap additional profit, while Enthusiastic Prospectors pay an even higher price for their excess coping capability. On the other hand, if environmental conditions become significantly more uncertain, the Enthusiastic Prospectors may be favored. They have a ready capacity for moving into new areas and experience in reshaping their structure and processes to meet new demands. Domain Defenders can survive under increasingly turbulent conditions only by (1) continuing to narrow the scope of their operations and concentrating on only the healthiest areas; or (2) attempting to move into new product or service areas (which they are likely to do hesitantly and clumsily). The first adjustment tack may ultimately prove impossible or unprofitable as the domain-narrowing process reaches its limits. Similarly, the second adjustment mechanism may prove extremely costly and time consuming, as it requires substantial restaffing and restructuring throughout the system. If the necessary changes are anticipated far enough in advance, a successful transition is possible. As suggested, however, Domain Defenders, in our research at least, typically do not maintain the sensing mechanisms necessary to identify and evaluate trends outside of their narrow domains and thus would be less likely to forecast environmental changes as effectively as would the Enthusiastic Prospectors. Consequently, it appears that if changes are particularly rapid or dramatic, Domain Defenders run the risk of major, perhaps disastrous losses. Our arguments here should not be construed as a blanket endorsement of growth and/or unconstrained diversification. Clearly not all "prospectors" strike gold and overextension of resources is a frequent cause of failure.

In sum, it appears that the price of excess adjustment capability is inefficiency, while the price of insufficient coping capacity is ineffectiveness. That is, an organization which adopts a flexible, highly adaptable structure and process in a stable environment may not minimize its costs (inefficiency), while an organization which maintains a bureaucratized structure and process in a highly turbulent environment runs the risk of major losses and even failure (ineffectiveness). Moreover, it would appear that it would be easier, particularly in the short run, to bureaucratize an organic structure than to develop coping capacity in a highly mechanized structure.

Extending this last point, Bennis has predicted the ultimate demise of all bureaucratic structures and processes in the face of ever-increasing environmental turbulence.[33] A more flexible argument seems to us more realistic—there are and will likely continue to be stable environments (or at least areas of stability) around many organizations which will prove quite amenable to specialized technologies, coordination by planning and standardized procedures, and control by policy and rule, but, at the same time, it seems likely that most organizations will also ultimately face the need for sizeable changes. Several available models (e.g., Perrow[34]) view organization structure and process as determined by, or contingent on, environmental and/or technological characteristics. A true contingency model, however, would not only describe the range of organizational structures and processes appropriate under various environmental conditions but also specify the costs, benefits, and means of maintaining an appropriate level of adjustment capability, given the choice of organizational structure and process.

CONCLUSIONS

We have attempted in this article to point out the areas where existing concepts and research concerning organization-environment relations appear to be deficient. Although we have no doubts that organizations must and do adjust their strategies, technologies, structures, and processes to meet changing environmental demands, we are convinced that current theories fail to clearly indicate how environmental conditions place constraints on adjustment alternatives and how each adjustment decision constrains those that follow. We are equally convinced that within these constraints there frequently exists the opportunity for managers to exercise considerable decision-making discretion (e.g., a variety of organizational structures and/or processes may meet the demands of a particular strategy or technology, and the choice among these is an exercise in managerial judgment). Thus, efforts to find direct linkages between, say, a given technology and a particular structural form are likely to be frustrated, with the possible unwarranted conclusion that no relationship exists.

We have also heavily emphasized managerial perceptions as a key variable at each of the decision points in the adjustment process. Top management clearly influences the process of domain definition, the choice of a basic operating strategy, the development of a core technology, and so on, and we believe that research in this area will make its largest contribution when it uncovers and displays for managers the implications of their current decisions for the longer-run adjustment capabilities of their organizations.

To provide information on the total adjustment process, researchers

---

[33] Warren G. Bennis, *Changing Organizations* (New York: McGraw-Hill, 1966).
[34] Perrow, *Organizational Analysis*.

will most likely be forced out of their current mode of cross-sectional survey studies and toward longitudinal analyses. Particularly important will be attempts to contrast the behavior of those organizations which appear to be at the leading and lagging edges of their particular industry or grouping and which describe not only the nature of their adjustment to environmental demands but the process by which these adjustments came about.

How G.M. Turned Itself Around*

CHARLES G. BURCK

The perpetuation of leadership is sometimes more difficult than the attainment of that leadership in the first place. This is the greatest challenge to be met by the leader of an industry. It is a challenge to be met by the General Motors of the future.

—former Chairman Alfred P. Sloan Jr.
My Years with General Motors (1963)

WITH giant corporations as with giant oil tankers, bigness confers advantages, but the ability to turn around easily is not one of them.

Though General Motors does some things very well, one just doesn't expect it to be nimble. In so huge an organization, decision-making processes are inherently complex, and sheer mass generates a great deal of inertia. Four years ago, however, G.M. came up against the sort of challenge foreseen by Alfred Sloan. Though the company seemed ill prepared for change, it not only met the challenge but did so with a resounding success that surprised many observers of the U.S. auto industry.

The clearest evidence of G.M.'s effective response to that challenge is the transformation of its product line to meet the demands of the marketplace—and the federal government—for better gas mileage. When the Arab oil embargo hit at the end of 1973, G.M. had the worst average gas mileage among U.S. automakers—a dismal twelve miles per gallon. As buyers turned away from gas-guzzlers in panic during the following year, G.M.'s share of the U.S. new-car market slid to 42 percent, the lowest point since 1952 (not counting the strike year of 1970). Just three years

---

* Reprinted by permission *Fortune,* January 16, 1978, pp. 87–89, 92, 96, 100.

later, in the 1977-model year, the average mileage of G.M. cars, 17.8 mpg, was the *best* among the Big Three automakers. G.M.'s big cars alone averaged 15 mpg, or 3 mpg better than the entire 1974 fleet. Largely as a result, the company's market share has rebounded to about 46 percent.

At the center of this product revolution was G.M.'s downsizing strategy, which began last year with the big cars. G.M. gambled that it could redefine the meaning of "big" in the American marketplace, from its traditional connotation of exterior bulk to a more functional, European-style definition based on interior space and driving quality. The gamble succeeded. In what proved to be a good year for big cars in general, G.M.'s more than held their own against the conventional offerings of Ford and Chrysler.

The downsizing strategy is also the key to G.M.'s hopes for the future. Despite the many difficulties and uncertainties of the auto market, General Motors is notably more confident than the other U.S. automakers of its ability to meet the government's tightening schedule of mileage laws for the years to come with cars that will still satisfy the American consumer. Says President Elliott M. Estes: "We're working on three or four scenarios for getting to 27.5 miles per gallon by 1985. It's a problem now of economics—how can we do it for the least cost?"

G.M.'s headquarters are awash in self-assurance these days. There is more than a hint of that spirit in Chairman Thomas Aquinas Murphy's outspoken optimism about the economy, the automobile industry, and General Motors itself. Most remarkable is Murphy's unabashed determination to increase market share as much as possible—indeed, he has said on more than one occasion that he will not be satisfied "until we sell every car that's sold." That's an astonishing departure from the posture of earlier G.M. chief executives, who avoided *any* talk about expanding market share for fear of unleashing the hounds of antitrust.

Murphy explains his outspokenness by asking and then answering a rhetorical question. "Should there be a limit to our return or our market penetration? I say no. The risks of the business today are as high as or higher than they've ever been, and the returns ought to be high. And if we're obeying the law, doing the best job of serving the customer, and discharging all the other responsibilities we have as a good employer and responsible citizen, then we've earned whatever we get."

Such spirit was nowhere to be found at G.M. four years ago. Nineteen seventy-four, in fact, seemed to confirm what many observers had been suspecting for some time—that G.M. was losing its capacity to lead the industry. Sloan, the man who established that leadership in the first place during the 1920s, had observed that "success may bring self-satisfaction . . . the spirit of venture is lost in the inertia of the mind against change," and it appeared in the early 1970s that his own company was fulfilling the prophecy.

Between 1962 and 1972, G.M.'s market share drifted down from its all-time high of 51.9 percent to 44.2 percent. Most of the lost sales went to imports and did not greatly trouble G.M. Following a strictly financial logic, the company concluded that it was sensible to stick with its traditional policies, which had earned it dominance of the highly profitable big-car market, rather than compete head-on in the less profitable small-car field.

For a while, events seemed to justify this reasoning. Measured in dollars, sales continued to rise. G.M. indisputably knew who the prime automobile customers were and how to make what they wanted.

But G.M. was slow to realize what besides efficiency made the imports so attractive: agility and a certain sporty functionalism were increasingly appealing to a broader public than what G.M. understood as the economy market. There were executives at G.M. in 1970 who actually thought that—as one explained to a reporter—"there's something wrong with people who like small cars." G.M.'s domestic and foreign competitors, knowing better, captured a lot of the growth while G.M.'s chosen territory was contracting. Ford's market share during those years slipped only two percentage points to 24.3, while Chrysler's actually rose.

G.M. also seemed fundamentally out of touch with the outside world. Its size made it a natural target for antibusiness critics—especially the militant autophobes who held the auto industry responsible for everything from urban pollution to suburban sprawl. The company's reaction to its critics, as well as to the pollution and safety legislation pushed forth by the government, was defensive and even uncomprehending. Its labor relations presented a similarly sorry sight. The problems of the highly automated plant at Lordstown, Ohio, for example, which began building Vegas in 1971, became celebrated as a classic management failure to understand or communicate with employees.

Yet despite G.M.'s insularity and self-preoccupation, managerial machinery was grinding along, resolutely if ponderously, in search of new directions. Sloan had, after all, set up a management system predicated upon change. But even important management decisions rarely show up visibly or dramatically on the outside. As Thomas Murphy says, "Drama in business lies mostly in doing well the job right before you."

New policies, moreover, like new cars, require lead times. Indeed, G.M.'s top officers are not inclined to react with high emotion to the events of any given year, for the practical reason that in so massive an institution there is little they can do to affect the short run in any case. Experience has taught patience. They know, for example, that even a new division head cannot do much that will influence his division's results for a good twenty to thirty months. Asked about the process of change at G.M., they invariably reply that it is "evolutionary, not revolutionary."

It is a characteristic of evolutionary processes, of course, that they are hard to perceive until after they have been going on for a while. G.M.'s first response to those social-minded critics was aloof and almost brusque. But after handily turning aside their most flamboyant challenge—"Campaign G.M." at the 1970 annual meeting—the company set up extensive machinery to bring new and critical thinking into its corporate planning process. It created a new public-policy committee, staffed entirely with outsiders, and the fresh viewpoints the committee brought to G.M. were listened to. The company also hired a number of important managers from outside—a radical departure from the tradition of near-exclusive reliance on internal management development. These people were assigned to key posts. For example, Stephen H. Fuller, who had been professor of business administration at Harvard Business School, was put in charge of the personnel administration and development staff. Ernest S. Starkman, from the school of engineering at the University of California, Berkeley, was made head of environmental activities.

The rapid turnaround of G.M.'s product line over the past three years could not have been accomplished without a good deal of earlier thinking and planning. As far back as 1972, the board of directors created an ad hoc group called the energy task force, headed by David C. Collier, then G.M.'s treasurer and now head of the Buick division. Collier's group included people from manufacturing, research, design, finance, and the economics staff, and it spent half a year on its research. "We came to three conclusions," said Collier. "First, that there was an energy problem. Second, the government had no particular plan to deal with it. Third, the energy problem would have a profound effect upon our business. We went to the board with those conclusions in March of 1973."

Collier's report made for a good deal of discussion throughout the company in the months following. "We were trying to get other people to think about it," says Richard C. Gerstenberg, who was then chairman of G.M. Meantime, Collier's group was assigned to examine G.M.'s product program, and when Collier reported back to the board again in October, the talk turned to what Gerstenberg refers to as "getting some downsizing in our cars."

The embargo, of course, intruded dramatically upon this rather studied planning process. But while no specific decisions had yet been made on the basis of Collier's report, the work of the task force had done much to create the right frame of mind at all levels of management. G.M.'s board was able within two months to approve several specific proposals. Two were "crash" decisions for the 1976-model year. The Chevette would be built, using component designs from Opel and other overseas divisions, mainly Brazil; and so would the car that would become the Seville, under consideration for more than a year. And then, as Gerstenberg says, "the possible long-term program was to find a way to redesign all of our regular lines so we could get them all in a much more fuel-efficient area.

G.M.'s product-policy committee had already decided, in April, to scale down the 1977 standard cars, but the reductions were to be modest, totaling about 400 pounds, and they were calculated to improve economy by only about one mile per gallon. By the end of 1973, however, mileage had suddenly become the overriding concern, and it was clear that practically the entire product line would eventually have to be redesigned. The biggest question, recalls Pete Estes, then executive vice president in charge of operations staffs, was where to begin. The committee's deliberaions were intense, but not lengthy. The consensus that emerged, says Estes, was that "our business was family cars, so we had to start there. If we had started at the bottom, there would have been a gap for a year or so where the competition could have moved in."

The policy committee's new proposals went to the executive committee, which makes all of G.M.'s major operational decisions (its members include the seven top officers). In December the executive committee instructed the company's engineers to come up with a plan for substantial reductions in the 1977 big cars, and to start on the reductions for other body sizes in the years after.

Even as the product plans were being redrawn, G.M. was taking a broader look at itself—investigating how it had failed to deal with its problems, and working up recommendations for change. Every summer, the executive committee undertakes what Gerstenberg calls "an inventory of people"—a review of the company's 6,000 or so top managers for possible promotion and replacement. In 1974, moreover, it was charged with picking successors to Gerstenberg and President Edward N. Cole, both of whom were retiring. In addition, the board asked the committee to take an inventory of G.M.'s problems. Both inventories, in turn, were presented to the newly created organization review committee, consisting mainly of the outside directors who serve on G.M.'s bonus and salary committee. The job of this review committee was to analyze the problems and propose organizational solutions.

Many of those problems were in the process of being dealt with, of course—particularly in the transformation of the product line. But some of the most important were not so easily defined or specifically addressed. The process of running G.M. had grown considerably more complex since the 1950's. The business environment was still uncertain, and outside constraints had to be taken increasingly into account. The review committee wrestled with the implications of such matters during that summer;

toward the end of its assignment, it was augmented by Murphy, who had been nominated to relace Gerstenberg as chairman.

What the committee recommended, in September 1974, was a major reorganization at the top. That reorganization, says Murphy, "expanded importantly the top management group. Looking beyond where we were at the time, we designed it to bring new executives into a higher echelon." Complicated in its details, the reorganization upgraded the responsibilities of the executive vice presidents, and added a fourth to the three already existing. The upgrading brought forward four relatively young men, all future prospects for the top, to serve on the board and the executive committee. Since the divisions now answer to top management through those executive vice presidents, the reorganization strengthened lines of authority and communication.

The reorganization also redefined and strengthened the jobs of the president and of the new vice chairman, Richard L. Terrell. Supervision of G.M.'s eight operating staffs had previously been split between the president and the vice chairman; all were brought together under Terrell. That move freed the new president, Estes, to concentrate more fully on operations—and especially upon overseas operations, which were transferred to him from the vice chairman. Along with Ford and Chrysler, G.M. is planning a growing number of "world cars"—essentially similar models that can be built in the U.S., Europe, or anywhere else. Though the first of those, the Chevette, was barely on the drawing boards for the U.S. that year, G.M. reasoned that overseas and domestic work could be more directly and effectively integrated if both divisions reported to Estes.

If the reorganization was a landmark event, it was in some ways less important than another change wrought in 1974—the adoption of the project center, a new concept in engineering management, devised to coordinate the efforts of the five automobile divisions. A G.M. project center, made up of engineers lent by the divisions, has no exact counterpart elsewhere in the auto industry—and perhaps in all of U.S. industry. NASA used the concept for the space program, and Terrell spotted it there when he was head of the nonautomotive divisions, one of which—Delco Electronics—was a NASA contractor. Sloan himself would have appreciated the concept, for it is right in line with the coordinated-decentralization approach to management.

G.M. adopted the project-center idea in order to meet the special demands created by the downsizing decision. Coordinating the development of a new body line among the various division is a complex undertaking even in normal times. To do what it wanted, the company would have to engineer its cars in a new way, using new design techniques and technologies, during a time when the margins for error and correction would be tighter than usual. Particularly under these circumstances, G.M. could no longer afford the old problem (by no means unique to G.M.) of what Estes calls "N-I-H, not invented here, a kind of disease engineers have." An engineer suffering from N-I-H resists new ideas that originate outside his bailiwick.

The project center is not a permanent group. Every time a major new effort is planned—a body changeover, say—a project center is formed, and it operates for the duration of the undertaking. Thus the A-body center, which shepherded this year's intermediates through development, ran from late 1975 until this past fall. The X-body center is now at work on next year's front-wheel-drive compacts. All project centers report to a board composed of the chief engineers of the automotive divisions.

Project centers work on parts and engineering problems common to all divisions, such as frames, electrical systems, steering gear, and brakes. Many of these are identical in every division; many others are what G.M. calls "common family parts"—e.g., shock absorbers—that are basically the same but are calibrated or adjusted to divisional specifications. The project center augments, but does not replace, G.M.'s traditional "lead division" concept, in which one division is assigned primary responsibility for bringing some technical innovation into production.

The project center was probably G.M.'s single most important managerial tool in carrying out that bold decision to downsize. It has eliminated a great deal of redundant effort, and has speeded numerous new technologies into production. Its success, however, rests on the same delicate balance between the powers of persuasion and coercion that underlies G.M.'s basic system of coordinated decentralization. "We become masters of diplomacy," says Edward Mertz, assistant chief engineer at Pontiac, who was manager of the now-disbanded A-body project center. "It's impossible to work closely on a design without influencing it somewhat. But the center can't force a common part on a division." Indeed, many of G.M.'s engineers feel the project-center innovation has actually helped enhance the divisions' individuality, by freeing some of them to work on divisional projects.

The turnaround of the past few years has worked powerfully to lift G.M.'s self-esteem and spirit. Spirit, of course, is a nebulous part of management, difficult to quantify. G.M.'s state of mind has always been particularly hard to assess. Its elaborate management systems seem designed to function almost regardless of the people who work in them, and G.M. officers rarely waste much time telling outsiders how they feel about themselves or their company. They are practical men who choose to be judged by results.

Indeed, the great defect of Sloan's landmark book as a management treatise was that it dealt exclusively with the practical aspects of professional management. As Peter Drucker pointed out in a critique of *My Years with General Motors*, "Something essential is lacking: people, ideas, and, above all, passion and compassion and a commitment to something more, and larger, than just the business." Sloan himself, Drucker was quick to observe, excelled at leading men and inspiring them, and was a man of ideas and large commitment. But he did not talk about such matters, and it may well be that his paper legacy outlasted his personal legacy, contributing to the rather impersonal quality that has seemed to characterize G.M.'s management during much of its recent history.

Nevertheless, there is an inescapable difference between the spirit at G.M. headquarters these days and what was observable a few years back. John DeLorean, who was one of G.M.'s rising management stars, quit the company in 1973 complaining that it had "gotten to be totally insulated from the world." And Edward N. Cole retired from the presidency in 1974 with the gloomy remark that "the fun is gone . . . I wouldn't go into the automobile business again."

Today it is hard to find a top executive at G.M. who does not evidence enthusiasm for what he or the company is doing. The enthusiasm is most often expressed as excitement over the current "challenge" of the automobile business, and it is especially common among engineers. They agree that some of the fun may indeed have gone out of the business—as Mertz says, "You haven't got the same freedom; more of the targets are set in Washington." But meeting those targets has required a great deal of ingenuity and hard work, and the job has been enormously satisfying.

Indeed, the bottom line of change at G.M. is the company's state of mind—which today reflects a revivified sense of purpose and a much sharper understanding of the external world. As a practical example, it was difficult for engineers to muster much enthusiasm for their work on safety and emissions controls when the company was publicly condemning the requirements as onerous and ill conceived. G.M. has long since stopped complaining and has adopted a deliberately cooperative stance, in good part to restore its credibility and its battered public image. In doing so, it has transformed a major problem—the need for compliance with illogical and unfair policies—into a managerial and technical challenge.

More fundamentally, G.M.'s entire approach to its business has changed. The company's downsizing plan was its first comprehensive new strategic attack upon the marketplace in many years. And it was shaped by a far better understanding of the market's changing nature than the strategies of the immediate past. The new top-management team that took over in 1974, moreover, was especially capable of making the new strategies work. To a degree rare among G.M. top managers over the years, Murphy, Estes, and Terrell are all confident, relaxed, and straightforward men, good at speaking and at listening, and broad in their vision and experience.

Indeed, a case can be made that G.M. has passed through one of the major turning points of its history. One authority who holds this view is Eugene E. Jennings, professor of management at Michigan State University, a consultant to top executives of numerous American corporations and a close observer of G.M. for more than twenty years. "In the late 1960s and early 1970s, G.M. was one of the most insular and inner-directed companies around," he says. "Now, more than any other company in the auto business, and more than most companies anywhere, it has moved up to a higher level of organizational effectiveness. It has learned how to be outer-directed and strategic—to use its head, rather than trying to use its clout." Jennings thinks those practical managers at G.M. don't fully realize as yet what they have accomplished—but he predicts that they will within a few years as they see the results accumulate.

There are tough years ahead for General Motors, unquestionably, as well as for the rest of the industry. The tug-of-war between emissions controls and fuel economy, for example, will intensify sharply under the proposed emissions standards for 1981. Publicly, G.M. is committed to good citizenship on the subject—the company has learned to its sorrow that credibility suffers badly when it complains about unreachable standards and then subsequently manages to meet them. But by any realistic measure, the 1981 standards are irrationally severe, and, in terms of their costs, will levy enormous social disbenefits. People at G.M. do not talk much about the problem at present, but they may have to make the issue public at some point in the future.

The coming year, moreover, may challenge G.M.'s downsizing strategy. The new G.M. intermediates are not the spectacular improvements over their predecessors that the standard cars were, and they face much stiffer competition. Ford's compact Fairmont and Zephyr, for example, are elegant designs, cleverly engineered, and are functionally comparable to the G.M. intermediates.

The costs of redoing the entire product line are enormous, of course. G.M.'s R. and D. expenditures are running at an annual rate of well over $1 billion, which is equivalent to more than a third of 1976 net income ($2.9 billion, on revenues of $47 billion). By 1980, G.M. estimates, capital expenditures for the decade will have amounted to more than $25 billion, most of which will go to meet the demands of emissions, safety, and downsizing. And some tactical requirements are costly too. The company is selling Chevettes at a loss right now, for example—G.M. feels it must pay that price to establish itself more securely in the small end of the market.

Along with the problems, however, come opportunties. By downsizing the top of its line first, while competitors started from the bottom, G.M. has ended up with the standard-car market almost to itself for the next year or so. And that market is hardly the dinosaur preserve it may seem to be. Although all American cars are growing smaller, some will always be bigger than others. G.M. estimates that around 25 percent of the public will continue to want six-passenger cars into the foreseeable future.

Small cars, moreover, are turning out to be a great deal more profitable than the industry once believed them to be. Consumers at all but the rock-bottom level are evidently opting for as much automotive luxury as they can afford. As domestic automakers emerge from the struggle of meeting a concentration of expensive government demands, they can almost surely look to climbing rates of return. Those enormous capital outlays will be making a positive contribution too—they are hastening plant overhaul, providing opportunities for productivity gains and new operating efficiencies. Murphy sees no reason why G.M.s' return on shareholders' equity should not climb back to the level of the mid-1960s—consistently above 20 percent.

Indeed, to G.M.'s officers these days, the problems of the future look pretty pallid in comparison with those of the past few years. The system that Sloan built, with its capacity for change and evolution, has weathered a major crisis of adaptation and emerged stronger than ever. It is hard to imagine what might come along in the foreseeable future that could test General Motors more severely.

18

Problems of Matrix Organizations*

STANLEY M. DAVIS and PAUL R. LAWRENCE

N o organization design or method of management is perfect. And any form can suffer from a variety of problems that develop because of the design itself. This is particularly true when a company tries a new form. In this article we look at one relatively new organization form —the matrix—which has gained considerable popularity in recent years but which has some significant pathologies. Before discussing its ills, however, let us look for a moment at matrix management and organization (see Exhibit 1) and at how widespread the matrix is in U.S. industry today.

The list of well-known companies that are using some form of a matrix is becoming long and impressive. Take, for example, a company that has annual sales of $14 billion and employs about 400,000 people in scores of diverse businesses—General Electric. For decades, despite the diversity of its businesses, GE used one basic structure throughout its organization: five functional managers reporting to one general manager. Employing the logic that a company must organize to meet the particular needs of each business, some GE groups, divisions, and departments, which have found the pyramid form cumbersome, have turned to the matrix as a fundamental alternative.

In projecting its organization over the next ten years, GE management states in its Organization Planning Bulletin (September 1976):

> We've highlighted matrix organization . . . not because it's a bandwagon that we want you all to jump on, but rather that it's a complex, difficult, and sometimes frustrating form of organization to live with. It's also, however, a bellwether of things to come. But, when implemented well,

* Stanley M. Davis and Paul R. Lawrence, "Problems of Matrix Organizations," *Harvard Business Review*, May–June 1978. Copyright © 1978 by the President and Fellows of Harvard College; all rights reserved.

it does offer much of the best of both worlds. And all of us are going to have to learn how to utilize organization to prepare managers to increasingly deal with high levels of complexity and ambiguity in situations where they have to get results from people and components *not* under their direct control. . . .

Successful experience in operating under a matrix constitutes better preparation for an individual to run a huge diversified institution like General Electric—where so many complex, conflicting interests must be balanced—than the product and functional modes which have been our hallmark over the past twenty years.

Other major corporations, in diverse activities, such as Bechtel, Citibank, Dow Chemical, Shell Oil, Texas Instruments, and TRW, to mention a few, have also turned to the matrix. Based on our studies of the matrix in these companies, we believe that while some of the matrix's popularity is simply a passing fad, most uses of it are founded on solid business reasons that will persist. The matrix's most basic advantage over the familiar functional or product structure is that it facilitates a rapid management response to changing market and technical requirements. Further, it helps middle managers make trade-off decisions from a general management perspective.

Because the matrix is a relatively new form, however, the companies that have adopted it have of necessity been learning on a trial and error basis. The mistakes as well as the successes of these pioneers can be very informative to companies that follow their lead. Here, we present some of the more common problems that occur when a company uses a matrix form. For the sake of easy reference, we diagnose each pathology first, then discuss its prevention and treatment. By using this format, however, we do not mean to suggest that simple first-aid treatment of pathologies will cure them.

ILLS OF THE MATRIX

Many of the ailments we discuss do arise in more conventional organizations, but the matrix seems somewhat more vulnerable to these particular ones. It is wise, therefore, for managers thinking of adopting a matrix to be familiar with the diagnoses, prevention, and treatment of nine particular pathologies: tendencies toward anarchy, power struggles, severe groupitis, collapse during economic crunch, excessive overhead, sinking to lower levels, uncontrolled layering, navel gazing, and decision strangulation.

Tendencies toward Anarchy

A formless state of confusion where people do not recognize a "boss" to whom they feel responsible.

Diagnosis. Many managers who have had no firsthand familiarity with matrix organizations tend to have half-expressed fears that a matrix leads to anarchy. Are these concerns based on real hazards? Actually today, a considerable number of organizations are successfully using the matrix form, so we need not treat anarchy as a general hazard of the matrix. However, there are certain conditions or major misconceptions that could lead a company into the formless confusion that resembles anarchy.

Through firsthand experience we know of only one organization that, using a "latent" matrix form, quite literally came apart at the seams during a rather mild economic recession. Following a fast-growth strategy, this company used its high stock multiple to acquire, and then completely assimilate, smaller companies in the recreation equipment field. Within a period of about six months the company changed from an exciting success to a dramatic disaster. Its entire manufacturing, distribution, and financial systems went out of control leaving unfilled orders, closed factories, distressed inventories, and huge debts in their wake.

Of course, there are many possible reasons why this might have happened, but one perfectly reasonable explanation is that the organization design failed under stress. What was that design?

Essentially, the organization used a functional structure. As it acquired each small company, top management first encouraged the owners and general managers to leave, and then it attached the company's three basic functions of sales, production, and engineering to their counterparts in the parent organization. Within the parent marketing department, a young aggressive product manager would be assigned to develop for the acquired product line a comprehensive marketing plan that included making sales forecasts, promotion plans, pricing plans, projected earnings, and so forth. Once top management approved the plan, it told the selected product manager to hustle around and make his plan come true. This is where the latent matrix came in.

The product manager would find himself working across functional lines to try to coordinate production schedules, inventories, cash flow, and distribution patterns without any explicit and formal agreements about the nature of his relationships with the functional managers. Because he was locked into his approved marketing plan, when sales slipped behind schedule, his response was to exhort people to try harder rather than to cut back on production runs.

But once one or two things began to crumble, there was not enough reserve in the system to keep everything else from going wrong. As the product manager lost control, a power vacuum developed, into which the functional managers fell, each grabbing for total control. The result was that a mild recession triggered conditions approaching anarchy.

Prevention. We believe the lesson of this experience is loud and clear.

Organizations should not rely too much on an informal or latent matrix to coordinate critical tasks. Relationships between functional and product managers should be explicit so that people are in approximate agreement about who is to do what under various circumstances. Properly used, a matrix does not leave such matters in an indefinite status; it is a definite structure and not a "free form" organization.

A useful "anarchy index" is how many people in an organization do not recognize one boss to whom they feel responsible for a major part of their work. In a study of five medical schools, which are notoriously anarchical, the one with the most explicit matrix structure was also the one with the least number of "bossless" people.[1]

Treatment. Should the worst happen and a company plunge into anarchy, true crisis management would be the best response. The crisis response is really no mystery. The CEO must pull all key people and critical information into the center. He or she must personally make all important decisions on a round-the-clock schedule until the crisis is over. Then and only then can he undertake the work of reshaping the organization so that it can withstand any future shock such as a minor recession.

Power Struggles

Managers jockey for power in many organizations, but a matrix design almost encourages them to do so.

Diagnosis. The essence of a matrix is dual command. For such a form to survive there needs to be a balance of power, where its locus seems to shift constantly, each party always jockeying to gain an advantage. It is not enough simply to create the balance, but there must also be continual mechanisms for checking the imbalances that creep in.

In business organizations that operate with a balance of power form, there is a constant tendency toward imbalance. As long as each group or dimension in an organization tries to maximize its own advantage vis-à-vis others, there will be a continual balancing struggle for dominant power. A power struggle in a matrix is qualitatively different from that in a traditionally structured hierarchy because in the latter it is clearly illegitimate. In the matrix, however, power struggles are inevitable; the boundaries of authority and responsibility overlap prompting people to maximize their own advantage.

Prevention. Most top managers will find it exceedingly difficult to forestall all power struggles. Equal strength on the part of the two parties, however, will prevent struggles from reaching destructive heights.

---

[1] From the forthcoming article by M. R. Weisbord, M. P. Charns, and P. R. Lawrence, "Organizational Dilemmas of Academic Medical Centers," *Journal of Applied Behavioral Science*, vol. 14, no. 3.

Exhibit 1

WHAT IS A MATRIX?

The identifying feature of a matrix organization is that some managers report to two bosses rather than to the traditional single boss; there is a dual rather than a single chain of command.

Companies tend to turn to matrix forms:

1. When it is absolutely essential that they be highly responsive to two sectors simultaneously, such as markets and technology;
2. When they face uncertainties that generate very high information processing requirements; and
3. When they must deal with strong constraints on financial and/or human resources.

Matrix structures can help provide both flexibility and balanced decision making, but at the price of complexity.

Matrix organization is more than a matrix structure. It must be reinforced by matrix systems such as dual control and evaluation systems, by leaders who operate comfortably with lateral decision making, and by a culture that can negotiate open conflict and a balance of power.

In most matrix organizations there are dual command responsibilities assigned to functional departments (marketing, production, engineering, and so forth) and to product or market departments. The former are oriented to specialized in-house resources while the latter focus on outputs. Other matrices are split between area-based departments and either products or functions.

Every matrix contains three unique and critical roles; the top manager who heads up and balances the dual chains of command, the matrix bosses (functional, product, or area) who share subordinates, and the managers who report to two different matrix bosses. Each of these roles has its special requirements.

Aerospace companies were the first to adopt the matrix form, but now companies in many industries (chemical, banking, insurance, packaged goods, electronics, computer, and so forth) and in different fields (hospitals, government agencies, and professional organizations) are adapting different forms of the matrix.

Friendly competition should be encouraged, but all-out combat severely punished. Managers in a matrix should push for their advantages but never with the intention of eliminating those with whom they share power, and always with a perspective that encompasses both positions.

Treatment. The best way to ensure that power struggles do not undermine the matrix is to make managers on the power axes aware that to win power absolutely is to lose it ultimately. These managers need to see that the total victory of one dimension only ends the balance, finishes the duality of command, and destroys the matrix. They must see this sharing of power as an underlying principle, before and during all of the ensuing and inevitable power struggles.

Matrix managers have to recognize that they need worthy adversaries, counterparts who can match them, to turn the conflict to constructive ends. For this successful outcome three things are necessary.

First, matrix managers always have to maintain an institutional point of view, seeing their struggles from a larger, shared perspective. Second, they have to jointly agree to remove other matrix managers who, through weakness or whatever inability, are losing irretrievable ground. And, third, that they replace these weak managers with the strongest available people —even if to do so means placing very strong managers in weakened parts of the organization and reversing their power initiatives.

Another key element in stopping power struggles before they get out of hand and destroy the balance is the top level superior to whom the duelling managers report. Because of this element, the matrix is a paradox—a shared-power system that depends on a strong individual, one who does not share the authority that is delegated to him (say by the board), to arbitrate between his power-sharing subordinates. The top manager has many vehicles for doing this: the amount of time he spends with one side of the matrix or the other, pay differentials, velocity of promotion, direct orders issued to one dimension and not to the other, and so forth. What he must do above all, however, is protect the weak dimension in the organization, not necessarily the weak manager in charge of that dimension.

Severe Groupitis

The mistaken belief that matrix management is the same as group decision making.

Diagnosis. The confusion of matrix behavior with group decision making probably arises from the fact that a matrix often evolves out of new project or business teams, which do suggest a group decision process. Under many circumstances, of course, it is perfectly sensible for managers to make decisions in groups. But managers should expect difficulties to arise if they believe group decision making to be the essence of matrix behavior.

We have seen one matrix organization that had a severe case of "groupitis." This multiproduct electronics company had a product manager and a product team, comprised of specialists drawn from the ranks of every functional department, assigned to every product. So far so good. But somehow the idea that the matrix structure requires that *all* business decisions be hammered out in group meetings became prevalent in the organization. To make decisions in other ways was considered illegitimate and not in the spirit of matrix operations.

Many of the decisions that had to be made about each product involved detailed matters with which only one or two people were regularly conversant. Yet all team members were constrained to listen to these issues being discussed until a decision was made, and were even expected to participate in the discussion and influence the choice. Some individuals seemed to enjoy the steady diet of meetings and the chance to practice being a generalist.

However, a large number of people felt that their time was being wasted and would have preferred leaving the decisions to the most informed people. The engineers, in particular, complained that the time they were spending in meetings was robbing them of opportunities to strengthen their special competence and identities. As well as noting these personal reactions, senior managers reported a general disappointment with the speed and flexibility of organizational responses.

Prevention.   Because the whole idea of a matrix organization is still unfamiliar to many managers, it is understandable that they confuse it with processes such as group decision making. The key to prevention is education. Top managers need to accompany their strategic choice to move toward a matrix with a serious educational effort to clarify to all participants what a matrix is and what it is not.

Treatment.   In the case of the multiproducts electronics company, the problem came to light while we were researching the matrix approach. Once senior people had clearly diagnosed the problem, it was 90 percent cured. Top management emphatically stated that there was nothing sacred about group decisions and that it was not sensible to have all product team members involved all the time. Once the line between individual and group matters was drawn according to who had information really relevant to a decision, meetings became fewer and smaller and work proceeded on a more economical and responsive basis. The concept of teamwork was put in perspective: as often as necessary and as little as possible.

Collapse during Economic Crunch

When business declines, the matrix becomes the scapegoat for poor management and is discarded.

Diagnosis.   Matrix organizations that blossom during periods of rapid growth and prosperity sometimes are cast away during periods of economic decline. On reflection, we can understand this. In prosperous times, companies often expand their business lines and the markets they serve. The ensuing complexity may turn them toward matrix management and organization.

However, if these companies follow the normal business cycle, there will be a period of two to five years before they experience another economic crunch which is more than enough time for the matrix concept to spread throughout a company. By that time the matrix occupies a central place in company conversations and is a familiar part of these organizations. Although there may still be some problems, the matrix seems there to stay.

When the down part of the economic cycle begins, senior management in these companies may become appreciably bothered by the conflict between subordinates as well as by the apparent slowness with which they respond to the situation. "We need decisive action" is their rallying cry.

In an authoritarian structure top management can act quickly because it need not consider the spectrum of opinion. Thinking there is no time for organizational toys and tinkering, the top level managers take command in an almost, but not quite, forgotten way, and ram their directives down the line. The matrix is "done in."

Prevention.   Top management can prevent this kind of collapse of the matrix by employing general managerial excellence, independent of the matrix, long before the crunch arrives. Good planning, for example, can often forecast downturns in the economic cycle. Corporate structures such as the matrix should not have to change because of standard changes in the business cycle. When management planning has been poor, however, the matrix is a readily available scapegoat.

Companies that experience severe economic crunches often make drastic changes in many directions at once: trimming product lines, closing offices, making massive personnel and budget cuts, and tightening managerial controls. The matrix is often done in during this period for several reasons: it represents too great a risk; "it never really worked properly" and giving it the coup de grace can disguise the failure of implementation; and the quality of decision making had not improved performance sufficiently to counterbalance the hard times. Measures management can take to prevent this pathology do not lie within the matrix itself, as much as with improvements in basic managerial skills and planning.

A real estate and construction company provides an example of how a company can anticipate and flexibly respond to an economic crunch that demonstrates the strength rather than the weakness of the matrix. The company has developed a structure as well as procedures that are especially well suited to the economic uncertainties of the business. These include a set of fully owned subsidiaries each the equivalent of a functional department in a manufacturing company and each the "home base" for varied specialists needed to execute all phases of a major building project. The heads of the subsidiaries act as chief salesmen for their various services, and often head up the bidding teams that put together sophisticated proposals.

As a proposal project proceeds, the selected project manager is drawn into the team in anticipation of securing the contract. This ensures an orderly transition to the project management phase. The project office is given first-line responsibility for control of costs, schedules, and quality of the project, but the top management team from the parent company reviews the project regularly as a backup.

The company has used the matrix to advantage in weathering major shifts in both the availability of business by market segment, for example, from schools to hospitals, and the level of construction activity. It maintains a cadre of professional specialists and project managers, who can be kept busy during the lows of the cycle, which it rapidly expands during the highs by subcontracting for temporary services.

Treatment.   This is one pathology that requires preventive treatment; we do not know of any cure. When the matrix does collapse during an economic crunch, it is very unlikely that it can be resurrected. At best, the organization will go back to its pendulum days, alternating between the centralized management of the crunch period and the decentralized freedoms of more prosperous times. Even if top management should try again, it is likely to get a negative response from lower level managers. "They said they were committed to the matrix, but at the first sign of hard times all the nice words about the advantages of the matrix turned out to be just that—nice words." If a company's conditioned response to hard times is to retrench, it should not attempt a matrix in the first place.

Excessive Overhead

The fear of high costs associated with a matrix.

Diagnosis.   On the face of it, a matrix organization would seem to double management costs because of its dual chain of command. This issue deserves thoughtful consideration.

The limited amount of research on matrix overhead costs indicates that in the initial phases overhead costs do in fact rise, but that, as a matrix matures, these extra costs disappear and are offset by productivity gains.[2] Our experience supports this finding. In a large electronics company we observed in some detail how initial overhead increases not only necessarily occur in a matrix but also how they can inflate unnecessarily. In this case, the company decided to employ the matrix design from the outset in setting up its new operating division at a new plant site.

This unique organizational experiment had a number of positive attributes, but one of its problems was with overhead costs. In staffing the new division, top management filled every functional office and every

---

[2] C. J. Middleton, "How to Set up a Project Organization," *Harvard Business Review*, March–April 1967, p. 73.

product manager's slot with one full-time person. This resulted in a relatively small division having top level managers as well as full-time functional group and full-time product managers. Within months, however, this top heavy division was pared down to more reasonable staffing levels; by assigning individuals to two or more slots, management got costs under control.

Prevention. The division's problem was caused by top management's assumption that each managerial slot requires a full-time incumbent. Overstaffing is much less liable to occur when an organization evolves gradually from a conventional design into a matrix, and managers perform as both functional and product managers. While this technique can be justified as a transition strategy, it also has its hazards. A safer route is to assign managers roles on the same side of the matrix (i.e., two functional jobs or two product management jobs).

As a final argument against the fear of overhead costs, consider that no well-run organization would adopt a matrix structure without the longer run expectation that, at a given level of output, the costs of operations would be lower than with other organizational forms. In what way can such economics be achieved?

The potential economies come from two general sources: fewer bad decisions and less featherbedding. First and most important, the matrix can improve quality of business decisions because it helps bring the needed information and emphasis to bear on critical decisions in a timely fashion. The second source, less featherbedding, is not so obvious, but potentially of greater significance. How can it work?

Treatment. Perhaps the clearest example of the matrix's potential to reduce redundancies in human resources is the way some consulting organizations employ it. These firms usually set up a matrix of functional specialists against client or account managers. The body of other consultants are grouped with their fellow specialists but are available for assignment to projects under the leadership of account or client managers.

From an accounting standpoint, therefore, consultants' time is directly billed to clients' accounts when they are working for an account or engagement manager. Otherwise, their time is charged against the budget of their function manager. The firm's nonbillable costs are, therefore, very conspicuous—both by department and by individual consultant. Of course, some time charged to functional departments, such as background study, research work, and time between assignments should by no means be thought of as wasted. But management can budget such time in advance so that it can scrutinize the variances from the budget.

As one senior manager in a consulting firm put it, "There is no place to hide in a matrix organization." This fact makes clear-cut demands on middle level people and consequently puts pressure on them to produce. For the long-term good of both the people involved and the organization, top managers need to keep such pressures from becoming too strong. Because it is perfectly possible to get too much as well as too little pressure, a creative tension is sought.

Sinking to Lower Levels

The matrix has some difficulty in staying alive at high levels of a corporation, and a corresponding tendency to sink to group and division level where it thrives.

Diagnosis.   Sinking may occur for two reasons. Either senior management has not understood or been able to implement the matrix concept as well as lower level managers, or the matrix has found its appropriate place. For example, if a company sets up a matrix between its basic functional and product groups, the product managers never truly relinquish their complete control, and the matrix fails to take hold at the corporate level.

But, say, one or two of the managers find the idea to be useful within their divisions. Their own functional specialists and project leaders can share the power they delegate and the design can survive within subunits of the corporation. For example, Dow Chemical's attempt to maintain the product/geography balance at the top failed, but the function/product balance held within the geographic areas for several years.

When sinking occurs because of top management misunderstanding, it is likely to occur in conjunction with other pathologies, particularly power struggles. For instance, if many senior executives consider adopting the matrix idea, but only one or a few really become convinced of its worth, there is a danger: those at the top who espouse a philosophy and method they did not employ themselves will be pitted against those who are able to show that it does work.

Prevention.   If the corporate top management thinks through which dimensions of the company it must balance, and at what level of aggregation, it can keep the matrix from sinking. For example, top managers should ask themselves if all the business units need to be balanced by central functional departments. If the answer is no, then some business units should operate as product divisions with the traditional pyramid of command, while others share functional services in a partial matrix. However, sinking is not always bad and should be prevented only when it indicates that an appropriate design is disintegrating.

Treatment.   Before matrix management can run smoothly, it must be in the proper location. As often as not, when a matrix sinks, it may simply be experiencing a healthy adjustment, and ought to be thought of as settling rather than as sinking. Settling is likely to occur during the early stages of a matrix's evolution and leads to manageable matrix units.

The question of size is a great concern for many managers who ask, in effect, "That sounds great for a $250-million company with a few thousand employees, but can it work for a $2-billion or $3-billion company with 50,000 employees? Its entire company is the size of one of our divisions." Our experience indicates that matrix management and organization seems to function better when no more than 500 managers are involved in matrix relationships. But that does not rule out the $2-billion to $3-billion company. In a company of 5,000 only about 50 managers are likely to be in the matrix; so in a company with 50,000 employees only about 500 may need to be involved in dual reporting lines. With that number, the people who need to coordinate regularly are able to do so through communication networks that are based on personal relations.

Whatever the size unit in which the matrix operates, the important thing is for management to have reasoned carefully from an analysis of the task to the design of the organization. Then, if settling occurs, it should be seen not as a pathology but as a self-adjustment that suggests the organization's capacity to evolve with growth.

Uncontrolled Layering

Matrices which lie within matrices which lie within matrices result frequently from the dynamics of power rather than from the logic of design.

Diagnosis. Sometimes matrices not only sink but also cascade down the organization and filter through several levels and across several divisions. This layering process may or may not be pathological. In fact, it may be a rational and logical development of the matrix, but we include it briefly here because it sometimes creates more problems than it solves. In terms of the metaphor we have used in this article, layering is a pathology only if the matrix begins to metastasize. When this occurs, organization charts began to resemble blueprints for a complex electronic machine, relationships become unnecessarily complex, and the matrix form may become more of a burden than it is worth.

Prevention and Treatment. The best remedies for uncontrolled layering are careful task analysis and reduced power struggles. We have seen a few cases where one dimension of a matrix was clearly losing power to the other, so, adapting an "if you can't beat 'em, join 'em" philosophy, it created a matrix within its own dimension. A product unit, for example, developed its own functional *expertise* distinct from the functional *units* at the next level up. The best defense was a good offense, or so it seemed.

In two other cases, the international divisions of two large companies each created its own matrix by adding business managers as an overlay to its geographic format, without reconciling these with the managers who ran the domestic product/service groups. In each case, adequate conceptualization by top managers would probably have simplified the organization design and forestalled the layering, which occurred because of power maneuvers. Management can treat this unhealthy state best by rebalancing the matrix so that no manager of one dimension is either too threatened or pushed too hard toward a power goal.

Matrix design is complex enough without the addition of power struggles. A well-conceptualized matrix is bound to be less complex and easier to manage than one that is illogically organized.

Navel Gazing

Managers in a matrix can succumb to excessive internal preoccupation and lose touch with the marketplace.

Diagnosis. Because a matrix fosters considerable interdependence of people and tasks and demands negotiating skills on the part of its members, matrix managers sometimes tend to get absorbed in internal relations at the expense of paying attention to the world outside the organization, particularly to clients. When this happens, an organization spends more energy ironing out its own disputes than in serving its customers. The outward focus disappears because the short-term demands of daily working life have yet to be worked through.

The navel gazers are not at all lethargic; rather they are involved in a heated fraternal love/hate affair with each other. This inward preoccupation is more common in the early phases of a matrix, when the new behaviors are being learned, than in matrices that have been operating for a few years.

Prevention. Whatever other pathologies develop in a matrix, attention to their cure is bound to increase the internal focus of the members; so prevention of other pathologies will certainly reduce the likelihood of this one occurring. Awareness of the tendency will also help. Since the product dimension of the organization generally has a more external focus than the resource dimension, the responsibility for preventing an excessive introspection is not equally distributed. The product dimension people can help the others keep perspective, but a strong marketing orientation is the best preventative of all.

Treatment. If the managers in the matrix are navel gazing, the first step in the treatment is to make these managers aware of the effects. Are customers complaining a lot, or at least more than usual? Managers need to confront internal conflict, but also to recognize that confrontation is secondary to maintaining effective external relationships. Navel gazing generally occurs when the matrix has been fully initiated but not yet debugged. People accept it, but they are engrossed in figuring out how to make it work.

The second step is to treat the inward focus as a symptom of the underlying issue: how to institutionalize matrix relationships so that they become familiar and comfortable routines, and so that people can work through them without becoming obsessed by them. Finally, it must always be remembered that any form of organization is only a means and should never become an end in itself.

Decision Strangulation

Too much democracy, not enough action?

Can moving into a matrix lead to the strangulation of the decision process, into endless delays for debate, for clearing with everybody in sight? Will decisions, no matter how well thought through, be made too late to be of use? Will too many people have power to water down all bold initiatives of veto them outright? Such conditions can arise in a matrix. We have in mind three situations—constant clearing, escalation of conflict, and unilateral style—each calling for slightly different preventive action and treatment.

Constant Clearing. In one company we know of, various functional specialists who reported to a second boss, a product manager, picked up the idea that they had to clear all issues with their own functional bosses before agreeing to product decisions. This meant that every issue had to be discussed in at least two meetings, if not more. During the first meeting, the specialists and the product manager could only review the facts of the issue, which was then tabled until, at the second meeting, the specialists cleared the matter with their functional bosses—who by this process were each given a de facto veto over product decisions.

This impossible clearing procedure represented, in our view, a failure of delegation, not of the matrix. One needs to ask why the functional specialists could not be trusted to act on the spot in regard to most product decisions in ways that would be consistent with the general guidelines of their functional departments? Either the specialists were poorly selected, too inexperienced and badly informed, or their superiors were lacking in a workable degree of trust of one another. Regardless, this problem, and its prevention and treatment, needs to be addressed directly without making a scapegoat of the matrix.

Escalation of Conflict. Another possible source of decision strangulation in matrix organizations occurs when managers frequently or constantly refer decisions up the dual chain of command. Seeing that one advantage of the conventional single chain of command is that two disagreeing peers can go to their shared boss for a resolution, managers unfamiliar with the matrix worry about this problem almost more than any other. They look at a matrix and realize that the nearest shared boss might be the CEO, who could be five or six echelons up. They realize that not too many problems can be pushed up to the CEO for resolution without creating the ultimate in information overload. So, they think, will not the inevitable disagreement lead to a tremendous pileup of unresolved conflict?

Certainly, this can happen in a malfunctioning matrix. Whether it does happen depends primarily on the depth of understanding that exists about required matrix behavior on the part of managers in the dual structure. Let us envision the following scene: a manager with two bosses gets sharply conflicting instructions from his product and his functional bosses. When he tries to reconcile his instructions without success, he quite properly asks for a session with his two bosses to resolve the matter. The three people meet, but the discussion bogs down, no resolution is reached, and neither boss gives way.

The two bosses then appeal the problem up a level to their respective superiors in each of the two chains of command. This is the critical step. If the two superiors properly understand matrix behavior, they will first ascertain whether the dispute reflects an unresolved broader policy issue. If it does not, they know their proper step is to teach their subordinates to resolve the problem themselves—not to solve it for them. In short, they would not let the unresolved problem escalate, but would force it back to the proper level for solution, and insist that the solution be found promptly.

Often, conflict cannot be resolved; it can, however, be managed, which it must be if the matrix is to work. Any other course of action would represent management's failure to comprehend the essential nature of the design.

Unilateral Style. A third possible reason for decision strangulation in a matrix system can arise from a very different source—personal style. Some managers have the feeling they are not truly managing if they are not in a position to make crisp, unilateral decisions. Identifying leadership with decisive action, they become very frustrated when they have to engage in carefully reasoned debates about the wisdom of what they want to do.

Such a manager is likely to feel frustrated even in regard to a business problem whose resolution will vitally affect functions other than his own, such as in a company that is experiencing critical dual pressure from the marketplace and from advancing technology. A matrix that deliberately induces simultaneous decision making between two or more perspectives is likely to frustrate such a person even further.

If managers start feeling emasculated by bilateral decision making, they are certain to be unhappy in a matrix organization. In such cases the strangulation is in the eye of the beholder. Such people must work on their personal decision-making style or look for employment in a nonmatrix organization.

AT LAST, LEGITIMACY

We do not recommend that every company adopt the matrix form. But where it is relevant, it can become an important part of an effective managerial process. Like any new method it may develop serious bugs, but the experiences that many companies are acquiring with this organization form can now help others realize its benefits and avoid its pitfalls.

The matrix seems to have spread despite itself and its pathologies: what was necessary was made desirable. It is difficult and complex, and human flexibility is required to arrive at organizational flexibility.

But the reverse is also true; success has given the form legitimacy, and, as the concept spreads, familiarity seems to reduce the resistance and difficulties people experience in using the matrix. Managers are now beginning to say, "It isn't that new or different after all." This familiarity is a sign of acceptance, more than of change or moderation of the design.

For generations, managers lived with the happy fiction of dotted lines, indicating that a second reporting line was necessary if not formal. The result had always been a sort of executive ménage à trois, a triangular arrangement where the manager had one legitimate relationship (the reporting line) and one that existed but was not granted equal privileges (the dotted line).

As executives develop greater confidence with the matrix form, they bring the dotted line relationship out of the closet, and grant it legitimacy.

Each time another organization turns to the matrix, it has a larger and more varied number of predecessors that have chartered the way. The examples of wider applicability suggest that the matrix is becoming less and less an experiment and more and more a mature formulation in organization design. As more organizations travel the learning curve, the curve itself becomes an easier one to climb. Similarly, as more managers gain experience operating in matrix organizations, they are bound to spread this experience as some of them move, as they inevitably will, into other organizations.

We believe that in the future matrix organizations will become almost commonplace and that managers will speak less of the difficulties and pathologies of the matrix than of its advantages and benefits.

_____ 19 ____

Organization Design:
An Information Processing View*

JAY R. GALBRAITH

THE INFORMATION PROCESSING MODEL

A basic proposition is that the greater the uncertainty of the task, the greater the amount of information that has to be processed between decision makers during the execution of the task. If the task is well understood prior to performing it, much of the activity can be preplanned. If it is not understood, then during the actual task execution more knowledge is acquired which leads to changes in resource allocations, schedules, and priorities. All these changes require information processing *during* task performance. Therefore *the greater the task uncertainty, the greater the amount of information that must be processed among decision makers during task execution in order to achieve a given level of performance.* The basic effect of uncertainty is to limit the ability of the organization to preplan or to make decisions about activities in advance of their execution. Therefore it is hypothesized that the observed variations in organizational forms are variations in the strategies of organizations to (1) increase their ability to preplan, (2) increase their flexibility to adapt to their inability to preplan, or (3) to decrease the level of performance required for continued viability. Which strategy is chosen depends on the relative costs of the strategies. The function of the framework is to identify these strategies and their costs.

* Reprinted from "Organizational Design: An Information Processing View," by Jay R. Galbraith, *Interfaces,* vol. 4, no. 3 (May 1974), pp. 28–36, published by the Institute of Management Sciences.

THE MECHANISTIC MODEL

This framework is best developed by keeping in mind a hypothetical organization. Assume it is large and employs a number of specialist groups and resources in providing the output. After the task has been divided into specialist subtasks, the problem is to integrate the subtasks around the completion of the global task. This is the problem of organization design. The behaviors that occur in one subtask cannot be judged as good or bad *per se*. The behaviors are more effective or ineffective depending upon the behaviors of the other subtask performers. There is a design problem because the executors of the behaviors cannot communicate with all the roles with whom they are interdependent. Therefore the design problem is to create mechanisms that permit coordinated action across large numbers of interdependent roles. Each of these mechanisms, however, has a limited range over which it is effective at handling the information requirements necessary to coordinate the interdependent roles. As the amount of uncertainty increases, and therefore information processing increases, the organization must adopt integrating mechanisms which increase its information processing capabilities.

1.   Coordination by Rules or Programs

For routine predictable tasks March and Simon have identified the use of rules or programs to coordinate behavior between interdependent subtasks [March and Simon, 1958, Chap. 6]. To the extent that job related situations can be predicted in advance, and behaviors specified for these situations, programs allow an interdependent set of activities to be performed without the need for interunit communication. Each role occupant simply executes the behavior which is appropriate for the task related situation with which he is faced.

2.   Hierarchy

As the organization faces greater uncertainty its participants face situations for which they have no rules. At this point the hierarchy is employed on an exception basis. The recurring job situations are programmed with rules while infrequent situations are referred to that level in the hierarchy where a global perspective exists for all affected subunits. However, the hierarchy also has a limited range. As uncertainty increases the number of exceptions increases until the hierarchy becomes overloaded.

3.   Coordination by Targets or Goals

As the uncertainty of the organization's task increases, coordination increasingly takes place by specifying outputs, goals or targets [March and Simon, 1958, p. 145]. Instead of specifying specific behaviors to be enacted, the organization undertakes processes to set goals to be achieved and the employees select the behaviors which lead to goal accomplishment. Planning reduces the amount of information processing in the hierarchy by increasing the amount of discretion exercised at lower levels. Like the use of rules, planning achieves integrated action and also eliminates the need for continuous communication among interdependent subunits as long as task performance stays within the planned task specifications, budget limits and within targeted completion dates. If it does not, the hierarchy is again employed on an exception basis.

The ability of an organization to coordinate interdependent tasks depends on its ability to compute meaningful subgoals to guide subunit action. When uncertainty increases because of introducing new products, entering new markets, or employing new technologies these subgoals are incorrect. The result is more exceptions, more information processing, and an overloaded hierarchy.

DESIGN STRATEGIES

The ability of an organization to successfully utilize coordination by goal setting, hierarchy, and rules depends on the combination of the frequency of exceptions and the capacity of the hierarchy to handle them. As the task uncertainty increases the organization must again take organization design action. It can proceed in either of two general ways. First, it can act in two ways to reduce the amount of information that is processed. And second, the organization can act in two ways to increase its capacity to handle more information. The two methods for reducing the need for information and the two methods for increasing processing capacity are shown schematically in Figure 1. The effect of all these actions is to reduce the number of exceptional cases referred upward into the organization through hierarchical channels. The assumption is that the critical limiting factor of an organizational form is its ability to handle the non-routine, consequential events that cannot be anticipated and planned for in advance. The non-programmed events place the greatest communication load on the organization.

1.   Creation of Slack Resources

As the number of exceptions begin to overload the hierarchy, one response is to increase the planning targets so that fewer exceptions occur.

Figure 1
Organization Design Strategies

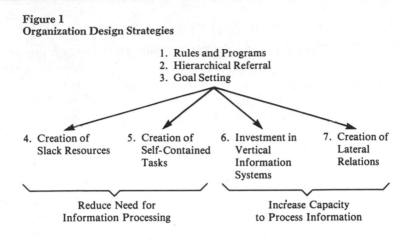

1. Rules and Programs
2. Hierarchical Referral
3. Goal Setting

4. Creation of Slack Resources
5. Creation of Self-Contained Tasks
6. Investment in Vertical Information Systems
7. Creation of Lateral Relations

Reduce Need for Information Processing

Increase Capacity to Process Information

For example, completion dates can be extended until the number of exceptions that occur are within the existing information processing capacity of the organization. This has been the practice in solving job shop scheduling problems [Pounds, 1963]. Job shops quote delivery times that are long enough to keep the scheduling problem within the computational and information processing limits of the organization. Since every job shop has the same problem standard lead times evolve in the industry. Similarly, budget targets could be raised, buffer inventories employed, etc. The greater the uncertainty, the greater the magnitude of the inventory, lead time or budget needed to reduce an overload.

All of these examples have a similar effect. They represent the use of slack resources to reduce the amount of interdependence between subunits [March and Simon, 1958, Cyert and March, 1963]. This keeps the required amount of information within the capacity of the organization to process it. Information processing is reduced because an exception is less likely to occur and reduced interdependence means that fewer factors need to be considered simultaneously when an exception does occur.

The strategy of using slack resources has its costs. Relaxing budget targets has the obvious cost of requiring more budget. Increasing the time to completion date has the effect of delaying the customer. Inventories require the investment of capital funds which could be used elsewhere. Reduction of design optimization reduces the performance of the article being designed. Whether slack resources are used to reduce information or not depends on the relative cost of the other alternatives.

The design choices are: (1) among which factors to change (lead time, overtime, machine utilization, etc.) to create the slack, and (2) by what amount should the factor be changed. Many operations research models are useful in choosing factors and amounts. The time-cost trade off problem in project networks is a good example.

2. Creation of Self-Contained Tasks

The second method of reducing the amount of information processed is to change the subtask groupings from resource (input) based to output based categories and give each group the resources it needs to supply the output. For example, the functional organization could be changed to product groups. Each group would have its own product engineers, process engineers, fabricating and assembly operations, and marketing activities. In other situations, groups can be created around product lines, geographical areas, projects, client groups, markets, etc., each of which would contain the input resources necessary for creation of the output.

The strategy of self-containment shifts the basis of the authority structure from one based on input, resource skill, or occupational categories to one based on output or geographical categories. The shift reduces the amount of information processing through several mechanisms. First, it reduces the amount of output diversity faced by a single collection of resources. For example, a professional organization with multiple skill specialties providing service to three different client groups must schedule the use of these specialties across three demands for their services and determine priorities when conflicts occur. But, if the organization changed to three groups, one for each client category, each with its own full complement of specialties, the schedule conflicts across client groups disappear and there is no need to process information to determine priorities.

The second source of information reduction occurs through a reduced division of labor. The functional or resource specialized structure pools the demand for skills across all output categories. In the example above each client generates approximately one-third of the demand for each skill. Since the division of labor is limited by the extent of the market, the division of labor must decrease as the demand decreases. In the professional organization, each client group may have generated a need for one-third of a computer programmer. The functional organization would have hired one programmer and shared him across the groups. In the self-contained structure there is insufficient demand in each group for a programmer so the professionals must do their own programming. Specialization is reduced but there is no problem of scheduling the programmer's time across the three possible uses for it.

The cost of the self-containment strategy is the loss of resource specialization. In the example, the organization forgoes the benefit of a specialist in computer programming. If there is physical equipment, there is a loss of economies of scale. The professional organization would require three machines in the self-contained form but only a large time-shared machine in the functional form. But those resources which have large economies of scale or for which specialization is necessary may remain centralized. Thus, it is the degree of self-containment that is the variable. The greater the degree of uncertainty, other things equal, the greater the degree of self-containment.

The design choices are the basis for the self-contained structure and the number of resources to be contained in the groups. No groups are completely self-contained or they would not be part of the same organization. But one product divisionalized firm may have eight of fifteen functions in the division while another may have twelve of fifteen in the divisions. Usually accounting, finance, and legal services are centralized and shared. Those functions which have economies of scale, require specialization or are necessary for control remain centralized and not part of the self-contained group.

The first two strategies reduced the amount of information by lower performance standards and creating small autonomous groups to provide the output. Information is reduced because an exception is less likely to occur and fewer factors need to be considered when an exception does occur. The next two strategies accept the performance standards and division of labor as given and adapt the organization so as to process the new information which is created during task performance.

3.   Investment in Vertical Information Systems

The organization can invest in mechanisms which allow it to process information acquired during task performance without overloading the hierarchical communication channels. The investment occurs according to the following logic. After the organization has created its plan or set of targets for inventories, labor utilization, budgets, and schedules, unanticipated events occur which generate exceptions requiring adjustments to the original plan. At some point when the number of exceptions becomes substantial, it is preferable to generate a new plan rather than make incremental changes with each exception. The issue is then how frequently should plans be revised—yearly, quarterly, or monthly? The greater the frequency of replanning the greater the resources, such as clerks, computer time, input-output devices, etc., required to process information about relevant factors.

The cost of information processing resources can be minimized if the language is formalized. Formalization of a decision-making language simply means that more information is transmitted with the same number of symbols. It is assumed that information processing resources are consumed in proportion to the number of symbols transmitted. The accounting system is an example of a formalized language.

Providing more information, more often, may simply overload the decision maker. Investment may be required to increase the capacity of the decision maker by employing computers, various man-machine combinations, assistants-to, etc. The cost of this strategy is the cost of the information processing resources consumed in transmitting and processing data.

The design variables of this strategy are the decision frequency, the degree of formalization of language, and the type of decision mechanism which will make the choice. This strategy is usually operationalized by creating redundant information channels which transmit data from the point of origination upward in the hierarchy where the point of decision rests. If data is formalized and quantifiable, this strategy is effective. If the relevant data are qualitative and ambiguous, then it may prove easier to bring the decision down to where the information exists.

4.   Creation of Lateral Relationships

The best strategy is to employ selectively joint decision processes which cut across lines of authority. This strategy moves the level of decision making down in the organization to where the information exists but does so without reorganizing around self-contained groups. There are several types of lateral decision processes. Some processes are usually referred to as the informal organization. However, these informal processes do not always arise spontaneously out of the needs of the task. This is particularly true in multinational organizations in which participants are separated by physical barriers, language differences, and cultural differences. Under these circumstances lateral processes need to be designed. The lateral processes evolve as follows with increases in uncertainty.

4.1.   Direct Contact.   Between managers who share a problem. If a problem arises on the shop floor, the foreman can simply call the design engineer, and they can jointly agree upon a solution. From an information processing view, the joint decision prevents an upward referral and unloads the hierarchy.

4.2.   Liaison Roles.   When the volume of contacts between any two departments grows, it becomes economical to set up a specialized role to handle this communication. Liaison men are typical examples of specialized roles designed to facilitate communication between two interdependent departments and to bypass the long lines of communication involved in upward referral. Liaison roles arise at lower and middle levels of management.

4.3.   Task Forces.   Direct contact and liaison roles, like the integration mechanisms before them, have a limited range of usefulness. They work when two managers or functions are involved. When problems arise involving seven or eight departments, the decision making capacity of direct contacts is exceeded. Then these problems must be referred upward. For uncertain, interdependent tasks such situations arise frequently. Task forces are a form of horizontal contact which is designed for problems of multiple departments.

The task force is made up of representatives from each of the affected departments. Some are full-time members, others may be part-time. The task force is a temporary group. It exists only as long as the problem remains. When a solution is reached, each participant returns to his normal tasks.

To the extent that they are successful, task forces remove problems from higher levels of the hierarchy. The decisions are made at lower levels in the organization. In order to guarantee integration, a group problem solving approach is taken. Each affected subunit contributes a member and therefore provides the information necessary to judge the impact on all units.

4.4. Teams. The next extension is to incorporate the group decision process into the permanent decision processes. That is, as certain decisions consistently arise, the task forces become permanent. These groups are labeled teams. There are many design issues concerned in team decision making such as at what level do they operate, who participates, etc. [Galbraith, 1973, Chaps. 6 and 7] One design decision is particularly critical. This is the choice of leadership. Sometimes a problem exists largely in one department so that the department manager is the leader. Sometimes the leadership passes from one manager to another. As a new product moves to the market place, the leader of the new product team is first the technical manager followed by the production and then the marketing manager. The result is that if the team cannot reach a consensus decision and the leader decides, the goals of the leader are consistent with the goals of the organization for the decision in question. But quite often obvious leaders cannot be found. Another mechanism must be introduced.

4.5 Integrating Roles. The leadership issue is solved by creating a new role—an integrating role [Lawrence and Lorsch, 1967, Chap. 3]. These roles carry the labels of product managers, program managers, project managers, unit managers (hospitals), materials managers, etc. After the role is created, the design problem is to create enough power in the role to influence the decision process. These roles have power even when no one reports directly to them. They have some power because they report to the general manager. But if they are selected so as to be unbiased with respect to the groups they integrate and to have technical competence, they have expert power. They collect information and equalize power differences due to preferential access to knowledge and information. The power equalization increases trust and the quality of the joint decision process. But power equalization occurs only if the integrating role is staffed with someone who can exercise expert power in the form of persuasion and informal influences rather than exert the power of rank or authority.

4.6. Managerial Linking Roles. As tasks become more uncertain, it is more difficult to exercise expert power. The role must get more power of the formal authority type in order to be effective at coordinating the joint decisions which occur at lower levels of the organization. This position power changes the nature of the role which for lack of a better name is labeled a managerial linking role. It is not like the integrating role because it possesses formal position power but is different from line managerial roles in that participants do not report to the linking manager. The power is added by the following successive changes:

a. The integrator receives approval power of budgets formulated in the departments to be integrated.
b. The planning and budgeting process starts with the integrator making his initiation in budgeting legitimate.
c. Linking manager receives the budget for the area of responsibility and buys resources from the specialist groups.

These mechanisms permit the manager to exercise influence even though no one works directly for him. The role is concerned with integration but exercises power through the formal power of the position. If this power is insufficient to integrate the subtasks and creation of self-contained groups is not feasible, there is one last step.

4.7. Matrix Organization. The last step is to create the dual authority relationship and the matrix organization [Galbraith, 1971]. At some point in the organization some roles have two superiors. The design issue is to select the locus of these roles. The result is a balance of power between the managerial linking roles and the normal line organization roles. Figure 2 depicts the pure matrix design.

The work of Lawrence and Lorsch is highly consistent with the assertions concerning lateral relations [Lawrence and Lorsch, 1967, Lorsch and Lawrence, 1968]. They compared the types of lateral relations undertaken by the most successful firm in three different industries. Their data are summarized in Table 1. The plastics firm has the greatest rate of new product introduction (uncertainty) and the greatest utilization of lateral processes. The container firm was also very successful but utilized only standard practices because its information processing task is much less formidable. Thus, the greater the uncertainty the lower the level of decision making and the integration is maintained by lateral relations.

Table 1 points out the cost of using lateral relations. The plastics firm has 22 percent of its managers in integration roles. Thus, the greater the

Figure 2
A Pure Matrix Organization

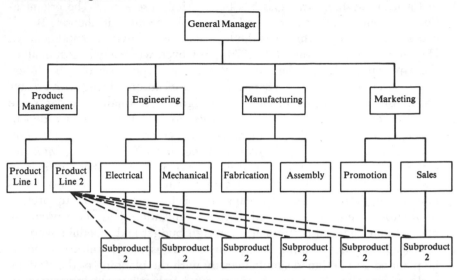

---- = Technical authority over product
——— = Formal authority over product (in product
organization, these relationships may be reversed)

use of lateral relations the greater the managerial intensity. This cost must be balanced against the cost of slack resources, self-contained groups and information systems.

Table 1

	Plastics	*Food*	*Container*
Percent new products in last ten years	35%	20%	0%
Integrating devices	Rules	Rules	Rules
	Hierarchy	Hierarchy	Hierarchy
	Planning	Planning	Planning
	Direct contact	Direct contact	Direct contact
	Teams at 3 levels	Task forces	
	Integrating dept.	Integrators	
Percent integrators/managers	22%	17%	0%

Source: Adopted from Lawrence and Lorsch, 1967, pp. 86–138 and Lorsch and Lawrence, 1968.

CHOICE OF STRATEGY

Each of the four strategies has been briefly presented. The organization can follow one or some combination of several if it chooses. It will choose that strategy which has the least cost in its environmental context. [For an example, see Galbraith, 1970.] However, what may be lost in all of the explanations is that the four strategies are hypothesized to be an exhaustive set of alternatives. That is, if the organization is faced with greater uncertainty due to technological change, higher performance standards due to increased competition, or diversifies its product line to reduce dependence, the amount of information processing is increased. *The organization must adopt at least one of the four strategies when faced with greater uncertainty.* If it does not consciously choose one of the four, then the first, reduced performance standards, will happen automatically. The task information requirements and the capacity of the organization to process information are always matched. If the organization does not consciously match them, reduced performance through budget and schedule overruns will occur in order to bring about equality. Thus the organization should be planned and designed simultaneously with the planning of the strategy and resource allocations. But if the strategy involves introducing new products, entering new markets, etc., then some provision for increased information must be made. Not to decide is to decide, and it is to decide upon slack resources as the strategy to remove hierarchical overload.

There is probably a fifth strategy which is not articulated here. Instead of changing the organization in response to task uncertainty, the organization can operate on its environment to reduce uncertainty. The organization through strategic decisions, long term contracts, coalitions, etc., can control its environment. But these maneuvers have costs also. They should be compared with costs of the four design strategies presented above.

SUMMARY

The purpose of this paper has been to explain why task uncertainty is related to organizational form. In so doing the cognitive limits theory of Herbert Simon was the guiding influence. As the consequences of cognitive limits were traced through the framework, various organization design strategies were articulated. The framework provides a basis for integrating organizational interventions, such as information systems and group problem solving, which have been treated separately before.

BIBLIOGRAPHY

Cyert, Richard, and March, James. *The Behavioral Theory of the Firm.* Prentice-Hall, Englewood Cliffs, N.J., 1963.

Galbraith, Jay.   "Environmental and Technological Determinants of Organization Design: A Case Study," in Lawrence and Lorsch (eds.), *Studies in Organization Design*. Richard D. Irwin Inc., Homewood, Ill., 1970.

Galbraith, Jay.   "Designing Matrix Organizations," *Business Horizons*, February 1971, pp. 29–40.

Galbraith, Jay.   *Organization Design*. Addison-Wesley Pub. Co., Reading, Mass., 1973.

Lawrence, Paul, and Lorsch, Jay.   *Organization and Environment*. Division of Research, Harvard Business School, Boston: 1967.

Lorsch, Jay, and Lawrence, Paul.   "Environmental Factors and Organization Integration." Paper read at the Annual Meeting of the American Sociological Association, August 27, 1967, Boston, Mass.

Match, James, and Simon, Herbert.   *Organizations*. John Wiley & Sons, New York, 1958.

Pounds, William. "The Scheduling Environment" in Muth and Thompson (eds.) *Industrial Scheduling*, Prentice-Hall Inc., Englewood Cliffs, N.J., 1963.

Simon, Herbert.   *Models of Man*. John Wiley & Sons, New York, 1957.

PART IV

PROCESSES WITHIN ORGANIZATIONS

T HIS part of the book contains articles related to fundamental processes which are vital to the effective functioning of every organization: evaluating, rewarding, communicating, and decision making. The flow of the preceding sections leads logically to a discussion of organizational processes. People behave as individuals and as members of groups within an organization structure and communicate for many reasons, one of which is to make decisions. The evaluation and reward processes of any organization rely upon communication and require that decisions be made. In fact, some of the most important purposes of an organization structure are to evaluate, reward, and to facilitate the processes of communication and decision making.

Alan H. Locher and Kenneth S. Teel, in "Performance Appraisal—A Survey of Current Practices," describe what kind of performance appraisal systems are being used today in private industry. Although their survey only covered organizations in California it provides some interesting results. Surprisingly, it revealed that large corporations are no more sophisticated than small ones in their appraisal programs. In addition, the lack of adequate training for appraisals was clearly indicated.

The second article in this section is "Appraisal of What Performance?" by Harry Levinson. In the paper the author discusses the three basic functions of performance evaluation—feedback, modifying behavior, and providing managers with usable data. The inadequacies of appraisal systems are also discussed. Levinson stresses the need for what he calls and describes as the upward appraisal process.

257

Edward Deci in "Paying People Doesn't Always Work the Way You Expect It to" emphasizes that money and motivation are not synonymous terms. He shows that it is necessary that pay be contingent on effective performance. Some interesting studies which the author conducted to look at the contingent theme of pay and performance are presented.

The next article examines the unintended consequences of many reward systems. Steven Kerr in "On the Folly of Rewarding A, While Hoping for B" examines why behaviors which are rewarded in many organizations are those which the administration of the rewards is really trying to discourage. Kerr presents data from a manufacturing firm and an insurance company.

One of the most interesting areas of study among behavioralists involves participation in decision making (PDM). Irving Bluestone in "Worker Participation in Decision Making" claims that in a society that prides itself on its democratic system, the workplace still stands as a solid example of authoritarianism. He describes what has to be done to minimize this autocratic rule and humanize the workplace.

It would be extremely difficult to find an aspect of a manager's job that does not involve communication. Serious problems arise when directives are misunderstood, when casual kidding leads to anger, or when informal remarks by a manager are distorted. Each of these is a result of a breakdown somewhere in the process of communication.

An article on this topic, "Communication Revisited," by Jay Hall, begins by stating that 74 percent of the managers sampled in a cross-cultural study reported communication breakdown as the single greatest barrier to organizational effectiveness. Hall notes that communication problems cited by people are not communication problems as such, but rather symptoms of difficulties at more fundamental levels of organizational life. He believes that the problems of communication in organizations are the feelings people have about where or with whom they work and that the quality of relationships in an organization greatly influence the effectiveness of communication. He then sets out to review what he believes is the critical factor underlying the quality of relationships in organizations: the interpersonal style of the parties to a relationship.

Performance Appraisal—A Survey of Current Practices*

ALAN H. LOCHER and KENNETH S. TEEL

I N recent years, many authors have pointed out the shortcomings of existing appraisal systems.[1][2][3][4] They have noted that many appraisal systems are not relevant to organizational objectives, are too subject to personal bias, and often are influenced more heavily by personality than by performance. Nevertheless, most have agreed that well designed and properly used appraisal systems are essential to the effective functioning of most organizations.[5][6] Furthermore, recent Equal Employment Commission actions and court decisions have underscored the necessity of organizations having accurate, objective records of employee performance to defend themselves against possible charges of discrimination in discharges, promotions and/or salary increases.[7][8]

---

* Reprinted with permission *Personnel Journal*, Copyright May 1977.

1 J. D. Colby, and R. L. Wallace, "Performance Appraisal—Help or Hindrance to Employee Productivity," *Personnel Administrator,* vol. 26 (1975), pp. 37–39.

2 H. J. Lasher, "The Employee Performance Syndrome—Is Improvement Possible?" *Personnel Journal,* vol. 53 (1974), pp. 897–901.

3 R. A. Morano, "Down with Performance Appraisal," *Supervisory Management,* vol. 19 (1974), pp. 18–22.

4 W. Oberg, "Make Performance Appraisal Relevant," *Harvard Business Review,* vol. 50 (1972), pp. 61–67.

5 G. A. Rieder, "Performance Review—A Mixed Bag," *Harvard Business Review,* vol. 51 (1973), pp. 61–67.

6 E. A. Slusher, "A Systems Look at Performance Appraisal," *Personnel Journal,* vol. 54 (1975), pp. 114–17.

7 R. I. Lazer, "The 'Discrimination' Danger in Performance Appraisal," *Conference Board Review,* vol. 13 (1976), pp. 60–64.

8 E. S. Stanton, "The Discharged Employee and the EEO Laws," *Personnel Journal,* vol. 55 (1976), pp. 128–29, 133.

The question then is not: Should an organization have an appraisal system? Instead, it is: What kind of appraisal system can best satisfy an organization's needs? A small, individual entrepreneur can undoubtedly get by with a completely informal system. As organizations grow, however, they need more formal systems to insure comparability of data from their many different departments.

PURPOSE

This study, of what kinds of performance appraisal systems are being used today in private industry, was limited to the private sector because a recent survey has already provided excellent data on appraisal practices of state government agencies.

METHOD

A 20-item questionnaire and a cover letter explaining the purpose of the study were sent to 696 organizations belonging to the Personnel and Industrial Relations Association (PIRA), Los Angeles. PIRA encompasses the Southern California counties of Los Angeles, Orange, Riverside, San Bernardino and Ventura. These counties comprise one of the largest population and industrial centers in the United States. Thus, although the survey was limited geographically its results may well be representative of appraisal practices throughout the country.[9]

Only one questionnaire was sent to each company, usually to the top personnel professional in the organization. Two-hundred-sixteen usable responses were received. This favorable response rate of 31 percent (216 of 696) was probably attributable to the fact that many of those to whom the questionnaires were sent have major responsibility for recommending and implementing their organizations' appraisal systems.

The summary of results which follows indicates the kinds of questions asked; consequently, the questions are not listed here. However, the questionnaire definitions of different types of appraisal systems are reproduced below so that the reader can clearly understand the meaning of the data that follow.

Rating Scale.   An appraisal form containing one or more ranges of performance qualities and characteristics. The rater evaluates the level of employee performance in each category by checking a box, circling a number or letter, or placing a mark along a continuum line.

Essay.   Usually open-ended questions regarding the employee's good and bad points, plus training needs and potential.

---

[9] H. S. Field and W. H. Holley, "Performance Appraisal—An Analysis of State-Wide Practices," *Public Personnel Management,* vol. 4 (1975), pp. 145–50.

Critical Incidents. The systematic recording of actual instances of significantly good or significantly poor performance as they occur.

Checklist. A list of statements describing employee behavior. The rater checks only those statements which accurately describe the performance of the employee being rated.

Forced-Choice. An appraisal form in which the rater chooses between pairs of equally positive or equally negative statements. The results are usually tabulated by personnel department staff.

Employee Comparison. The comparison of employees resulting in a rank ordering from best to worst in the order of their relative performance.

Results-oriented (MBO). The appraisal of results achieved as compared with quantifiable and measurable performance goals or standards established in advance. The goals may be set by the employer, employee, or both.

THE RESPONDENTS

Sixty-nine percent of the responding organizations were engaged in manufacturing, while the remaining 31 percent were not. Both groups were almost evenly divided above and below the 500-employee level, which was used to distinguish between small and large organizations. Significant differences were noted between the responses of small and large organizations, but not between those of manufacturing and non-manufacturing. Consequently, in the tables which follow, data are presented separately only for small and large organizations.

HOW PREVALENT ARE FORMAL PROGRAMS?

Eighty-nine percent of the respondents reported that they have formal performance appraisal programs. Most, as shown in Table 1, have more than one program in use. The most common practice among multiple program firms is to have one program for exempt employees and a different one for nonexempt. Furthermore, executives typically are excluded from

Table 1
Program Status of Responding Organizations

	Small Organizations		Large Organizations		All	
	No.	Percent	No.	Percent	No.	Percent
No program	18	15.7	5	4.9	23	10.6
Single program	34	29.9	33	32.4	67	31.0
Multiple programs	62	54.4	64	62.7	126	58.4

formal appraisal programs, as are members of the bargaining unit whose agreements often dictate that wages be based on longevity rather than on performance.

HOW ARE APPRAISALS USED?

One of the goals of this study was to identify the ways in which individual appraisals are used by different organizations. Respondents were asked to indicate the primary functions served by their programs; interpretation of the term "primary" was left to them. A list of 11 traditional appraisal functions was provided in the questionnaire. Respondents were invited to identify as many primary functions as they considered appropriate. The entries in Table 2, therefore, do not add up to 100 percent; instead, they simply show the percentages of respondents who identified each function as a primary one.

Table 2 indicates that performance appraisals are by far most widely used as bases for compensation decisions and individual performance improvement programs. It also indicates that small organizations make significantly greater use of appraisals in compensation and promotion decisions, while large organizations make greater use of appraisals for performance improvement and feedback. These differences are statistically significant at the .01 level.

Table 2 also reveals that neither large nor small organizations make much use of appraisal data for personnel planning or reassignment. In short, the data suggest that performance appraisals are being used today for essentially the same purposes that they have served for many years in the past. New and/or more sophisticated uses of appraisal data are still quite limited.

Table 2
Primary Uses of Appraisals

Use	Small Organizations (Percent)	Large Organizations (Percent)	All (Percent)
Compensation	80.6	62.2	71.3
Performance improvement	49.7	60.6	55.2
Feedback	20.6	37.8	29.3
Promotion	29.1	21.1	25.1
Documentation	11.4	10.0	10.7
Training	8.0	9.4	8.7
Transfer	7.4	8.3	7.9
Manpower planning	6.3	6.1	6.2
Discharge	2.3	2.2	2.3
Research	2.9	0.0	1.4
Layoff	0.6	0.0	0.3

WHAT TECHNIQUES ARE BEING USED?

Appraisal techniques in use today are also essentially the same as those that have been used for many years. The typical appraisal technique consists of a rating scale, with space for narrative comments to justify ratings and to elaborate on employee strengths, weaknesses and developmental plans. This fact was noted by the respondents and verified by our personal inspection of appraisal forms provided by approximately three-fourths of the respondents. Table 3 shows the percentages of responding organizations using rating scales, essays and management-by-objectives (MBO) as their primary appraisal techniques. The other techniques covered in the questionnaire—checklists, critical incidents, employee comparison and forced-choice scales—are used so infrequently that they are lumped together into an "All Others" category.

Perhaps the most surprising finding of the survey was the limited use of MBO as an appraisal technique. Because of the extensive literature advocating the use of MBO, we had expected far more than 12.7 percent of the respondents to identify MBO as their primary appraisal technique. Although our results indicate that large organizations are significantly (p .05) more likely to use MBO than are small, they nevertheless suggest that the difficulties encountered in identifying and agreeing upon measurable behavioral objectives still stand in the way of widespread implementation of MBO. They therefore support the conclusion of another recent survey[10] that there often are ". . . great differences between what companies 'preach' and the practice of collaborative techniques like Management by Objectives."

Table 3
Appraisal Techniques

Technique	Small Organizations (Percent)	Large Organizations (Percent)	All (Percent)
Rating scale	59.5	54.2	56.7
Essay	25.8	24.2	24.9
MBO	8.5	16.6	12.7
All others	6.2	5.0	5.7
Total	100.0	100.0	100.0

WHO DOES THE APPRAISING? HOW OFTEN?

In 98.9 percent of the responding organizations, appraisals are made by the employee's immediate supervisor, either alone or in conjunction with

---

[10] R. A. Zawacki and R. L. Raylor, "A View of Performance Appraisal from Organizations Using It," *Personnel Journal*, vol. 55 (1976), pp. 290–92, 299.

others. In 78 percent of the cases, the supervisor has sole responsibility for the appraisal. In the remainder, the supervisor's appraisal is supplemented by, in decreasing order of probability, appraisals made by his/her own superior, by the employee being appraised, by a committee, or by a personnel department staff member. In 63.4 percent of the programs, it is standard practice for the appraisal to be reviewed and approved by the appraiser's superior.

Again, it was interesting to discover that, despite emphasis in the management literature on the importance of a collaborative approach to appraisal, few employees are actively involved in their own appraisal. Employees have direct inputs to their own appraisals in only 5.4 percent of the programs. In the others, they must accept, willingly or otherwise, the appraisals made by their supervisors.

Appraisals are conducted annually in 52 percent of the responding organizations, semi-annually in 24 percent, and at variable intervals depending upon organizational level and salary in the remaining 24 percent. An annual appraisal apparently is still the most common.

ARE APPRAISERS WELL PREPARED?

The appraiser is the key to the success or failure of any appraisal system. If an appraiser does not know how to observe behavior objectively, does not understand how to use the system, or is not willing to devote enough time to the appraisal task, the appraisal system will be ineffective. No system, regardless of its features, can be effective unless appraisers are capable and motivated.

We did not attempt, in this survey, to measure the motivation of appraisers. Instead, we assumed that they probably would be well motivated if they understood the systems, were properly trained in their objectives and uses, and were monitored by management to see that they were using the appraisal systems properly. We therefore asked questions about written instructions for appraisers, formal training, and management monitoring of appraisal programs.

Written instructions on how to use the appraisal system are provided in 76.6 percent of the organizations; none is provided in the remaining 23.4 percent. Where instructions are provided, 46 percent are on the appraisal forms only; 35 percent are separate; and 19 percent are both on the forms and separate. Our review of these instructions reveals that most are clear and complete. Thus, most organizations provide adequate information on how their appraisal systems should be used.

The same, however, cannot be said for training. The percentages of organizations providing formal training for appraisers are shown in Table 4.

For many years, research results have documented the widespread existence of appraiser bias and the fact that such bias can be significantly

Table 4
Appraiser Training

Type of Training	Small Organizations (Percent)	Large Organizations (Percent)	All (Percent)
None	54.1	55.6	54.8
Initial	24.1	16.6	20.3
Refresher	21.8	27.8	24.9
Total	100.0	100.0	100.0

reduced through training. Recent research[11] has underscored the need for such training by pointing out that appraisers often are biased by employee race and sex, as well as by personality characteristics unrelated to job performance. We were quite surprised, therefore, to discover that over half of the organizations with formal programs provide no appraiser training whatsoever. Even most of those who do provide training limit it to short (one or two hour) refresher sessions scheduled at variable intervals. Thus, most appraisers must "sink or swim" on the basis of what they can learn from written instructions and/or informal comments from their colleagues. We must agree with the statement[12] that appraiser training "... is probably the most neglected in modern management education."

The picture is somewhat brighter in terms of management monitoring to see that appraisals are being conducted in accord with organizational policies. In 78.5 percent of the responding organizations, the personnel department is responsible for monitoring appraisal practices. In 14.1 percent, line management alone is responsible. In the remaining 7.4 percent, personnel and line management share the responsibility. Methods of monitoring range from completely informal to sophisticated computerized systems. In most cases, though, personnel sends the forms to appraisers, maintains a log to see that they are returned, and reviews the forms as they are returned.

In short, our results indicate that most organizations with formal appraisal programs provide adequate written instructions and check to see that appraisals are completed as required, but do *not* provide adequate training for appraisers. Consequently, their appraisal programs probably are far less effective than they could be. Further investments in appraiser training would undoubtedly yield more favorable cost/benefit ratios for their appraisal programs.

---

[11] W. J. Bigoness, "Effect of Applicant's Sex, Race and Performance on Employers' Performance Ratings—Some Additional Findings," *Journal of Applied Psychology*, vol. 61 (1976), pp. 80–84.

[12] N. B. Winstanley, "Performance Appraisal, Another Pollution Problem," *Conference Board Record*, vol. 9 (1972), pp. 59–63.

CONCLUSIONS AND RECOMMENDATIONS

Our conclusions can be summarized briefly as follows: (1) Most organizations have formal appraisal programs and use two or more different appraisal techniques for different groups of employees. (2) Large corporations (500 employees) are no more sophisticated than small in their appraisal programs. Although they emphasize different uses of appraisal information, their programs are essentially the same. (3) The graphic rating scale, despite its well-known limitations, is still by far the most widely used appraisal technique. (4) MBO, despite its widespread publicity, is not widely used; only about one-eighth of the responding organizations use it. (5) Most appraisals are annual. They are made by the immediate supervisor of the employee being appraised, without any direct employee input. (6) Very few organizations provide adequate training for appraisers.

Our overall recommendation for improvement is simple to state, but probably difficult to implement: Place more emphasis on defining appraisal objectives and training of appraisers, but less on techniques. It is easy to debate the relative merits of rating scales vs. MBO, or to argue whether a rating scale should have five, seven or nine points. It is far more difficult to go through the iterative analytical process of determining exactly what objectives are to be achieved by an appraisal program, as well as what type of program can best achieve them. As a result, many organizations seem to have adopted the appraisal technique that most impressed them or was readily available at little cost and then tried to figure out how best to use it.

What is needed instead is more of a "systems approach," in which effort is first devoted to deciding exactly what is to be accomplished and then how best to accomplish it. Appraisal techniques, like organizational structures, are merely tools to be used in achieving organizational objectives. Consequently, the choice of one or more techniques should follow, not precede, the definition of objectives. Then, after objectives have been defined and techniques selected, appraisers must be given enough formal training to insure that they clearly understand both the objectives and the mechanics of the system. If training time is limited because of costs, emphasize objectives; the mechanics are easier to explain in writing. Finally, encourage appraisers to provide feedback on how well the system is working for them, as well as to suggest ways in which it might be improved.

Our recommendations can be summarized as follows:

1. Identify in detail the objectives of your appraisal program.
2. Audit your current program to see if it is achieving those objectives. Establish a continuing research program to provide feedback to management on how well your appraisal program is working and when it needs to be changed.

3. Modify it whenever your objectives change, or data indicate that it is no longer satisfying your objectives. Choose techniques to suit your objectives; don't choose one simply because someone says it's good.
4. Provide formal training for appraisers, to insure that they understand both the objectives and mechanics of the program. Without such training, the most carefully-conceived program is likely to be ineffective.

In short, place more emphasis on defining appraisal objectives and on training appraisers, and less on techniques. Finally, appraisal programs should be dynamic; as objectives, employee expectations and other such factors change, appraisal programs also must change.

21

Appraisial of What Performance?*

HARRY LEVINSON

A corporate president put a senior executive in charge of a failing operation. His only directive was "Get it in the black." Within two years of that injunction, the new executive moved the operation from a deficit position to one that showed a profit of several million. Fresh from his triumph, the executive announced himself as a candidate for a higher-level position, and indicated that he was already receiving offers from other companies.

The corporate president, however, did not share the executive's positive opinions of his behavior. In fact, the president was not at all pleased with the way the executive had handled things. Naturally the executive was dismayed, and when he asked what he had done wrong, the corporate president told him that he had indeed accomplished what he had been asked to do, but he had done it singlehandedly, by the sheer force of his own personality. Furthermore, the executive was told, he had replaced people whom the company thought to be good employees with those it regarded as compliant. In effect, by demonstrating his own strength, he had made the organization weaker. Until the executive changed his authoritarian manner, his boss said, it was unlikely that he would be promoted further.

Implicit in this vignette is the major fault in performance appraisal and management by objectives—namely, a fundamental misconception of what is to be appraised.

Performance appraised has three basic functions: (1) to provide adequate feedback to each person on his or her performance; (2) to serve as a basis for modifying or changing behavior toward more effective working

* Harry Levinson, "Appraisal of What Performance?" *Harvard Business Review* (July–August 1976), pp. 30–48. Copyright 1976 by the President and Fellows of Harvard College; all rights reserved.

habits; and (3) to provide data to managers with which they may judge future job assignments and compensation. The performance appraisal concept is central to effective management. Much hard and imaginative work has gone into developing and refining it. In fact, there is a great deal of evidence to indicate how useful and effective performance appraisal is. Yet present systems of performance appraisal do not serve any of these functions well.

As it is customarily defined and used, performance appraisal focuses not on behavior but on outcomes of behavior. But even though the executive in the example achieved his objective, he was evaluated on *how* he attained it. Thus, while the system purports to appraise results, in practice, people are really appraised on how they do things—which is not formally described in the setting of objectives, and for which there are rarely data on record.

In my experience the crucial aspect of any manager's job and the source of most failures, which is practically never described, is the "how." As long as managers appraise the ends yet actually give greater weight to the means, employ a static job description base which does not describe the "how," and do not have support mechanisms for the appraisal process, widespread dissatisfaction with performance appraisal is bound to continue. In fact, one personnel authority speaks of performance appraisal as "the Achilles heel of our profession. . . ."[1]

Just how these inadequacies affect performance appraisal systems and how they can be corrected to provide managers with realistic bases for making judgments about employees' performance is the subject of this article.

INADEQUACIES OF APPRAISAL SYSTEMS

It is widely recognized that there are many things inherently wrong with most of the performance appraisal systems in use. The most obvious drawbacks are:

1. No matter how well defined the dimensions for appraising performance on quantitative goals are, judgments on performance are usually subjective and impressionistic.
2. Because appraisals provide inadequate information about the subtleties of performance, managers using them to compare employees for the purposes of determining salary increases often make arbitrary judgments.

---

[1] Herbert Heneman, "Research Roundup," *The Personnel Administrator,* June 1975, p. 61.

3. Ratings by different managers, and especially those in different units, are usually incomparable. What is excellent work in one unit may be unacceptable in another in the same company.
4. When salary increases are allocated on the basis of a curve of normal distribution, which is in turn based on rating of results rather than on behavior, competent employees may not only be denied increases, but may also become demotivated.[2]
5. Trying to base promotion and layoff decisions on appraisal data leaves the decisions open to acrimonious debate. When employees who have been retired early have complained to federal authorities of age discrimination, defendant companies have discovered that there were inadequate data to support the layoff decisions.
6. Although managers are urged to give feedback freely and often, there are no built-in mechanisms for ensuring that they do so. Delay in feedback creates both frustration, when good performance is not quickly recognized, and anger, when judgment is rendered for inadequacies long past.
7. There are few effective established mechanisms to cope with either the sense of inadequacy managers have about appraising subordinates, or the paralysis and procrastination that result from guilt about playing God.

Some people might argue that these problems are deficiencies of managers, not of the system. But even if that were altogether true, managers are part of that system. Performance appraisal needs to be viewed not as a technique but as a process involving both people and data, and as such the whole process is inadequate.

Recognizing that there are many deficiencies in performance appraisals, managers in many companies do not want to do them. In other companies there is a great reluctance to do them straightforwardly. Personnel specialists attribute these problems to the reluctance of managers to adopt new ways and to the fear of irreparably damaging their subordinates' self-esteem. In government, performance appraisal is largely a joke, and in both private and public enterprise, merit ratings are hollow.[3]

One of the main sources of trouble with performance appraisal systems is, as I have already pointed out, that the outcome of behavior rather than the behavior itself is what is evaluated. In fact, most people's jobs are described in terms that are only quantitatively measurable; the job description itself is the root of the problem.

---

[2] Paul H. Thompson and Gene W. Dalton, "Performance Appraisal: Managers Beware," *Harvard Business Review*, January–February 1970, p. 149.

[3] Herbert S. Meyer, "The Pay for Performance Dilemma," *Organizational Dynamics*, Winter 1975, p. 39.

THE STATIC JOB DESCRIPTION

When people write their own job descriptions (or make statements from which others will write them) essentially they define their responsibilities and basic functions. Then on performance appraisal forms, managers comment on these functions by describing what an individual is supposed to accomplish. Forms in use in many companies today have such directions as:

1. "List the major objectives of this person's job that can be measured qualitatively or quantitatively."
2. "Define the results expected and the standards of performance—money, quantity, quality, time limits, or completion dates."
3. "Describe the action planned as a result of this appraisal, the next steps to be taken—reevaluation, strategy, tactics, and so on."
4. "List the person's strong points—his assets and accomplishments—and his weak points—areas in which improvement is needed. What are the action plans for improvement?"

In most instances the appraiser is asked to do an overall rating with a five-point scale or some similar device. Finally, he is asked to make a statement about the person's potential for the next step or even for higher-level management.

Nowhere is this set of questions or in any of the performance appraisal systems I have examined is anything asked about *how* the person is to attain the ends he or she is charged with reaching.

While some may assert that the ideal way of managing is to give a person a charge and leave him or her alone to accomplish it, this principle is oversimplified both in theory and practice. People need to know the topography of the land they are expected to cross, and the routes as perceived by those to whom they report.

Every manager has multiple obligations, not the least of which are certain kinds of relationships with peers, subordinates, and various consumer, financial, government, supplier, and other publics. Some of these are more important than others, and some need to be handled with much greater skill and aplomb than others. In some situations a manager may be expected to take a vigorous and firm stand, as in labor negotiations; in others he may have to be conciliative; in still others he may even have to be passive. Unless these varied modes of expected behavior are laid out, the job description is static. Because static job descriptions define behavior in gross terms, crucially important differentiated aspects of behavior are lost when performance appraisals are made.

For example, in one of the more progressive performance appraisal systems, which is used by an innovative company, a manager working out his own job description prepares a mission or role statement of what he is supposed to do according to the guide which specifically directs him to concentrate on the what and the when, not on the why and the how.[4] The guide instructs him to divide his mission into four general areas: (1) innovation; (2) problem solving; (3) ongoing administration; and (4) personal.

In still another company, a manager appraising a subordinate's performance is asked to describe an employee's accomplishments, neglected areas, goals, and objectives. The manager is told that he is to recognize good work, suggest improvement, get agreement on top priority elements of the task, clarify responsibility, verify and correct rumors, and talk about personal and long-range goals.

In another company's outstanding performance appraisal guide, which reflects great detail and careful consideration, the categories are: work, effectiveness with others, problem solving, decision making, goal setting, organizing and planning, developing subordinates, attending to self-development, and finding initiatives. Each of these categories is broken down into example statements such as: "exhibits high level of independence in work"; "identifies problems and deals with them"; "appropriately subordinates departmental interest to overall company goal"; or "gives people genuine responsibility, holds them accountable, and allows them freedom to act."

Some personnel researchers have advocated role analysis techniques to cope with static job descriptions, and this is a step in the right direction.[5]

But even these techniques are limited because they lean heavily on what other people—supervisors, subordinates, peers—expect of the manager. These expectations are also generalized; they do not specify behavior.

Nowhere in these examples is an individual told what *behavior* is expected of him in a range of contexts. Who are the sensitive people with whom certain kinds of relationships have to be maintained? What are the specific problems and barriers? What have been the historic manufacturing blunders or frictions? How should union relationships and union leaders be dealt with? What are the specific integrative problems to be resolved and what are the historical conflicts? These and many more similar pieces of behavior will be the true bases on which a person will be judged, regardless of the questions an appraisal form asks.

Static job descriptions are catastrophic for managers. Job proficiency and goal achievement usually are necessary but not sufficient conditions for advancement; the key elements in whether one makes it in an organization are political. The collective judgments made about a person, which rarely find their way into performance appraisals, become the social web

[4] John B. Lasagna, "Make Your MBO Pragmatic," *Harvard Business Review*, November–December 1971, p. 64.

[5] Ishwar Dayal, "Role Analysis Techniques in Job Descriptions," *California Management Review*, Summer 1969, p. 47.

in which he or she must live. Therefore, when a person is placed in a new situation, whether in a different geographical site, at a different level in the hierarchy, or in a new role, he must be apprised of the subtleties of the relationships he will have with those who will influence his role and his career. Furthermore, he must be helped to differentiate the varied kinds of behavior required to succeed.

Some people develop political diagnostic skill very rapidly; often, however, these are people whose social senses enable them to move beyond their technical and managerial competence. And some may be out-and-out manipulative charlatans who succeed in business without really trying, and whose promotion demoralizes good people. But the great majority of people, those who have concentrated heavily on their professional competence at the expense of acquiring political skill early, will need to have that skill developed, ideally by their own seniors. That development process requires: (1) a dynamic job description; (2) a critical incident process; and (3) a psychological support system.

DYNAMIC JOB DESCRIPTION

If a static job description is at the root of the inadequacies of performance appraisal systems, what is needed is a different kind of job description. What we are looking for is one that amplifies statements of job responsibility and desired outcome by describing the emotional and behavioral topography of the task to be done by the individual in the job.

Psychologists describe behavior in many ways, each having his or her own preferences. I have found four major features of behavior to be fundamentally important in a wide range of managerial settings. These features have to do with how a person characteristically manages what some psychologists call aggression, affection, dependency, and also the nature of the person's ego ideal.[6]

Using his preferred system, one can begin formulating a dynamic job description by describing the characteristic behavior required by a job. This is what these terms mean with respect to job descriptions:

1. How does this job require the incumbent to handle his aggression, his attacking capacity?

    Must he or she vanquish customers? Must he hold on to his anger in the face of repeated complaints and attacks from others? Will she be the target of hostility and, if so, from whom? Must he give firm direction to others? Must she attack problems vigorously, but handle some areas with great delicacy and finesse? Which problems are to be attacked with vigor and immediacy and which coolly and analytically?

---

[6] Harry Levinson, *The Great Jackass Fallacy* (Cambridge, Mass.: Harvard University Press, 1973), chap. 3.

2. How does this job require the incumbent to manage affection, the need to love and be loved?

    Is the person required to be a socially friendly leader of a close-knit group? Should the person work closely and supportively with subordinates for task accomplishment? Is the task one in which the person will have to be content with the feeling of a job well done, or is it one which involves more public display and recognition? Will he be obscure and unnoticed, or highly visible? Must she lavish attention on the work, a product, a service, or customers? Must he be cold and distant from others and, if so, from whom?

3. How does this job require the incumbent to manage dependency needs?

    Will the individual be able to lean on others who have skill and competencies, or will he have to do things himself? How much will she be on her own and in what areas? How much support will there be from superiors and staff functions? How well defined is the nature of the work? What kind of feedback provisions are there? What are the structural and hierarchical relationships? How solid are they and to whom will the person turn and for what? With which people must he interact in order to accomplish what he needs to accomplish, and in what manner?

4. What ego ideal demands does this job fulfill?

    If one does the task well, what are the gratifications to be gained? Will he achieve considerable organizational and public recognition? Will she be eligible for promotion? Will he feel good about himself and, if so, in what ways? Why? Will she acquire a significant skill, an important element of reputation, or an organizational constituency? Will he acquire power?

Individuals may be described along the same four dynamic dimensions: How does this person characteristically handle aggression? How does he or she characteristically handle affection? How does he or she characteristically handle dependency needs? What is the nature of his or her ego ideal?

Once the subtleties of the task are defined and individuals described, people may be matched to tasks. I am not advocating a return to evaluation of personality traits. I am arguing for a more dynamic conception of the managerial role and a more dynamic assessment of an employee's characteristics. And only when a person's behavior is recognized as basic to how he performs his job will performance appraisal systems be realistic.

CRITICAL INCIDENT PROCESS

Having established a dynamic job description for a person, the next step is to evolve a complementary performance appraisal system that will provide feedback on verifiable behavior, do so in a continuous fashion, and serve coaching-, promotion-, and salary-data needs.

Ideally, a manager and his subordinate will have defined together the objectives to be attained in a certain job, and the criteria by which each will know that those objectives have been attained, including the more qualitative aspects of the job. Then they will have spelled out the subtleties of how various aspects of the job must be performed. They will in this way have elaborated the *behavioral* requirements of the task.

In order for performance appraisal to be effective for coaching, teaching, and changing those aspects of an employee's behavior that are amenable to change, an employee needs to know about each piece of behavior that is good, as well as that which for some reason is not acceptable or needs modification. Such incidents will occur randomly and be judged randomly by his manager.

So that there will be useful data, the manager needs to quickly write down what he has said to the subordinate, describing in a paragraph what the subordinate did or did not do, in what setting, under what circumstances, about what problem. This information forms a *behavioral* record, a critical incident report of which the subordinate already has been informed and which is now in his folder, open to his review. Examples of two incidents can be found in the boxed material below.

EXAMPLES OF CRITICAL INCIDENTS

On May 15, the director of manufacturing, together with the president of the union, met with a group of shop stewards and the international business agent who were irate about the temporary 10 percent cutback in working hours. The cutback had been prematurely announced by corporate personnel without local consultation. The director of manufacturing heard them out, did not get hot under the collar about their tirade, and then explained the need to use up inventories. By reassuring them of the company's true intention, the director of manufacturing reduced tension in the plants.

Executive Vice President

The director of manufacturing and I met today (August 13th) to review his development plans for his subordinates. While these are broadly defined on paper, the director does not hear enough from his subordinates about *their* objectives or ask enough about what *they* are up against. He is impatient with this aspect of his responsibility. I suggested that he allot regular meeting times for such discussions and take more time to listen. He agreed to do so.

Executive Vice President

This critical incident technique is not new.[7] In the past it has been used largely for case illustrations and, in modified forms, has been suggested as a method for first-level supervisors to evaluate line employees. Supervisors already record negative incidents concerning line employees because warnings and disciplinary steps must be documented. However, efforts to develop scales from critical incidents for rating behavior have not worked well.[8] Behavior is too complex to be scaled along a few dimensions and then rated.

But instead of scaling behavior, one might directly record the behavior of those being appraised, and evaluate it at a later date. There are other good reasons for adopting this technique as well. At last, here is a process that provides data to help managers perform the basic functions of performance appraisal systems—namely, provide feedback, coaching, and promotion data. Another plus is that recorded data live longer than the manager recording them.

Here is how behavioral data might be put to use in the critical incident process:

1. *Feedback Data.* When there is a semiannual or annual review, an employee will have no surprises, and the manager will have on paper what he is using as a basis for making his summary feedback and appraisal. Because the data are on record, an employee cannot deny having heard what was said earlier, nor must the manager try to remember all year what have been the bases of his judgments.

    Also, as each critical incident is recorded, over time there will be data in an individual's folder to be referred to when and if there are suits alleging discrimination. Critical incidents of behavior, which illustrate behavior patterns, will be the only hard evidence acceptable to adjudicating bodies.

2. *Coaching Data.* When employees receive feedback information at the time the incident occurs, they may be able to adapt their behavior more easily. With this technique, the employee will receive indications more often on how he is doing, and will be able to correct small problems before they become large ones. Also, if the employee cannot change his behavior, that fact will become evident to him through the repetitive critical incident notes. If the employee feels unfairly judged or criticized, he may appeal immediately rather than long after the

---

[7] John C. Flanagan, "The Critical Incident Technique," *Psycological Bulletin*, vol. 51 (1954), p. 327; and John C. Flanagan (coauthor Robert K. Burns), "The Employee Performance Record: A New Appraisal and Development Tool," *Harvard Business Review*, September–October 1955, p. 95.

[8] Donald P. Schwab, Herbert G. Heneman III, and Thomas A. DeCotiis, "Behavioral Anchored Rating Scales: A Review of the Literature," *Personnel Psychology*, vol. 28 (1975), p. 549.

fact. If there are few or no incidents on record, that in itself says something about job behavior, and may be used as a basis for discussion. In any event, both manager and employee will know which behavior is being appraised.

3. *Promotion Data.* With such an accumulation of critical incidents, a manager or the personnel department is in a position to evaluate repeatedly how the person characteristically manages aggression, affection, and dependency needs, and the nature of his ego ideal. These successive judgments become cumulative data for better job fit.

When a person is provided continuously with verifiable information, including when he has been passed over for promotion and why, he is able to perceive more accurately the nuances of his behavior and his behavioral patterns. Thus, when offered other opportunities, the employee is in a better position to weigh his own behavioral configurations against those required by the prospective job. A person who knows himself in this way will be more easily able to say about a given job, "That's not for me." He will see that the next job in the pyramid is not necessarily rightfully his. In recognizing his own behavioral limitations he may save himself much grief as well as avoid painful difficulty for his superiors and the organization.

But the most important reason for having such information is to increase the chances of success of those who are chosen for greater responsibility. In most personnel folders there is practically no information about how a manager is likely to do when placed on his own. Data about dependency are noticeably absent, and many a shining prospect dims when there is no one to support him in a higher-level job. Managements need to know early on who can stand alone, and they cannot know that without behavioral information.

4. *Long-Term Data.* Frequently, new managers do not know their employees and all too often have little information in the folder with which to appraise them. This problem is compounded when managers move quickly from one area to another. For his part, the employee just as frequently has to prove himself to transient bosses who hold his fate in their hands but know nothing of his past performance. With little information, managers feel unqualified to make judgments. With the critical incident process, however, managers can report incidents which can be summarized by someone else.

Some may object to "keeping book" on their people or resist a program of constant reviews and endless reports—both extreme views. Some may argue that supervisors will not follow the method. But if managers cannot get raises for or transfer employees without adequate documentation, they will soon learn the need to follow through. The critical incident process compels superiors to face subordinates, a responsibility too many shirk.

While it might seem difficult to analyze performance in terms of aggression, affection, dependency, the ego ideal, or other psychological concepts, to do so is no different from learning to use economic, financial, or accounting concepts. Many managers already talk about these same issues in other words, for example: "taking charge" versus "being a nice guy"; "needing to be stroked" versus the "self-starter"; "fast track" versus the "shelf-sitter." A little practice, together with support mechanisms, can go a long way.

SUPPORT MECHANISMS

Performance appraisal cannot be limited to a yearly downward reward-punishment judgment. Ideally, appraisal should be a part of a continuing process by which both manager and employee may be guided. In addition, it should enhance an effective superior-subordinate relationship.

To accomplish these aims, performance appraisal must be supported by mechanisms that enable the manager to master his inadequacies and to cope with his feelings of guilt; have a record of that part of his work that occurs outside the purview of his own boss (e.g., task force assignments which require someone to appraise a whole group); and modify those aspects of his superior's behavior which hamper his performance. All of this requires an upward appraisal process.

1. *Managing the Guilt.* The manager's guilt about appraising subordinates appears when managers complain about playing God, about destroying people. A great crippler of effective performance appraisal is the feeling of guilt, much of which is irrational, but which most people have when they criticize others.[9] Guilt is what leads to the fear of doing appraisals. It is the root of procrastination, of the failure to appraise honestly, and of the overreaction which can demolish subordinates.

   Fortunately, there are group methods for relieving guilt and for helping managers and supervisors understand the critical importance, indeed the necessity, of accurate behavioral evaluations. One way is by having people together at the same peer level discuss their problems in appraisal and talk about their feelings in undertaking the appraisal task. In addition, rehearsals of role playing increase a manager's sense of familiarity and competence and ease his anxiety.

   In fact, a five-step process, one step per week for five weeks, can be extremely helpful:

   Week One. Group discussion among peers (no more than 12) about their feelings about appraising subordinates.

---

[9] Harry Levinson, "Management by Whose Objectives?" *Harvard Business Review*, July–August 1970, p. 125.

Week Two. Group discussions resulting in advice from each other on the specific problems that each anticipates in appraising individuals.

Week Three. Role playing appraisal interviews.

Week Four. Actual appraisals.

Week Five. Group discussion to review the appraisals, problems encountered, both anticipated and unanticipated, lessons learned, and skill needs that may have surfaced.

2. *Group Appraisal.* By group appraisal, I do not mean peer approval of each other, which usually fails; rather, I mean appraisal of a group's accomplishment. When people work together in a group, whether reporting to the same person or not, they need to establish criteria by which they and those to whom they report will know how well the task force or the group has done—in terms of behavior as well as results. Group appraisals provide information that is helpful both in establishing as well as in providing each individual with feedback.

At the end of a given task, a group may do a group appraisal or be appraised by the manager to whom they report, and that appraisal may be entered into folders of each of the people who are involved. It will then serve as another basis for managerial- and self-judgment.

3. *Upward Appraisal.* Finally, there should be upward appraisal. Some beginning voluntary steps in this direction are being taken in the Sun Oil Company, and by individual executives in other companies. Upward appraisal is a very difficult process because most managers do not want to be evaluated by their subordinates. As a matter of fact, however, most managers *are* evaluated indirectly by their employees, and these evaluations are frequently behavioral.

The employees' work itself is a kind of evaluation. Their work may be done erratically or irresponsibly. Or they may be poorly motivated. Negative behavior is a form of appraisal, and one from which a manager gains little. A manager cannot be quite sure what precipitated the behavior he sees, let alone be sure what to do about it.

If, however, the manager is getting dynamic behavioral appraisal from his employees, then he, too, may correct his course. But if he asks his subordinates for upward appraisal without warning, he is likely to be greeted with dead silence and great caution. A helpful way to deal with this situation is to ask one's employees to define the criteria by which they would appraise the manager's job, not to judge his actual performance.

This process of definition may require a manager to meet with employees weekly for months to define the criteria. By the end of three months, say, the employees should be much more comfortable working with their manager on this issue. And if the manager can be trusted at all, then when he or she finally asks them to evaluate the performance, including specific behaviors, along the dimensions they have worked out together, they are likely to be more willing to do so. Of course, if there is no trust, there is no possibility of upward appraisal. In any event, the upward performance appraisal should go to the manager's superior so that people do not jeopardize themselves by speaking directly.

Under present performance appraisal systems, it is difficult to compensate managers for developing people because the criteria are elusive. With a developing file of upward appraisals, however, executives can judge how well a manager has done in developing his people. The employees cannot evaluate the whole of their manager's job, but they can say a great deal about how well he or she has facilitated their work, increased their proficiency, cleared barriers, protected them against political forces, and raised their level of competence—in short, how the manager has met their ministration, maturation, and mastery needs.[10] A top executive can then quantify such upward evaluations and use the outcome as a basis for compensating a manager for his effectiveness in developing his employees.

When a group of manager peers experiments with upward appraisal and works it out to their own comfort, as well as to that of their employees, then it might be tried at the next lower level. When several successive levels have worked out their own systems, the process might be formalized throughout the organization. Acceptance of the upward appraisal concept is likely to be greater if it has been tested and modeled by the very people who must use it, and if it has not been imposed on them by the personnel department. With appropriate experience, the managers involved in the process would ultimately evolve suitable appraisal forms.

WHAT ABOUT RESULTS?

What does adopting the critical incident technique and the dynamic job description mean for judging a person's ability to obtain results? Does quantitative performance lose its importance?

My answer is an unqualified no. There will always be other issues that managers will have to determine, such as level of compensation or promotability—issues which should be dealt with in other sessions after the basic behavioral performance appraisal.[11]

Some of the performance appraisal information may be helpful in making such determinations, but neither of these two functions should con-

---

[10] Harry Levinson, *The Exceptional Executive* (Cambridge, Mass.: Harvard University Press, 1968).

[11] Herbert H. Meyer, Emanual Kay, and John R. P. French, Jr., "Split Roles in Performance Appraisal," *Harvard Business Review*, January–February 1965, p. 123.

taminate the performance appraisal feedback process. There can still be an annual compensation evaluation, based not only on behavior, which is the basis for coaching, but also on outcome. Did an employee make money? Did he reach quantitative goals? Did she resolve problems in the organization that were her responsibility?

No doubt, there will be some overlapping between behavior and outcome, but the two are qualitatively different. One might behave as it was expected he should, but at the same time not do what had to be done to handle the vagaries of the marketplace. He might not have responded with enough speed or flexibility to a problem, even though his behavior corresponded to all that originally was asked of him in the job description and goal-setting process.

Both behavior and outcome are important, and neither should be overlooked. It is most important, however, that they not be confused.

22

Paying People Doesn't Always Work the Way You Expect It to*

EDWARD L. DECI

FOR many people, the words *money* and *motivation* are nearly synonymous. An abundance of research indicates, however, that this is not the case. Paying workers doesn't necessarily motivate them. Furthermore, money is not the only reward which workers seek to achieve. In order to use money as a motivator, it is necessary that pay be contingent on effective performance. That is, the reward system must be structured so that receiving pay depends on good performance. Money will then motivate performance because performance is instrumental to receiving payments. If money and performance are not tied together, money will not serve as an effective motivator.

Two areas of psychological research have provided support for this assumption about motivation. (1) Behaviorists have substantiated and refined the Law of Effect which states simply that when a response is followed by a reinforcement it will have an increased probability of recurrence. Contingent payments presumably reinforce the response of producing output and should, therefore, strengthen that response. (2) The use of contingent payments can also be defended by cognitive theories of motivation. These theories state that man's behavior is goal-directed; in other words, man will engage in behavior which he believes will lead him to desired goals. Since money is probably one goal all workers accept, cognitive theories would suggest that a worker would produce efficiently in order to get substantial wages, if that was the easiest way he could get them.

One approach to management which has recognized the importance of

---

* Reprinted from *Human Resource Management,* Summer 1973, pp. 28–32. Reprinted with permission. Graduate School of Business Administration, University of Michigan, Ann Arbor, Michigan 48109.

tying rewards to performance is Scientific Management which was developed by Frederick Winslow Taylor over half a century ago. He used piece-rate payments (i.e., wage incentives) which involve paying people a set rate for each unit of output. Sales commissions and bonus plans work similarly. The motivational assumption underlying these pay schemes is that a person will perform effectively to the extent that his rewards are made contingent upon effective performance. For this motivational system to work effectively, it is necessary that there be clear standards for performance which the workers understand. Then, performance has to be monitored, and rewards must be administered consistently. Further, the output must be quantifiable so that performance can be measured, and jobs should be relatively independent so that a worker has control of his own production rate.

The rewards in these systems are money, promotions, fringe benefits, etc. These rewards are of course extrinsically mediated, that is, they are given to the employee by someone other than himself. Management administers them to try to control (or motivate) the behavior of the employees. Although this system seems to have advantages for motivating employees, there are also many limitations to it. Perhaps the most serious is that there are many rewards which *cannot* be administered by management. Money is *not* the only reward which workers are looking for. People also need what we call *intrinsic rewards;* that is, internal rewards which the person derives from doing what he likes or meeting a challenge. They give him a feeling of satisfaction and accomplishment. Many studies have reported that employees consider these intrinsic rewards to be important. It follows then that there are many important motivators of human behavior which are not under the direct control of managers and, therefore, cannot be contingently administered in a system such as piece-rate payments.

More recent approaches to management—often referred to as participative management, Theory Y Management, Management by Objectives— have assumed that man can be intrinsically motivated to perform effectively. These approaches focus on structuring jobs so that workers will become ego-involved in their work and committed to doing it well.

There are two essential aspects to motivating intrinsically. The first involves designing tasks which are interesting and which necessitate creativity and resourcefulness. The second involves allowing workers to participate in decisions which concern them so they will feel like they have a say about what they do. The newer participative management theories, then, stress the importance of giving employees a voice in decisions which affect them, and giving them greater latitude in the way they do their jobs. There is less reliance on authority as a control mechanism, and employees are judged by their results. These theories suggest that jobs should be enlarged or enriched so as to be more challenging.

These behavioral scientists believe that participative management is the most effective way of achieving high performance and is also more conducive to satisfied and mentally healthy employees. There are some experimental results which substantiate that organizations which have implemented these practices are more productive and have higher levels of employee satisfaction.

Theories of work motivation which recognize the importance of intrinsic motivation often suggest that work should be structured to elicit this intrinsic motivation and that workers should be rewarded extrinsically for doing well. This presumably has the advantage of motivating employees both intrinsically and extrinsically at the same time, and it assumes that the effects of intrinsic and extrinsic motivation are additive.

It now seems appropriate to ask whether piece-rate payments or other extrinsic reward systems which tie rewards (especially money) to performance are compatible with participative management, which focuses on intrinsic motivation? That is, will a person's intrinsic motivation to do a job remain unaffected by extrinsic rewards?

To investigate this question I have conducted a number of experiments where subjects worked on an intrinsically interesting activity and were given extrinsic rewards for doing so.[1] Then I assessed their intrinsic motivation after their experience with the extrinsic rewards. The hundreds of college students who served as subjects worked on an intrinsically interesting spatial relations puzzle which has seven differently shaped, three dimensional pieces, each of which is made to look like it is composed of three or four one-inch cubes. Subjects used these puzzle pieces to reproduce various configurations which had been drawn on paper for them. Pilot testing showed clearly that subjects found the activity of puzzle-solving highly interesting and enjoyable.

In the experiments to be reported, the experimenter gave each person four configurations to solve and allowed ten minutes to solve each. If a subject were unable to solve one of the puzzles within the ten minutes, he was stopped and shown how to do it. He then proceeded to the next puzzle. At the end of the session with the four puzzles he was left alone in the room to read magazines, solve more puzzles, or do whatever he liked, while the experimenter ostensibly was at a computer terminal.

It was reasoned that subjects were intrinsically motivated if they spent time working on the puzzles when they were alone and when there were other things they could do such as reading magazines. Hence, the amount

---

[1] For a fuller presentation of these experiments, see my papers "The Effects of Contingent and Non-Contingent Rewards and Controls on Intrinsic Motivation," *Organizational Behavior and Human Performance*, vol. 8 (1972), pp. 217–29; and "The Effects of Externally Mediated Rewards on Intrinsic Motivation," *Journal of Personality and Social Psychology*, vol. 18 (1971), pp. 105–15.

of time they spent working on the puzzles while they were alone was a measure of their intrinsic motivation.

Some of the subjects were told at the beginning of the experimental session that they would receive $1 for each of the four puzzles which they solved within the ten minutes; some were not. Earnings for the puzzle-solving (which took about 20 minutes) ranged from $1 to $4 (average was over $2), and this was paid to subjects in cash at the end of the session. It is important to note that, for those who were promised pay, these money payments were contingent upon performance ($1 per puzzle solved).

Those students who had been paid spent significantly less time working on the puzzles when they were alone in the room than did those who had worked on the same puzzles for no pay. Once subjects began to receive contingent monetary payments for doing an interesting activity their intrinsic motivation to perform the activity decreased. That is, they were less willing to perform the activity in the absence of the external rewards than were subjects who had not been paid. The paid subjects had, to some extent, become dependent on the external rewards (money), and their intrinsic motivation had decreased. Or in other words, the locus of causality of their behavior seems to have shifted from within themselves to the external reward.

In another experiment which Wayne Cascio and I conducted,[2] subjects were told that if they were unable to solve any of the puzzles within the ten minutes, a buzzer would sound indicating that their time on that puzzle had expired. They were then given a short exposure to the buzzer so they would realize that it was truly noxious. Consequently, these subjects were performing the activity because of intrinsic motivation and also because they wanted to avoid a punishment (the buzzer). The results indicate that subjects who had performed under the threat of buzzer condition were also less intrinsically motivated than subjects who had received no threats. Since most subjects were able to solve all or all but one of the puzzles, they received little or no punishment (the buzzer) and they experienced little or no failure in doing the task, so it appears that the threat of punishment was the crucial element in decreasing intrinsic motivation in this experiment.

Their behavior, like the behavior of the paid subjects, had apparently become dependent on the external causes (avoiding punishment), and their intrinsic motivation decreased. In summation, one process by which intrinsic motivation can be affected is to have the intrinsically-motivated behavior become dependent on external causes such as tangible rewards

---

[2] Wayne Cascio, now an assistant professor of psychology at Florida International University, assisted me in these experiments while he was my student.

like money or the avoidance of punishment. The perceived locus of causality shifts from within the person to the external reward and causes a decrease in intrinsic motivation.

In the studies involving money payments, the money was made contingent upon performance ($1 per puzzle solved). In another study, subjects were paid $2 for participating in the experiment regardless of their performance, and they showed no change in intrinsic motivation. This seems consistent with the change in perceived locus of causality proposition mentioned above. With the contingent payments, the subject's performance of the activity is instrumental to his receiving the reward, so he is likely to come to perceive the rewards as the *reason* for his performing the activity. With non-contingent payments, however, the payments are not directly tied to performance, so he is less likely to perceive the money as the reason for his performance. Hence, he is less likely to experience a decrease in intrinsic motivation.

We've said that a change in perceived locus of causality is one process by which intrinsic motivation can be affected; the second process involves feedback. Through this process, intrinsic motivation can either be enhanced or decreased. Subjects in one experiment were males who were reinforced with verbal statements such as "Good, that's very fast for that one," each time they solved a puzzle. The intrinsic motivation in these subjects increased due to the experience with positive verbal feedback. They liked the task more and spent more free time working on it than non-rewarded subjects. To understand why verbal reinforcements increase intrinsic motivation, we need to look at what underlies intrinsic motivation. Being intrinsically motivated involves doing an activity not because it will lead to an extrinsic reward but rather because it will allow a person to have internal feelings of competence and self-determination. Therefore, any feedback which is relevant to the person's feelings of competence and self-determination has potential for affecting his intrinsic motivation. This means, then, that external rewards can have at least two functions. One is a "controlling function" which makes a person dependent on the reward, and the other is a "feedback function" which affects his feelings of competence and self-determination.

Money and threats are commonly perceived as controllers of behavior. As a result, subjects become dependent on these controls and lose intrinsic motivation even though the money or avoided punishment *could* provide them with positive information about their competence and self-determination. On the other hand, a subject is less likely to become dependent on verbal reinforcements because he is less likely to perceive the feedback as the reason for his performance. In fact, the effect of verbal feedback may not be distinguishable from the internal feedback which he gives himself (namely, recognizing that he is competent and self-determining). So, in the experiment described above, the positive feedback would indeed have strengthened the subjects' feelings of competence and self-determination, thereby increasing their intrinsic motivation.

In a replication of the verbal reinforcement experiment we used both male and female subjects and were surprised to find a sex difference. Positive verbal feedback increases the intrinsic motivation of males, but it decreased the intrinsic motivation of females. Apparently, due to socialization processes, females more readily become dependent on verbal praise than males do. For females, we see a change in perceived locus of causality which causes a decrease in intrinsic motivation; however, the same does not happen for males.

Now imagine a situation in which the feedback is negative. It should decrease intrinsic motivation because it decreases the subjects' feelings of competence and self-determination. Wayne Cascio and I did an experiment which utilized a different set of puzzles that were much more difficult. The subjects failed badly in solving these puzzles, and afterward, they were less intrinsically motivated than subjects who had worked on somewhat easier puzzles with a higher success rate. The negative feelings associated with failure had offset some of the internal rewards associated with the activity causing a decrease in intrinsic motivation. Failing at an activity made the people less motivated to do it.

We have seen that intrinsic motivation appears to be affected by two processes: change in locus of causality, and change in feelings of competence and self-determination. Intrinsic motivation decreases when a person's behavior becomes dependent on an extrinsic reward or threat. It also decreases when a person receives negative feedback about his performance on an intrinsically motivated activity. But it increases in males as a result of positive feedback.

To understand the importance of these results for organizations, it is necessary to distinguish between keeping a person on the job and motivating him to perform effectively on that job. To attract and keep a person in an organization, it is necessary to satisfy his needs. He will have to be paid a competitive salary and given other comforts. However, satisfying a worker does not guarantee that he will be motivated to perform well on the job. Let us, therefore, consider how payments and intrinsic factors relate to satisfaction on the one hand and effective performance on the other. Paying workers is necessary to attract them to jobs and keep them satisfied with those jobs. However, in order to use money as a motivator of performance, the performance has to be perceived by the worker as being instrumental to his receiving the money. As we've said, this is generally accomplished by making pay contingent upon performance. In other words, it is not the money *per se* which motivates performance but rather the way that it is administered. To use money as an extrinsic motivator (or controller) of behavior, it has to be administered contingently. However, we've seen that not only are there many difficulties in making such a system work effectively, but also such a system decreases intrinsic motivation.

On the other hand, a system for motivating employees such as participative management, which—through participation and job enlargement—attempts to arouse intrinsic motivation, appears to motivate effective performance at the same time that it satisfies intrinsic needs. Since advocates of participative management stress the importance of intrinsic motivation, the experimental results which demonstrate that money decreases intrinsic motivation have led some antagonists to the conclusion that workers should not be payed. Clearly, such a prescription is absurd. The importance of the non-contingent payment study is that money does not decrease intrinsic motivation if it is paid non-contingently. It is possible to pay workers and still have them intrinsically motivated. So we are left with a dilemma. To use money and other extrinsic rewards as effective motivators they must be made contingent on performance. However, doing this decreases intrinsic motivation.

This suggests then that we must choose between trying to utilize either intrinsic or extrinsic reward systems. I personally favor the prescription that we concentrate on structuring situations and jobs to arouse intrinsic motivation, rather than trying to structure piece-rate and other contingency payment schemes. This preference is based on the evidence which indicates that intrinsic approaches seem to lead to greater productivity and more satisfied workers.

_____ 23 _____

On the Folly of Rewarding A,
While Hoping for B*

STEVEN KERR

W HETHER dealing with monkeys, rats, or human beings, it is hardly
controversial to state that most organisms seek information concerning what activities are rewarded, and then seek to do (or at least
pretend to do) those things, often to the virtual exclusion of activities not
rewarded. The extent to which this occurs of course will depend on the
perceived attractiveness of the rewards offered, but neither operant nor
expectancy theorists would quarrel with the essence of this notion.

Nevertheless, numerous examples exist of reward systems that are fouled
up in that behaviors which are rewarded are those which the rewarder is
trying to *discourage*, while the behavior he desires is not being rewarded
at all.

In an effort to understand and explain this phenomenon, this paper presents examples from society, from organizations in general, and from
profit-making firms in particular. Data from a manufacturing company
and information from an insurance firm are examined to demonstrate
the consequences of such reward systems for the organizations involved,
and possible reasons why such reward systems continue to exist are
considered.

SOCIETAL EXAMPLES

Politics

Official goals are "purposely vague and general and do not indicate . . .
the host of decisions that must be made among alternative ways of achiev-

---

* Reprinted from *Academy of Management Journal*, 1975, vol. 18, pp. 769–83.

ing official goals and the priority of multiple goals . . ." (8, p. 66). They usually may be relied on to offend absolutely no one, and in this sense can be considered high-acceptance, low-quality goals. An example might be "build better schools." Operative goals are higher in quality but lower in acceptance, since they specify where the money will come from, what alternative goals will be ignored, etc.

The American citizenry supposedly wants its candidates for public office to set forth operative goals, making their proposed programs "perfectly clear," specifying sources and uses of funds, etc. However, since operative goals are lower in acceptance, and since aspirants to public office need acceptance (from at least 50.1 percent of the people), most politicians prefer to speak only of officials goals, at least until after the election. They of course would agree to speak at the operative level if "punished" for not doing so. The electorate could do this by refusing to support candidates who do not speak at the operative level.

Instead, however, the American voter typically punishes (withholds support from) candidates who frankly discuss where the money will come from, rewards politicians who speaks only of official goals, but hopes that candidates (despite the reward system) will discuss the issues operatively. It is academic whether it was moral for Nixon, for example, to refuse to discuss his 1968 "secret plan" to end the Vietnam war, his 1972 operative goals concerning the lifting of price controls, the reshuffling of his cabinet, etc. The point is that the reward system made such refusal rational.

It seems worth mentioning that no manuscript can adequately define what is "moral" and what is not. However, examination of costs and benefits, combined with knowledge of what motivates a particular individual, often will suffice to determine what for him is "rational."[1] If the reward system is so designed that it is irrational to be moral, this does not necessarily mean that immorality will result. But is this not asking for trouble?

War

If some oversimplification may be permitted, let it be assumed that the primary goal of the organization (Pentagon, Luftwaffe, or whatever) is to win. Let it be assumed further that the primary goal of most individuals on the front lines is to get home alive. Then there appears to be an important conflict in goals—personally rational behavior by those at the bottom will endanger goal attainment by those at the top.

But not necessarily! It depends on how the reward system is set up.

---

[1] In Simon's (10, pp. 76–77) terms, a decision is "subjectively rational" if it maximizes an individual's valued outcomes so far as his knowledge permits. A decision is "personally rational" if it is oriented toward the individual's goals.

The Vietnam war was indeed a study of disobedience and rebellion, with terms such as "fragging" (killing one's own commanding officer) and "search and evade" becoming part of the military vocabulary. The difference in subordinates' acceptance of authority between World War II and Vietnam is reported to be considerable, and veterans of the Second World War often have been quoted as being outraged at the mutinous actions of many American soldiers in Vietnam.

Consider, however, some critical differences in the reward system in use during the two conflicts. What did the GI in World War II want? To go home. And when did he get to go home? When the war was won! If he disobeyed the orders to clean out the trenches and take the hills, the war would not be won and he would not go home. Furthermore, what were his chances of attaining his goal (getting home alive) if he obeyed the orders compared to his chances if he did not? What is being suggested is that the rational soldier in World War II, *whether patriotic or not*, probably found it expedient to obey.

Consider the reward system in use in Vietnam. What did the man at the bottom want? To go home. And when did he get to go home? When his tour of duty was over! This was the case *whether or not* the war was won. Furthermore, concerning the relative chance of getting home alive by obeying orders compared to the chance if they were disobeyed, it is worth noting that a mutineer in Vietnam was far more likely to be assigned rest and rehabilitation (on the assumption that fatigue was the cause) than he was to suffer any negative consequence.

In his description of the "zone of indifference," Barnard stated that "a person can and will accept a communication as authoritative only when ... at the time of his decision, he believes it to be compatible with his personal interests as a whole" (1, p. 165). In light of the reward system used in Vietnam, would it not have been personally irrational for some orders to have been obeyed? Was not the military implementing a system which *rewarded* disobedience, while *hoping* that soldiers (despite the reward system) would obey orders?

Medicine

Theoretically, a physician can make either of two types of error, and intuitively one seems as bad as the other. A doctor can pronounce a patient sick when he is actually well, thus causing him needless anxiety and expense, curtailment of enjoyable foods and activities, and even physical danger by subjecting him to needless medication and surgery. Alternately, a doctor can label a sick person well, and thus avoid treating what may be a serious, even fatal ailment. It might be natural to conclude that physicians seek to minimize both types of error.

Such a conclusion would be wrong.[2] It is estimated that numerous Americans are presently afflicted with iatrogenic (physician *caused*) illnesses (9). This occurs when the doctor is approached by someone complaining of a few stray symptoms. The doctor classifies and organizes these symptoms, gives them a name, and obligingly tells the patient what further symptoms may be expected. This information often acts as a self-fulfilling prophecy, with the result that from that day on the patient for all practical purposes is sick.

Why does this happen? Why are physicians so reluctant to sustain a type 2 error (pronouncing a sick person well) that they will tolerate many type 1 errors? Again, a look at the reward system is needed. The punishments for a type 2 error are real: guilt, embarrassment, and the threat of lawsuit and scandal. On the other hand, a type 1 error (labeling a well person sick) "is sometimes seen as sound clinical practice, indicating a healthy conservative approach to medicine" (9, p. 69). Type 1 errors also are likely to generate increased income and a stream of steady customers who, being well in a limited physiological sense, will not embarrass the doctor by dying abruptly.

Fellow physicians and the general public therefore are really *rewarding* type 1 errors and at the same time *hoping* fervently that doctors will try not to make them.

GENERAL ORGANIZATIONAL EXAMPLES

Rehabilitation Centers and Orphanages

In terms of the prime beneficiary classification (2, p. 42) organizations such as these are supposed to exist for the "public-in-contact," that is, clients. The orphanage therefore theoretically is interested in placing as many children as possible in good homes. However, often orphanages surround themselves with so many rules concerning adoption that it is nearly impossible to pry a child out of the place. Orphanages may deny adoption unless the applicants are a married couple, both of the same religion as the child, without history of emotional or vocational instability, with a specified minimum income and a private room for the child, etc.

If the primary goal is to place children in good homes, then the rules ought to constitute means toward that goal. Goal displacement results when these "means become ends-in-themselves that displaces the original goals" (2, p. 229).

To some extent these rules are required by law. But the influence of

---

[2] In one study (4) of 14,867 films for signs of tuberculosis, 1,216 positive readings turned out to be clinically negative; only 24 negative readings proved clinically active, a ratio of 50 to 1.

the reward system on the orphanage's management should not be ignored. Consider, for example, that the:

1. Number of children enrolled often is the most important determinant of the size of the allocated budget.
2. Number of children under the director's care also will affect the size of his staff.
3. Total organizational size will determine largely the director's prestige at the annual conventions, in the community, etc.

Therefore, to the extent that staff size, total budget, and personal prestige are valued by the orphanage's executive personnel, it becomes rational for them to make it difficult for children to be adopted. After all, who wants to be the director of the smallest orphanage in the state?

If the reward system errs in the opposite direction, paying off only for placements, extensive goal displacement again is likely to result. A common example of vocational rehabilitation in many states, for example, consists of placing someone in a job for which he has little interest and few qualifications, for two months or so, and then "rehabilitating" him again in another position. Such behavior is quite consistent with the prevailing reward system, which pays off for the number of individuals placed in any position for 60 days or more. Rehabilitation counselors also confess to competing with one another to place relatively skilled clients, sometimes ignoring persons with few skills who would be harder to place. Extensively disabled clients find that counselors often prefer to work with those whose disabilities are less severe.[3]

Universities

Society *hopes* that teachers will not neglect their teaching responsibilities but *rewards* them almost entirely for research and publications. This is most true at the large and prestigious universities. Clichés such as "good research and good teaching go together" notwithstanding, professors often find that they must choose between teaching and research-oriented activities when allocating their time. Rewards for good teaching usually are limited to outstanding teacher awards, which are given to only a small percentage of good teachers and which usually bestow little money and fleeting prestige. Punishments for poor teaching also are rare.

Rewards for research and publications, on the other hand, and punishments for failure to accomplish these, are commonly administered by universities at which teachers are employed. Furthermore, publication-oriented resumés usually will be well received at other universities, whereas teaching credentials, harder to document and quantify, are much less

---

[3] Personal interviews conducted during 1972–73.

transferable. Consequently it is rational for university teachers to concentrate on research, even if to the detriment of teaching and at the expense of their students.

By the same token, it is rational for students to act based upon the goal displacement which has occurred within universities concerning what they are rewarded for. If it is assumed that a primary goal of a university is to transfer knowledge from teacher to student, then grades become identifiable as a means toward that goal, serving as motivational, control, and feedback devices to expedite the knowledge transfer. Instead, however, the grades themselves have become much more important for entrance to graduate school, successful employment, tuition refunds, parental respect, etc., than the knowledge or lack of knowledge they are supposed to signify.

It therefore should come as no surprise that information has surfaced in recent years concerning fraternity files for examinations, term-paper writing services, organized cheating at the service academies, and the like. Such activities constitute a personally rational response to a reward system which pays off for grades rather than knowledge.

BUSINESS-RELATED EXAMPLES

Ecology

Assume that the president of XYZ Corporation is confronted with the following alternatives:

1. Spend $11 million for antipollution equipment to keep from poisoning fish in the river adjacent to the plant; or
2. Do nothing, in violation of the law, and assume a one in ten chance of being caught, with a resultant $1 million fine plus the necessity of buying the equipment.

Under this not unrealistic set of choices it requires no linear program to determine that XYZ Corporation can maximize its probabilities by flouting the law. Add the fact that XYZ's president is probably being rewarded (by creditors, stockholders, and other salient parts of his task environment) according to criteria totally unrelated to the number of fish poisoned, and his probable course of action becomes clear.

Evaluation of Training

It is axiomatic that those who care about a firm's well-being should insist that the organization get fair value for its expenditures. Yet it is commonly known that firms seldom bother to evaluate a new GRID, MBO, job enrichment program, or whatever, to see if the company is getting its money's worth. Why? Certainly it is not because people have not pointed out that this situation exists; numerous practitioner-oriented articles are written each year to just this point.

The individuals (whether in personnel, manpower planning, or wherever) who normally would be responsible for conducting such evaluations are the same ones often charged with introducing the change effort in the first place. Having convinced top management to spend the money, they usually are quite animated afterwards in collecting arigorous vignettes and anecdotes about how successful the program was. The last thing many desire is a formal systematic and revealing evaluation. Although members of top management may actually *hope* for such systematic evaluation, their reward systems continue to *reward* ignorance in this area. And if the personnel department abdicates its responsibility, who is to step into the breach? The change agent himself? Hardly! He is likely to be too busy collecting anecdotal "evidence" of his own, for use with his next client.

Miscellaneous

Many additional examples could be cited of systems which in fact are rewarding behaviors other than those supposedly desired by the rewarder. A few of these are described briefly below.

Most coaches disdain to discuss individual accomplishments, preferring to speak of teamwork, proper attitude, and a one-for-all spirit. Usually, however, rewards are distributed according to individual performance. The college basketball player who feeds his teammates instead of shooting will not compile impressive scoring statistics and is less likely to be drafted by the pros. The ballplayer who hits to right field to advance the runners will win neither the batting nor home run titles, and will be offered smaller raises. It therefore is rational for players to think of themselves first, and the team second.

In business organizations where rewards are dispensed for unit performance or for individual goals achieved, without regard for overall effectiveness, similar attitudes often are observed. Under most Management by Objectives (MBO) systems, goals in areas where quantification is difficult often go unspecified. The organization therefore often is in a position where it *hopes* for employee effort in the areas of team building, interpersonal relations, creativity, etc., but it formally *rewards* none of these. In cases where promotions and raises are formally tied to MBO, the system itself contains a paradox in that it "asks employees to set challenging, risky goals, only to face smaller paychecks and possibly damaged careers if these goals are not accomplished" (5, p. 40).

It is *hoped* that administrators will pay attention to long-run costs and opportunities and will institute programs which will bear fruit later on. However, many organizational reward systems pay off for short-run sales and earnings only. Under such circumstances it is personally rational for officials to sacrifice long-term growth and profit (by selling off equipment and property, or by stifling research and development) for short-term advantages. This probably is most pertinent in the public sector, with the result that many public officials are unwilling to implement programs which will not show benefits by election time.

As a final, clear-cut example of a fouled-up reward system, consider the cost-plus contract or its next of kin, the allocation of next year's budget as a direct function of this year's expenditures. It probably is conceivable that those who award such budgets and contracts really hope for economy and prudence in spending. It is obvious, however, that adopting the proverb "to him who spends shall more be given," rewards not economy, but spending itself.

TWO COMPANIES' EXPERIENCES

A Manufacturing Organization

A midwest manufacturer of industrial goods had been troubled for some time by aspects of its organizational climate it believed dysfunctional. For research purposes, interviews were conducted with many employees and a questionnaire was administered on a company-wide basis, including plants and offices in several American and Canadian locations. The company strongly encouraged employee participation in the survey, and made available time and space during the workday for completion of the instrument. All employees in attendance during the day of the survey completed the questionnaire. All instruments were collected directly by the researcher, who personally administered each session. Since no one employed by the firm handled the questionnaires, and since respondent names were not asked for, it seems likely that the pledge of anonymity given was believed.

A modified version of the Expect Approval scale (7) was included as part of the questionnaire. The instrument asked respondents to indicate the degree of approval or disapproval they could expect if they performed each of the described actions. A seven-point Likert scale was used, with 1 indicating that the action would probably bring strong disapproval and 7 signifying likely strong approval.

Although normative data for this scale from studies of other organizations are unavailable, it is possible to examine fruitfully the data obtained from this survey in several ways. First, it may be worth noting that the questionnaire data corresponded closely to information gathered through interviews. Furthermore, as can be seen from the results summarized in Table 1, sizable differences between various work units, and between employees at different job levels within the same work unit, were obtained.

This suggests that response bias effects (social desirability in particular loomed as a potential concern) are not likely to be severe.

Most importantly, comparisons between scores obtained on the Expect Approval scale and a statement of problems which were the reason for the survey revealed that the same behaviors which managers in each division thought dysfunctional were those which lower level employees claimed were rewarded. As compared to job levels 1 to 8 in Division B (see Table 1), those in Division A claimed a much higher acceptance by management of "conforming" activities. Between 31 and 37 percent of Division A employees at levels 1-8 stated that going along with the majority, agreeing with the boss, and staying on everyone's good side brought approval; only once (level 5-8 responses to one of the three items) did a majority suggest that such actions would generate disapproval.

Furthermore, responses from Division A workers at levels 1-4 indicate that behaviors geared toward risk avoidance were as likely to be rewarded as to be punished. Only at job levels 9 and above was it apparent that the reward system was positively reinforcing behaviors desired by top management. Overall, the same "tendencies toward conservatism and apple-polishing at the lower levels" which divisional management had complained about during the interviews were those claimed by subordinates to be the most rational course of action in light of the existing reward system. Management apparently was not getting the behaviors it was *hoping* for, but it certainly was getting the behaviors it was perceived by subordinates to be *rewarding*.

An Insurance Firm

The Group Health Claims Division of a large eastern insurance company provides another rich illustration of a reward system which reinforces behaviors not desired by top management.

Attempting to measure and reward accuracy in paying surgical claims, the firm systematically keeps track of the number of returned checks and letters of complaint received from policyholders. However, underpayments are likely to provoke cries of outrage from the insured, while overpayments often are accepted in courteous silence. Since it often is impossible to tell from the physician's statement which of two surgical procedures, with different allowable benefits, was performed, and since writing for clarifications will interfere with other standards used by firm concerning "percentage of claims paid within two days of receipt," the new hire in more than one claims section is soon acquainted with the informal norm: "When in doubt, pay it out!"

The situation would be even worse were it not for the fact that other features of the firm's reward system tend to neutralize those described.

Table 1
Summary of Two Divisions' Data Relevant to Conforming and Risk-Avoidance Behaviors (extent to which subjects expect approval)

Dimension	Item	Division and Sample	Total Responses	Percentage of Workers Responding		
				1, 2, or 3 (disapproval)	4	5, 6, or 7 (approval)
Risk avoidance	Making a risky decision based on the best information available at the time, but which turns out wrong.	A, levels 1–4 (lowest)	127	61	25	14
		A, levels 5–8	172	46	31	23
		A, levels 9 and above	17	41	30	30
		B, levels 1–4 (lowest)	31	58	26	16
		B, levels 5–8	19	42	42	16
		B, levels 9 and above	10	50	20	30
Risk	Setting extremely high and challenging standards and goals, and then narrowly failing to make them.	A, levels 1–4	122	47	28	25
		A, levels 5–8	168	33	26	41
		A, levels 9 +	17	24	6	70
		B, levels 1–4	31	48	23	29
		B, levels 5–8	18	17	33	50
		B, levels 9 +	10	30	0	70
	Setting goals which are extremely easy to make and then making them.	A, levels 1–4	124	35	30	35
		A, levels 5–8	171	47	27	26
		A, levels 9 +	17	70	24	6

	B, levels 1–4	31	58	26	16
	B, levels 5–8	19	63	16	21
	B, levels 9 +	10	80	0	20
Being a "yes man" and always agreeing with the boss.	A, levels 1–4	126	46	17	37
	A, levels 5–8	180	54	14	31
	A, levels 9 +	17	88	12	0
	B, levels 1–4	32	53	28	19
	B, levels 5–8	19	68	21	11
	B, levels 9 +	10	80	10	10
Always going along with the majority.	A, levels 1–4	125	40	25	35
	A, levels 5–8	173	47	21	32
	A, levels 9 +	17	70	12	18
	B, levels 1–4	31	61	23	16
	B, levels 5–8	19	68	11	21
	B, levels 9 +	10	80	10	10
Being careful to stay on the good side of everyone, so that everyone agrees that you are a great guy.	A, levels 1–4	124	45	18	37
	A, levels 5–8	173	45	22	33
	A, levels 9 +	17	64	6	30
	B, levels 1–4	31	54	23	23
	B, levels 5–8	19	73	11	16
	B, levels 9 +	10	80	10	10

For example, annual "merit" increases are given to all employees, in one of the following three amounts:

1. If the worker is "outstanding" (a select category, into which no more than two employees per section may be placed): 5 percent
2. If the worker is "above average" (normally all workers not "outstanding" are so rated): 4 percent
3. If the worker commits gross acts of negligence and irresponsibility for which he might be discharged in many other companies: 3 percent.

Now, since (a) the difference between the 5 percent theoretically attainable through hard work and the 4 percent attainable merely by living until the review data is small and (b) since insurance firms seldom dispense much of a salary increase in cash (rather, the worker's insurance benefits increase, causing him to be further overinsured), many employees are rather indifferent to the possibility of obtaining the extra one percent reward and therefore tend to ignore the norm concerning indiscriminant payments.

However, most employees are not indifferent to the rule which states that, should absences or latenesses total three or more in any six-month period, the entire 4 or 5 percent due at the next "merit" review must be forfeited. In this sense the firm may be described as *hoping* for performance, while *rewarding* attendance. What it gets, of course, is attendance. (If the absence-lateness rule appears to the reader to be stringent, it really is not. The company counts "times" rather than "days" absent, and a ten-day absence therefore counts the same as one lasting two days. A worker in danger of accumulating a third absence within six months merely has to remain ill (away from work) during his second absence until his first absence is more than six months old. The limiting factor is that at some point his salary ceases, and his sickness benefits take over. This usually is sufficient to get the younger workers to return, but for those with 20 or more years' service, the company provides sickness benefits of 90 percent of normal salary, tax-free! Therefore . . . .)

CAUSES

Extremely diverse instances of systems which reward behavior A although the rewarder apparently hopes for behavior B have been given. These are useful to illustrate the breadth and magnitude of the phenomenon, but the diversity increases the difficulty of determining commonalities and establishing causes. However, four general factors may be pertinent to an explanation of why fouled-up reward systems seem to be so prevalent.

Fascination with an "Objective" Criterion

It has been mentioned elsewhere that:

Most "objective" measures of productivity are objective only in that their subjective elements are (*a*) determined in advance, rather than coming into play at the time of the formal evaluation, and (*b*) well concealed on the rating instrument itself. Thus industrial firms seeking to devise objective rating systems first decide, in an arbitrary manner, what dimensions are to be rated, . . . usually including some items having little to do with organizational effectiveness while excluding others that do. Only then does Personnel Division churn out official-looking documents on which all dimensions chosen to be rated are assigned point values, categories, or whatever (6, p. 92).

Nonetheless, many individuals seek to establish simple, quantifiable standards against which to measure and reward performance. Such efforts may be successful in highly predictable areas within an organization, but are likely to cause goal displacement when applied anywhere else. Overconcern with attendance and lateness in the insurance firm and with number of people placed in the vocational rehabilitation division may have been largely responsible for the problems described in those organizations.

Overemphasis on Highly Visible Behaviors

Difficulties often stem from the fact that some parts of the task are highly visible while other parts are not. For example, publications are easier to demonstrate than teaching, and scoring baskets and hitting home runs are more readily observable than feeding teammates and advancing base runners. Similarly, the adverse consequences of pronouncing a sick person well are more visible than those sustained by labeling a well person sick. Team-building and creativity are other examples of behaviors which may not be rewarded simply because they are hard to observe.

Hypocrisy

In some of the instances described the rewarder may have been getting the desired behavior, notwithstanding claims that the behavior was not desired. This may be true, for example, of management's attitude toward apple polishing in the manufacturing firm (a behavior which subordinates felt was rewarded, despite management's avowed dislike of the practice). This also may explain politicians' unwillingness to revise the penalties for disobedience of ecology laws, and the failure of top management to devise reward systems which would cause systematic evaluation of training and developing programs.

Emphasis on Morality or Equity Rather than Efficiency

Some consideration of other factors prevents the establishment of a system which rewards behaviors desired by the rewarder. The felt obligation of many Americans to vote for one candidate or another, for example, may impair their ability to withhold support from politicians who refuse to discuss the issues. Similarly, the concern for spreading the risks and costs of wartime military service may outweigh the advantage to be obtained by commiting personnel to combat until the war is over.

It should be noted that only with respect to the first two causes are reward systems really paying off for other than desired behaviors. In the case of the third and fourth causes the system *is* rewarding behaviors desired by the rewarder, and the systems are fouled up only from the standpoints of those who believe the rewarder's public statements (cause 3), or those who seek to maximize efficiency rather than other outcomes (cause 4).

CONCLUSIONS

Modern organization theory requires a recognition that the members of organizations and society possess divergent goals and motives. It therefore is unlikely that managers and their subordinates will seek the same outcomes. Three possible remedies for this potential problem are suggested.

Selection

It is theoretically possible for organizations to employ only those individuals whose goals and motives are wholly consonant with those of management. In such cases the same behaviors judged by subordinates to be rational would be perceived by management as desirable. State-of-the-art reviews of selection techniques, however, provide scant grounds for hope that such an approach would be successful (for example, see 12).

Training

Another theoretical alternative is for the organization to admit those employees whose goals are not consonant with those of management and then, through training, socialization, or whatever, alter employee goals to make them consonant. However, research on the effectiveness of such training programs, though limited, provides further grounds for pessimism (for example, see 3).

Altering the Reward System

What would have been the result if:

1. Nixon had been assured by his advisors that he could not win reelection except by discussing the issues in detail?

2. Physicians' conduct was subjected to regular examination by review boards for type 1 errors (calling healthy people ill) and to penalties (fines, censure, etc.) for errors of either type?

3. The President of XYZ Corporation had to choose between (*a*) spending $11 million for antipollution equipment, and (*b*) incurring a 50-50 chance of going to jail for five years?

Managers who complain that their workers are not motivated might do well to consider the possibility that they have installed reward systems which are paying off for behaviors other than those they are seeking. This, in part, is what happened in Vietnam, and this is what regularly frustrates societal efforts to bring about honest politicians, civic-minded managers, etc. This certainly is what happened in both the manufacturing and the insurance companies.

A first step for such managers might be to find out what behaviors currently are being rewarded. Perhaps an instrument similar to that used in the manufacturing firm could be useful for this purpose. Chances are excellent that these managers will be surprised by what they find—that their firms are not rewarding what they assume they are. In fact, such undesirable behavior by organizational members as they have observed may be explained largely by the reward systems in use.

This is not to say that all organizational behavior is determined by formal rewards and punishments. Certainly it is true that in the absence of formal reinforcement some soldiers will be patriotic, some presidents will be ecology minded, and some orphanage directors will care about children. The point, however, is that in such cases the rewarder is not *causing* the behaviors desired but is only a fortunate bystander. For an organization to *act* upon its members, the formal reward system should positively reinforce desired behaviors, not constitute an obstacle to be overcome.

It might be wise to underscore the obvious fact that there is nothing really new in what has been said. In both theory and practice these matters have been mentioned before. Thus in many states Good Samaritan laws have been installed to protect doctors who stop to assist a sticken motorist. In states without such laws it is commonplace for doctors to refuse to stop, for fear of involvement in a subsequent lawsuit. In college basketball additional penalties have been instituted against players who foul their opponents deliberately. It has long been argued by Milton Friedman and others that penalties should be altered so as to make it irrational to disobey the ecology laws, and so on.

By altering the reward system the organization escapes the necessity of selecting only desirable people or of trying to alter undesirable ones. In Skinnerian terms (as described in 11, p. 704), "As for responsibility and goodness—as commonly defined—no one . . . would want or need them.

They refer to a man's behaving well despite the absence of positive reinforcement that is obviously sufficient to explain it. Where such reinforcement exists, 'no one needs goodness.'"

REFERENCES

1. Barnard, Chester I. *The Functions of the Executive.* Cambridge, Mass.:
   Harvard University Press, 1964.
2. Blau, Peter M., and W. Richard Scott. *Formal Organizations.* San Fran-
   cisco: Chandler, 1962.
3. Fiedler, Fred E. "Predicting the Effects of Leadership Training and Experience from the Contingency Model," *Journal of Applied Psychology,*
   vol. 56 (1972), pp. 114–19.
4. Garland, L. H. "Studies of the Accuracy of Diagnostic Procedures,"
   American Journal Roentgenological Radium Therapy Nuclear Medicine,
   vol. 82 (1959), pp. 25–38.
5. Kerr, Steven. "Some Modifications in MBO as an OD Strategy," *Academy
   of Management Proceedings,* 1973, pp. 39–42.
6. Kerr, Steven. "What Price Objectivity?" *American Sociologist,* vol. 8
   (1973), pp. 92–93.
7. Litwin, G. H., and R. A. Stringer, Jr. *Motivation and Organizational
   Climate.* Boston: Harvard University Press, 1968.
8. Perrow, Charles. "The Analysis of Goals in Complex Organizations," in
   A. Etzioni, ed., *Readings on Modern Organizations.* Englewood Cliffs,
   N.J.: Prentice-Hall, 1969.
9. Scheff, Thomas J. "Decision Rules, Types of Error, and Their Consequences in Medical Diagnosis," in F. Massarik and P. Ratoosh, eds.,
   Mathematical Explorations in Behavioral Science. Homewood, Ill.: Irwin,
   1965.
10. Simon, Herbert A. *Administrative Behavior.* New York: Free Press, 1957.
11. Swanson, G. E. "Review Symposium: Beyond Freedom and Dignity,"
    American Journal of Sociology, vol. 78 (1972), pp. 702–05.
12. Webster, E. *Decision Making in the Employment Interview.* Montreal:
    Industrial Relations Center, McGill University, 1964.

Worker Participation in
Decision Making*

IRVING BLUESTONE

THE history of mankind has been marked by struggle between those who govern and those who are governed. In each major conflict, regardless of time, place, and circumstances, the voice of rebellion against authority has manifested itself in the cry for freedom, liberty, human rights, and human dignity. The underlying motivation is the desire for the right to participate in the decisions that affect one's welfare.

Monarchs once claimed to rule by the "divine right of kings." And who would be so brave as to challenge the right of rulers claiming divine guidance? Yet challengers there were, and challengers there will be. The yearning of people to have something to say about how they will be governed is unceasing, even as history records setbacks along the road.

The same drive that has moved people and nations toward political freedom exists as well in the workplace—between employer and employee. The owner of capital in the early years of the Industrial Revolution assumed the same mantle in his firm as had monarchs in an earlier day. We are, of course, familiar with the oppression and oppressiveness in the factories of the early Industrial Revolution. Control over the employees was almost absolute—short of the worker's right to quit and take a chance of being blackballed from other employment.

Zachary U. Geiger, proprietor of the Mt. Cory Carriage and Wagon Works, listed rules and regulations for his employees in April 1872. Today they appear ludicrous, yet they were the norm in their day.

1. Employes will daily sweep the floors, dust the furniture, shelves, and showcases.

---

* This article first appeared in *The Humanist,* September–October 1973, pp. 11–15, and is reprinted by permission.

2.   Each day fill lamps, clean chimneys and trim wicks; wash the windows once a week.

3.   Each clerk will bring in a bucket of water and skuttle of coal for the day's business.

4.   Make your own pens carefully. You may whittle nibs to your individual taste.

5.   This office will open at 7 a.m. and close at 8 p.m. daily except on the Sabbath, on which day it will remain closed.

6.   Men employes will be given an evening off each week for courting purposes, or two evenings if they go regularly to church.

7.   Every employe should lay aside from each pay a goodly sum of his earnings for his benefits during his declining years so that he will not become a burden upon the charity of his betters.

8.   Any employe who smokes Spanish cigars, uses liquors in any forms, gets shaved at a barber shop, or frequents public halls will give good reason to suspect his worth, intentions, integrity, and honesty.

9.   The employe who has performed his labors faithfully and without fault for a period of five years in my service and who has been thrifty and attentive to his religious duties and is looked upon by his fellowmen as a substantial and law-abiding citizen will be given an increase of 5 cents per day in his pay providing that just returns in profits from the business permit it.

Contrast this relationship with the following. In 1967, the UAW was negotiating with each of the three big automobile companies—General Motors, Ford, and Chrysler. These negotiations took place separately, since the auto industry and the UAW do not engage in industry-wide national-contract bargaining. When the contracts were about to come to their terminal date (each of them had the same date of termination), the union proposed to each automobile company that the contracts be extended on a day-to-day basis while negotiations continued toward a conclusion. The companies refused this proposal. As a result, the contracts expired, and the workers were free to strike at any time. One of the union's tactics was to curtail overtime work in order to forestall the buildup of car inventories.

In one of the plants, the local management called a meeting with the committee after the workers had walked out rather than work overtime. The management said to the committee: "You fellows won't let us set our own schedules; so, okay, you set the schedules."

The chairman of the union committee pondered this a moment and asked, "You mean you want to give up management's prerogative to schedule overtime? You want the workers to make that decision?" The company spokesman replied, "Look, we are asking you to do it." The union chairman, without blinking an eye, retorted, "The hell with you. You set the schedules, and we won't work them!"

Authoritarian Rule in the Workplace

In a society that prides itself on its democratic system of freedom for the individual and rejection of dictatorial rule, the workplace still stands as an island of authoritarianism. The organizational mold of business, especially big business, and the material objective of maximizing profits serve to obstruct, or at least deter, the fulfillment of democracy in the workplace. In fact, the workplace is probably the most authoritarian environment in which the adult finds himself in a free society. Its rigidity leads people to live a kind of double life: at home, they enjoy a reasonable measure of autonomy and self-fulfillment; at work, they are subject to regimentation, supervision, and control by others.

A society anchored in democratic principles should ensure each individual the dignity, respect, and liberty worthy of free people; it should afford opportunity for self-expression and participation in the shaping of one's own life. At work, however, personal freedom is severely curtailed, each worker having to adapt himself to tasks, work speeds, and behavior decided upon by others or by machines.

The American way of life rests on the concept that in public life the "governors" are subject to the will of the "governed." In the private life of business, however, leadership does not stem from the confidence of the "governed" (the workers); rather, it is directed toward protection of the interests of the firm, most often against the "governed," whose activities and patterns of life at work are organized, directed, and dominated by the "governors."

In a democracy, the rules of society are fashioned with the consent of those who must live by them, and the individual is guaranteed a fair trial and is "innocent until proved guilty." In the workplace, management decides the rules to be lived by, then exercises its authority to impose sanctions in cases of individual transgression.

The argument used to support authoritarianism in the workplace is that the organization of production and the goal of maximizing profit make it mandatory. Ownership means control. Ownership means rule by decree. Thus, the pattern of relations between the "governors" and the "governed" in business is contradictory to democracy.

Moreover, the power of ownership is reinforced in society by custom, tradition, and law. The rights of property often supersede the rights of people, and these property rights are buttressed by protective legislation.

This is the heart of the problem that labor-management relations must grapple with. Workers who organize into unions bring an increasing measure of democracy into the workplace. In the broadest possible sense, this is an essential task of unionism and collective bargaining. Moreover, once organized, the workers, as citizens, move to alter the law and to make the rights of people superior to the rights of property and profit. This, too, is an essential task of unionism.

Present-day industrialized society holds to certain economic precepts. Among them are: (1) technological progress is inevitable and desirable; (2) a better living standard for all depends on increased productivity and an expanding gross national product; (3) the purpose of business is to make and maximize profit.

Thus, the underlying thrust of our economic system, anchored in these precepts, has motivated management to develop a production system that is maximally advanced technologically, with maximum production at the lowest possible unit cost, and maximum profitability.

The pursuit of maximum profit received remarkable stimulus with the advent of industrial organization and its system of production. Very soon, individuals and their needs became extensions of that tool. Skills were broken down to the least common denominator so that humans became as interchangeable as machine parts. Specialization through fractioning the job into the simplest, most repetitive acts of performance reduced skill requirements to the minimum. This production process evolved into scientific management.

The granddaddy of the principles of scientific management, Frederick Taylor, once observed that the average workingman is "so stupid and so phlegmatic that he more resembles the ox in his mental makeup than any other type." Obviously, this is more than mere exaggeration. It is a cynical expression concerning human beings who happen to be workers.

Over the years, scientific management evolved refinements that have robotized workers, removing to the greatest degree possible requirements of education, knowledge, skill, creativity, brain power, and muscle power. The assembly line, with its repetitive, monotonous sameness, developed into the ultimate symbol of scientific management. Taylor's principles have served industry well as a guide toward ever increasing productivity, lower unit costs, and higher profits. They also dovetailed neatly into the concept of "profits before people."

WINDS OF CHANGE IN THE PRODUCTION SYSTEM

Times and circumstances are now beginning to modify the eighty-year-old practices of refined technology—in part because workers' attitudes toward the meaning of work are changing, but also because society as a whole is paying closer attention to the total environment and the quality of life.

About the time that Henry Ford announced the "five-dollar day," he remarked, "The assembly line is a haven for those who haven't got the brains to do anything else." His "enlightened" wage scale was accompanied by rules reminiscent of Geiger's rules of 1872. Mr. Ford's hiring practices were strict and stifling. No women were to work in his factories; they belonged at home in the kitchen and with their children. Men who failed to support their dependents would find no work at Ford, nor would divorced men or others who were "living unworthily"—those who smoked or drank hard liquor. Once hired, the workers were subjected to a spy system. "Social workers" on the Ford payroll visited workers' homes and reported on living habits: Did the man raise his own garden as instructed? Did his family house male boarders (which was taboo)? Did the worker complain to his family about his job and factory conditions? And so forth.

Today, the employer no longer has control of the worker outside the workplace, and unionization has wrested from the employer a measure of the control he exercises at the workplace. The next step is to provide the worker with a more meaningful measure of control over his job through participation in decisions affecting the job.

Contrast Henry Ford's stifling authoritarianism with the words of Richard Gerstenberg, chairman of the board of directors of General Motors Corporation, in 1972: "Productivity is not a matter of making employees work longer or harder . . . We must improve working conditions and take out the boredom from routine jobs . . . We must increase an employee's satisfaction with his job, heightening pride of workmanship, and, as far as is feasible, involve the employee personally in decisions that relate directly to his job. . . ."[1]

Within its limited meaning, this statement marked an unfashionable awareness of Robert Heilbroner's thesis that ". . . the ultimate challenge to the institutions, motivations, political structures, lifeways, and ideologies of capialist nations is whether they can accommodate themselves to the requrements of a society in which an attitude of 'social fatalism' is being replaced by one of social purpose."[2]

Mr. Gerstenberg's statement hopefully represents a conscious departure from the historic trickle-down theory that profits come first, that profits exemplify good in themselves and can only redound to the benefit of all society. Yet, more income and more material wealth, in and of themselves, do not guarantee a life of satisfaction or worth, and certainly cannot compensate for lives converted into deadened extensions of the tools of production.

New directions emerge as new problems arise. Cracks are occurring in the traditional discipline of the workplace. Absenteeism has been increasing. The Monday and Friday absentee is more commonplace. Tardiness

[1] Richard C. Gerstenberg, speech to the Annual Meeting of the American Publishers Association, New York, April 26, 1972.

[2] Robert Heilbroner, "The Future of Capitalism," *World Magazine*, September 12, 1972, p. 30.

also shows a generally upward trend. Labor turnover increases. Job boredom and repetitiveness are accompanied by "job alienation." Departure
from the "work ethic" in turn results in a deterioration of production and
quality. Workers feel a loss of individuality, dignity, and self-respect. Job
dissatisfaction grows, and workers question the current ways of doing
things as they seek to change the inflexible restrictions the production
process puts upon them.

In 1969, the Survey Research Center of the University of Michigan
reported the results of a study of 1,533 workers at various occupational
levels. It concluded that workers ranked interesting work and enough
equipment, information, and authority to get the job done ahead of good
pay and job security.

An extensive study by Harold Sheppard and Neal Herrick, *Where Have
All the Robots Gone?*, concluded that job dissatisfaction is indeed widespread—and not only among blue-collar workers; that workers entering
the labor force are increasingly anti-authoritarian, better educated, less
income oriented than past generations of workers, and more resistant to
meaningless, repetitive and boring job assignments. They expect to enhance the quality of their working lives.

Each year, the Gallup organization has been taking a poll aimed at determining "job satisfaction." Between 1969 and 1971, those indicating satisfaction with their work dropped by seven points, from eighty-eight to
eighty-one. Still further, the Bureau of Labor Statistics indicates that absentee rates have increased an average of 35 percent since 1961.

One significant aspect of American life that has been undergoing rapid
change relates to freedom to enjoy the autonomy of self-employment. In
1950, 16 percent of the labor force was self-employed. This figure dropped
to about 12 percent in 1960, and to 8 percent in 1970. Thus, the percentage
of the self-employed dropped by half in two decades. Increasingly, people
have been losing even this bastion of control over their working lives.

A study undertaken by HEW, published in 1973 as *Work in America*,
leaves no doubt that worker dissatisfaction with jobs, both blue-collar and
white-collar, is widespread, is on the rise, and presents an urgent problem
for management, union, and government. The report notes: "And significant numbers of American workers are dissatisfied with the quality of
their working lives. Dull, repetitive, seemingly meaningless tasks, offering
little challenge or autonomy, are causing discontent among workers at all
occupational levels."[3]

The report makes a point that the failure to solve this problem will mean
increased social costs. It points to the relationship between job dissatisfaction on the one hand and mental health, alcohol and drug abuse, heart

---

[3] *Work in America*, Report of a Special Task Force to the Secretary of Health, Education, and Welfare (Cambridge, Mass.: MIT Press, 1973), p. xv.

disease, early death, and other factors on the other; it concludes that unless the situation is corrected society can expect these costs to impose on increasing tax burden on the total community.

It is important to understand that reasonable satisfaction with meaningless, repetitive work may simply mean that man, highly adaptable creature that he is, has made his peace with an unhappy situation. There is strong evidence that workers write off deadening jobs as "inevitable" and seek their satisfaction in other pursuits. The HEW study makes a point of the relationship between the meaninglessness of the job and the adverse effect on the physical and mental well-being of the worker.

It is also important to note that workers who have been given the opportunity to enlarge their horizons at work, to participate in the decisions affecting their jobs, and to lend their innovative input toward getting the job done have a focal point against which to compare their previous work experience. These workers usually do not want to return to the simple monotonous tasks of little or no responsibility. They have tried a better way and they like it.

The increase in job dissatisfaction is not only rooted in the production system of scientific management; it feeds as well on the growing cynicism and frustration that citizens express toward public life. An increasing number feel alienated toward their government and public leaders as they become more remote from decision making in a complex world and as they sense their inability to affect economic and political decisions. With the exception of a Ralph Nader, the average citizen feels impotent to influence the direction and thrust of society.

How widespread are complaints about the hypocrisy of elected leaders and the disillusionment over promises made but never kept? And how often are voices raised against corruption, dissembling, and the lack of moral leadership "on high"? Until Watergate, even political spying, bugging, and bribery on a large scale raised less of a ripple than a deep freezer or a vicuna coat. It is too early to assess the long-term impact of Watergate on these feelings of impotency and disillusionment.

It is axiomatic that people respond more affirmatively to their role in society as they share in the opportunity to participate significantly in decisions affecting their welfare. History teaches, moreover, that at some point people who are denied this opportunity will reach out to grasp it.

This is equally true in the workplace. The stirrings of job dissatisfaction, in my judgment, relate in large measure to denial of participation in the decision-making process, denial of the opportunity to be creative and innovative and to control the machine, instead of being controlled by it.

The ferment of union activity in the 1930s and 1940s consolidated the organizing strength of industrial workers. It was the first stage toward accomplishment of a larger goal: industrial democracy. It provided the base on which workers were then able to improve their standard of living, win better working conditions, and achieve a greater measure of dignity and security as important members of society. Every gain constituted an incursion into the traditional authority wielded by management. The vast array of benefits won in collective bargaining over the years relates essentially to protecting the worker and his family against the hazards of economic insecurity. Workers, young and old, continue to aspire toward a better life, to be won at the bargaining table and through legislation. Their unions will, of course, persist in innovative collective-bargaining efforts as well as in improving upon already established benefit programs. They mobilize politically, cognizant of the intimate relationship between the bread box and the ballot box.

There is little need to spell out the enormously important progress workers have made through their unions. In *quantitative* terms, organized workers have won, and continue to win, a larger share of economic well-being. Unorganized workers have, of course, reaped the advantages of the gains made by unionized workers. Working conditions have also been vastly improved under the pressure of collective bargaining. Yet in *qualitative* terms, workers have not made as marked progress and are still struggling to play a more meaningful role in the decisions that affect their welfare in the business enterprise. Emphasis on qualitative improvement of life on the job is, I believe, the next step on the road toward industrial democracy.

WHITHER WORKER PARTICIPATION?

Two distinct, somewhat overlapping directions are indicated. One relates to "managing the enterprise"; the other relates to "managing the job." The latter is part and parcel of the former, but it is of more immediate concern to the worker.

Experiments with worker participation in "managing the enterprise" are under way in Yugoslavia (worker control of management), Germany (*Mitbestimmung*—codetermination established by law), Sweden (voluntary acceptance of worker representation on a company's board of directors), and Israel (union owned and operated cooperative enterprises). But in the United States, labor contracts, with their hundreds of provisions establishing and protecting workers' rights, leave substantially to management the "sole responsibility" to determine the products to be manufactured, the location of plants, production schedules, the methods, processes, and means of manufacture, as well as administrative decisions governing finances, marketing, purchasing, pricing, and the like. Unions traditionally have moved in the direction of improving wages, benefits, and working conditions. Generally, they have left "managing the enterprise" to management, only *reacting* to managerial acts objectionable to the workers. They have not embraced a political philosophy to motivate their overall policies and programs. This is not to say that American unions have no socioeconomic political concepts. Quite the contrary; but they are not married to an "ism" governing and directing their behavior.

Rather, American unions move to meet practical problems with practical solutions. It is highly improbable that they will approach the problem of worker participation in decision making via fierce ideological struggle founded in socioeconomic theory. They are not prone to beat their wings in ideological or doctrinaire frustration. Where workers feel victimized, they combine their forces to correct the situation, case by case, problem by problem. Gradual persistent change, not revolutionary upheaval, has marked the progress of the American worker. When explosions occur, as in the 1930s, they are responses to specific problems and are searches for specific solutions. We can anticipate that worker participation in managing the enterprise or job will manifest itself in a smilar way.

Decisions regarding purchasing, advertising, selling, and financing, for instance, are far more remote from the immediate problems facing the worker than are decisions concerning his or her job. In the vast range of managerial decisions, the immediacy of impact on the worker varies enormously. Thus, the average worker in a gigantic enterprise usually displays less interest in the selection of the chairman of the board than in the amount of overtime he receives.

What direction, then, will the drive toward worker participation in decision making take? To begin with, it seems safe to say that any further encroachment on so-called management prerogatves will spell "revolution" to management, while to the worker it will simply represent a non-ideological effort to resolve a bothersome problem.

Certain areas of possible confrontation come to mind. By way of example, management makes a decision to shut down a plant or move all or part of it to another location, often hundreds of miles away. The union bargains for severance pay, early retirement, the right of the worker to transfer with the job and to receive moving allowance, and so forth. But the worker, often with long years of service, is the victim of such a decision. He is permanently thrown out of work, or even if he is given the right to transfer with the job, he must pull up stakes, cut his roots in the community, leave friends, perhaps break family ties, and begin a new life in a strange place, with no assurance of permanence. Management wields the decision-making authority; the workers and the community dangle at the end of that decision.

Similarly, management generally controls the final decision to subcontract work or to shuffle work among its facilities in a multiplant corporation. The worker faces the ultimate insecurity. Management also holds the authority to discipline. All places of work (as in society at large) require rules and regulations for people to live by; but discipline can be a fearful weapon in the hands of a ruthless employer, even when subject to a collectively bargained grievance procedure.

Production scheduling can be a serious source of friction. In an auto-assembly plant, for instance, changes in line speed to meet changes in production schedules or changes in model mix require rebalancing of jobs and operations. This in turn gives rise to disputes over production standards and manpower. Frequent changes in line speed or model mix disturb agreed-upon settlements about production standards and manpower agreements, often resulting in crisis bargaining and, on occasion, strike action.

The never ending yet necessary introduction of technological innovation and the concomitant alteration of jobs, cutbacks in manpower, and effect on skill requirements are a constant source of new problems, emphasizing the concern workers naturally have for their job security. Furthermore, the call for excessive overtime is a constant source of unhappiness and discontent.

These are but a handful of the kinds of confrontation issues that directly affect workers and that are increasingly subject to "worker participation" bargaining.

Other types of issues, also relating directly to life in the workplace, will command attention, for democratizing the workplace carries considerations beyond the worker's immediate job. The double standard for managers and workers is being questioned. Symbols of elitism, traditionally taken for granted in industrial society, are challenged: salaries and their normally recognized advantages (versus hourly payment and the punching of time clocks), paneled dining rooms (versus spartan cafeterias), privileged parking facilities nearest the plant entrance, and so forth.

Democratizing the workplace may entail organizing the work schedule to enable the worker to manage his personal chores: visiting the dentist or doctor, getting his car repaired, visiting his children's school during teaching and conference hours, for example.

Worker participation in decision making will be demanded more often with regard to those aspects of working life most immediately and noticeably affected. "Managing the job" is more immediate and urgent. Worker concern for "managing the enterprise" is more variable and is best measured by the immediacy of impact on the worker's welfare.

Increasing attention is currently being devoted to this problem of "managing the job." Rising rates of absenteeism, worker disinterest in the quality and quantity of production, job alienation, and the insistence on unit-cost reduction are motivating some employers to reevaluate current practices and customs governing management-worker relationships. Concurrently workers rebel against the authoritarian atmosphere of the workplace and the subordination of their personal dignity, desires, and aspirations to the drive for more production at lower cost; they find little challenge, satisfaction, or interest in their work. While the worker's rate of pay may dominate his relationship to the job, he can be responsive to the opportunity for playing an innovative, creative, and imaginative role in the production process.

One of the essential tasks of the union movement is to "humanize the workplace." A pleasant, decent management is desirable but does not alter the basic managerial design. "Human engineering" concepts may make for more comfortable employer-employee relationships, but here, too, managerial administration of the workplace remains fundamentally unchanged. "Humanizing the workplace" not only must include the normally recognized amenities of life in the workplace but it also must move to a higher plateau and relate to job satisfaction—a closing of the widening gap between the mechanization of production by scientific management and the worker's participation in the production and decision-making process. "Humanizing the workplace" in this sense represents one additional step toward the fulfillment of industrial democracy.

But humanizing the workplace must not become simply another gimmick designed essentially to "fool" the worker by having as its primary goal or hidden agenda an increase in worker productivity. Manipulation of the worker will be recognized for what it is—another form of exploitation; it will breed suspicion and distrust.

In this regard, Delmar Landan, an expert in personnel development for General Motors, has said: ". . . where we have to aim is participation—it is the only way to work in this increasingly complex society. The man at the top can't have all the answers. The man doing the job will have some of them."[4]

Worker participation in decision making about his job is one means of achieving democratization of the workplace. It should result in a change from the miniaturization and oversimplification of the job to the evolution of a system embracing broader distribution of authority, increasing rather than diminishing responsibility and accountability. It should combine the imaginative creation of more-interesting jobs with the opportunity to exercise a meaningful measure of autonomy and utilization of more-varied skills. It requires tapping the creative and innovative ingenuity of the worker to the maximum.

Hundreds of experiments have been and are being undertaken in American industry, following the European lead. They are directed toward opening up opportunities for meaningful worker participation. The HEW report describes some of them. In the auto industry, the industry with which I am most closely associated, a myriad of demonstration projects are under way. They cover innumerable facets of the problem and some are a sharp departure from the assembly-line concept.

----

[4] Delmar Landan in Judson Gooding, *The Job Revolution* (New York: Walker Publishing Co., 1972), p. 111.

It is too early to describe precisely what form or forms humanizing the workplace will take. Certain criteria, however, deserve serious consideration.

1. The worker should genuinely feel that he or she is not simply an adjunct to the tool, but that his or her bent toward being creative, innovative, and inventive plays a significant role in the production (or service) process.
2. The worker should be assured that his or her participation in decision making will not erode job security or that of fellow workers.
3. Job functions should be adapted to the worker; the current system is designed to make the worker fit the job, on the theory that this is a more efficient production system and that, in any event, economic gain is the worker's only reason for working. This theory may be proved wrong on both counts.
4. The worker should be assured the widest possible latitude of self-management, responsibility, and opportunity to use her or his brain. Gimmickery and manipulation of the worker must be ruled out.
5. Changes in job content and the added responsibility and involvement in decision making should be accompanied by upgrading pay rates.
6. The worker should be able to foresee opportunities for growth in his or her work and for promotion.
7. The worker's role in the business should enable her or him to relate to the product or services rendered, as well as to their meanings in society; in a broader sense, it should also enable her or him to relate constructively to her or his role in society.

The union, as the workers' representative, will naturally share with management in implementing these and other criteria. But crisis negotiating—settling a wage dispute before a midnight strike deadline—is not the time to seek precise means of humanizing the workplace. This task requires careful experiment and analysis. While issues of economic security (wages, fringe benefits) and continuing encroachment on what management terms its sole prerogatives will remain adversary in nature, there is every reason why humanizing the workplace should be undertaken as a joint, cooperative, constructive, nonadversary effort by management and the union. The initial key to achieving this goal may well be open, frank, and enlightened discussion between the parties, recognizing that democratizing the workplace and humanizing the job need not be matters of confrontation but of mutual concern for the worker, the enterprise, and the welfare of society.

25

Communication Revisited*

JAY HALL

Hɪɢʜ on the diagnostic checklist of corporate health is communication; and the prognosis is less than encouraging. In a recent cross-cultural study,[1] roughly 74 percent of the managers sampled from companies in Japan, Great Britain, and the United States cited communication breakdown as the single greatest barrier to corporate excellence.

Just what constitutes a problem of communication is not easily agreed upon. Some theorists approach the issue from the vantage point of information bits comprising a message; others speak in terms of organizational roles and positions of centrality or peripherality; still others emphasize the directional flows of corporate data. The result is that more and more people are communicating about communication, while the achievement of clarity, understanding, commitment, and creativity—the goals of communication—becomes more and more limited.

More often than not, the communication dilemmas cited by people are not communication problems at all. They are instead *symptoms* of difficulties at more basic and fundamental levels of corporate life. From a dynamic standpoint, problems of communication in organizations frequently reflect dysfunctions at the level of *corporate climate*. The feelings people have about where or with whom they work—feelings of impotence, distrust, resentment, insecurity, social inconsequence, and all the other very human emotions—not only define the climate which prevails but the manner in which communications will be managed. R. R. Blake and Jane S. Mouton[2] have commented upon an oddity of organizational life: when management

---

* Copyright 1973 by the Regents of the University of California. Reprinted from *California Management Review,* vol. 15, no. 3, pp. 56–67 by permission of the Regents.

[1] R. R. Blake and Jane S. Mouton, *Corporate Excellence through Grid Organization Development* (Houston, Tex.: Gulf Publishing Co., 1968), p. 4.

[2] Ibid., pp. 3–5.

is effective and relationships are sound, problems of communication tend not to occur. It is only when relationships among members of the organization are unsound and fraught with unarticulated tensions that one hears complaints of communication breakdown. Thus, the quality of relationships in an organization may dictate to a great extent the level of communication effectiveness achieved.

INTERPERSONAL STYLES AND THE QUALITY OF RELATIONSHIPS

The critical factor underlying relationship quality in organizations is in need of review. Reduced to its lowest common denominator, the most significant determinant of the quality of relationships is the interpersonal style of the parties to a relationship. The learned, characteristic, and apparently preferred manner in which individuals relate to others in the building of relationships—the manner in which they monitor, control, filter, divert, give, and seek the information germane to a given relationship—will dictate over time the quality of relationships which exist among people, the emotional climate which will characterize their interactions, and whether or not there will be problems of communication. In the final analysis, individuals are the human links in the corporate network, and the styles they employ interpersonally are the ultimate determinants of what information goes where and whether it will be distortion-free or masked by interpersonal constraints.

The concept of interpersonal style is not an easy one to define; yet, if it is to serve as the central mechanism underlying the quality of relationships, the nature of corporate climate, managerial effectiveness, and the level of corporate excellence attainable, it is worthy of analysis. Fortunately, Joseph Luft[3] and Harry Ingham—two behavioral scientists with special interests in interpersonal and group processes—have developed a model of social interaction which affords a way of thinking about interpersonal functioning, while handling much of the data encountered in everyday living. The Johari Window, as their model is called, identifies several interpersonal styles, their salient features and consequences, and suggests a basis for interpreting the significance of style for the quality of relationships. An overview of the Johari model should help to sharpen the perception of interpersonal practices among managers and lend credence to the contention of Blake and Mouton that there are few communication problems as such, only unsound relationships. At the same time, a normative statement regarding effective interpersonal functioning and, by extension, the foundations of corporate excellence may be found in the model as well. Finally, the major tenets of

---

[3] Joseph Luft, *Of Human Interaction* (Palo Alto, Calif.: National Press Books, 1969), passim.

the model are testable under practical conditions, and the latter portion of this discussion will be devoted to research on the managerial profile in interpersonal encounters. The author has taken a number of interpretive liberties with the basic provisions of the Johari Awareness model. While it is anticipated that none of these violate the integrity of the model as originally described by Luft, it should be emphasized that many of the inferences and conclusions discussed are those of the author, and Dr. Luft should not be held accountable for any lapses of logic or misapplications of the model in this paper.

THE JOHARI WINDOW: A GRAPHIC MODEL OF INTERPERSONAL PROCESSES

As treated here, the Johari Window is essentially an information processing model; interpersonal style and individual effectiveness are assessed in terms of information processing tendencies and the performance consequences thought to be associated with such practices. The model employs a four celled figure as its format and reflects the interaction of two interpersonal sources of information—Self and Others—and the behavioral processes required for utilizing that information. The model, depicted in Figure 1, may be thought of as representing the various kinds of data available for use in the establishment of interpersonal relationships. The squared field, in effect, represents a personal space. This in turn is partitioned into four regions, with each representing a particular combination or mix of relevant information and having special significance for the quality of relation-

Figure 1
The Johari Window: A Model of Interpersonal Processes

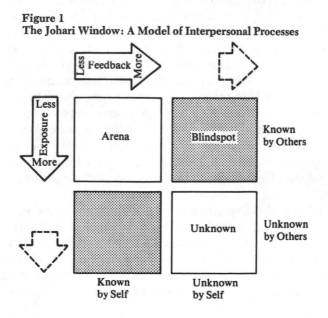

ships. To fully appreciate the implications that each informational region has for interpersonal effectiveness, one must consider not only the size and shape of each region but also the reasons for its presence in the interpersonal space. In an attempt to "personalize" the model, it is helpful to think of oneself as the *Self* in the relationship for, as will be seen presently, it is what the Self does interpersonally that has the most direct impact on the quality of resulting relationships. In organizational terms, it is how the management-Self behaves that is critical to the quality of corporate relationships.

Figure 1 reveals that the two informational sources, Self and Others, have information which is pertinent to the relationship, and at the same time, each lacks information that is equally germane. Thus, there is relevant and necessary information which is *Known by the Self, Unknown by the Self, Known by Others,* and *Unknown by Others.* The Self/Other combinations of known and unknown information make up the four regions within the interpersonal space and, again, characterize the various types and qualities of relationships possible within the Johari framework.

Region I, for example, constitutes that portion of the total interpersonal space which is devoted to mutually held information. This Known-by-Self-Known-by-Others facet of the interpersonal space is thought to be the part of the relationship which, because of its shared data characteristics and implied likelihood of mutual understanding, controls interpersonal productivity. That is, the working assumption is that productivity and interpersonal effectiveness are directly related to the amount of mutually held information in a relationship. Therefore, the larger Region I becomes, the more rewarding, effective, and productive the relationship. As the informational context for interpersonal functioning, Region I is called the "Arena."

Region II, using the double classification approach just described, is that portion of the interpersonal space which holds information Known-by-Others but Unknown-by-Self. Thus, this array of data constitutes an interpersonal handicap for the Self, since one can hardly understand the behaviors, decisions, or potentials of others if he doesn't have the data upon which these are based. Others have the advantage of knowing their own reactions, feelings, perceptions, and the like while the Self is unaware of these. Region II, an area of hidden unperceived information, is called the "Blindspot." The Blindspot is, of course, a limiting factor with respect to the size of Region I and may be thought of, therefore, as inhibiting interpersonal effectiveness.

Region III may also be considered to inhibit interpersonal effectiveness, but it is due to an imbalance of information which would seem to favor the Self; as the portion of the relationship which is characterized by information Known-by-Self but Unknown-by-Others, Region III constitutes a protective feature of the relationship for the Self. Data which one perceives as potentially prejudicial to a relationship or which he keeps to himself out of fear, desire for power, or whatever, make up the "Façade." This protective front, in turn, serves a defensive function for the Self. The question is not one of whether a Façade is necessary but rather how much Façade is required realistically; this raises the question of how much conscious defensiveness can be tolerated before the Arena becomes too inhibited and interpersonal effectiveness begins to diminish.

Finally, Region IV constitutes that portion of the relationship which is devoted to material neither known by the self nor by other parties to the relationship. The information in this Unknown by-Self–Unknown-by-Others area is thought to reflect psychodynamic data, hidden potential, unconscious idiosyncrasies, and the data-base of creativity. Thus, Region IV is the "Unknown" area which may become known as interpersonal effectiveness increases.

Summarily, it should be said that the information within all regions can be of any type—feeling data, factual information, assumptions, task skill data, and prejudices—which are relevant to the relationship at hand. Irrelevant data are not the focus of the Johari Window concept: just those pieces of information which have a bearing on the quality and productivity of the relationship should be considered as appropriate targets for the information processing practices prescribed by the model. At the same time, it should be borne in mind that the individuals involved in a relationship, particularly the Self, control what and how information will be processed. Because of this implicit personal control aspect, the model should be viewed as an open system which is *dynamic* and amenable to change as personal decisions regarding interpersonal functioning change.

BASIC INTERPERSONAL PROCESSES: EXPOSURE AND FEEDBACK

The dynamic character of the model is critical; for it is the movement capability of the horizontal and vertical lines which partition the interpersonal space into regions which gives individuals control over what their relationships will become. The Self can significantly influence the size of his Arena in relating to others by the behavioral processes he employs in establishing relationships. To the extent that one takes the steps necessary to apprise others of relevant information which he has and they do not, he is enlarging his Arena in a downward direction. Within the framework of the model, this enlargement occurs in concert with a reduction of one's Façade. Thus, if one behaves in a non-defensive, trusting, and possibly risk-taking manner with others, he may be thought of as contributing to increased mutual awareness and sharing of data. The process one employs toward this end has been called the "Exposure" process. It entails the open and candid disclosure of one's feelings, factual knowledge, wild guesses, and the like in a conscious attempt to share. Frothy, intentionally untrue, diversionary sharing does not constitute exposure; and as personal experience will attest, it does nothing to help mutual understanding. The Exposure process is under the direct control of the Self and may be used as a mechanism for building trust and for legitimizing mutual exposures.

The need for mutual exposures becomes apparent when one considers the behavioral process required for enlarging the Arena laterally. As a behavior designed to gain reduction in one's Blindspot, the Feedback process entails an active solicitation by the Self of the information he feels others might have which he does not. The active, initiative-taking aspect of this solicitation behavior should be stressed, for again the Self takes the primary role in setting interpersonal norms and in legitimizing certain acts within the relationship. Since the extent to which the Self will actually receive the Feedback he solicits is contingent upon the willingness of others to expose their data, the need for a climate of mutual exposures becomes apparent. Control by the Self of the success of his Feedback-seeking behaviors is less direct therefore than in the case of self-exposure. He will achieve a reduction of his Blindspot only with the cooperation of others; and his own prior willingness to deal openly and candidly may well dictate what level of cooperative and trusting behavior will prevail on the part of other parties to the relationship.

Thus, one can theoretically establish interpersonal relationships characterized by mutual understanding and increased effectiveness (by a dominant Arena) if he will engage in exposing and feedback soliciting behaviors to an optimal degree. This places the determination of productivity and amount of interpersonal reward—and the quality of relationships—directly in the hands of the Self. In theory, this amounts to an issue of interpersonal competence; in practice, it amounts to the conscious and sensitive management of interpersonal processes.

INTERPERSONAL STYLES AND MANAGERIAL IMPACTS

While one can theoretically employ Exposure and Feedback processes not only to a great but to a similar degree as well, individuals typically fail to achieve such an optimal practice. Indeed, they usually display a significant preference for one or the other of the two processes and tend to overuse one while neglecting the other. This tendency promotes a state of imbalance in interpersonal relationships which, in turn, creates disruptive tensions capable of retarding productivity. Figure 2 presents several commonly used approaches to the employment of Exposure and Feedback processes. Each of these may be thought of as reflecting a basic interpersonal style—that is fairly consistent and preferred ways of behaving interpersonally. As might be expected, each style has associated with it some fairly predictable consequences.

Figure 2
Interpersonal Styles as Functions of Exposure and Feedback
Solicitation

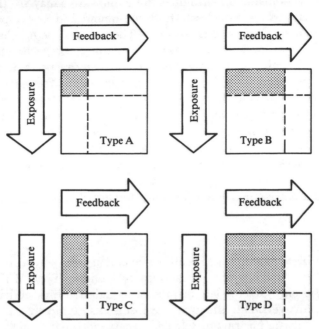

Type A

This interpersonal style reflects a minimal use of both Exposure and Feedback processes; it is a fairly impersonal approach to interpersonal relationships. The Unknown region dominates under this style; and unrealized potential, untapped creativity, and personal psychodynamics prevail as the salient influences. Such a style would seem to indicate withdrawal and an aversion to risk-taking on the part of its user; interpersonal anxiety and safety-seeking are likely to be prime sources of personal motivation. Persons who characteristically use this style appear to be detached, mechanical, and uncommunicative. They may often be found in bureaucratic, highly structured organizations of some type where it is possible, and perhaps profitable, to avoid personal disclosure or involvement. People using this style are likely to be reacted to with more than average hostility, since other parties to the relationship will tend to interpret the lack of Exposure and Feedback solicitation largely according to their own needs and how this interpersonal lack affects need fulfillment.

Subordinates whose manager employs such a style, for example, will often feel that his behavior is consciously aimed at frustrating them in their work. The person in need of support and encouragement will often view a Type A manager as aloof, cold, and indifferent. Another individual in need of firm directions and plenty of order in his work may view the same manager as indecisive and administratively impotent. Yet another person requiring freedom and opportunities to be innovative may see the Type A interpersonal style as hopelessly tradition-bound and as symptomatic of fear and an overriding need for security. The use of Type A behaviors on a large scale in an organization reveals something about the climate and fundamental health of that organization. In many respects, interpersonal relationships founded on Type A uses of exposure and feedback constitute the kind of organizational ennui about which Chris Argyris[4] has written so eloquently. Such practices are, in his opinion, likely to be learned ways of behaving under oppressive policies of the sort which encourage people to act in a submissive and dependent fashion. Organizationally, of course, the result is lack of communication and a loss of human potentials; the Unknown becomes the dominant feature of corporate relationships, and the implications for organizational creativity and growth are obvious.

Type B

Under this approach, there is also an aversion to Exposure, but aversion is coupled with a desire for relationships not found in Type A. Thus, Feedback is the only process left in promoting relationships and it is much overused. An aversion to the use of Exposure may typically be interpreted as a sign of basic mistrust of self and others, and it is therefore not surprising that the Façade is the dominant feature of relationships resulting from neglected Exposure coupled with overused Feedback. The style appears to be a probing, supportive interpersonal ploy, and once the Façade becomes apparent, it is likely to result in a reciprocal withdrawal of trust by other parties. This may promote feelings of suspicion on the part of others; such feelings may lead to the manager being treated as a rather superficial person without real substance or as a devious sort with many hidden agenda.

Preference for this interpersonal style among managers seems to be of two types. Some managers committed to a quasi-permissive management may employ Type B behaviors in an attempt to avoid appearing directive. Such an approach results in the manager's personal resources never being fully revealed or his opinions being expressed. In contrast—but subject to many of the same inadequacies—is the use of Type B behaviors in an attempt to gain or maintain one's personal power in relationships. Many managers build a façade to maintain personal control and an outward appearance of confidence. As the Johari model would suggest, however, persons who employ such practices tend to become isolated from their subordinates and colleagues alike. Lack of trust predominates and consolidation of power and promotion of an image of confidence may be the least

---

[4] C. Argyris, *Interpersonal Competence and Organizational Effectiveness* (Homewood, Ill.: Dorsey, 1962), passim.

likely results of Type B use in organizations. Very likely, the seeds of distrust and conditions for covert competitiveness—with all the implications for organizational teamwork—will follow from widespread use of Type B interpersonal practices.

Type C

Based on an overuse of Exposure to the neglect of Feedback, this interpersonal style may reflect ego-striving and/or distrust of others' competence. The person who uses this style usually feels quite confident of his own opinions and is likely to value compliance from others. The fact that he is often unaware of his impact or of the potential of others' contributions is reflected in the dominant Blindspot which results from this style. Others are likely to feel disenfranchised by one who uses this style; they often feel that he has little use for their contributions or concern for their feelings. As a result, this style often triggers feelings of hostility, insecurity, and resentment on the part of others. Frequently, others will learn to perpetuate the manager's Blindspot by withholding important information or giving only selected feedback: as such, this is a reflection of the passive-aggressiveness and unarticulated hostility which this style can cause. Labor-management relations frequently reflect such Blindspot dynamics.

The Type C interpersonal style is probably what has prompted so much interest in "listening" programs around the country. As the Johari model makes apparent, however, the Type C over-use of Exposure and neglect of Feedback is just one of several interpersonal tendencies that may disrupt communications. While hierarchical organizational structure or centrality in communication nets and the like may certainly facilitate the use of individual Type C behaviors, so can fear of failure, authoritarianism, need for control, and over-confidence in one's own opinions; such traits vary from person to person and limit the utility of communication panaceas. Managers who rely on this style often do so to demonstrate competence; many corporate cultures require that the manager be *the* planner, director, and controller and many managers behave accordingly to protect their corporate images. Many others are simply trying to be helpful in a paternalistic kind of way; others are, of course, purely dictatorial. Whatever the reason, those who employ the Type C style have one thing in common: their relationships will be dominated by Blindspots and they are destined for surprise whenever people get enough and decide to force feedback on them, solicited or not.

Type D

Balanced Exposure and Feedback processes are used to a great extent in this style; candor, openness, and a sensitivity to others' needs to participate are the salient features of the style. The Arena is the dominant characteristic, and productivity increases. In initial stages, this style may promote some defensiveness on the part of others who are not familiar with honest and trusting relationships; but perseverance will tend to promote a norm of reciprocal candor over time in which creative potential can be realized.

Among managers, Type D practices constitute an ideal state from the standpoint of organizational effectiveness. Healthy and creative climates result from its widespread use, and the conditions for growth and corporate excellence may be created through the use of constructive Exposure and Feedback exchanges. Type D practices do not give license to "clobber," as some detractors might claim; and for optimal results, the data explored should be germane to the relationships and problems at hand, rather than random intimacies designed to overcome self-consciousness. Trust is slowly built, and managers who experiment with Type D processes should be prepared to be patient and flexible in their relationships. Some managers, as they tentatively try out Type D strategies, encounter reluctance and distrust on the part of others, with the result that they frequently give up too soon, assuming that the style doesn't work. The reluctance of others should be assessed against the backdrop of previous management practices and the level of prior trust which characterizes the culture. Other managers may try candor only to discover that they have opened a Pandora's box from which a barrage of hostility and complaints emerges. The temptation of the naive manager is to put the lid back on quickly; but the more enlightened manager knows that when communications are opened up after having been closed for a long time, the most emotionally laden issues—ones which have been the greatest source of frustration, anger, or fear—will be the first to be discussed. If management can resist cutting the dialogue short, the diatribe will run its course as the emotion underlying it is drained off, and exchanges will become more problem-centered and future-oriented. Management intent will have been tested and found worthy of trust, and creative unrestrained interchanges will occur. Organizations built on such practices are those headed for corporate climates and resource utilization of the type necessary for true corporate excellence. The manager's interpersonal style may well be the catalyst for this reaction to occur.

Summarily, the Johari Window model of interpersonal processes suggests that much more is needed to understand communication in an organization than information about its structure or one's position in a network. People make very critical decisions about what information will be processed, irrespective of structural and network considerations. People bring with them to organizational settings propensities for behaving in certain ways interpersonally. They prefer certain interpersonal styles, sharpened and honed by corporate cultures, which significantly influence—if not dictate entirely—the flow of information in organizations. As such, individuals and their preferred styles of relating one to another amount to the synapses in the corporate network which control and co-ordinate the human system. Central to an understanding of communication in organizations, therefore, in an appreciation of the complexities of those human interfaces which comprise organizations. The work of Luft and Ingham, when brought to bear on management practices and corporate cultures, may lend much needed insight into the constraints unique to organizational life which either hinder or facilitate the processing of corporate data.

RESEARCH ON THE MANAGERIAL PROFILE: THE PERSONAL RELATIONS SURVEY

As treated here, one of the major tenets of the Johari Window model is that one's use of Exposure and Feedback soliciting processes is a matter of personal decision. Whether consciously or unconsciously, when one employs either process or fails to do so he has decided that such practices somehow serve the goals he has set for himself. Rationales for particular behavior are likely to be as varied as the goals people seek; they may be in the best sense of honest intent or they may simply represent evasive logic or systems of self-deception. The *purposeful* nature of interpersonal styles remains nevertheless. A manager's style of relating to other members of the organization is never simply a collection of random, unconsidered acts. Whether he realizes it or not, or admits it or denies it, his interpersonal style *has purpose* and is thought to serve either a personal or interpersonal goal in his relationships.

Because of the element of decision and purposeful intent inherent in one's interpersonal style, the individual's inclination to employ Exposure and Feedback processes may be assessed. That is, his decision to engage in open and candid behaviors or to actively seek out the information that others are thought to have may be sampled, and his Exposure and Feedback tendencies thus measured. Measurements obtained may be used in determining the manager's or the organization's Johari Window configuration and the particular array of interpersonal predictions which underlie it. Thus, the Luft-Ingham model not only provides a way of conceptualizing what is going on interpersonally, but it affords a rationale for actually assessing practices which may, in turn, be coordinated to practical climate and cultural issues.

Hall and Williams have designed a paper-and-pencil instrument for use with managers which reveals their preferences for Exposure and Feedback in their relationships with subordinates, colleagues, and superiors. The *Personnel Relations Survey*,[5] as the instrument is entitled, has been

---

[5] J. Hall and Martha S. Williams, *Personnel Relations Survey* (Conroe, Tex.: Teleometrics International, 1967).

used extensively by industry as a training aid for providing personal feedback of a type which "personalizes" otherwise didactic theory sessions on the Johari, on one hand, and as a catalyst to evaluation and critique of on-going relationships, on the other hand. In addition to its essentially training oriented use, however, the *Personnel Relations Survey* has been a basic research tool for assessing current practices among managers. The results obtained from two pieces of research are of particular interest from the standpoint of their implications for corporate climates and managerial styles.

Authority Relationships and Interpersonal Style Preferences

Using the *Personnel Relations Survey*, data were collected from 1,000 managers. These managers represent a cross section of those found in organizations today; levels of management ranging from company president to just above first-line supervisor were sampled from all over the United States. Major manufacturers and petroleum and food producers contributed to the research, as well as major airline, state and federal governmental agencies, and nonprofit service organizations.

Since the *Personnel Relations Survey* addresses the manner in which Exposure and Feedback processes are employed in one's relationships with his subordinates, colleagues, and superiors, the data from the 1,000 managers sampled reveal some patterns which prevail in organizations in terms of downward, horizontal, and upward communications. In addition, the shifting and changing of interpersonal tactics as one moves from one authority relationship to another is noteworthy from the standpoint of power dynamics underlying organizational life. A summary of the average tendencies obtained from managers is presented graphically in Figure 3.

Of perhaps the greatest significance for organizational climates is the finding regarding the typical manager's use of Exposure. As Figure 3 indicates, one's tendency to deal openly and candidly with others is directly influenced by the amount of power he possesses relative to other parties to the relationship. Moving from relationships with subordinates in which the manager obviously enjoys greater formal authority, through colleague relationships characterized by equal authority positions, to relationships with superiors in which the manager is least powerful, the plots of Exposure use steadily decline. Indeed, a straight linear relationship is suggested between amount of authority possessed by the average manager and his use of candor in relationships.

While there are obvious exceptions to this depiction, the average managerial profile on Exposure reveals the most commonly found practices in organizations which, when taken diagnostically, suggest that the average

Figure 3
Score Plots on Exposure and Feedback for the "Average" Manager
from a Sample of 1,000 Managers in the United States

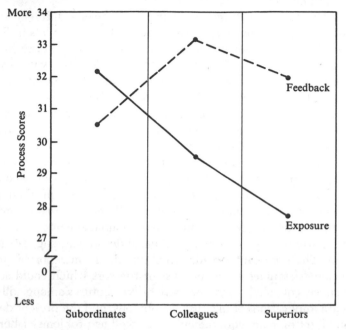

manager in today's organizations has a number of "hang-ups" around authority issues which seriously curtail his interpersonal effectiveness. Consistent with other findings from communication research, these data point to power differences among parties to relationships as a major disruptive influence on the flow of information in organizations. A more accurate interpretation, however, seems to be that it is not power differences as such which impede communication, but the way people *feel* about these differences and begin to monitor, filter, and control their contributions in response to their own feelings and apprehensions.

Implications for overall corporate climate may become more obvious when the data from the Exposure process are considered with those reflecting the average manager's reliance on Feedback acquisition. As Figure 3 reveals, Feedback solicitation proceeds differently. As might be expected, there is less use of the Feedback process in relationships with subordinates than there is of the Exposure process. This variation on the Type C interpersonal style, reflecting an overuse of Exposure to some neglect of Feedback, very likely contributes to subordinate feelings of resentment, lack of social worth, and frustration. These feelings—which are certain to manifest themselves in the *quality* of subordinate performance if not in production quantity—will likely remain as hidden facets of corporate climate, for a major feature of downward communication revealed in Figure 3 is that of managerial Blindspot.

Relationships at the colleague level appear to be of a different sort with a set of dynamics all their own. As reference to the score plots in Figure 3 will show, the typical manager reports a significant preference for Feedback seeking behaviors over Exposure in his relationships with his fellow managers. A quick interpretation of the data obtained would be that, at the colleague level, everyone is seeking information but very few are willing to expose any. These findings may bear on a unique feature of organizational life—one which has serious implications for climate among corporate peers. Most research on power and authority relationships suggests that there is the greatest openness and trust among people under conditions of equal power. Since colleague relationships might best be considered to reflect equal if not share distributions of power, maximum openness coupled with maximum solicitation of others' information might be expected to characterize relationships among management coworkers. The fact that a fairly pure Type B interpersonal style prevails suggests noise in the system. The dominant Façade which results from reported practices with colleagues signifies a lack of trust of the sort which could seriously limit the success of collaborative or cooperative ventures among colleagues. The climate implications of mistrust are obvious, and the present data may shed some light on teamwork difficulties as well as problems of horizontal communication so often encountered during inter-departmental or intergroup contacts.

Interviews with a number of managers revealed that their tendencies to become closed in encounters with colleagues could be traced to a competitive ethic which prevailed in their organizations. The fact was a simple one: "You don't confide in your 'buddies' because they are bucking for the same job you are! Any worthwhile information you've got, you keep to yourself until a time when it might come in handy." To the extent that this climate prevails in organizations, it is to be expected that more effort goes into façade building and maintenance than is expended on the projects at hand where colleague relationships are concerned.

Superiors are the targets of practices yielding the smallest, and therefore least productive, Arena of the three relationships assessed in the survey. The average manager reports a significant reluctance to deal openly and candidly with his superior while favoring the Feedback process as his major interpersonal gambit; even the use of Feedback, however, is subdued relative to that employed with colleagues. The view from on high in organizations is very likely colored by the interpersonal styles addressed to them; and based on the data obtained, it would not be surprising if many members of top management felt that lower level management was submissive, in need of direction, and had few creative suggestions of their own. Quite aside from the obvious effect such an expectation might have on performance reviews, a characteristic reaction to the essentially Type B style directed at superiors is, on their part, to invoke Type C behaviors. Thus, the data obtained call attention to what may be the seeds of a self-reinforcing cycle of authority-obedience-authority. The long-range consequences of such a cycle, in terms of relationship quality and interpersonal style, has been found to be corporate-wide adoption of Type A behaviors which serve to depersonalize work and diminish an organization's human resources.

Thus, based on the present research at least, a number of interpersonal practices seem to characterize organizational life which limit not only the effectiveness of communication within, but the attainment of realistic levels of corporate excellent without. As you will see, which style will prevail very much depends upon the individual manager.

Interpersonal Practices and Managerial Styles

In commenting upon the first of their two major concerns in programs of organization development, Blake and Mouton[6] have stated: "The underlying causes of communication difficulties are to be found in the character of supervision. . . . The solution to the problem of communication is for men to manage by achieving production and excellence through sound utilization of people." To the extent that management style is an important ingredient in the communication process, a second piece of research employing the Johari Window and Managerial Grid models in tandem may be of some interest to those concerned with corporate excellence.

Of the 1,000 managers sampled in the *Personnel Relations Survey*, 384 also completed a second instrument, the *Styles of Management Inventory*,[7] based on the Managerial Grid (a two-dimensional model of management styles).[8] Five "anchor" styles are identified relative to one's concern for production vis-à-vis people, and these are expressed in grid notation as follows: 9,9 reflects a high production concern coupled with high people concern; 5,5 reflects a moderate concern for each; 9,1 denotes high production coupled with low people concerns, while 1,9 denotes the opposite orientation; 1,1 reflects a minimal concern for both dimensions. In an attempt to discover the significance of one's interpersonal practices for his overall approach to management, the 40 individuals scoring highest on each style of management were selected for an analysis of their interpersonal styles.

---

[6] R. R. Blake and Jane S. Mouton, *Corporate Excellence*, p. 5.

[7] J. Hall, J. B. Harvey, and Martha S. Williams, *Styles of Management Inventory* (Conroe, Tex.: Teleometrics International 1963).

[8] R. R. Blake and Jane S. Mouton, *The Managerial Grid* (Houston, Tex.: Gulf Publishing Co., 1964), *passim*.

Thus, 200 managers—40 each who were identified as having dominant managerial styles of either 9,9; 5,5; 9,1; 1,9; or 1,1—were studied relative to their tendencies to employ Exposure and Feedback processes in relationships with their subordinates. The research question addressed was: how do individuals who prefer a given managerial style differ in terms of their interpersonal orientations from other individuals preferring other managerial approaches?

The data were subjected to a discriminant function analysis, and statistically significant differences were revealed in terms of the manner in which managers employing a given dominant managerial style also employed the Exposure and Feedback processes. The results of the research findings are presented graphically in Figure 4. As the bar graph of Exposure and Feedback scores reveals those managers identified by a dominant management style of 9,9 displayed the strongest tendencies to employ both Exposure and Feedback in their relationships with subordinates. In addition, the Arena which would result from a Johari plotting of their scores would be in a fairly good state of balance, reflecting about as much use of one process as of the other. The data suggest that the 9,9 style of management—typically described as one which achieves effective production through the sound utilization of people—also entails the sound utilization of personal resources in establishing relationships. The Type D interpersonal style which seems to be associated with the 9,9 management style is fully consistent with the open and unobstructed communication which Blake and Mouton view as essential to the creative resolution of differences and sound relationships.

Figure 4
A Comparison of Exposure and Feedback Use among Managers with Different Dominant Managerial Styles

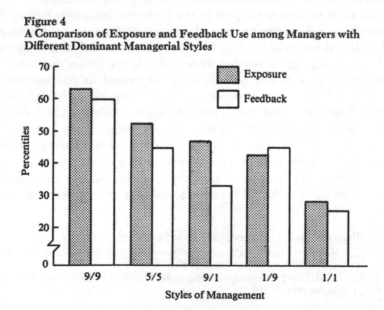

The 5,5 style of management appears, from the standpoint of Exposure and Feedback employment, to be a truncated version of the 9,9 approach. While the reported scores for both processes hover around the 50th percentile, there is a noteworthy preference for Exposure over Feedback. Although a Johari plotting of these scores might also approach a Type D profile, the Arena is less balanced and accounts for only 25 percent of the data available for use in a relationship. Again, such an interpersonal style seems consistent with a managerial approach based on expediency and a search for the middle ground.

As might be expected, the 9,1 managers in the study displayed a marked preference for Exposure over Feedback in their relationships with subordinates. This suggests that managers who are maximally concerned with production issues also are given to an overuse of Exposure—albeit not maximum Exposure—and this is very likely to maintain personal control. In general, a Type C interpersonal style seems to underlie the 9,1 approach to management; and it is important that such managerial practices may be sustained by enlarged Blindspots.

Considering the opposing dominant concerns of the 1,9 manager as compared to the 9,1, it is not too surprising to find that the major interpersonal process of these managers is Feedback solicitation. As with the 9,1 style, the resulting Arena for 1,9 managers is not balanced; but the resulting tension likely stems from less than desired Exposure, leading to relationships in which the managerial Façade is the dominant feature. The Type B interpersonal style may be said to characterize the 1,9 approach to management, with its attendant effects on corporate climate.

Finally, the use of Exposure and Feedback processes reported by those managers identified as dominantly 1,1 is minimal. A mechanical impersonal approach to interpersonal relationships which is consistent with the low profile approach to management depicted under 1,1 is suggested. The Unknown region apparently dominates relationships, and hidden potential and untapped resources prevail. The consequences of such practices for the quality of relationships, climates, and communication effectiveness have already been described in the discussion of Type A interpersonal behaviors.

In summary, it appears that one's interpersonal style is a critical ingredient in his approach to management. While the uses of Exposure and Feedback reported by managers identified according to management style seem to be quite consistent with what one might expect, it is worthy to mention that the test items comprising the *Personnel Relations Survey* have very little, if anything, to do with production versus people concerns. Rather, one's willingness to engage in risk-taking disclosures of feelings, impressions, and observations coupled with his sensitivity to others' participative needs and a felt responsibility to help them become involved via Feedback solicitation were assessed. The fact that such purposive behaviors coincide with one's treatment of more specific context-bound issues like production and people would seem to raise the question: which comes first, interpersonal or managerial style? The question is researchable, and management practices and information flow might both be enhanced by the results obtained.

CORPORATE CLIMATE AND PERSONAL DECISION

The major thesis of this article has been that interpersonal styles are at the core of a number of corporate dilemmas: communication breakdowns, emotional climates, the quality of relationships, and even managerial practices have been linked to some fairly simple dynamics between people. The fact that the dynamics are simple should not be taken to mean that their management is easy—far from it. But, at the same time, the fact that individuals can and do change their interpersonal style—and thereby set in motion a whole chain of events with corporate significance—should be emphasized. A mere description of one's interpersonal practices has only limited utility, if that is as far as it goes. The value of the Johari Window model lies not so much with its utility for assessing what is but, rather, in its inherent statement of what might be.

Although most people select their interpersonal styles as a *reaction* to what they anticipate from other parties, the key to effective relationships lies in "pro-action"; each manager can be a norm setter in his relationships if he will but honestly review his own interpersonal goals and undertake the risks necessary to their attainment. Organizations can criticize their policies—both formal and unwritten—in search for provisions which serve to punish candor and reward evasiveness while equating solicitation of data from others with personal weakness. In short, the culture of an organization and the personal and corporate philosophies which underlie it may be thought of as little more than a *decision product* of the human system. The quality of this decision will directly reflect the quality of the relationships existing among those who fashion it.

If the model and its derivations make sense, then corporate relationships and managerial practices based on candor and trust, openness and spontaneity, and optimal utilization of interpersonal resources are available options to every member of an organizational family. As we have seen, power distributions among people may adversely influence their interpersonal choices. Management styles apparently constrain individuals, but the choice is still there. Type A practices require breaking away from the corporate womb into which one has retreated; personal experiments with greater Exposure and Feedback, however anxiety-producing, may be found in the long-run to be their own greatest reward. For the manager locked into Type B behaviors, the task is more simple; he already solicits Feedback to an excellent degree. Needed is enough additional trust in others—whether genuine or forced—to allow a few experiences with Exposure. Others may be found to be less fragile or reactionary than one imagined. Learning to listen is but part of the task confronting managers inclined toward Type C styles; they must learn to seek out and encourage the exposures of others. This new attention to the Feedback process should not be at the expense of Exposure, however. Revamping Type C does not mean adopting Type B. These are all forms of low-risk high-potential-yield personal experiments. Whether they will ever be undertaken and their effects on corporate excellence determined depends upon the individual; the matter is one of personal decision.

PART V

DEVELOPING INDIVIDUAL, GROUP, AND ORGANIZATIONAL EFFECTIVENESS

THE process by which managers sense and respond to the necessity for change has been the focus of much research and practical attention in recent years. If managers were able to design and to perfect social and technical organizations and if the scientific, market, and technical environments were stable and predictable, there would be less pressure for change. But such is not the case. In fact the statement that "we live in the midst of constant change" has become a well-worn cliché despite its relevance. Of course, the need for change affects organizations differently; those which operate in relatively certain environments need to be less concerned with change than those which operate in less certain environments. But even managers in relatively certain environments must continually combat the problems of complacency.

The literature which deals with the process of organizational change cannot be conveniently classified because of the yet unsettled nature of this aspect of organizational behavior. We have various conceptualizations and theories whose meanings and interpretations are subject to considerable disagreement. The current trend is to use the term *"organizational development"* (OD) to refer to the process of preparing for and managing change.

Organizational development as we will use the term refers to (1) a planned, systematic program initiated by an organization's management, (2) with the aim of making the organization more effective, (3) through the use of a variety of methods designed to change environmental behavior, and (4) based upon the assumption that organizational effectiveness is enhanced to the extent that the program facilitates the integration of individual and organizational objectives. These four statements capture the essence of OD. It is admittedly broader than some experts would like, since it permits the inclusion of methods other than sensitivity training. Our view is consistent with others who note the trend toward a more "eclectic approach" utilizing a number of methods depending upon the situation.

It is apparent that OD is oriented toward problem-solving where the underlying problem is defined in terms of actual or potential organizational ineffectiveness. As such we can cast OD in the managerial language of problem-solving:

1. What is the problem? (diagnosis)
2. What are the alternatives? (methods)
3. How should the method be implemented? (implementation)
4. Did it work? (evaluation)

The articles included in this part deal with aspects of those four questions.

In the first article, "Organizational Development: Some Problems and Proposals," Robert L. Kahn reviews the current state of OD in terms of its research. He questions the validity of much of the research that has sought to determine the outcome of OD programs. Khan's discussion provides the reader with an overview of many of the popular OD methods, such as sensitivity training, team development, and encounter groups. He also distinguishes between the target and the means of organizational change, a distinction which allows for an integration of the process-structure dichotomy.

In the second article, "Red Flags in Organization Development," Larry E. Greiner cautions readers by examining six trends in OD. He discusses the warning signals of (1) placing the individual before the organization, (2) assuming that the informal organization takes precedence over the formal organization, (3) overemphasizing behavioral change before diagnosis, (4) placing primary emphasis upon improving the behavioral processes of decision making while de-emphasizing or ignoring the content and task issues, (5) placing expert knowledge before managerial knowledge, and (6) imposing on a company programs of OD that have been designed by outsiders who do not know the organization. After discussing these six caution flags. Greiner suggests alternative courses of action for those involved in OD programs.

In the third article "The Management of Change Part Three: Planning and Implementing Change" by Paul Hersey and Kenneth H. Blanchard, some examples of change are examined. The authors first look at the dilemma facing organizations. That is, there is a shortage of successful marriages. They also present the force field analysis approach to change. In addition, the impact of change on the total system is considered.

The fourth article looks at the Non Linear Systems study. Edmund R. Gray in "The Non Linear Systems Experience: A Requiem" traces over time the successes and fortunes of one organization involved in change. The original use of many behavioral principles offered by Likert, Maslow, and McGregor are identified. The author offers some cogent explanations about the reasons for later failures in the Non Linear Systems change experiments.

In the fifth article Gary P. Latham and Gary A. Yukl in "A Review of Research on the Application of Goal Setting in Organizations" an excellent example of integrating a literature base is presented. The authors look at, analyze, and suggest improvements for goal-setting research in organizations. The article presents a summary of goal-setting field studies and illustrates the sample, criteria, and goal measure. One of the highlights of the paper is the discerning discussion and conclusions which offer managers and readers insights about the future research needs in goal setting.

In the final article of the book James L. Gibson, John M. Ivancevich, and James H. Donnelly, Jr. in "Behavior, Structure, and Processes in Two Organizations," illustrate how the behavioral sciences have influenced managerial practices in two different organizations. A public utility and a state health agency were used to make comparisons and as reference points to discuss behavior, structure, and process.

Organizational Development: Some Problems and Proposals*

ROBERT L. KAHN

INTRODUCTION

Advising people in power about how they can better attain their goals is a very old occupation. Organizational Development (OD), on the other hand, is a new label for a conglomerate of things an increasing number of consultants do and write about. What that label refers to depends to a considerable extent upon the doer or writer. Among the critics and practitioners of organizational development, who are often the same people, there is a continuing argument over the state of the art, its proper definition, and the requisite skills for practicing it.

For example, Harry Levinson (1972), a clinical psychologist writing in the journal *Professional Psychology*, criticized OD practice for its neglect of diagnostic procedures, along with other theoretical and methodological shortcomings. He was answered in the same journal by Marshall Sashkin (1973a) and by Warner Burke (1973b), both of whom undertook a specific rebuttal of Levinson's criticisms and a general defense of organizational development as practiced. Levinson (1973a) responded; Sashkin (1973b) replied; Burke (1973a) commented further; and Levinson (1973b) offered summary comments, which included the inarguable observation that the discussion had reached the point of diminishing returns.

Such exchanges reveal a good deal about current practice and preference, and several recent review articles provide more comprehensive statements. One of the most instructive is Friedlander and Brown's chapter in

---

* Reproduced by special permission from the *Journal of Applied Behavioral Science*, "Organizational Development: Some Problems and Proposals," Robert L. Kahn, 485–502. Copyright 1974 by NTL Institute Publications.

the current *Annual Review of Psychology* (1974), which is built around the familiar dichotomy between people-oriented ("human processual") and technology-oriented ("technostructural") approaches to organizational change. Comprehensive reviews have also been written by Alderfer (1974), Sashkin et al., (1973), Strauss (1975), and Hornstein et al. (1971). Leavitt's earlier chapter (1965) speaks in terms of applied organizational change rather than development, but the difference is more terminological than substantive, and the review remains a useful commentary on what is now called OD.

More numerous than such reviews are books and articles that describe a preferred approach to organizational development, sometimes in very general terms, sometimes with a good deal of theoretical elaboration, occasionally with some substantiating empirical data. Examples are provided by Argyris (1970, 1971) on intervention theory, Blake and Mouton (1968, 1969) on grid organization development, Schein (1969) on process consultation, Schmuck and Miles (1971) on the OD Cube, and others.

My present purpose is neither to rehearse the OD arguments nor to review the reviews. Much less do I wish to dispute whether the practice of organizational development has been nearly completed, is well en route, or has barely begun the long transition from being a miscellany of uncertain devices to becoming a mature, useable set of principles and procedures for organizational change. I want instead to cite some problems, the resolution of which will facilitate that transition and thus make organizational development better than it is, in theory and practice.

OMISSIONS AND REDUNDANCIES

No reasonable person can complain that written material on organizational change and development is meager. In 1962 Everett Rogers (Rogers and Shoemaker, 1962, 1971), working in an admittedly broader area, the communication of innovations, generated a bibliography of some 1,500 items. In 1968 Ronald Havelock (Havelock et al., 1968, 1972) found almost 4,000 titles in the area of planned innovation and offered the terrifying bibliographic projection that the number was increasing at the rate of 1,000 per year. Such volume invites specialization; in the more circumscribed area of organizational development, Jerome Franklin (1973) lists about 200 books, chapters, and articles. That is the body of material most relevant for our present purposes; what does it tell us?

About 15 years ago, March and Simon (1958) observed that rather little had been said about organizations but that little had been said repeatedly and in many different ways. In the years since then, I believe that caustic judgment has become less accurate for organizational research in general, but it remains unhappily true of writings on organizational development. A few theoretical propositions are repeated without additional data or development; a few bits of homey advice are reiterated without proof or disproof, and a few sturdy empirical generalizations are quoted with reverence but without refinement or explication.

For example, Kurt Lewin's (1947 a,b) suggestion that the process of planned change be conceptualized in terms of three successive phases— unfreezing, moving, and freezing—is often quoted or paraphrased as a preamble to research, but seldom with any clear indication of how that formulation determined the design of the research that follows its invocation. The Lewinian concept of quasi-stationary equilibrium (1947c) is also frequently mentioned, but without any systematic conceptualization or measurement of the alleged opposing forces. Gordon Lippitt (1969) presents this model as "force-field analysis," and 40 driving and restraining forces are represented by opposing arrows in a diagram (p. 156). The forces, however, are unidentified; their identification and measurement is left to the reader. Such presentations are common. The Lewinian schema thus remains not only unelaborated and untested, but really unused. It deserves more serious attention.

The OD literature contains other slogans, less theoretical but recited no less often. Consider, for example, the advice that the "change agent" should "start at the top" of the organization he intends to change. Beckhard (1969) makes "management from the top" one of five defining characteristics of organizational development; Blake and Mouton (1969) assert that "to change a company, it is necessary for those who head the company to lead the change of it." Argyris' recent cases (1971) begin with discussions between the author and chief executives of the companies described.

I have neither experience nor data to challenge the advice that one should start at the top, and certainly it has a pleasant ring. Nevertheless, it would benefit from specification and test. Does it mean that the top of the organization must change before any other part can do so? Does it mean that the people at the top of the organization must actively support the proposed program of change without necessarily becoming "trainees" themselves? Or does it mean merely that some degree of top-echelon sanction for the new enterprise of organizational development must be visible in order for others to accept the proposed changes? One can readily imagine research to answer these questions, but it has yet to be done. Nor can it be, until the homily about starting at the top is stated with enough specificity to be tested.

As an example of a third sort of redundancy without development, empirical generalization, let us take the proposition that organizational changes are more likely to be accepted by people who have had a voice in determining their content. This is the principle of participation, perhaps the best established and most widely accepted empirical generalization in the literature of organizational change. The research pedigree for this principle dates back at least to 1948, when Coch and French published their classic article on overcoming resistance to change. Their experiment demonstrated that varying degrees of employee's participation in changes of work methods were related to their expressed acceptance of the new methods, to the rapidity with which they learned those methods, and to their decision to remain as employees of the company.

As good research should, the Coch and French experiment not only answered old questions; it raised new ones. Some of them—the interaction of participation with individual personality differences, for example— have been the subject of subsequent investigations (Tannenbaum and All-port, 1956; Vroom, 1960). Others remain unstudied; for example, the important question of distinguishing the motivational effects of participation from substantive effects of participative decisions.

It would be exciting to see an organizational development program that included research designed to obtain separate estimates of the effects of identical substantive changes generated under participative and non-participative conditions. Such data could be provided, I think, by means of a design using "master" and "slave" groups. (I use the terms only in their figurative, mechanical sense.) Work groups would be chosen in sets of three, one in each set randomly designated master, one slave, and one control. If one of the master groups decided in the course of an OD program that the group should have the authority to set its own standards or choose its own methods of work or have access to current cost data, these same changes would be initiated in the slave group, but by conventional managerial instruction. An increase in productivity or satisfaction in the master groups, as compared to control groups, would be interpreted as the combined consequence of the participative experience and the substantive participative decisions. An increase in productivity or satisfaction in the slave groups, as compared to control groups, would be interpreted as the effect of the substance of the decisions without the motivational effect of participation. The difference in criterion changes in a master group as compared to the matched slave group would be interpreted as reflecting the effect of participation alone, the effects of decision content having been held constant experimentally within each such pair of groups.

Whether or not readers share my enthusiasm for this particular case of unexplored research is not important. The foregoing examples of omission and redundancy in the literature of organizational development and change are not intended to urge some particular research project. Rather, they are intended to rouse in the reader a thirst for movement—for elaboration and strengthening of old theoretical formulations, for systematic test of old injunctions, for the refinement and extension of old empirical generalizations. Argument by example, however, is always judgmental; let us state the criticism of redundancy in more objective terms. Of the 200 items in the Franklin (1973) bibliography of organizational development, only 25 percent include original quantitative data; the remaining 75 percent consist for the most part of opinions, narrative material, and theoretical fragments. No branch of science can long afford such a ratio. Ideas and personal impressions need desperately to be tested by collision with facts. The mill of science grinds only when hypotheses and data are in continuous and abrasive contact.

PACKAGES AND CONCEPTS

Organizational development is not a concept, at least not in the scientific sense of the word: it is not precisely defined; it is not reducible to specific, uniform, observable behaviors; it does not have a prescribed and verifiable place in a network of logically related concepts, a theory. These statements hold, I believe, in spite of some serious efforts to provide a workable definition and a meaningful theoretical context.

Lawrence and Lorsch (1969) provided one such example, building on their earlier work on differentiation and integration (1967) and describing organizational development in terms of activities at three interfaces—organization and environment, group to group, and individual in relation to organization. Argyris (1970) provides another example, in his sustained effort to conceptualize and describe his own experience in organizational change. His emphasis is on the autonomy and "health" of the client organization, and on OD as a means of increasing those valued characteristics by increasing the capacity of the organization to generate and utilize valid information about itself.

Argyris, like Lawrence and Lorsch, is stating his own definition and theoretical position; he is not attempting a formulation that accommodates everything that goes by the name of organizational development. Attempts at such broader and more eclectic statements sacrifice a good deal in precision and theoretical connectedness. For example, Bennis (1969) says that "organization development is a response to change, a complex educational strategy intended to change the beliefs, attitudes, values, and structure of organizations so that they can better adapt to new technologies, markets, and challenges, and the dizzying rate of change itself." His co-editor, Richard Beckhard (1969) says that "organizational development is the name that is being attached to *total-system*, planned-change efforts for coping with the above-mentioned conditions." (These conditions include four assertions about "today's changing world," five about "today's business environment," and six about "today's changing values.") I find those definitions too inclusive to be helpful, and others go still farther. Margulies and Raia (1972) offer a definition broad enough to include everything from market research to industrial espionage. They define organizational development as consisting of "data gathering, organizational diagnosis, and action interventions."

Other authors give us other descriptions, and their variety serves to underline my assertion that *organizational development* is not a concept. This assertion is in itself neither praise nor damnation; it merely reminds us that the term is a convenient label for a variety of activities. When we remember that fact about the term *OD*, we benefit from its convenience, as we do from the convenience of other colloquial terms—*mental health* and *illness*, for example. Scientific research and explanation, however, require concepts that get beneath convenient labels and represent explicitly defined and observable events and behaviors. The literature of organizational development is disappointed in this respect; it is tied too closely to the labels in terms of which the varied services of organizational development are packaged and marketed.

Moreover, this criticism holds even when we consider more specific terms. *Sensitivity training*, for example (also known as *laboratory method* or *T-Group training*, and partially inclusive of such variants as *encounter groups* and *personal development groups*), is itself a convenience term for a number of activities that probably vary as much with the preferences of the trainer as with anything else (Back, 1972). *Grid organization development* is another such term; it refers to those consulting and training activities marketed by Blake and Mouton and their colleagues (1964, 1968, 1969). Indeed, their firm has registered the term as a trademark or brand name— the antithesis of scientific conceptualization.

One of the persisting problems with research on organizational development is that it has incorporated such colloquial and commercial terms as independent variables. I have noted that of the more than 200 bibliographic entries on organizational development, about 25 percent (53) present quantitative data. Within that subset, more than 65 percent (35) utilized independent variables that must be considered packages rather than concepts. In most of those, the package was "the T-group," variously employed and mingled with lectures, skill-practice, and other training activities. In about 10 percent of the data-reporting articles, the "independent variable" was "Managerial Grid Training."

In a few cases the experimental treatment was simply—or rather, complicatedly—"Organizational Development." And a few others offer as the independent variable a sort of omnibus treatment in which the social scientist and management seem to have done a variety of things—T-groups, consultation, lectures, surveys, explicit changes in formal policies, and the like, which they hoped might produce wanted changes in employee attitudes and behavior. Evidence of such changes is presented, but we are left in doubt as to the potent ingredient or synergistic combination of ingredients that produced the effect.

Such aggregate treatments need not be bad, but they can be made scientifically good only when the package treatment is sufficiently described to permit replication and "dissection" of its ingredients. I have found no examples of sustained refinement of independent variables in the articles that make up the bibliography of organizational development, although some beginnings have been made from time to time. In 1965, Bunker, for example, showed that conventional T-group experience produced changed interpersonal behavior in the back-home work situation, as measured in terms of the perceptions of co-workers, not merely the perceptions of the trainees themselves. Shortly thereafter, Bunker and Knowles (1967) replicated those findings, with variations in the duration of the experimental treatment. They compared the effects of two-week with three-week T-groups, and found that the latter generated the greater perceived changes in behavior. We could wish for more work along these lines, especially in view of the tendency toward shorter and more intensive use of T-groups and encounter groups—a tendency that appears to be based on administrative convenience rather than evaluative research.

There is another encouraging sign in the research that uses packages as independent variables: a few experiments or quasi-experiments have compared packages. Perhaps the best example of such comparative work is Bowers' (1973) article "OD Techniques and Their Results in 23 Organizations." This research is based on data from 14,000 respondents in 23 industrial organizations and reports gain scores (before and after treatment) for four patterns of developmental activity—Survey Feedback, Interpersonal Process Consultation, Task Process Consultation, Laboratory (T-group) Training—and two "control" treatments, "data handback" and "no treatment." Bowers found that "Survey Feedback was associated with statistically significant improvements on a majority of measures, that Interpersonal Process Consultation was associated with improvement on a majority of measures, that Task Process Consultation was associated with little or no change, and that Laboratory Training and No Treatment were associated with declines."

These findings are not definitive, nor are they presented as such. There are the now-familiar problems with raw gain scores (Cronbach, Gleser et al., 1972), although Bowers has done supplementary analyses to control for initial differences in the several treatment groups and to test for the plausibility of the alternative hypothesis that his results merely reflect the regression of extreme scores toward the mean. There are other explicit limitations: the treatments are defined only approximately; there is confounding of change agents with treatment differences (since each change agent conducted the treatment of his choice); there is some self-selection of treatments by populations as well as change agents; and there is the absence of hard criteria of organizational change (productivity, profit, turnover, and the like). Finally, a sociologist of knowledge might express some lurking skepticism that Survey Feedback had been discovered by its proponents to be the most effective form of organizational development. Nevertheless, the comparison of treatments is most welcome; I applaud it and only wish that it were more frequent.

Friedlander and Brown (1974), in a careful review article of some 18 pages, require only three paragraphs to summarize comparative studies of OD interventions. Moreover, of the three studies summarized, two (Greiner, 1967; Buchanan, 1971) do not evaluate alternative interventions; the third study cited is that of Bowers.

Even such comparative studies, however, leave us with needs for explanation that can be satisfied only by research that clarifies the nature of the independent variable, the experimental treatment itself. Such conceptualization and explicit definition of the experimental treatment is well illustrated in three field experiments that are widely regarded as classics in organizational change—Coch and French's (1948) work on the effects of participation, Morse and Reimer's (1956) on hierarchical locus of decision-making power, and Trist and Banforth (1951) on changes in sociotechnical structure. There are other and more recent examples, of course, but the list remains short. Let us hope that it will lengthen.

AUTOBIOGRAPHY AND ORGANIZATION

My third criticism of research on organizational development may seem to include a contradiction in terms: the research on organizational development is not sufficiently organizational. It is too autobiographical a literature, too concentrated on the experience of the trainees and change agents. It is a literature of training episodes, and those episodes are often nonorganizational or extraorganizational.

Research that carries the term *organizational* in its title often consists of the group experience of a few people, far from the organizations that are allegedly being developed. More often than not, the criteria by which the success of the developmental process is judged are the reactions of these participants to the temporary group experience. Let us be specific: of the projects (in the Franklin [1973] bibliography) reporting empirical data interpreted in terms of organizational development, about 60 percent are based on data from the training episode only; 40 percent include some measure of the persistence of the training effect to some later time. A much smaller proportion, 15 percent, trace the training effect in terms of behavior in the organization itself. Forty percent measure the effect of the experimental treatment only in terms of self-report, and an equal proportion include no control or comparison group, either as part of an experimental design or in the statistical analysis of a larger population.

Friedlander and Brown (1974) report similar conclusions in the three kinds of process-oriented intervention that have been most researched—survey feedback, group development, and intergroup development. They find "little evidence that survey feedback alone leads to changes in individual behavior or organizational performance," but considerable evidence for reported attitudinal change, at least in the short run. They speak of research on group development intervention in comparable terms: "There remains a dearth of evidence for the effects of team building external to the group developed." As for intergroup relations development—

> . . . there is very little systematic research on the effectiveness of such interventions in the field. Case studies abound [e.g., Blake, Mouton, and Sloma (1965)], but they leave many questions about the efficacy of the intervention unresolved.

Most OD activities seem to emphasize process rather than structure as the primary target of change, and most research describing the effects of structural changes in organizations seems to exemplify a different tradition from organizational development. However, definitional distinctions are difficult to make when definitions are unclear. If one includes in the realm of organizational development those studies that Friedlander and Brown call "technostructural," the evidence for persisting organizational effects increases. Certainly such effects were attained in the coal-mine experiments of Trist and his colleagues (1951, 1963) and in the textile-mill experiments of Rice (1958, 1969). Thorsrud (1969), working in the same theoretical tradition, reported still broader and more ramifying changes in a series of Norwegian field experiments. In all these cases, the primary aim was to improve the goodness of fit between the social and the technical aspects of the work organizations. The improvement involved changes in both organizational aspects.

Significant increases in performance, attendance, and satisfaction have also been accomplished by organizational changes that begin with the division of labor, the definition of individual jobs. Such approaches include job design, job enlargement, and job enrichment, the distinctions among which are not always clear. All three share the assumption that many industrial jobs have been fragmented beyond the point of maximum efficiency, and that gains in performance and satisfaction are obtainable by reducing the fragmentation and increasing the variety of content. Results of such work are described by Davis and Taylor (1972) and Ford (1969), and are summarized by Stewart (1967) and Friedlander and Brown (1974). The findings are not uniform, nor are the changes in job content that serve as independent variables or the organizational circumstances in which the experiments were attempted. One must conclude, nevertheless, that the content of the job makes a difference, and that intervention in terms of job content is likely to have effects.

Our present point, however, is not where OD intervention should begin but rather where it should end. As the term *organizational development* reminds us, the organization is the major target of change. Persisting change in the organization must therefore be the criterion of OD success or failure.

STRUCTURE AND PROCESS

The penultimate problem that I wish to raise about organizational development is the separation of structure and process. It is a familiar enough distinction in organizational theory and in writings on organizational change. Friedlander and Brown (1974) classify all efforts at organizational development as either "technostructural" or "human processual." Leavitt (1965) had earlier proposed a trichotomy: a similar distinction between structure and process, and an additional distinction between technological structure and social structure. As classifications that remind us of the different emphases or starting points of various approaches to change, I find these schemes useful. As classifications that imply the separation of organizational process and structure, however, I find them misleading.

We have argued elsewhere (Katz and Kahn, 1966) that human organizations be viewed as a class of open systems which lack the usual properties of physical boundedness and therefore lack structure in the physical or "anatomical" sense of the term. The structures of an organization can thus be said to consist in the pattern of interdependent events or activities, cyclical and repetitive in nature, that in combination create the organizational product or service. Organizational structures can therefore be well described in terms of roles, those activities expected of persons occupying certain positions in a network of such expectations and behaviors.

The structure of the living organization is not the charts and job descriptions and work-flow diagrams usually employed to describe those roles and the relationships among them. The structure of an organization is the pattern of actual behaviors as that pattern is created and re-created by the human beings we call members of the organization.

It may be useful for some purposes to distinguish this actual organization from some idealized or preferred structure, to distinguish the paper organization from the living organization, for example. There are many ways of making such distinctions—formal versus informal organizational behavior, role prescriptions versus role elaborations, and the like. But the central point remains: the structure of the organization *is* the pattern of actual recurring behaviors.

If we are agreed on that point, the issue of structural versus processual approaches to organizational development takes on a new and clearer form. To change an organization means changing the pattern of recurring behavior, and that is by definition a change in organizational structure. For example, suppose that an OD practitioner somehow gets all the supervisors in an organization to tell employees in advance about any developments that may affect their jobs. Suppose that the giving of such advance information becomes a continuing supervisory practice, a norm among supervisors, and an expectation on the part of subordinates. It will then be part of the role structure of the organization.

Providing such information may or may not be written into the job descriptions of supervisory duties, may or may not be included among criteria for promotion of supervisors. Likelihood of providing such information may or may not be built into the selection procedures for supervisors. To the extent that these things are also done, the giving of advance information becomes more a part of the "formal" structure of the organization, by which I mean management's representation of the organization. The incorporation of some change into the formal structure of the organization—that is, into the management-prescribed roles—has its own significance. But the main issue is change in the enactment of roles; if there is change in those recurring behavior patterns, then the structure of the living organization has changed. Organizational development, if it implies change at all, must change those behaviors, regardless of whether it calls itself structural or processual.

I believe that these issues become clearer if we discuss separately the target and the means of organizational change, and if we do so in terms of role concepts. There is by now some consensus about these concepts and their definition. A role consists simply of the expected behaviors associated with a particular position or office. The people who occupy positions somehow interdependent with that office typically hold and communicate expectations about the behaviors they want enacted by its occupant. The job description thus becomes a special case of such role expectations, probably sent to the occupant by someone in the personnel department acting as a surrogate for upper management. The actual behavior of a person in a role is likely to be a complex combination of responses to the expectations of relevant others and spontaneous activities that are neither prescribed nor proscribed by others. These latter activities are referred to as role elaborations, in contrast to role prescriptions.

Now let us use these terms to discuss first the target of change and then the means of change. I assume that when people speak of the target as structural change, they mean changing the roles and the official or formal expectations associated with them. The number of jobs, their formally prescribed activities, and their prescribed relationships to other positions are examples of such changes.

When people speak of changes in process rather than structure, I assume that they are referring to aspects of role behavior that are not usually prescribed but left to the discretion of the occupant—role elaborations rather than role prescriptions. For example, in most organizations, the extent to which supervisors express consideration and interest toward workers is a matter of role elaboration—unspecified in the formal description of the supervisory job and not included in the role expectations expressed by the workers themselves. If an OD program increases supervisory consideration, the changes might ordinarily be referred to as processual. It might be argued, of course, that what the OD program has done is to move certain consideration-expressing behaviors from role elaborations (options) to role prescriptions (managerial expectations, in this case), and that the target is therefore the formal structure of the organization after all. I would not disagree except to point out that the observation illustrates my point about the special meaning of structure in human organizations, and the ultimate fusion of structure and process.

A similar distinction and unity with respect to structure and process is involved in the means of organizational change. One can, for example, attempt to bring about change by altering the formal role prescriptions, introducing new technology, new written policies, new division of labor, and the like. Or one can attempt to bring about change by means of process interventions—counseling, consultation, encounter groups, and the like.

But in the means of change, as in the target, we see some blurring of the usual dichotomy between structure and process. Even Frederick W. Taylor (1923), that classic exemplar of the structural approach to organizational change, began with process-like persuasion and interaction, first at the top of the company and then with the immortal Schmidt. Morse and Reimer (1956) used counseling, role playing, T-groups, and other process-emphasizing activities to bring about and anchor the systemic organizational change they sought.

On the other hand, the most process-oriented OD practitioner necessarily enters the organizational structure in which he hopes to encourage change. He creates a role for himself in that structure and probably changes the role expectations and prescriptions of the people with whom he meets —if only because they are expected to speak with him, attend the group sessions he arranges, and the like. Moreover, his processual interventions, to the extent they are successful, are likely to lead to changes in formal policies, role prescriptions, and other representations of organizational structure.

The process-oriented OD specialist is likely to avoid specifying what structural changes he prefers; he expects those decisions to emerge from the heightened sensitivity and problem-solving abilities of the individuals and groups with which he has worked. He thus illustrates a certain complementarity with his structure-emphasizing counterpart. One OD specialist speaks in terms of process and says little about the structural end-state that he hopes to see the organization attain. The other concentrates on advocated changes in formal structure (job size, division of labor, and the like) and tells us little about the process by which changes are to be attained.

If there is a lesson for us as researchers and as observers of organizational development, it is to avoid being too absorbed with terminological distinctions and to concentrate instead on what is actually done by the change agent, what subsequent behavioral changes in the organization can be identified, their duration, and their ramifying or receding effects.

CHANGING THE UNWRITTEN CONTRACT

I believe that the body of material on organizational development, with its distinctive strengths and weaknesses, is itself the product of special conditions—the concentration of developmental experience in business and industry, and the nature of the role relationship between managements and researcher-consultants. A management, typically concerned with the productivity and profitability of its enterprise, with secondary interests in job satisfaction and the meaningfulness of work, pays a specialist in organizational development to do certain agreed-upon things in expectation of improved productivity and profit. If these results can be brought about with concomitant gains in satisfaction and worker identification with task and mission, all the better; hence the special appeal of approaches that promise some explicit linkage of satisfaction and productivity. Management also assumes in most cases that the process of organizational development will not alter or infringe traditional managerial prerogatives in matters of personnel, resource allocation, and the like.

The change agent, in his writings about organizational development, gives more emphasis to humanistic values in organizational life. He accepts his role in relation to management in the hope of contributing to the realization of those values, in the hope of increasing the satisfaction and meaningfulness of work. He also wishes to add to the store of things known about human organizations and to learn how they can be influenced. He usually enters into the relationship with management as a paid consultant, and with implied agreement about areas of activity and reservation. Too often, in my view, that implies agreement to induce some change in satisfaction, motivation, and productivity without becoming involved in resource allocation, availability of equipment, choice of supervisors, content of jobs, allocation of rewards, and the like. In the extreme case, the organizational developer agrees to leave the role structure alone and to induce changes in role elaboration—those activities and stylistic characteristics that are left to the discretion of individuals.

Progress in organizational change and the knowledge about change has been made sometimes in spite of those limitations, and sometimes because of welcome exceptions to them. Now there are numerous signs that the contract between management and behavioral science is being redrawn. Managements are less insistent on tangible results from intangible manipulations, and behavioral scientists are less willing to attempt such legerdemain. As one visible sign of this tendency, I welcome the work on job design (Davis and Taylor, 1972), which approaches organizational improvement through change in one of the major aspects of organizational structure—the division of labor. I hope that more research is done on job design and that comparable lines of research develop on other aspects of formal organizational structure. Not only will this strengthen the practice of organizational development; it will also bring the language of organizational development into the larger realm of organizational theory and research. It is a long awaited convergence.

REFERENCES

Alderfer, C. P. Change processes in organizations. In M. D. Dunnette (ed.), *Handbook of industrial and organizational psychology.* Chicago: Rand McNally, 1974.

Argyris, C. *Intervention theory and methods.* Reading, Mass.: Addison-Wesley, 1970.

Argyris, C. *Management and organizational development: The path from Xa to Yb.* New York: McGraw-Hill, 1971.

Back, K. W. *Beyond words.* New York: Russell Sage, 1972.

Beckhard, R. *Organizational development—Strategies and models.* Reading, Mass.: Addison-Wesley, 1969.

Bennis, W. G. *Organization development: Its nature, origins, and perspectives.* Reading, Mass.: Addison-Wesley, 1969.

Blake, R. R., and Mouton, J. S. *Corporate excellence through grid organizational development.* Houston: Gulf Publishing Co., 1968.

Blake, R. R., and Mouton, J. S. *Building a dynamic organization through grid organization development.* Reading, Mass.: Addison-Wesley, 1969.

Blake, R. R., Mouton, J. S., and Sloma, R. The union-management intergroup laboratory: Strategy for resolving intergroup conflict. *Journal of Applied Behavioral Science,* 1965, 1, 25–57.

Blake, R. R., Mouton, J. S., Barnes, L., and Greiner, L. Breakthrough in organizational development. *Harvard Business Review,* 1964, 42, 37–59.

Bowers, D. OD techniques and their results in 23 organizations: The Michigan ICL study. *Journal of Applied Behavioral Science,* 1973, 9, 21–43.

Buchanan, P. C. Crucial issues in OD. In *Social intervention: A behavioral science approach.* New York: Free Press, 1971, Pp. 386–400.

Bunker, D. R. Individual application of laboratory training. *Journal of Applied Behavioral Science,* 1965, 1, 131–147.

Bunker, D. R., and Knowles, E. S. Comparison of behavioral changes resulting from human relations training laboratories of different lengths. *Journal of Applied Behavioral Science,* 1967, 3, 505–523.

Burke, W. W. Further comments by Burke. *Professional Psychology,* May 1973, pp. 207–208. (a)

Burke, W. W. Organization development. *Professional Psychology,* May 1973, pp. 194–199. (b)

Coch, L., and French, J. R. P., Jr. Overcoming resistance to change. *Human Relations,* 1948, 1 (4), 513–533.

Cronbach, J., Gleser, G., Nanda, H., and Rajartnam, N. *The dependability of behavioral generalizability for scopes and profiles.* New York: John Wiley, 1972.

Davis, L. E., and Taylor, J. C. (eds.) *Design of jobs.* New York: Penguin Books, 1972.

Ford, R. N. *Motivation through work itself.* New York: American Management Association, 1969.

Franklin, J. L. Organizational development: An annotated bibliography. Ann Arbor, Mich.: Center for Research on the Utilization of Scientific Knowledge, Institute for Social Research, University of Michigan, 1973.

Friedlander, F., and Brown, L. D. Organization development. *Annual Review of Psychology,* vol. 25. Palo Alto, Calif.: Annual Reviews, 1974.

Greiner, L. E. Patterns of organizational change. *Harvard Business Review,* 1967, 45, 119–128.

Havelock, R., et al. *Bibliography on knowledge utilization and dissemination.* Ann Arbor, Mich.: Institute for Social Research, 1968. Rev. 1972.

Hornstein, H. A., et al. Some conceptual issues in individual and group oriented strategies of intervention into organizations. *Journal of Applied Behavioral Science,* 1971, 7, 557–567.

Katz, D., and Kahn, R. L. *The social psychology of organizations.* New York: John Wiley, 1966.

Lawrence, P. R., and Lorsch, J. W. *Organization and environment.* Boston: Division of Research, Harvard Business School, 1967.

Lawrence, P. R., and Lorsch, J. W. *Developing organizations: Diagnosis and action.* Reading, Mass.: Addison-Wesley, 1969.

Leavitt, H. J. Applied organizational change in industry: Structural, technological, and humanistic approaches. In J. G. March (ed.), *Handbook of organizations.* Chicago: Rand McNally, 1965.

Levinson, H. The clinical psychologist as organizational diagnostician. *Professional Psychology,* 1972, 3, 34–40.

Levinson, H. Levinson's response to Sashkin and Burke. *Professional Psychology,* May 1973, pp. 200–204.(a)

Levinson, H. Summary comments. *Professional Psychology.* May 1973, p. 208.(b)

Lewin, K. Frontiers in group dynamics I. *Human Relations,* 1947, 1, 5–41.(a)

Lewin, K. Frontiers in group dynamics II. *Human Relations,* 1947, 1, 143–153.(b)

Lewin, K. Group decision and social change. In T. M. Newcomb and E. L. Hartley (eds.), *Readings in social psychology.* New York: Holt, 1947.(c)

Lippitt, G. L. *Organization renewal.* New York: Appleton-Century-Crofts, 1969.

March, J., and Simon, H. *Organizations.* New York: John Wiley, 1958.

Margulies, N., and Raia, A. P. *Organization development: Values, process, and technology.* New York: McGraw-Hill, 1972.

Morse, N., and Reimer, E.   The experimental change of a major organizational variable. *Journal of Abnormal and Social Psychology*, 1956, 52, 120–129.

Rice, A. K.   *Productivity and social organization: The Ahmedabad experiment.* London: Tavistock, 1958.

Rice, A. K.   Individual group and intergroup processes. *Human Relations*, 1969, 22, 565–584.

Rogers, E., and Shoemaker, F.   *Communication of innovations.* New York: The Free Press, 1962. Rev. 1971.

Sashkin, M.   Organization development practices. *Professional Psychology*, May 1973, pp. 187–192.(a)

Sashkin, M.   Sashkin's reply to Levinson. *Professional Psychology*, May 1973, pp. 204–207.(b)

Sashkin, M., et al.   A comparison of social and organizational change models: Information flow and data use processes. *Psychological Review*, 1973, 80 (6), 510–526.

Schein, E. H.   *Process consultation: Its role in organization development.* Reading, Mass.: Addison-Wesley, 1969.

Schmuck, R. A., and Miles, M. B. (eds.)   *Organization development in schools.* Palo Alto: National Press, 1971.

Stewart, P. A.   *Job enlargement.* Iowa City: College of Business Administration, University of Iowa, 1967.

Strauss, G.   Organization development. In R. Dubin (ed.), *Handbook of work organization in society.* Chicago: Rand McNally, 1975.

Tannenbaum, A., and Allport, F. H.   Personality, structure and group structure: An interpretative study of their relationship through an event structure hypothesis. *Journal of Abnormal and Social Psychology*, November 1956, 53, (3), 272–280.

Taylor, F. W.   *The principles of scientific management.* New York: Harper, 1923.

Thorsrud, E.   A strategy for research and social change in industry: A report on the industrial democracy project in Norway. *Social Science Inform*, 1969, 9 (5), 65–90.

Trist, E. L., and Bamforth, R.   Some social and psychological consequences of the long wall method of coal-getting. *Human Relations*, 1951, 4 (1), 3–38.

Trist, E. L., Higgin, G. W., Murray, H., and Pollack, A. B.   *Organizational choice.* London: Tavistock, 1963.

Vroom, V.   *Some personality determinants of the effects of participation.* Englewood Cliffs, N.J.: Prentice-Hall, 1960.

Red Flags in
Organization Development*

LARRY E. GREINER

M ANY organizations have embarked in recent years on ambitious programs of large-scale change labeled with the high-sounding title
of "organization development" (or OD, as it has come to be called
by its devotees). A very special meaning has become attached to OD,
usually referring to the widespread application of an intensive educational program within an organization for the twin purposes of changing
managerial behavior and improving the total performance of the organization.

A basic proposition underlying these OD programs centers around the
notion that if an educational program can cause a large number of individual managers to alter their behavioral styles in working with others,
then the organization as a whole will be transformed—and so will its overall effectiveness.

Although some of these programs have been uniquely designed for a
particular organization, a great majority are prepacked by outside consultants. Such packaged programs include the managerial grid, versions
of sensitivity training, synectics, and a host of lesser known programs designed by small consulting companies and academics who have moved
forward to meet the demand.

Despite the differences between one OD program and the next, there
are some common features that apply to all of them. Basically, they center
around an educational training program attended by, preferably, a large
number of managers and even nonmanagerial employees from a single organization. These training laboratories concentrate on presenting a new

---

* Reprinted by permission from *Business Horizons* (June 1972), pp. 17–24.

role model or behavioral style for managers and employees to emulate back on the job when solving problems in interpersonal settings. The role model tends to be universally prescribed for all who attend the laboratory sessions—that is, if you change your individual styles to this one "best" approach, then you and the organization will perform better.

This learning experience is intensive and intended to be long range; the learning message is not imparted in a one-day session, but begins with a one- to two-week educational laboratory conducted away from the job. It is usually followed by numerous on-the-job learning activities after the initial training session in order to make the reeducation "stick."

NEED FOR PERSPECTIVE

For the last few years, two colleagues of mine, Louis Barnes of Harvard and Paul Leitch, formerly of Harvard, have joined me in studying and learning about the application of various approaches to OD. Out of these efforts has come an increasing concern with some disturbing trends recurring in the design and conduct of many organization development programs.

My purpose in this article is to build on this experience by taking a critical look at these trends and offering some additional perspective on them. To date, this perspective seems to be lacking. Too many organizations have embarked on OD for a number of ill-founded reasons—because it is the "thing to do," or because "change is the watchword of the day," or because "I went to one of their laboratory training sessions; it was good for me, and it will be good for my managers."

To an extent this new initiative has been healthy. A growing number of consultants and companies have at least taken the leap to utilize nontraditional approaches for improving behavioral conditions within their firms. No longer can the behavioral scientist be condemned for sitting in his ivory tower conducting meaningless experiments on his students. Nor can the manager be criticized for forgetting about the human aspects of his organization while drumming away on production at all costs.

But there is also much to be concerned about when examining such an enthusiastic rush into organization development. Numerous methods used in these programs are relatively untested; their deficiencies have not been weeded out through long experience or research.

Moreover, disturbing symptoms of the failure of current brands of OD have been appearing frequently in research studies, in anecdotal comments by managers, and in the literature of organizations. Some skeptics contend that OD is a luxury afforded only by affluent organizations, but which is usually discarded when a major crisis arises. One study has shown that a major OD effort in a government agency failed to make any impact on the climate of the organization, although it did produce small increments in behavioral change.[1] In this case, one wonders how long the individual changes will last.

A thoughtful review of many studies of OD by Dunnette and Campbell has concluded:

> . . . none of the studies yields any evidence that the changes in job behavior have any favorable effect on actual performance effectiveness. Thus, there is little to support a claim that T-group or laboratory education effects any substantial behavior change back on the job for any large proportion of trainees. Whatever change does occur seems quite limited in scope and may not contribute in any important way to changes in overall job effectiveness.[2]

Of considerable concern, in the absence of more convincing research, has been the tendency for consultants and organizations to "freeze" prematurely on particular approaches, indicating that they have already found the one "best" approach. Vested interests no doubt help to explain this absence of self-critique; if I as a consultant design a program, I have a strong commitment and personal interest in its success. Therefore, while I may make small refinements in my methodology, I am not likely to alter its basic approach. Similarly, if I as a manager have committed funds and support to a particular program, I am not likely to treat it as an academic experiment where the chips fall as they may. Rather, I want it to succeed just as I do with any program implemented within my organization.

It is this unhealthy trend toward premature commitment that should be questioned, especially in terms of what has been working and not working. Such a reexamination seems essential if we are to benefit from our experience instead of slipping back into the pitfall of making the same mistakes again.

SIX RED FLAGS

I wish to raise red flags by questioning six trends that may be preventing the very changes that are being sought. For each warning signal, I will suggest an alternative way of thinking that might open up other directions for future OD programs.

---

[1] Larry Greiner, D. Paul Leitch, Louis B. Barnes, "The Simple Complexity of Organizational Climate in a Government Agency," in R. Tagiuri and George Litwin, eds., *Organizational Change: Exploration of a Concept* (Boston: Division of Research, Harvard Business School, 1968).

[2] Marvin D. Dunnette and John P. Campbell, "Laboratory Education: Impact on People and Organizations," in Gene Dalton and others, eds., *Organization Change and Development* (Homewood, Ill.: Richard D. Irwin, 1970).

Flag 1—Individual before the Organization

Many OD programs are characterized by a seemingly logical sequence of learning and behavior change, beginning typically with an exclusive focus on the individual employee and his style of behavior. Next, attention is given to the small group in which the employee works, assuming that if the individual is to change his behavior, there must be support in his immediate work surroundings. Third, once many individuals and small groups are changing, emphasis shifts to intergroup issues, such as resolving conflicts between R&D and production. Finally, after these basic subunits of the organization have been reeducated, consideration is given to issues affecting the entire organization, such as its corporate strategy.[3]

There are two principal reasons why I wish to question this gradually expanding sequence from individual to organization. First, the problems of a particular organization may not fit this exact sequence. It could well be that issues of over-all company strategy are dominant in the beginning and that, until these are more clearly resolved, there can be little clarity of direction for specific changes within basic subunits. A second concern with the "individual first" logic is that spontaneity of problem solving can easily be stifled. I have seen organizations in which certain managers have discovered a serious interdepartmental problem early in their OD program, only to be told by higher management to "cool it" and work on their own team first, since this was the prescribed stage of OD at that time.

To replace the individual-to-organization sequence, I would suggest a more situational and issue-centered approach. That is, if the management of the organization is not using OD to attack major problems affecting a majority of employees, then employees are likely to turn off quite rapidly on OD. For example, if problems center more around formal organization structure, it makes little sense for OD to begin with the behavioral styles of individual managers. Why not change the structure instead of beating around the bush?

Another important guideline is to work simultaneously on both the individual and his surroundings. We know from research on the dynamics of learning and psychotherapy, that individuals do not make changes in their behavior entirely on their own initiative. They require strong support from all levels of their environment. Thus, employees in organizations need reinforcement from not only their immediate work groups, but also from the climate of their departments and the formal organization itself. For instance, if a centralized structure is being adjusted to be more decentralized, individual managers will usually have to be assisted in learning through reeducation new behavior skills for acting more autonomously.

---

[3] A clear statement of this sequence is described in Robert R. Blake and Jane S. Mouton, *The Managerial Grid* (Houston: Gulf Publishing Co., 1964).

Flag 2—Informal before Formal Organization

A strong assumption among many OD advocates is that informal organization takes precedence over formal organization. Therefore, they concentrate their educational efforts primarily on the teaching of new "values" or social norms which, if accepted by many colleagues, create social pressure for conformity to new behavior patterns.

Clearly, the informal culture of an organization is a strong determinant of how individuals behave; therefore, it must be addressed in organization change efforts. Yet any manager can tell you that the formal aspects of his organization are also quite important. An OD program may teach the value of participative behavior, but it will not make much headway if managers in this same organization are working under a very rigid and autocratic budget-setting method.

A major reason why formal organization is omitted from many OD efforts is that a taboo frequently exists among OD proponents which says that formal organization is bad or unimportant. This is largely a hangover from the old human relations days when humanistic behavioral scientists preferred to believe that formal organization was only something written on paper or that it was a tool of scientific management to produce mass conformity among employees.

Now we know a great deal more about formal organization, and it is not necessarily as bad as the humanists have contended. Several researchers have shown that formal organization can, indeed, significantly affect the behavior of employees, and that much of this behavior cannot be described as oppressive. For example, Lawrence and Lorsch have shown that formal project teams with considerable delegated formal responsibility can operate in a participative and creative manner. Or advocates of management by objectives have shown how informal participation can be incorporated into formal goal-setting methods.[4]

Therefore, we need to design OD efforts that incorporate a closer connection between formal and informal organization. During the educational phases of OD, managers need to be taught more about formal organization and how it can be used to complement and reinforce changes in their behavior. Many alternative forms of structure are available to managers, not just pyramids with limits on span of control; there are also product, project, and matrix forms of organization. Assumptions that there is one best type of formal organization are as parochial as the mentality that believes in one best type of organization development.

---

[4] Paul Lawrence and Jay Lorsch, *Organization and Environment* (Cambridge, Mass.: Harvard Business School, 1967); Joan Woodward, *Management and Technology* (London: Her Majesty's Stationery Office, 1958); John Humble, *Management by Objectives in Action* (New York: McGraw-Hill Book Co., 1970).

Flag 3—Behavior before Diagnosis

Most OD programs stress a new behavioral model in reeducating managers. Whether the program be based on sensitivity training, the managerial grid, or management by objectives, the learning content of these programs is based on the assimilation of a new form of work behavior that will supposedly be more effective in decision making.

In other words, they are teaching managers to *act* differently—to be more "participative," "open," "confronting," or "authentic," depending upon the value orientation of the program.

What concerns me about this behavioral emphasis is that the thinking side of managers is frequently overlooked. Where their outward behavior is considered by OD, their conceptual thought process are neglected in terms of how they analyze problems or think about their organizations. This oversight can result in some interesting dilemmas once managers begin to behave differently.

One organization with which I am acquainted began an OD effort that stressed team problem solving and the open confrontation of troublesome issues. This was a big step forward for the organization, whose key managers had previously avoided discussions of important problems because of vested interests among them. However, once these managers took the step and placed the issues on the table, they were not particularly adept at making a thorough intellectual analysis of their problems, which were extremely complicated, interwoven with both emotional and technical aspects.

OD programs need to stress the cognitive along with the behavioral and emotional dimensions of more effective problem solving. For example, at the Harvard Business School, we work very hard in the classroom to teach two important aspects of managerial thinking. First, the student must learn to conceive of an organization as an open system and to think in terms of the important conceptual variables that are relevant to a systemic way of thinking about behavior in organizations.

Second, we see a need to practice over and over again a systematic diagnosis of numerous case situations so that these future managers can more quickly ferret out the problems of a situation and design unique solutions. Sharp and objective intellectual insights into management problems seldom come through brilliant lectures or interesting books on problem solving.

Flag 4—Process before Task

A large majority of OD programs place primary emphasis on improving the behavioral processes of decision making while deemphasizing or ignoring the content and task aspects of operating issues facing the organization. Thus, for example, it is assumed that if a manager can learn to participate more skillfully in team meetings, the content of team decisions will be dealt with more effectively.

While attention to behavioral processes is indeed a worthy focal point, there is a danger that managers will become preoccupied with, and even oversensitive to, their own behavior. As a consequence, meetings will be called to discuss the most trivial of issues in order to avoid affronting people; at the opposite extreme, personal issues will be put on the agenda for team discussion when they might better be discussed privately between two individuals.

This new norm of openness, as taught in many OD programs, is frequently abused in a carte blanche manner without thoughtful attention being paid to questions of whom to be open with, about what, and where and when. In order to make these decisions, one must also keep in mind the task aspects of the job. It makes little sense to call a meeting when knowledge for making a decision rests outside the group or when little content preparation has been done ahead of time to shed light on difficult problem issues.

It is no wonder that some managers are frequently turned off by OD programs that place exclusive stress on behavioral processes. These same managers are often dismissed by the consultants as being afraid or insensitive. Yet another plausible explanation is that these managers are understandably concerned about making progress toward solving difficult operating problems. They want to get on with the work, not just sit around contemplating their navels. Of course, this work-oriented preoccupation can be an obstacle too, since these same managers may ignore the importance of building behavioral commitment to decisions they wish to make.

My suggestion to the OD advocates is for them to strive for a better understanding of how task demands influence the behavioral process, not just the other way around. I have seen great OD progress made in one company when a group of conflicting functional managers were brought together for one day to discuss a single operating problem. Prior to this meeting, they had argued mainly over the telephone or behind the backs of other managers about the problem.

In this situation, the OD advocate with a process orientation might have focused the meeting on the question of "Why are you in conflict?" Yet the consultant involved here made no explicit reference to interpersonal conflicts. Instead, he focused the group's attention on analyzing the particular operating problem and reaching a consensus solution by the end of the day. And this is just what the group did, although it took a great deal of argument and soul searching.

What is fascinating about the outcome of this meeting is that a lot of individual stereotypes about other people were changed, as each manager's preconceived opinions began to break down under a more constructive arrangement for problem solving. In other words, behavioral processes were facilitated by a productive task discussion, even when behavioral problems were not the explicit agenda.

Flag 5—Experts before the Manager

Since the technology of OD is often elaborate, wordy, and known only to outside consultants (or staff personnel responsible for OD), these professionals are tempted to presume more than they know and to "talk down" to practicing managers. It is a reflection of the old dichotomy of we (the consultants or staff) are the experts and you (the Managers) are the doers. Therefore, the "knowledge guys," are here to tell you, the "practitioners," how to improve your organization.

There are understandable reasons for this point of view. The experts will often argue convincingly that OD is such powerful stuff that, if directed by untrained people, it can result in very naïve applications that can hurt rather than help an organization. And managers will often subscribe to this argument too, preferring to believe that the experts know more about their concepts and methods than they do; therefore, we, the managers, who know more about action taking, will confine ourselves to carrying out their recommendations.

Several pitfalls are hidden in this rather arbitrary role division. First, there is the possibility that managers will become overdependent on the experts. As a result, dependent managers do not question or argue with the professionals; they just keep looking to them for direction. Second, the experts seldom know the particular organization as well as the managers themselves. Therefore, the outsiders often end up recommending general methods and techniques that have been useful in prior situations, but which may or may not be relevant to the problems at hand. Third, the experts are removed from responsibility for daily operating decisions, thereby making it difficult for them to respond continuously to the important issues that come up daily while OD is in progress. Finally, and perhaps most serious, the experts usually feel more responsibility for and have more commitment to what they are doing than the managers. The OD program, in essence, becomes the experts' program rather than the organization's.

One way out of this dilemma is to share and develop more expertise and commitment between experts and managers. Organizations which have recognized this need have sought to train not only their own internal staff people but also their line managers for assuming a more active role in the conduct of organization development.

Early in the planning of OD, there is a special need to involve key managers in the diagnosis and planning of the direction and methods for implementing the program. Here the managers must exercise sufficient independence to tell the experts that they are "all wet" when foreign ideas seem irrelevant. To do this requires more knowledge than managers typically have about organization development; hence, their own background should contain an exposure to various methods for introducing OD. This does not mean that they should become OD experts, but that they should have sufficient exposure to see through the jargon that so often pervades the OD field.

In addition, managers should be prepared to make known what they are most familiar with—the specific characteristics of the operation they manage and what they perceive to be the main development needs. Here is where the experts would be advised to sit still and listen carefully.

Flag 6—The Package before the Situation

Underlying much of what has been said so far is the deductive fallacy of imposing a program of organization development that has been designed by outsiders who do not know the organization. As a result, there is an insensitive application of a nicely packaged program, based on general theories or misleading past experiences. The organization is asked to fit itself to the package, not vice versa.

This deductive approach is not unknown in the consulting world. Consulting firms, like any other business organization, develop a product to sell. Moreover, they find that the more specific and tangible their product, the more the customer will be attracted to it. Only a few large management consulting firms, such as McKinsey and Booz, Allen & Hamilton, have been able to develop multiple services that can be applied flexibly, though even here each of these firms is frequently identified as being keen on certain solutions which they have grown accustomed to over the years.

I would suggest a more tailor-made approach to the design of OD programs. Here the program is fitted to the situation. This does not mean that a completely new package has to be designed for each customer. Rather, the OD expert must have a large number of tools in his kit so that he can apply a wrench, not a hammer, when only bolts need tightening. Another guideline, as urged earlier, is to encourage managers from within the organization to provide more data and suggestions on what needs to be done. They may have a much more intimate knowledge of company problems than do the outsiders. Their handicap is that they are seldom mobilized to put their heads together, due largely to barriers in communication processes within the organization.

A nice combination of an outsider-insider approach is reflected in the work of Beckhard.[5] He provides a learning structure for managers to get together but does not define their problems and solutions for them.

---

[5] Richard Beckhard, "The Confrontation Meeting," *Harvard Business Review* (May–June 1967).

Rather the managers, by being asked to meet in small groups to confront and identify major issues facing the organization, are the ones who give substance to their organization development efforts. In such cases, Beckhard uses his position as an outside expert to convene the meeting and arrange a focus for productive discussion, but he does not presume to have the answers.

FUTURE ACTIONS

New directions in organization development depend upon a critical assessment of where we are today. I have pointed to six questionable trends that give rise for concern. These include tendencies for OD to begin with the individual before the organization, stress informal values over formal organization, prescribe behavioral actions without diagnostic skills, focus more on behavioral relationships than task accomplishment, adhere to standardized programs over situational needs, and place the expert ahead of the manager. Failure to take account of these other realities of organization life has, I believe, seriously limited the promised impact of organization development. So where do we go from here?

It would be a serious mistake to swing over completely to the other end of the themes; this would only raise six more flags. In doing so, we would prevent the use of the very real expertise that currently resides with experts in the field of organizational development. Instead, I have suggested alternative actions that attempt to build on the strengths from both extremes, since each points to a piece of reality that should be considered in organization development.

First, begin OD with specific and major problem issues founded in the developmental needs facing the organization and many of its employees. These needs may lie in the individual domain with the styles of managers or they may lie in the strategy of the firm. Whichever the case, we know that at some point in any organization change the units of individual, group, intergroup, and organization will have to be addressed, but we should not prescribe the exact sequence ahead of time.

Second, be ready to achieve a more complementary relationship between formal and informal organization during organization development. New informal values will not be accepted for long unless they are reinforced by parallel changes in formal prescriptions. Nor will changes in formal structure be sufficient unless the informal culture is adjusted to accept and encourage the directions implied by new formal designs.

Third, stress a closer integration of diagnostic and action-oriented role models so that we "look while we leap," and we keep on looking as we continue to act. If an educational program is called for, then do not simply stress a single action model, one that, for example, relies exclusively on team problem solving. Instead, sharpen a manager's intellectual insights so that he may choose his actions more appropriately and flexibly.

Yet his action skills should not be neglected, since bright insights are not always equivalent to skillful behavior. Let him know, for instance, that participative behavior can produce certain beneficial results, but also inform him that, under certain conditions, participation can be inappropriate.

Fourth, place more emphasis on the task concerns of managers while educating them in behavioral processes. We cannot ignore the reality of work and the continuing pressure upon managers to deal with the immediate task issues facing them. They may show greater appreciation for the behavioral dynamics in decision making if they can more directly experience task accomplishment at the same time.

Fifth, achieve a more collaborative planning and problem-solving relationship between experts and managers in designing OD programs. Avoid the arbitrary role division of expert as planner and manager as doer. Managers have much to contribute in diagnosing their own ills while experts can provide new tools and fresh perspectives for enlivening managerial insight—without going so far as to recommend one "best" solution.

Sixth, improve the integration of packaged OD materials with the unique demands of each organizational situation. OD tools are just that —handy to have available but applied only when needed. A greater variety of tools must be developed so that they can deal with all points on the continua described in the six flag dimensions. These tools must not be overdesigned, however, since their more important function may be to spade up the data in each situation, not mold the organization or its members in a predetermined fashion.

A little more emphasis on development for OD could head us in a more promising direction.

28

The Management of Change Part Three: Planning and Implementing Change*

PAUL HERSEY and KENNETH H. BLANCHARD

I N evaluating effectiveness, perhaps more than 90 percent of managers in organizations look at measures of output alone. Thus, the effectiveness of a business manager is often determined by net profits, the effectiveness of a college professor may be determined by the number of articles and books he has published, and the effectiveness of an athletic coach may be determined by his won-lost record.

Others feel that it is unrealistic to think only in terms of productivity or output in evaluating effectiveness. According to Rensis Likert,†[13] another set of variables should be taken into consideration in determining effectiveness. These are *intervening variables* which reflect the current condition of the human resources in an organization and are represented in its skills, loyalty, commitment to objectives, motivations, communications, decision-making and capacity for effective interaction. These intervening variables are concerned with building and developing the organization and tend to be long-term considerations. Managers are often promoted, however, on the basis of short-run output variables such as increased production and earnings, without concern for the long-run and organizational development. This creates a dilemma.

---

* From *Training and Development Journal*, March 1972. Copyright 1972 by The American Society for Training and Development, Inc. Reprinted by permission.

† Note: Footnotes 1–12 appear in Parts 1 and 2 of this series of articles which are not published in this book.

[13] Rensis Likert, *New Patterns of Management*, McGraw-Hill, New York (1961), p. 7.

ORGANIZATIONAL DILEMMA

One of the major problems in industry today is that there is a shortage of successful managers. Therefore, it is not uncommon for a manager to be promoted in six months or a year if he is a "producer." Let's look at the example of Mr. X, a manager who realizes that the basis on which top management promotes is often short-run output, and therefore attempts to achieve high levels of productivity by over-emphasizing task accomplishment and placing extreme pressure on everyone, even when it is inappropriate.

The immediate or short-run effect on Mr. X's behavior will probably be increased productivity. Yet if his task-oriented style is inappropriate for those involved, and if it continues over a long period, the morale and climate of the organization will deteriorate. Some indications of deterioration resulting from these intervening variables may be turnover, absenteeism, increased accidents, scrap loss and numerous grievances. Not only the number of grievances, but the nature of grievances is important. Are grievances really significant problems or do they reflect pent-up emotions due to anxieties and frustration? Are they settled at the complaint stage between the employee and supervisor or are they pushed up the hierarchy to be settled at higher levels or by arbitration? The organizational dilemma is that in many instances a manager like Mr. X, who places pressure on everyone and produces in the short run, is promoted out of this situation before the disruptive aspects of the intervening variables catch up.

TIME LAG

There tends to be a time lag between declining intervening variables and significant restriction of output by employees under such management climate. Employees tend to feel "things will get better." Thus, when Mr. X is promoted rapidly, he often stays "one stop ahead of the wolf."

The real problem is faced by the next manager, Mr. Y. Although productivity records are high, he has inherited many problems. Merely the introduction of a new manager may be enough to collapse the slowly deteriorating intervening variables. A tremendous drop in morale and motivation leading almost immediately to significant decrease in output can occur. Change by its very nature is frightening; to a group whose intervening variables are declining, it can be devastating.

Regardless of Mr. Y's style, the present expectations of the followers may be so distorted, that much time and patience will be needed to close the now apparent "credibility gap" between the goals of the organization and the personal goals of the group. No matter how effective Mr. Y might be in the long run, his superiors, in reviewing a productivity drop, may give him only a few months to improve performance. But as Likert's studies indicate, rebuilding a group's intervening variables in a small organization may take one to three years, and in a large organization, may extend to seven years.

SHORT AND LONG TERM

It should be made clear that the choice for a manager is not whether to concentrate on output or intervening variables but often a matter of how much emphasis to place on each. The decision is between short- and long-range goals. If the accepted goal is building and developing an organization for the future, then the manager should be evaluated on these terms and not entirely on his present productivity.

While intervening variables do not appear on balance sheets, sales reports or accounting ledgers, we feel that these long-term considerations can be just as important to an organization as short-term output variables. Therefore, although difficult to measure, intervening variables should not be overlooked in determining organizational effectiveness.

In summary, we feel that effectiveness is actually determined by whatever the manager and the organization decide are their goals and objectives, but should consider these factors: output variables, intervening variables, short-range goals and long-range goals.

FORCE FIELD ANALYSIS

Force field analysis, a technique for diagnosing situations developed by Kurt Lewin, may be useful in looking at the variables involved in determining effectiveness and in developing strategies for changing in particular the condition of the output or intervening variables.[14]

Lewin assumes that in any situation there are both driving and restraining forces which influence any change which may occur. *Driving forces* are those forces affecting a situation which are "pushing" in a particular direction; they tend to initiate a change and keep it going. In terms of improving productivity in a work group, pressure from a supervisor, incentive earnings and competition may be examples of driving forces. *Restraining forces* are forces acting to restrain or decrease the driving forces. Apathy, hostility and poor maintenance of equipment may be examples of restraining forces against increased production. Equilibrium is reached when the sum of the driving forces equals the sum of the restraining forces. In our example, equilibrium represents the present level of productivity as shown in Figure 1.

[14] Kurt Lewin, "Frontiers in Group Dynamics: Concept, Method and Reality in Social Science; Social Equilibria and Social Change," *Human Relations*, vol. 1, no. 1 (June, 1947), pp. 5–41.

Figure 1
Driving and Restraining Forces in Equilibrium

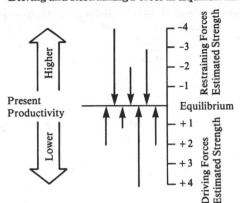

This equilibrium or present level of productivity can be raised or low-ered by changes in the relationship between the driving and restraining forces. For illustrations, let us look again at the dilemma of Mr. Y, the new manager who takes over a work group where productivity is high but Mr. X, his predecessor, drained the human resources (intervening vari-ables). Mr. X had upset the equilibrium by increasing the driving forces (i.e., being autocratic and keeping continual pressure on his men) and thus achieving increases in output in the short run. By doing this though, new restraining forces developed, such as increased hostility and antago-nism, and at the time of his departure the restraining forces were beginning to increase and the results manifested themselves in turnover, absenteeism and other restraining forces which lowered productivity shortly after Mr. Y arrived. Now a new equilibrium at a significantly lowered productivity is faced by the new manager.

Now just assume that Mr. Y decides not to increase the driving forces, but to reduce the restraining forces. He may do this by taking time away from the usual production operation and engaging in problem-solving and training and development. In short run, output will tend to be lowered still further. However, if commitment to objectives and technical know-how of his group are increased in the long run, they may become new driving forces, and that, along with the elimination of the hostility and apathy which were restraining forces, will now tend to move the balance to a higher level of output.

A manager, in attempting to implement change, is often in a position where he must consider not only output but also intervening variables, not only short-term but also long-term goals, and a framework which is useful in diagnosing these interrelationships is available through force field analysis.

PROCESS OF CHANGE

In developing a change strategy, another important aspect that must be taken into consideration is the process of change. Kurt Lewin, in his pioneer work in change, identified three phases of the change process.[15] These are unfreezing, changing and refreezing.

UNFREEZING

The aim of unfreezing is to motivate and make the individual or group ready to change. It is a "thawing out" process where the forces acting on an individual are rearranged so now he sees the need for change. According to Edgar H. Schein, some elements that unfreezing situations seem to have in common are: (1) the physical removal of the individual being changed from his accustomed routines, sources of information and social relationships; (2) the undermining and destruction of all social supports; (3) demeaning and humiliating experience to help the individual being changed to see his old self as unworthy and thus to be motivated to change; (4) the consistent linking of reward with willingness to change and of punishment with unwillingness to change.[16]

In brief, unfreezing is the breaking down of the mores, customs, and traditions of an individual—the old ways of doing things so he is ready to accept new alternatives. In terms of force field analysis, unfreezing may occur when either the driving forces are increased or the restraining forces that are resisting change are reduced.

CHANGING

Once the individual has become motivated to change, he is now ready to be provided with new patterns of behavior. This process is most likely to occur by one of two mechanisms; identification and internalization.[17] *Identification* occurs when one or more models are provided in the environment from whom an individual can learn new behavior patterns by identifying with them and trying to become like them. *Internalization* occurs when an individual is placed in a situation where new behaviors are demanded of him if he is to operate successfully in that situation. He learns

---

15 Ibid.

16 Edgar H. Schein, "Management Development as a Process of Influence" in David R. Hampton, *Behavioral Concepts in Management,* Dickinson Publishing Co., Belmont, Cal. (1968), p. 110. Reprinted from the *Industrial Management Review,* vol. II, no. 2 (May, 1961), pp. 59–77.

17 The mechanisms are taken from H. C. Kelman, "Compliance, Identification and Internalization: Three Processes of Attitude Change," *Conflict Resolution,* vol. 2 (1958), pp. 51–60.

these new behavior patterns not only because they are necessary to survive but as a result of new high strength needs induced by coping behavior.

> Internalization is a more common outcome in those influence settings where the direction of change is left more to the individual. The influence which occurs in programs such as Alcoholics Anonymous, in psychotherapy or counseling for hospitalized or incarcerated populations, in religious retreats, in human relations training of the kind pursued by the National Training Laboratories (1953), and in certain kinds of progressive education programs is more likely to occur through internalization or, at least, to lead ultimately to more internalization.[18]

Identification and internalization are not either/or courses of action and effective change is often the result of combining the two into a strategy for change.

Force or compliance is sometimes discussed as another mechanism for inducing change.[19] It occurs when an individual is forced to change by the direct manipulation of rewards and punishment by someone in a power position. In this case, behavior appears to have changed when the change agent is present, but often is dropped when supervision is removed. Thus, rather than discussing force as a mechanism of changing, we would rather think of it as a tool for unfreezing.

REFREEZING

The process by which the newly-acquired behavior comes to be integrated as patterned behavior into the individual's personality and/or ongoing significant emotional relationships is referred to as *refreezing*. As Schein contends, if the new behavior has been internalized while being learned, "this has automatically facilitated refreezing because it has been fitted naturally into the individual's personality. If it has been learned through identification, it will persist only so long as the target's relationship with the original influence model persists and new surrogate models are found or social support and reinforcement is obtained for expressions of the new attitudes."[20]

This highlights how important it is for an individual engaged in a change process to be in an environment which is continually reinforcing the desired change. The effect of many a training program has been shortlived when the person returns to an environment that does not reinforce the new patterns or, even worse, is hostile toward them.

What we are concerned about in refreezing is that the new behavior

---

[18] Schein, op. cit., p. 112.

[19] Kelman discussed compliance as a third mechanism for attitude change.

[20] Schein, op. cit., p. 112.

does not get extinguished over time. To insure this not happening, reinforcement (rewards and incentives) must be scheduled in an effective way. There seem to be two main reinforcement schedules: continuous and intermittent.[21] Continuous reinforcement means that the individual being changed is rewarded every time he engages in the desired new pattern. With intermittent reinforcement on the other hand, not every desired response is reinforced. Reinforcement can be either completely random or scheduled according to a prescribed number of responses occurring or a particular interval of time elapsing before reinforcement is given.

With continuous reinforcement, the individual learns the new behavior quickly, but if his environment changes to one of nonreinforcement, extinction (elimination of the behavior) can be expected to take place relatively soon. With intermittent reinforcement, extinction is much slower because the individual has been conditioned to go for periods of time without any reinforcement. Thus for fast learning, a continuous reinforcement schedule should be used. But once the individual has learned the new pattern, a switch to intermittent reinforcement should insure a long lasting change.

CHANGE PROCESS—SOME EXAMPLES

To see the change process in operation, several examples could be cited.

A college basketball coach recruited for his team Bob Anderson, a 6' 4" center from a small town in a rural area. In his district, 6' 4" was a good height for a college center. This fact, combined with his deadly turnaround-jump shot, made Anderson the rage of his league and enabled him to average close to 30 points a game.

Recognizing that 6' 4" is small for a college center, the coach hoped that he could make Anderson a forward, moving him inside only when they were playing a double pivot. One of the things the coach was concerned about, however, was when Anderson would be used in the pivot, how he could get his jump shot off when he came up against other players ranging in height from 6' 8" to 7'. He felt that Anderson would have to learn to shoot a hook shot, which is much harder to block, if he was going to have scoring potential against this kind of competition.

The approach that many coaches use to solve this problem would probably be as follows: The first day of practice when Anderson arrived, the coach would welcome Anderson and then explain the problem to him as he had analyzed it. As a solution he would probably ask Anderson to start to work with the varsity center, Steve Cram, who was 6' 10" and had an excellent hook. "Steve can help you start working on that new shot, Bob," the

---

[21] See C. B. Ferster and B. F. Skinner, *Schedules of Reinforcement*, Appleton-Century-Crofts, New York (1957).

coach would say. Anderson's reaction to this interchange might be one of resentment and he would go over and work with Cram only because of the coach's position power. After all, he might think to himself, "Who does he think he is? I've been averaging close to 30 points a game for three years now and the first day I show up here the coach wants me to learn a new shot." So he may start to work with Cram reluctantly, concentrating on the hook shot only when the coach is looking but taking his favorite jump shot when he wasn't being observed. Anderson is by no means unfrozen or ready to learn to shoot another way.

ANOTHER APPROACH

Let's look at another approach the coach could have used to solve this problem. Suppose on the first day of practice he sets up a scrimmage between the varsity and freshmen. Before he starts the scrimmage he gets big Steve Cram, the varsity center, aside and tells him, "Steve, we have this new freshman named Anderson who has real potential to be a fine ball player. What I'd like you to do today though, is not to worry about scoring or rebounding, just make sure every time Anderson goes up for a shot you make him eat it. I want him to see that he will have to learn to shoot some other shots if he is to survive against guys like you."

So when the scrimmage starts, the first time Anderson gets the ball and turns around to shoot Cram leaps up and "stuffs the ball right down his throat." Time after time this occurs. Soon Anderson starts to engage in some coping behavior, trying to fall away from the basket, shooting from the side of his head rather than the front, in an attempt to get his shot off.

After the scrimmage, Anderson comes off the court dejected. The coach says, "What's wrong Bob?" He replies, "I don't know, Coach, I just can't seem to get my shot off against a man as big as Cram. What do you think I should do, Coach?" he asks. "Well, Bob, why don't you go over and start working with Steve on a hook shot. I think you'll find it much harder to block. And with your shooting eye I don't think it will take long for you to learn." How do you think Anderson feels about working with Cram now? He's enthusiastic and ready to learn. Having been placed in a situation where he learns for himself that he has a problem, Anderson is already in the process of unfreezing his past patterns of behavior. Now he's ready for identification. He has had an opportunity to internalize his problem and is ready to work with Steve Cram.

So often the leader who has knowledge of an existing problem forgets that until the people involved recognize the problem as their own, it is going to be much more difficult to produce change in their behavior. Internalization and identification are not either/or alternatives but can be parts of developing specific change strategies appropriate to the situation.

THE MILITARY EXAMPLE

Another example of the change processes in operation can be seen in the military, particularly in the induction phase. There are probably few organizations that have entering their ranks people who are less motivated and committed to the organization than the recruits the military gets. Yet in a few short months, they are able to mold these men into a relatively effective combat team. This is not an accident. Let's look at some of the processes that help accomplish this.

The most dramatic and harsh aspects of the training are the unfreezing phase. All four of the elements that Schein claims unfreezing situations have in common are present. A specific example follows.

1. The recruits are *physically removed from their accustomed routines, sources of information and social relationships* in the isolation of a place such as Parris Island.

   During this first week of training at Parris Island, the recruit is . . . hermetically sealed in a hostile environment, required to rise at 4:55 A.M., do exhausting exercises, attend classes on strange subjects, drill for hours in the hot sun, eat meals in silence and stand at rigid attention the rest of the time; he has no television, no radio, no candy, no coke, no beer, no telephone —and can write letters only during one hour of free time a day.[22]

2. *The undermining and destruction of social supports* is one of the DI's (Drill Instructor) tasks. "Using their voices and the threat of extra PT (physical training), the DI . . . must shock the recruit out of the emotional stability of home, pool hall, street corner, girl friend or school."[23]

3. *Demeaning and humiliating experiences* are commonplace during the first two weeks of the training as the DI's help the recruits *see themselves as unworthy and thus motivated to change* into what they want a Marine to be. "It's a total shock . . . Carrying full seabags, 80 terrified privates are herded into their 'barn,' a barracks floor with 40 double-decker bunks. Sixteen hours a day, for two weeks, they will do nothing right."[24]

4. *Throughout the training there is consistent linking of reward with willingness to change and punishment with unwillingness to change.*

   Rebels or laggards are sent to the Motivation Platoon to get "squared away." A day at Motivation combines constant harassment and PT (physical training), ending the day with the infiltration course. This hot, 225-yard ordeal of crawling, jumping and screaming through ditches and obstacles is climaxed by recruits dragging two 30-pound ammo boxes 60 yards in mud and water. If he falters he starts again. At the end, the privates are lined up and asked if they are ready to go back to their home platoons . . . almost all go back for good.[25]

---

[22] "Marine Machine," *Look Magazine,* August 12, 1969.
[23] Ibid.
[24] Ibid.
[25] Ibid.

While the recruits go through a severe unfreezing process, they quickly move to the changing phase, first identifying with the DI and then emulating informal leaders, as they develop. "Toward the end of the third week a break occurs. What one DI calls 'that five per cent—the slow fat, dumb or difficult' have been dropped. The remaining recruits have emerged from their first-week vacuum with one passionate desire—to stay with their platoon at all costs."[26]

Internalization takes place when the recruits through their forced interactions develop different high strength needs. "Fear of the DI gives way to respect, and survival evolves into achievement toward the end of training." "I learned I had more guts than I imagined" is a typical comment.[27]

Since the group tends to stay together throughout the entire program, it serves as a positive reinforcer which can help refreeze the new behavior.

IMPACT OF CHANGE ON TOTAL SYSTEM

The focus in [this three-part] article has been on the management of human resources and as a result we have spent little time on how technical change can have an impact on the total system. And yet, the importance of combining the social and technical into a unified social systems concept is stressed by Robert Guest.

> On his part the social scientist often makes the error of concentrating on human motivation and group behavior without fully accounting for the technical environment which circumscribes, even determines, the roles which the actors play. Motivation, group structure, interaction processes, authority—none of these abstractions of behavior take place in a technological vacuum.[28]

A dramatic example of the consequences of introducing technical change and ignoring its consequences on the social system is the case of the introduction of the steel axe to a group of Australian aborigines.[29]

This tribe remained considerably isolated, both geographically and socially, from the influence of Western cultures. In fact, their only contact was an Anglican mission established in the adjacent territory.

The polished stone axe was a traditionally basic part of the tribe's technology. Used by men, women and children, the stone axe was vital to the subsistence economy. But more than that, it was actually a key to the smooth running of the social system; it defined interpersonal relationships

---

26 Ibid.

27 Ibid.

28 Guest, op. cit. p. 4.

29 Lauriston Sharp, "Steel Axes for Stone Age Australians," in *Human Problems in Technological Change*, ed. Edward H. Spicer, Russell Sage Foundation, New York (1952), pp. 69–94.

and was a symbol of masculinity and male superiority. "Only an adult male could make and own a stone axe; a woman or a child had to ask his permission to obtain one."[30]

The Anglican mission in an effort to help improve the situation of the aborigines introduced the steel axe, a product of European technology. It was given indiscriminately to men, women and children. Because the tool was more efficient than the stone axe, it was readily accepted but it produced severe repercussions unforeseen by the missionaries or the tribe. As Stephan R. Cain reports:

> The adult male was unable to make the steel axe and no longer had to make the stone axe. Consequently, his exclusive axe-making ability was no longer a necessary or desirable skill, and his status as sole possessor and dispenser of a vital element of technology was lost. The most drastic overall result was that traditional values, beliefs, and attitudes were unintentionally undermined.[31]

This example illustrates that an organization is an "open social system," that is, all aspects of an organization may have an impact on other parts or the organization itself. Thus a proposed change in one part of an organization must be carefully assessed in terms of its likely impact on the rest of the organization.

---

[30] Stephen R. Cain, "Anthropology and Change," taken from *Growth and Change*, vol. 1, no. 3 (July, 1970), University of Kentucky.

[31] Ibid.

29

The Non Linear Systems
Experience: A Requiem*

EDMUND R. GRAY

THE organizational changes instituted in 1960–1961 at Non Linear Systems, Inc. (NLS), a small manufacturer and marketer of digital electrical measuring instruments, represent one of the most celebrated
and ambitious "field experiments" in a business firm since the famous Hawthorne Studies performed by the Western Electric Company between
1927 and 1932. NLS instituted a package of drastic changes, the most important of which were the following:[1]

Organizational Structure. A flat structure with wide spans of management consisting of three levels was established: an executive council made
up of the president and seven vice-presidents; approximately thirty managers of departments, project teams, and marketing regions; and the
worker level, including assistant managers in some of the larger departments. The executive council functioned primarily as a planning and
policy-making body. The several department managers reported to the
whole council rather than to individual members and were delegated almost complete authority for operational matters. Prior to the organizational changes, NLS had a traditional hierarchical structure with typical
reporting arrangements.

Work Organization. Assembly line operations were eliminated and
replaced by instrument assembly teams. A typical team consisted of three
to twelve workers and an assistant manager. Under this arrangement,
batches of instruments were completely built and checked out by a single

---

* Reprinted by permission from *Business Horizons,* February 1978, pp. 31–36.

[1] For a more complete description of these organizational changes, see Cyril O'Donnell, *Cases in General Management,* rev. ed. (Homewood, Ill.: Richard D. Irwin, 1965).
pp. 36–59.

team. Ideally, the teams would plan their own work and the members would assist each other in performing the overall task.

Wage Changes.   Hourly wages were eliminated, and all workers were placed on straight salary with a minimum of $100 per week established (this was $24 higher than the lowest wage on the hourly scale in 1960). Time clocks were eliminated and workers were not docked for absence. Moreover, a policy of continuous employment without layoffs was announced.

Accounting Changes.   The accounting department as such was expunged. The record-keeping function was reduced to a minimum and placed with the individual departments. A policy of "say it, don't write it" was established.

During the early years after the initiation of the changes, both the company and its president, Andrew F. Kay, were praised lavishly by scholars, journalists, and practitioners for their willingness to engage in such an ambitious experiment. It was frequently suggested that the results proved the validity of the underlying behavioral theory.

In 1965, with diminishing sales and increasingly unfavorable competitive conditions, NLS introduced such extensive structural modifications "as to signify the end of the experiment."[2] Again, in 1970, additional reactionary changes were initiated.

With the abandonment of the "experiment," critics were quick to blame the behavioral theories presumably being tested. Richard Farson, for example, asserted, "I think we now know that human relations don't have a lot to do with profit or productivity."[3] Erwin Malone in his analysis suggested that the NLS experience demonstrates that participative management does not work.

In my opinion the early advocates of the experiment were engaging in wishful thinking rather than dispassionate judgment, while the more recent critics have been too sweeping in their denouncement of the applicability of behavioral theory to industrial settings. In this paper I have attempted to place the NLS experience in a more objective perspective. To do this it is necessary to dispel three popular misconceptions: that it was a scientific experiment, that it tested participative management, and that it tested the theories of the leading behavioral writers of the day.

NOT AN EXPERIMENT

Although the term "experiment" is usually applied to the organizational changes at NLS in 1960–1961, those changes cannot be considered an

---

[2] Erwin L. Malone, "The Non Linear Systems Experiment in Participative Management," *The Journal of Business of the University of Chicago* (January 1975), p. 57.

[3] *Business Week* (January 20, 1973), pp. 99–100.

experiment in the scientific sense of the word. James L. Gibson and associates state that for an investigation to be considered an experiment, it must contain two essential elements—the manipulation of some variable (independent variable) by the researcher, and the observation or measurement of the results (dependent variable) while maintaining all other factors unchanged.[4] Where possible it is advisable to establish separate control and experimental groups to monitor unanticipated variables. The experimental methodology permits the researcher to conclude that any changes in the dependent variable are attributable to changes in the independent variable.

A well-known example of a field experiment in industry is the Sears, Roebuck study on "flat" versus "tall" organization structures in the late 1940s. Two groups of similar stores were observed. In the experimental group of stores, 30 departmental managers reported to the store manager and assistant manager. The other group of stores (the control group) was structured in the traditional way with an additional level of management between the department heads and the store manager. The quantitative results clearly showed that, at least for Sears, Roebuck, the flat structure was more effective.[5]

Unlike Sears, NLS failed to meet the requirements of scientific experimentation in two fundamental ways. First, a single independent variable was not manipulated. Instead, numerous major changes were introduced into the organization almost simultaneously, so that it would have been impossible to attribute results at a later date to specific independent variables. Second, dependent variables were not established prior to the introduction of the changes and then later measured. Malone has emphasized that one of the principal problems in attempting to evaluate the NLS experience is the fact that the company kept few records; hence, measurable data for analysis was not available.

If the NLS executives had been interested in scientific experimentation (and there is no indication they were), they could have introduced changes one at a time, establishing experimental and control groups where feasible, and observed changes in selected dependent variables. It is regrettable that the firm did not proceed with this approach; opportunities for experimentation in ongoing business firms have been extremely limited, principally because managers are hesitant to interrupt operations and risk poorer results. NLS management was perfectly willing to accept the risks of experimentation but was unwilling to practice the patience, discipline, and reservation of judgment required by scientific methodology.

---

[4] James L. Gibson, John M. Ivancevich, and James H. Donnelly, *Organizations: Structure, Process Behavior* (Dallas: Business Publications, 1973), p. 14.

[5] Harold Koontz and Cyril O'Donnell, *Management: A Systems and Contingency Analysis of Managerial Functions*, 6th ed. (New York: McGraw-Hill, 1976), pp. 291–292.

Apparently, they had made up their minds that certain theories and applications would work and wanted to demonstrate this to the world as soon as possible.

TESTING PARTICIPATIVE MANAGEMENT

In his analysis, Malone suggests that the NLS experience represents a test of participative management. Moreover, he seems to conclude that the evidence demonstrates the bankruptcy of the participative approach in all but the most environmentally favorable situations. A basic problem I have with this conclusion is that participative management is not a single technique or approach but rather a generic term encompassing several different approaches. NLS encouraged and practiced some forms of participation but discouraged other forms.

Marshall Sashkin has distinguished four basic types of participation: goal-setting, decision-making, problem-solving, and the development and implementation of change. He also has asserted that participation may be implemented on an individual, dyadic, or group basis.[6] The principal form of participation designed into the structure at NLS was problem-solving, defined as nonprogrammed decision-making. Group problem-solving was encouraged and, in fact, demanded by the system at all levels. Thus, at the executive council level, decisions affecting the company as a whole were made by the entire council. In the instrument assembly department, with specialization eliminated, group problem-solving became a way of organizational life. The several engineering project teams also relied heavily on group problem-solving. The company salesmen, on the other hand, tended to utilize individual goal-setting and problem-solving approaches.

Horizontal problem-solving among the various departments was especially critical because of the lack of direct supervision from the vice-presidential level. To facilitate this coordination, formal weekly meetings of the managers of the five production-oriented departments were held. These managers also interacted during the week as problems arose.

Surprisingly, some of the more successful forms of participation practiced in organizations today, particularly joint goal-setting, problem-solving, and decision-making between hierarchical levels, were discouraged at NLS. In other words, participation was primarily lateral at each scalar level rather than vertical between levels. Goal-setting for the instrument assembly department is illustrative of this lack of vertical participation. The executive council would establish production quotas for instrument assembly on a quarterly basis. The department manager would then

---

[6] Marshall Sashkin, "Changing toward Participative Approaches: A Model and Methods," *Academy of Management Review* (July 1976), p. 76.

distribute the work load among the various teams who, in turn, would work out the detailed plans.

In another example, the executive council unilaterally set maximum and minimum inventory levels for the materials department at $200,000 and $175,000. The department was then free to plan its purchases within these limits.[7]

Vertical interaction was probably greatest between the executive council and the engineering project teams. The typical procedure was for a team to be assigned the development of a new instrument with preliminary specifications prepared by the council. Upon receiving the specifications, the project manager would negotiate with the council until mutual agreement was reached as to exactly what the team would do. But even under these conditions, engineers were heard to complain that vertical communication was difficult because they were dealing with a faceless plural executive rather than a single superior.[8]

Perhaps the most startling omission in participation was the fact that the organizational changes were planned and executed solely by top management, primarily Andrew Kay, with the aid of outside consultants. Discussions were held with employees prior to the changes, but it would appear that the primary purpose of these meetings was to "sell" and educate the employees rather than to gain their imput.[9] Although it is recognized that participation is not universally necessary for successful change, it is incongruous that such dramatic changes based on behavioral management theory would be introduced without significant employee participation.

TESTING BEHAVIORAL THEORY

NLS executives publicly stated that the organizational changes of 1961–1962 were based on the writings of Abraham Maslow, Douglas McGregor, Peter Drucker, and other leading behavioral scholars of the day. Let us now look at what these writers said and how it relates to what NLS did.

The concepts which appeared to have the greatest influence on Kay and his advisors were Maslow's "hierarchy of needs" and McGregor's "Theory Y." Maslow states that human needs are structured in a series of levels—physiological, safety, social, esteem, and self-realization—and when those on a lower level are generally fulfilled, those on the next level will demand satisfaction. "Theory Y" is a set of assumptions about human

---

[7] *Business Week,* p. 100.

[8] O'Donnell, *Cases in General Management,* p. 58.

[9] During my research at the firm I learned that several members of the executive council as well as others in the organization were highly skeptical of the package of changes.

nature which asserts that people are not inherently lazy or dishonest, and that they have the capacity to learn and accept responsibility under proper conditions. McGregor contrasted it with "Theory X," which states that the average individual inherently dislikes work, avoids responsibility, and must be controlled and coerced to put forth a fair day's work.

The NLS reorganization was to a large degree aimed at creating a working environment in which employees could satisfy their full range of needs and thereby realize the assumptions of "Theory Y." Thus, the elimination of hourly wages, raising the general wage level, and the no-lay-off policy were directed at fully satisfying the employee's lower-level needs. The elements of autonomy, ambiguity, and job enrichment were designed into the system for the purpose of providing the opportunity for higher-level need satisfaction.

In designing a structure to accomplish their goals, the NLS executives had to innovate because Maslow and McGregor provided little guidance. Maslow was a psychologist who developed a general theory of human motivation. He did not concern himself with business firms and the practical problems of creating an internal environment where high-level needs could be fulfilled.[10] McGregor, on the other hand, was concerned with the business firm and its management. His focus, however, was not on suggested applications but, rather, was on the assumptions of managers and a critique of their traditional practices, which were a logical consequence of what he believed to be faulty assumptions ("Theory X"). He did, however, endorse two specific techniques, the "Scanlon Plan" and "Management by Integration and Self-Control."

The Scanlon Plan has two essential features: a profit-sharing scheme based on cost reduction, and an employee-suggestion system which utilizes a series of committees to receive and evaluate ideas for improving productivity.[11] NLS, curiously, did not incorporate either of these features into its new structure. Instead of profit sharing, all workers were placed on a high straight salary, as noted earlier. Moreover, there was no formal suggestion system at NLS. Of course, the high degree of horizontal interaction encouraged the flow of ideas at the operating level, but the paucity of interaction between the departments of the executive council tended to hinder the consideration of more far-reaching suggestions.

"Management by Integration and Self-Control" was McGregor's version of Peter Drucker's "Management by Objectives." It required subordinate input into the establishment of specific goals for a limited time period and

---

10 (Maslow was a Visiting Fellow at NLS during the summer of 1962, well after the major organizational change had been put into effect. While there, he developed the impressions which became the basis for his book, *Eupsychian Management* (Homewood, Ill.: Richard D. Irwin, 1965).

11 Douglas McGregor, *The Human Side of Enterprise* (New York: McGraw-Hill, 1960), pp. 110–123.

joint appraisal by the superior and subordinate of the results.[12] Conversely, major objectives and guidelines at NLS were set from above and formal appraisals were not required.

An important influence on the thinking of the organization designers at NLS was Drucker's classic, *The Practice of Management*. This book is replete with original concepts, the most significant of which was "Management by Objectives." However, as demonstrated above, NLS completely eschewed this idea.

The Drucker concept with which Kay and his advisors were most intrigued was "the eight objectives of business." Drucker argued convincingly that it is a basic fallacy for a firm to concentrate on profit as its sole objective, as economists have traditionally asserted, because it tends to misdirect managers' attention to the short run at the expense of the long run. As an alternative to profit maximization, Drucker suggested eight critical areas where objectives should be set: market standing, innovation, productivity, physical and financial resources, profitability, manager performance and development, worker performance and attitude, and public responsibility.[13] He saw these as areas where planning and control were essential to the long-run viability of the business. In essence he was recommending a comprehensive strategic planning focus for the firm. NLS, however, carried his idea a step further and incorporated it directly into its formal organization structure. Thus, the executive council was created with each position corresponding to one of Drucker's key planning areas.[14]

In my opinion, this corruption of Drucker's concept led to some of the major internal problems at NLS. The executive council became essentially an aloof, top heavy, eight-man planning group. Its members were former line executives, most of whom were uncomfortable in their new staff assignments. Moreover, their ill-defined position descriptions caused confusion, frustration, and, in one or two cases, guilt feelings resulting from a perceived lack of contribution. In any event, the structure that emerged at NLS went far beyond what Drucker had in mind.

Rensis Likert was another important behavioral scholar whose ideas were occasionally linked to the thinking at NLS. His early book, *New Patterns in Management*, presented the results of his research on the principles and practices followed by managers achieving the best results. The most famous concept to come out of this work is the "Linking Pin Function," which stresses the need for effectively functioning interlocking groups that connect the various hierarchical levels in the organization. The importance

---

[12] McGregor, *The Human Side* . . . , pp. 61–76.

[13] Peter F. Drucker, *The Practice of Management* (New York: Harper and Bros., 1954).

[14] Actually, manager performance and development and worker performance and attitude were handled by the same executive, and the eighth member of the council was the president, whose primary function was to coordinate the council's activities.

of the "Linking Pin Function," according to Likert, is that it provides for upward communication and influence in the organization.[15] However, as discussed earlier, the NLS structure mediated against vertical groups and upward communication.

According to company executives, the accounting changes instituted were inspired to a large degree by Carl F. Braun's succinct little monograph, *Objective Accounting*.[16] Braun pleads for internal accounting information that is significant, timely, and understandable. He severely criticizes standard cost accounting procedures and offers a number of practical suggestions for improving the effectiveness of internal accounting. Predictably, however, nowhere in the book does he recommend eliminating the accounting department or reducing accounting information to the minimum that is required for government reports. As with many of the other NLS innovations, these changes involved rather questionable extensions of an author's ideas.

What can be learned from the NLS experience? The most obvious conclusion is that a favorable environment and sagacious strategy can overcome the inadequacies of structure, but once the environment turns hostile, structural faults quickly become manifest and untenable. But what were the structural inadequacies at NLS? Malone has suggested that the executive council concept, the dearth of vertical communication, and the wage and lay-off policies were major flaws in the system. He also seems to feel that the team production concept was a moderate success. Subjectively, I tend to agree with him. Objectively, however, almost nothing about the experience can be concluded with any degree of certainty because of three fundamental errors in the design of the new structure. First, many changes were implemented simultaneously, thereby confounding any results which might have been obtained. Second, little, if any, usable data upon which to draw conclusions was generated. Contrast this with the Hawthorne studies, where various changes were introduced sequentially, and data was systematically collected for future scholarly analysis. Finally, the various behavioral theories that supposedly were being implemented were to a large degree misapplied. Hence, all that was being tested was the organization architects' unique interpretations of these concepts.

NLS is one of the few firms that has been willing to incur the risk of large-scale behavioral experimentation. It is unfortunate that the undertaking failed, but the real tragedy is that so little was learned from it. Perhaps the most important lesson to emerge from the experience is how *not* to proceed with organizational experimentation or change.

---

[15] Rensis Likert, *New Patterns in Management* (New York: McGraw-Hill, 1961).

[16] Carl F. Braun, *Objective Accounting: A Problem of Communication* (Alhambra, Calif.: C. F. Braun & Co., 1958).

A Review of Research on the Application of Goal Setting in Organizations*

GARY P. LATHAM and GARY A. YUKL

L OCKE'S (36) theory of goal setting deals with the relationship between conscious goals or intentions and task performance. The basic premise of the theory is that an individual's conscious intentions regulate his actions. A goal is defined simply as what the individual is consciously trying to do. According to the theory, hard goals result in a higher level of performance than do easy goals, and specific hard goals result in a higher level of performance than do no goals or a generalized goal of "do your best." In addition, the theory states that a person's goals mediate how performance is affected by monetary incentives, time limits, knowledge of results (i.e., performance feedback), participation in decision making, and competition. Goals that are assigned to a person (e.g., by a supervisor) have an effect on behavior only to the degree that they are consciously accepted by the person. Thus, Locke states, "It is not enough to know that an order or request was made; one has to know whether or not the individual heard it and understood it, how he appraised it, and what he decided to do about it before its effects on his behavior can be predicted and explained" (36, p. 174).

Locke's theory is based primarily on a series of well-controlled laboratory experiments with college students who performed relatively simple tasks (e.g., adding numbers) for short periods of time. Some psychologists legitimately have questioned whether something so deceptively simple as setting specific hard goals can increase the performance of employees in real organizational settings, where experimental "demand effects" are ab-

* Reprinted from *Academy of Management Journal*, 1975, vol. 18, pp. 824–45.

sent and acceptance of goals cannot be obtained so easily (5, 15). Although Locke (36) cites a large number of laboratory studies in support of his theory, only four field studies are discussed in his article. Most of the field research on goal setting has been conducted since Locke's 1968 theoretical article was published.

The purpose of the present article is to review research on the application of goal setting in organizations, particularly in industry. The article is concerned with evaluating the practical feasibility of goal setting as well as with evaluating Locke's theory. The review includes 27 published and unpublished reports of field research. The major characteristics of these studies are summarized in Table 1.

Table 1
Summary of Goal Setting Field Studies

Investigators	Type of Study[a]	Sample	Criterion	Goal Measure or Manipulation
Blumenfield and Leidy (2)	C	55 vending machine servicemen	Supervisor report of typical output quantity	Supervisor report of assigned goal level or absence of goals
Burke and Wilcox (4)	C	323 female telephone operators	Self-rated performance improvement	Employee perception that specific goals were set and perceived participation
Carroll and Tosi (6, 7, 8, 9)	C	150 managers	Self-reported goal attainment and effort increase	Self-reported goal difficulty, participation, and feedback
Dachler and Mobley (14)	C	596 production employees	Output quantity[b]	Employees' stated goals
Duttagupta (16)	C	18 R&D managers	Self-reported motivation	Self-reported participation and feedback
French, Kay, and Meyer (17)	E	92 managers	Self-rated goal acceptance, self and superior-rated goal attainment	Assigned vs. participative goal setting in MBO and perceived participation
Ivancevich (22)	QE	166 managers	Change in self-rated need satisfaction	Goal setting in MBO programs
Ivancevich (23)	QE	181 groups of salesmen and production workers	Sales; output quantity and quality[b]	MBO with and without reinforcement versus comparison group
Ivancevich, Donnelly, and Lyon (24)	QE	166 managers	Change in self-rated need satisfaction	Goal setting in MBO programs
Kolb and Boyatzis (26)	C	111 management students in T-groups	Self- and trainer-rated behavior change	Self-reported goal for behavior change
Kolb, Winters, and Berlew (27)	E-C	79 management students in T-groups	Self- and trainer-rated behavior change	Self-reported goal for behavior change

Table 1 (*continued*)

Investigators	Type of Study[a]	Sample	Criterion	Goal Measure or Manipulation
Latham and Baldes (29)	QE	36 truck drivers	Net weight of truck loads[b]	Assigned individual goals versus prior no-goal condition
Latham and Kinne (30)	E	20 logging crews	Quantity of output[b]	Assigned group goals versus no-goal control condition
Latham and Yukl (32)	E	48 logging crews	Quantity of output[b]	Assigned group goals, participative group goals, and no-goal control condition
Latham and Locke (31)	QE	379 logging crews	Quantity of output[b]	Time limitations on output disposal
Lawrence and Smith (33)	E	22 office and garment factory workers	Improvement in output quantity[b]	Participative group goal setting versus discussion without goal setting
Mendleson (42)	C	25 superior-subordinate pairs in 8 companies	Superior ratings of subordinate performance	Superior-subordinate reported degree of goal setting
Raia (48)	QE	112 managers and supervisors	Output quantity[b]	MBO participative goal setting versus prior no-goal condition
Raia (49)	QE	74 managers and supervisors	Output quantity[b]	(See above)
Ronan, Latham, and Kinne (50)	C	1184 logging crews	Quantity of output[b]	Supervisor reported goal specificity
Shetty and Carlisle (52)	C	109 professors in a public university	Perceived improvement in performance and commitment	Goal setting in MBO
Sorcher (53)	QE	14 assembly work groups	Improvement in output quality[b]	Participative goal setting versus prior no-goal condition
Stedry and Kay (54)	E-C	19 manufacturing work groups	Productivity and rework costs[b]	Assigned goals for two performance criteria
Steers (55)	C	133 female first-line supervisors	Superior ratings of performance	Perceived goal specificity, goal difficulty, and participation
Wexley and Nemeroff (58)	E	27 managers and 125 subordinates	Absenteeism,[b] LBDQ, and JDI	Assigned goals versus no goals
Zander, Forward, and Albert (63)	C	255 members of 64 United Fund campaigns	Dollars collected[b]	Official annual goal set by each local committee
Zander and Newcomb (62)	C	149 United Fund campaign	Dollars collected[b]	Official annual goal set by each local committee

[a] E = experiment, C = correlational study, QE = quasi-experimental study.
[b] Denotes "hard" objective criterion.

A few laboratory studies conducted since 1968 also are discussed when the research appears to be particularly relevant for evaluating the theory. The review is divided into sections corresponding to the following aspects of Locke's theory: (a) the effects of specific goals versus generalized goals or no goals; (b) the effects of goal difficulty on performance; and (c) goals as mediators of performance feedback, monetary incentives, and time limits. Some research on goal setting within the context of a management by objectives (MBO) program also is examined. Finally, studies on the relative effectiveness of assigned versus participative goal setting are reviewed. The article concludes with a general evaluation of the theory and a discussion of desirable directions for future research on goal setting.

SPECIFIC VERSUS GENERALIZED GOALS OR NO GOALS

One of the earliest field studies providing information on the effects of goal setting was conducted by Lawrence and Smith (33). The objective of the study was to investigate the effects of employee participation in decision making and goal setting, rather than to determine the effects of setting specific goals. However, since the researchers compared a participative goal setting condition with a condition in which work problems and company policy were discussed without any explicit goal setting, the study can appropriately be interpreted as an assessment of the effects of goal setting. Lawrence and Smith found that employees were equally satisfied in both conditions, but production (quantity) increased significantly more in the goal setting condition than in the no-goal condition.

Sorcher (53) conducted a study to evaluate the effects of a program consisting of employee participation in goal setting together with "role training" (i.e., an explanation of the importance of each employee's job). This program resulted in substantial improvement in the quality of production, as well as in some increases in quantity of production. A possible limitation of both this and the preceding study is the difficulty in determining the extent to which the improvements were due to the goal setting rather than to other features of the experimental treatment, such as the role training.

A study by Burke and Wilcox (4) assessed the effects of goal setting during the appraisal interview. Data were obtained by means of a questionnaire survey of a sample of nonmanagerial female employees. Burke and Wilcox found that employee perception of the extent to which an employee and her supervisor set mutual goals was correlated with the employee's self-reported desire to improve her performance ($r = .45$) and her self-ratings of actual performance improvement ($r = .29$).

In another correlational study, Blumenfeld and Leidy (2) found that soft drink salesmen and servicemen checked more vending machines when specific hard goals were assigned than when no goals were assigned. However, assignment of easy goals did not result in better performance than no goals.

In a factor analysis of data obtained from 292 independent pulpwood producers, Ronan, Latham, and Kinne (50) found that the effects of goal setting depended on the extent to which logging crews were closely supervised. Goal setting was correlated with high performance only when it was accompanied by close supervision. Goal setting without supervision correlated with labor turnover but not with performance. Supervision that did not include goal setting was not correlated with any performance criterion. In a follow-up study by the same authors, an analysis of variance was performed on the man-day production of 892 producers. These producers were classified on the basis of the three factor patterns cited above: (a) producers who supervise their men and set production goals; (b) "absentee" producers who set production goals only; and (c) producers who supervise their men but do not set production goals. The results indicated that producers who supervise their employees and set production goals have higher productivity than do producers who supervise their men but do not set production goals. The difference between "absentee producers" who set production goals only, and producers who set production goals and supervise their men was in the expected direction. In summarizing the results of these two studies, Ronan, Latham, and Kinne (50) interpreted their findings as supporting the conclusion that setting a specific task goal does not affect performance in an industrial setting unless a supervisor is present to encourage goal acceptance.

A limitation of the studies on pulpwood producers is that they were correlational in nature, and inferences about causality could not be made with confidence. In order to overcome this limitation, Latham and Kinne (30) matched and randomly assigned 20 pulpwood producers and their crews to either a one day training program in goal setting or to a control condition. Data on cords per man-hour production, turnover, absenteeism, and injuries then were collected for 12 consecutive weeks. Analyses of variance revealed that those individuals who received training in goal setting had a significant increase in production and a decrease in absenteeism compared to workers in the control condition. No significant trend effects over time were found. There were no significant differences between conditions with respect to injuries or turnover, which were very low in both conditions.

Latham and Baldes (29) conducted a quasi-experimental study of a goal setting program with unionized truck drivers. The goal setting program was designed to increase the net weight of truckloads of logs, which previously had been considerably below the legal limit. A specific hard goal of 94 percent of the legal maximum was assigned to the drivers, which resulted in an immediate increase in average net weight from approximately

60 percent of the legal maximum to approximately 94 percent. Performance remained relatively stable at this improved level over the nine month study period, resulting in a cost savings of over a quarter of a million dollars for the company. Although the performance improvement was attributed primarily to goal specificity, anecdotal information suggested that goal setting also led to informal competition among drivers, and this competition probably helped to maintain goal commitment over the nine month period.

Latham and Yukl (32) conducted an experiment in which two methods of goal setting were compared to a control condition in which no specific goals were set. Goal setting resulted in higher performance of logging crews in only one of the four goal setting conditions. Some problems in the implementation of the goal setting program, such as a lack of support by local management, were cited as the likely reason for the failure of goal setting in the other three conditions. This study is discussed in more detail in the section "Assigned Versus Participative Goal Setting."

Mendleson (42) conducted a questionnaire survey of goal setting in eight companies and analyzed the responses of 25 pairs of superior-subordinate managers. The extent of goal setting, as perceived by both the superior and the subordinate was positively correlated with superior ratings of subordinate promotability, but not with superior ratings of subordinate performance. Due to the lack of consistency in these results, and the low reliability of the goal setting measure developed by Mendleson for use in this study, it is difficult to draw firm conclusions.

In a study differing in several respects from those preceding, Kolb and Bayatzis (26) examined the effect of goal setting on behavior change and attainment of personal development goals, rather than on performance and task goal attainment. In a management course requiring extensive T-group participation, each student established a personal development goal relevant to his behavior in groups and formulated a method for measuring goal attainment. At the end of each T-group session, the students filled out a form recording relevant feedback received from other group members during the session. Behavior change after the 30 hours of T-group sessions was reported by each student and was rated by the group trainers. Positive behavior change was greater for behavior dimensions related to the students' goals than for behavior dimensions not related to the goals.

Wexley and Nemeroff (58) evaluated the effects of goal setting and feedback when used in conjunction with role playing exercises in a two day supervisory training program. In two variations of the experimental treatment, hospital supervisors were assigned goals for behavior improvement, and they received coaching and feedback regarding their performance as leaders in the role playing exercises. The supervisors also were assigned specific behavioral goals after the first and third weeks back on the job, and additional feedback and coaching were provided. A control group of supervisors participated in the role playing, but were not assigned goals or given feedback either during or after the training. Wexley and Nemeroff found that supervisors in the experimental conditions had less subordinate absenteeism and more positive improvement in leadership behavior than did supervisors in the control group.

In summary, eleven studies in organizations have examined the effects of setting specific goals. In ten of these studies, evidence in support of the effectiveness of setting specific goals was obtained, although some possible limiting conditions also were discovered. Only one study (42) failed to find any support for the goal specificity proposition of Locke's theory, and the measure of goal setting in this study was of dubious validity.

EFFECTS OF SPECIFIC GOALS IN MBO PROGRAMS

Indirect evidence on the effectiveness of setting specific goals is provided by studies of MBO programs in organizations. Management by objectives is an approach to planning and performance appraisal that attempts to clarify employee role requirements, relate employee performance to organization goals, improve manager-subordinate communication, facilitate objective evaluation of employee performance, and stimulate employee motivation. An essential feature of the MBO approach is the setting of specific performance goals and, in many cases, goals for personal development of the employee. Employees are expected to be more committed to goals as a result of participation in setting them and involvement in the development or criteria for assessing goal attainment. Most of the published literature on MBO consists of anecdotal reports about employee reactions and the problems encountered in implementing an MBO program in a particular organization, or of discussions about the best procedures for implementing MBO (e.g., 3, 18, 19, 20, 25, 28, 46, 59). Only eight studies were found in which the effects of specific goals versus generalized goals or no goals were assessed with an acceptable degree of scientific rigor.

The first of these studies was conducted by Raia (48) in 15 plants of the Purex Corporation. The MBO program resulted in an increase in productivity over a 10-month period, even though the goals had to be revised downward several times during the fiscal year. Some improvements in absenteeism, accidents, grievances, turnover, and customer service also were noted in the plants that set goals for these criteria. The percentage of plants reporting an improvement for these criteria ranged from 33 percent for absenteeism to 80 percent for accident reduction.

Raia (49) obtained an additional 12 months of data from a follow-up study in the same company. These data indicated a stabilization of productivity at the higher level attained during the earlier period, and the attainment of budgetary goals continued to improve. The major weakness of

Raia's research is that, with neither a control group nor an immediate large improvement in the performance curve following implementation of the MBO program, it is impossible to determine if the improvement was due to MBO. The gradual improvements in performance could have been due to extraneous conditions unrelated to the MBO program.

French, Kay, and Meyer (17) conducted an experiment on goal setting within an MBO program at General Electric Company. The sample consisted of 92 low-level managers who either participated in goal setting with their boss or were assigned goals during an appraisal interview. Regardless of how the goals were set, when criticisms of the subordinate manager were translated into specific goals, both the subordinate and the boss reported that twice as much improvement in performance occurred than when criticisms were made without being formulated as specific goals. No objective criterion measures were obtained in this study, however.

Shetty and Carlisle (52) evaluated an MBO program in a public university by means of a questionnaire survey of faculty opinions. There was no indication that the MBO program resulted in any substantial improvement in performance or commitment to the university. However, it should be noted that the criterion measures were entirely subjective and of questionable validity, and no measure of the extent of goal setting was obtained.

Ivancevich, Donnelly, and Lyon (24) did a comparative study of two companies with an MBO program. Managers in both companies were asked to complete a Porter-type job satisfaction questionnaire before the MBO programs were initiated and again after the programs were in effect for a year. Need satisfaction improved in one company but not in the other. Interviews with the managers to obtain their reactions to the program revealed that MBO was used primarily at the top management level in the second company. The MBO program was never effectively implemented with lower level managers, due in part to a lack of top management involvement in setting up the program. Some problems also were found in the first company, despite the improvement in need deficiency scores. The most frequent complaints were an excess of paperwork and the difficulty of stating quantitative goals for all aspects of the job. These same problems have been noted in some of the case study and discussion articles on MBO; they also were found by Raia (49).

In what was essentially a follow-up study, Ivancevich (22) measured need satisfaction again in the two companies 18 to 20 months after the MBO program had been initiated. He found that any improvements in need satisfaction were short-lived and had disappeared by the time of his final measurement. This extinction phenomenon was attributed to a lack of sustained top management commitment to the program and the absence of any additional training or reinforcement after the program was initiated. Although this research by Ivancevich and his associates suggests some conditions which may prevent an MBO program from being implemented and maintained, the absence of a performance criterion makes it impossible to determine whether MBO ever really had an effect on the behavior and performance of the managers in these companies.

In a more recent study, Ivancevich (23) used objective measures of employee performance to evaluate an MBO program in a manufacturing company. The performance of production departments in three plants was compared. One plant had an MBO program for supervisors which included encouragement and support from top management in the form of letters, memos, telephone conversations, and meetings. The second plant had an MBO program that was not given encouragement and support by top management. The third plant did not have an MBO program and served as a control condition. Only the production department in the first plant had a sustained improvement in quantity and quality of performance over the course of the three year study. In addition, there was a significant decrease in absenteeism and grievances in this one plant.

Ivancevich also compared the performance of marketing departments in the three plants. Unlike the production workers, salesmen in the two plants with an MBO program were involved in the goal setting process along with their supervisors. The results indicated that sales performance improved in both MBO programs, but there was no improvement in the plant without an MBO program.

In the final MBO study, by Steers (55), questionnaire data on task-goal perceptions and need strength were obtained from 133 female first-line supervisors in a company with an ongoing MBO program. In addition, ratings of goal effort and performance for the supervisors were obtained from each supervisor's boss. Steers found that a supervisor's perception of goal specificity was significantly correlated with goal effort but not with the rating of overall performance. Steers also found that these relationships were moderated by the supervisor's need for achievement. Goal specificity was significantly correlated with goal effort and overall performance only for those supervisors with a high need for achievement.

In summary, the eight studies on MBO appear to provide a diverse set of findings. However, if we disregard the studies which had no measure of performance or goal attainment, the results are more consistent. French et al. (17), Ivancevich (23), Steers (55), and Raia (48, 49) all found some support for the proposition that setting specific goals can result in improved performance although some limiting conditions were present. The major problem with this MBO research as a means of evaluating goal setting is that MBO programs typically involve other changes besides the introduction of goal setting. Therefore, it is difficult to determine the extent to which performance improvements in these studies were due to goal setting rather than to other changes.

THE EFFECTS OF GOAL DIFFICULTY ON PERFORMANCE

Locke (36) proposed that, as long as goals are accepted, the more difficult the goals the higher the level of performance. This proposition is supported by results from a number of laboratory studies reported by Locke (36), including correlations between stated goals and subsequent performance and experiments with different levels of assigned goals. Seven field studies also have attempted to determine the effects of goal difficulty.

In the first study, by Stedry and Kay (54), goal difficulty was manipulated for two different performance criteria: productivity and rework cost. Performance goals were set either at the average level of performance attained during the previous six months (easy goal) or at a level substantially higher than average previous performance (difficult goal). The 19 foremen were assigned in a nonrandom manner to one of the following four experimental conditions: (a) easy productivity goal and difficult rework goal; (b) difficult productivity goal and easy rework goal; (c) both goals easy; (d) both goals difficult. In addition to the experimental manipulation, Stedry and Kay measured the extent to which the foremen actually perceived the assigned goals to be easy, challenging, or impossible, and these perceptions corresponded closely to actual difficulty. Performance improvement was defined as the difference between average performance during the 13 weeks after the manipulation and the 13 weeks before the manipulation. The data were analyzed first for each criterion separately. Performance improved more for the goals perceived to be easy or challenging than for the goals perceived to be impossible; and for the impossible goals, performance actually decreased. This finding is consistent with Locke's theory if it can be assumed that impossible goals are not accepted. Performance improvement was not significantly related to the difficulty of the productivity goal or the difficulty of the rework goal when analyzed separately. However, the theory may be tested more appropriately by an analysis of the combined difficulty of both goals since they are independent and a person must decide how to allocate his effort between them. Stedry and Kay conducted a regression analysis and found that total perceived difficulty for both goals was significantly related to a composite criterion of performance improvement ($R^2 = .59$), which is clearly in support of Locke's theory.

Zander and Newcomb (62) examined the effects of goals set in United Fund campaigns in 149 communities. They found a significant relationship between the difficulty of the goal, in terms of how far it was above the previous year's performance, and subsequent performance improvement. When the sample was subdivided according to the frequency of goal attainment success in the previous four years, prior success was found to be a moderator of the effects of goal difficulty. Goal difficulty was significantly correlated with subsequent performance improvement for communities with more prior successes than failures $(r = .76)$ and for communities with an equal number of successes and failures $(r = .73)$. However, for communities with more prior failures than successes in goal attainment, goal difficulty was not significantly correlated with performance improvement.

One explanation for these results is provided in a follow-up study by Zander, Forward, and Albert (63). They compared consistently successful and consistently unsuccessful United Funds and found that the successful Funds set higher absolute goals and attained a higher absolute level of performance. However, expressed as a percentage of the prior year's performance, the goals of successful Funds were more reasonable than were those of unsuccessful Funds. Furthermore, members of the successful Funds attributed more importance to attainment of the goal than did members of failing Funds. The unreasonableness of the goal and the lack of importance attributed to it by the members of consistently failing Funds suggest that there was little goal acceptance and commitment in these Funds. Therefore, it is not surprising that goal difficulty was unrelated to performance for the unsuccessful Funds.

Blumenfeld and Leidy (2) evaluated the effect of goal difficulty in an incentive program designed to motivate salesmen and servicemen to check and adjust soft drink vending machines to an optimal temperature. Employees who were assigned hard goals checked more vending machines than did employees who were assigned easy goals.

Steers (55) surveyed female first-line supervisors in a company with an MBO program and analyzed the relationship between perceived goal difficulty and performance ratings made by each supervisor's boss. No significant correlation was obtained, even when the sample was subdivided according to measures of supervisor needs.

In another survey of managers in an MBO program, Carroll and Tosi (6, 7) found that perceived goal difficulty was positively correlated with the self-rated effort of managers who were high in self-assurance $(r = .26)$ and maturity $(r = .31)$ and who perceived rewards to be contingent upon performance $(r = .26)$. For managers with low scores on self-assurance and maturity or who did not perceive a strong contingency between rewards and performance, goal difficulty was negatively correlated $(r = -.25, -.26, -.19)$ with self-rated effort. For the combined sample of managers, there was no significant correlation between goal difficulty and self-rated effort. Although Carroll and Tosi used a different criterion measure from that used by Steers (55), these results suggest that Steers also might have found significant correlations if he had used similar moderator variables.

Dachler and Mobley (14) examined the relationship between stated performance goals and objective performance of production workers in two organizations. Performance was measured in terms of piece rate earnings in the first organization and work rate as a percentage of standard in the second organization. A significant positive correlation ($r = .46$) between an employee's stated current goal and his performance was found in the first organization. This relationship was moderated by employee tenure. The correlation was significant ($r = .44$) for employees who had been on the job for more than two years but not for employees who had been on the job for less than two years ($r = .13$). This difference was consistent with the additional finding that long tenure employees perceived desirable outcomes to be contingent upon performance, whereas short tenure employees did not, presumably because of their limited experience in their current job situation.

The current performance goal stated by an employee also was significantly correlated with performance in the second organization. However, the correlation was very low ($r = .16$), and the relationship was not moderated by job tenure. The difference in magnitude of relationships between goal level and performance for the two organizations may have been due to differences in criterion measures, but more likely it is due to the lower perceived contingency of desirable outcomes on performance in the second organization, in which jobs were less structured and where there was no incentive system. This interpretation is consistent with the tenure results found in the first organization and with the findings of Carroll and Tosi (6, 7) summarized earlier.

In summary, seven studies have examined the relationship between goal difficulty and performance. With one exception (55), support was found in each study for Locke's (36) proposition that hard goals lead to greater performance than do easy goals, as long as the goals are accepted. The major limitation of this research is that, except for the study by Stedry and Kay (54), the effects of goal difficulty were assessed by means of a correlational design rather than by manipulation of goal difficulty. Some of the correlational studies attempted to deal with the problem of determining causality when there is likely to be an influence of prior performance on goals by measuring both difficulty and performance in relation to prior performance. Since the results from these studies, most other correlational studies, the experiment by Stedry and Kay (54), and a large number of laboratory experiments are generally consistent, it can be concluded that there is strong support for Locke's goal difficulty proposition.

Because goal acceptance is a necessary condition of this proposition, it is important to identify the factors that determine whether employees will accept hard goals. Some of the studies reviewed in this section provide insights into the nature of these determinants. The variables found to moderate the effects of goal difficulty probably also influence goal acceptance. These variables include the employee's perception that the goal is reasonable, and the perceived contingency between goal attainment and desirable outcomes. Hard goals are more likely to be perceived as challenging rather than impossible if the employee has a high degree of self-assurance and has previously had more successes in goal attainment than failures. The perceived instrumentality of goal attainment depends largely upon the type of incentive systems and the objectivity of performance appraisal in the organization.

GOALS AS MEDIATORS OF PERFORMANCE FEEDBACK, MONETARY INCENTIVES, AND TIME LIMITS

Locke's (36) theory proposes that the effects of performance feedback, monetary incentives, and time limits are mediated by goal setting and conscious intentions. Performance feedback or "knowledge of results" can lead to an increase in effort and performance for at least four different reasons: (a) feedback may induce a person who previously did not have specific goals to set a goal to improve performance by a certain amount; (b) feedback may induce a person to raise his goal level after attaining a previous goal; (c) feedback that informs a person that his current level of effort is insufficient to attain his goal may result in greater effort; and (d) feedback may inform a person of ways in which to improve his methods of performing the task. Locke's theory is concerned primarily with the first three "motivational" aspects of feedback and not with the final "cueing" aspect. Locke also proposed that the form or quality of feedback partly determines what effect the feedback will have. These feedback propositions are supported by a substantial number of laboratory studies that are reviewed in the article by Locke, Cartledge, and Koeppel (38). Some recent laboratory studies have provided additional support and insight (e.g., 13, 37, 60).

Field studies in which goal setting and performance feedback are independently manipulated, or feedback is manipulated and the effects of goals are controlled, would provide evidence as to the validity of Locke's feedback propositions in real organizations. Unfortunately, no studies of this type were found. In fact, only a few field studies have investigated the effects of performance feedback on subsequent performance. Since use of feedback alone may be viewed by some persons as an alternative approach to goal setting, it is worthwhile to briefly review studies on the effects of feedback in comparison to no feedback. In addition, since the amount and frequency of feedback necessary for an effective goal setting program have not been established, it also is useful to examine studies on the effects of feedback in combination with goal setting.

Three studies investigated the effects of feedback on performance in the absence of explicit goal setting. Hundal (21) found that feedback resulted in increased productivity of industrial workers with a repetitive task;

productivity also was higher than was that of a no-feedback control group. However, Chapanis (11) failed to find any effect of feedback on the performance of students hired to work an hour per day for 24 days on a repetitive job. Miller (44) found that feedback regarding errors resulted in only a temporary improvement in performance quality for manufacturing employees, unless used in conjunction with incentives or the threat of negative consequences for failure to improve. The improvement that occurred with feedback plus incentives may well have been due to employees setting goals to reduce errors. However, since the subjects in these studies were not asked if they set private goals, no firm conclusions can be drawn in relation to Locke's theory. With so few studies and the inconsistent results, it also would be premature to reach any conclusions about the effectiveness of feedback as a motivational technique when used without explicit goal setting. Of course, the importance of feedback for learning, as opposed to motivation, has been well established in the literature on training research.

A study on the effects of feedback in conjunction with goal setting was conducted by Kolb, Winters, and Berlew (27). Explicit goals for behavior change were set by students in a management course with extensive T-group participation. In T-groups instructed to provide relevant feedback, more positive change (self-rated and trainer-rated) occurred than in T-groups instructed not to discuss the behavior change projects of their members. The results also supported the importance of feedback quality (e.g., timing, relevance, and manner of presentation) for goal attainment. In a study of managers in a company with an MBO program, Carroll and Tosi (8) found that the amount and frequency of perceived feedback were positively correlated with self-rated goal attainment, but not with an increase in self-rated effort level. Duttagupta (16) found that frequency and amount of feedback were associated with greater self-reported motivation and a better perceived understanding of job requirements by the R&D managers in a company with an MBO program. Finally, Steers (55) found that the amount of perceived feedback in a company with an MBO program was positively correlated with goal effort and overall performance ratings for supervisors with high achievement motivation, but not for supervisors with low achievement motivation. Although these results tend to support the conclusion that frequent, relevant feedback is needed for a successful goal setting program, the evidence is limited, and further research clearly is warranted.

In contrast to performance feedback, monetary incentives are more likely to increase goal acceptance and commitment than to induce a person to set a harder goal. "Offering an individual money for output may motivate him to set his goals higher than he would otherwise, but this will depend on how much money he wishes to make and how much effort he wishes to expend to make it" (36, p. 185). Locke's propositions about goals as mediators of monetary incentives are based on a series of five laboratory studies in which he found that, when goal level was controlled or partialled out, incentives did not affect performance. Also, a particular goal level resulted in the same performance, regardless of whether monetary incentives were provided. A similar type of field study would provide evidence regarding the generalizability of these findings to real organizations. Unfortunately, no studies of this type have been conducted in an organizational setting. However, a recent laboratory study by Prichard and Curtis (47) appears to be relevant to evaluating Locke's proposition. Prichard and Curtis point out that Locke used small incentives with little potential for motivating his subjects. In a study designed to overcome this potential limitation, the effects of assigned goals were compared for three levels of incentive (large, small, and no incentive). Prichard and Curtis found, as did Locke, that small incentives did not increase performance in comparison to no incentive when goal level was held constant. However, contrary to Locke, large incentives resulted in higher performance than did small or no incentives when goal level was held constant. Moreover, the self-reported commitment of subjects to the goal was not greater in the larger incentive condition than in the small and no-incentive conditions. In other words, Prichard and Curtis found that incentives can affect performance independently of goal level and goal commitment.

Latham and Locke (31) conducted a study which provided evidence in support of Locke's theory that time limits affect performance only to the degree that they lead to goal setting. The authors found that when pulp and paper mills limited their buying of wood to one or two days per week, they implicitly urged a higher production goal (per man-hour) on independent harvesting crews. To minimize income loss, the crews tried to harvest as much wood in one or two days as they normally harvested in five days. Thus logging crews with limitations on the number of days they could sell timber had higher productivity than crews without such restrictions. These findings are in basic agreement with the results of the early British studies (51) which found that a reduction in the work week led to a higher hourly rate of production.

In summary, there is little relevant data for evaluating Locke's proposition that goals mediate the effects of performance feedback. The few field studies on the effects of feedback alone or in combination with goal setting are not directly relevant for testing the mediation hypothesis. The three studies on the consequences of feedback without explicit goal setting do not yield consistent results. The four studies on feedback in combination with goal setting tend to support the importance of frequent, relevant feedback for goal setting effectiveness. No field studies have been conducted to provide a direct test of Locke's mediation proposition concerning monetary incentives, but one laboratory study provides evidence contrary to the proposition and raises doubts about the external validity of the earlier supporting results found by Locke and associates. One field study provides indirect support for the hypothesis that goals mediate the effects of time limits on performance.

ASSIGNED VERSUS PARTICIPATIVE GOAL SETTING

Locke's (36) theory specifies that goals mediate the effects of employee participation in decision making. The theory is not directly concerned with the manner in which goals are set. However, the most appropriate manner of setting goals is an important practical question. The consequences of subordinate participation in decision making have been the subject of considerable speculation in the leadership and management literature. According to the classical management theories (40), it is the leader's responsibility to assign goals and ensure that they are attained. Humanistic organization theories (35, 41) favor substantial subordinate participation in decision making, and such participation is believed to increase acceptance of the decision and commitment to implement it. More recently, various contingency theories (39, 45, 56, 57, 61) have proposed that participation is effective in some situations but not in others. Leadership research on the effects of employee participation in decision making tends to support the contingency approach.

Several studies have attempted to assess the effects of different amounts of subordinate participation in goal setting. In the first of these studies, French, Kay, and Meyer (17) compared assigned and participative goal setting during performance appraisal interviews with lower-level managers. In addition to the experimental manipulation of participation, the perceived participation of the managers and observer judgments of the amount of participation during the appraisal interview also were measured, as well as the managers' perception of the usual amount of participation they previously had been allowed. Perception of the usual amount of participation, which was measured prior to the appraisal interview, was positively related to acceptance of job goals. However, goal acceptance and goal attainment were not significantly related to the other participation measures and were not affected by the experimental manipulation. A number of limitations of this study make it difficult to reach any clear conclusions. The participation manipulation was not always successful, the participation treatment was somewhat confounded with the usual level of participation that occurred between the supervisor and his subordinates, and no objective performance measures were obtained. Despite these problems and the scarcity of significant differences, the authors reach the following conclusions in another report of this research (43): (a) subordinates who received a high participation level in the performance interview in most cases achieved a greater percentage of their improvement goals; (b) men who usually worked under high participation levels performed best on goals they set for themselves, and men who usually worked under low participation levels performed best on goals that their boss set for them.

Carroll and Tosi (6, 7) included a measure of perceived influence in establishing goals in their questionnaire survey of managers in an MBO program. The results indicate that participation in goal setting was not significantly correlated with the amount of goal attainment or effort increase. However, there was some indication that a manager's self-assurance moderated the effects of participation. Participation in goal setting tended to be positively correlated ($r = .33$) with effort increase for managers with high self-assurance but not for managers with low self-assurance ($r = .08$).

In a study by Duttagupta (16) R&D managers in an MBO program were interviewed and answered a short questionnaire. No relationship was found between self-reported motivation and perceived influence in the goal setting process.

In a questionnaire survey of first-line supervisors, Steers (55) found that perceived participation was significantly correlated with goal effort and overall performance ratings for supervisors with low need for achievement ($r = .41$), but was not significantly correlated for supervisors with a high need for achievement. For the overall sample, there was only a low correlation ($r = .20$). The major limitation of this study and the study by Carroll and Tosi is the subjective nature of the participation in goal setting measures. The leadership literature suggests that subordinate judgments about their influence in decision making are of questionable accuracy. Furthermore, since the conclusions reached in these studies are based on a large number of correlations and correlational comparisons, there also is a strong possibility that some significant findings occurred by chance. Therefore, the results should be regarded as tentative until they are replicated.

Latham and Yukl (32) conducted a field experiment on the effects of assigned and participative goal setting. Specifically, they attempted to determine which method of goal setting was most effective for independent logging crews with different levels of education. Twenty-four "educated" crews were randomly assigned to a participative goal setting condition, an assigned goal setting condition, or a "do your best" condition. Twenty-four educationally disadvantaged crews in another geographical location were randomly assigned to the same three conditions. In the sample of educationally disadvantaged crews, the participative goal setting condition yielded higher performance and more frequent goal attainment during the eight week period of the study than did the assigned goal setting condition. The average goal level was significantly higher for the participative condition than for the assigned goal condition, which suggests that the performance difference was due in part to greater goal difficulty in the participative condition. The fact that goal attainment was higher in the participative condition than in the assigned condition, despite more difficult goals, suggests that goal acceptance was increased by participation in the goal setting process.

In the sample of educated crews, performance, goal attainment, and average goal level were not significantly different for the participative and assigned conditions. Due to the unavoidable confounding of education level with geographical region and other factors in this study, it is not clear whether the failure to find a significant difference in the educated sample was due to education level or to other factors. Anecdotal evidence suggested that the goal setting program was not effectively implemented for this sample due to the lack of support by local management.

In summary, five studies in organizations provide data on the effects of participation in goal setting, but each of these studies has major limitations or problems. None of the studies provides an adequate test of Locke's mediation proposition regarding the effects of participation. With respect to the more applied question of whether participative goal setting results in higher performance than assigned goals, the results are not consistent. Although most of the studies found some evidence supporting the superiority of participative goal setting, a significant difference is found only under certain conditions or with certain types of employees. The most satisfactory way of explaining these discrepancies probably is in terms of a contingency model, but further research is needed to clarify the nature of the limiting conditions and the manner in which the moderating variables operate.

DISCUSSION AND CONCLUSIONS

The organizational research reviewed in this article provides strong support for Locke's (36) propositions that specific goals increase performance and that difficult goals, if accepted, result in better performance than do easy goals. The field studies do not provide relevant evidence concerning Locke's propositions that goal setting mediates the effects of participation, monetary incentives, and performance feedback. With respect to monetary incentives, the results from a laboratory experiment by Prichard and Curtis (47) are contrary to the mediation proposition. Field research designed to test the mediation propositions and to investigate the possibility that participation, monetary incentives, and feedback affect performance independently of goal setting, or interact with goal setting, is clearly desirable.

Perhaps the greatest deficiency of Locke's theory is the failure to specify the determinants of goal acceptance and goal commitment. In recent research, investigators have used expectancy theory concepts to aid in explaining how goal acceptance is determined. In field studies by Dachler and Mobley (14) and Steers (55) and in a laboratory study by Cartledge (10), goal acceptance and performance appeared to be predictable from measures of a person's expectancy that effort will lead to goal attainment, his expectancy that goal attainment will lead to various outcomes, and the subjective values (valence) assigned to those outcomes. These studies and the accompanying efforts to develop a model integrating goal theory with expectancy theory appear to be the most promising direction for further elaboration of goal theory.

Another important gap in theory development and research is the manner in which goal acceptance, goal difficulty, and other aspects of goal setting combine to determine a person's task effort. This subject takes on added complexity as a history of successes or failures in goal attainment is accumulated. For example, if pressures exist to set excessively hard goals or to prevent a downward revision of goals that have proved to be unreasonable, a series of failures in goal attainment is likely, and this in turn will greatly reduce the likelihood of subsequent goal acceptance by subordinates. There clearly is a need for more longitudinal research on the complex interactions that determine if goal setting will be effective. An understanding of *why* goal setting affects employee performance has only begun.

Another promising approach for elaboration of Locke's theory is the inclusion of propositions concerning the cueing function of goals. The usefulness of goal setting for clarifying role requirements and the effects of goals on the employee's allocation of effort to different aspects of his job have been emphasized in the MBO literature. The effects of goals and feedback on learning as well as motivation, specifically the development of better job procedures by employees, also have been noted in some of the goal setting studies. As yet, these processes have not been incorporated into Locke's goal setting theory in any systematic fashion.

As for the practical feasibility of goal setting as a means of improving employee performance, the research shows goal setting programs to be effective over an extended time period in a variety of organizations, at both the managerial and nonmanagerial levels. Substantial increases in performance were obtained in some of the studies without any special prizes or incentives for goal attainment, although in other studies reward contingencies were an important consideration. Assigned goal setting and participative goal setting each was effective in several studies. In the few studies where the relative effectiveness of these two goal setting methods could be compared, the results were not conclusive. Further research on the consequences of subordinate participation in goal setting and on variables moderating these effects is highly desirable.

Although goal setting was found to be effective in many situations, some limiting conditions and moderating variables also were identified. One determinant of goal setting feasibility may be the complexity of the job and the availability of reasonably accurate performance measures. Goal setting for simple jobs with only one or two important performance dimensions may be much easier and more effective than goal setting for jobs with many performance dimensions, especially when some of these dimensions cannot be measured quantitatively. Since managerial jobs usually are of this complex nature, it is not surprising that goal setting programs with managers have encountered more problems and have been less successful than goal setting with nonmanagerial employees. One problem found by Levinson (34) is the tendency to neglect aspects of the job that are not easily quantified, such as customer service. The way in which multiple goals direct behavior and effort allocation is an important applied question that has received little attention except for the initial exploration of this subject by Charnes and Stedry (12) and Stedry and Kay (54). Additional research is needed to determine what goal setting procedures are most effective for very complex jobs, and to determine if there are some jobs for which goal setting may be impractical or even dysfunctional.

Another type of limiting condition found in several studies is the degree of managerial attention and support received by a goal setting program. In some of the studies in which goal setting was unsuccessful, the failure was attributed to a lack of strong support by key managerial personnel. The importance of management support and involvement in all types of organizational interventions has been emphasized in the organization development literature as well as the MBO literature.

The interrelationships among jobs in an organization are another possible limiting condition for effective goal setting. There first is the problem of evaluating individual performance and goal attainment by employees with highly interdependent jobs. As Levinson has pointed out, "The more a man's effectiveness depends upon what other people do, the less he himself can be held responsible for the outcome of his efforts" (34, p. 127). Group goals can be used instead of individual goals for some types of interdependent jobs, but this remedy would not be applicable to many types of jobs. An additional problem with setting specific goals for interdependent jobs was found by Baumler (1). He conducted a laboratory study of simulated organizations with either independent or interdependent jobs and compared the effects of defined criteria (i.e., specific goals) and no defined criteria in both types of organizations. Specific goals facilitated performance when jobs were independent but inhibited performance when jobs were interdependent. The inhibiting effects in the latter case were attributed to coordination difficulties and a preoccupation with individual goals at the expense of overall organizational effectiveness. The possibility that individual goal setting can be dysfunctional for interdependent jobs is important enough to warrant further investigation in actual as opposed to simulated organizations.

Even when goal setting is feasible for a job, it may not be effective for all types of employees who hold that job. Individual traits were found to be moderators of goal setting effectiveness in several studies. Needs, attitudes, personality, and perhaps education and cultural background may determine whether an employee will respond favorably to goal setting, and such traits also may moderate the effects of goal difficulty and participation in goal setting. However, the research to date on this subject should be regarded as exploratory rather than definitive, and additional studies on employee traits as moderators of goal setting effectiveness are clearly needed.

In conclusion, the laboratory and field research on goal setting has provided impressive support for portions of Locke's theory and has demonstrated the practical feasibility of goal setting programs as a means of improving employee performance. Nevertheless, much still remains to be learned, and several lines of research are essential for further validation and elaboration of the theory. Such research is likely to result eventually in the formulation of a contingency model of goal setting effectiveness.

REFERENCES

1. Baumler, J. V. "Defined Criteria of Performance in Organizational Control." *Administrative Science Quarterly,* vol. 16 (1971), 340–350.

2. Blumenfeld, W. E., and T. E. Leidy. "Effectiveness of Goal Setting as a Management Device: Research Note," *Psychological Reports,* vol. 24 (1969), 24.

3. Brady, R. H. "MBO Goes to Work in the Public Sector," *Harvard Business Review,* vol. 51 (1973), 65–74.

4. Burke, R. J., and D. S. Wilcox. "Characteristics of Effective Employee Performance Reviews and Developmental Interviews," *Personnel Psychology,* vol. 22 (1969), 291–305.

5. Campbell, J. P., M. D. Dunnette, E. E. Lawler, and K. E. Weick, Jr. *Managerial Behavior, Performance and Effectiveness* (New York: McGraw-Hill, 1970).

6. Carroll, S. J., and H. L. Tosi. "Relationship of Goal Setting Characteristics as Moderated by Personality and Situational Factors to the Success of the Management by Objectives Approach," *Proceedings of the 77th Annual Convention,* American Psychological Association, 1969.

7. Carroll, S. J., and H. L. Tosi. "Goal Characteristics and Personality Factors in a Management by Objectives Program," *Administrative Science Quarterly,* vol. 15 (1970), 295–305.

8. Carroll, S. J., and H. L. Tosi. "Relationship of Characteristics of the Review Process to the Success of the MBO Approach," *Journal of Business,* vol. 44 (1971), 299–305.

9. Carroll, S. J., and H. L. Tosi. *Management by Objectives: Applications and Research* (New York: Macmillan, 1973).

10. Cartledge, N. D. *An Experimental Study of the Relationship between Expectancies, Goal Utility, Goals, and Task Performance* (Ph.D. dissertation, University of Maryland, 1973).

11. Chapanis, A. "Knowledge of Performance as an Incentive in Repetitive, Monotonous Tasks," *Journal of Applied Psychology,* vol. 48 (1964), 263–267.

12. Charnes, A., and A. C. Stedry. "Exploratory Models in the Theory of Budgetary Control," in W. W. Cooper, H. J. Leavitt, and M. W. Shelly (eds.), *New Perspectives in Organizational Research* (New York: Wiley, 1964).

13. Cummings, L. L., D. P. Schwab, and M. Rosen. "Performance and Knowledge of Results as Predeterminants of Goal Setting," *Journal of Applied Psychology,* vol. 55 (1971), 526–530.

14. Dachler, H. P., and W. H. Mobley. "Construct Validation of an Instrumentality-Expectancy-Task-Goal Model of Work Motivation," *Journal of Applied Psychology,* vol. 58 (1973), 397–418.

15. Dobmeyer, T. W. "A Critique of Edwin Locke's Theory of Task Motivation and Incentives," in H. L. Tosi, R. J. House, and M. D. Dunnette (eds.), *Managerial Motivation and Compensation* (East Lansing, Mich.: MSU Business Studies, 1971), pp. 244–259.

16. Duttagupta, D. *An Empirical Evaluation of Management by Objectives* (Master's thesis, Baruch College, 1975).

17. French, J. R. P., E. Kay, and H. H. Meyer. "Participation and the Appraisal System," *Human Relations,* vol. 19 (1966), 3–19.

18. Gell, T., and C. F. Molander. "Beyond Management by Objectives," *Personnel Management,* vol. 2 (1970), 18–20.

19. Howell, R. A. "A Fresh Look at Management by Objectives," *Business Horizons,* vol. 10 (1967), 51–58.

20. Howell, R. A. "Managing by Objectives—A Three Stage System," *Business Horizons,* vol. 13 (1970), 41–45.

21. Hundal, P. S. "Knowledge of Performance as an Incentive in Repetitive Industrial Work," *Journal of Applied Psychology,* vol. 53 (1969), 244–226.

22. Ivancevich, J. M. "A Longitudinal Assessment of Management by Objectives," *Administrative Science Quarterly,* vol. 17 (1972), 126–138.

23. Ivancevich, J. M. "Changes in Performance in a Management by Objectives Program," *Administrative Science Quarterly,* vol. 19 (1974), 563–574.

24. Ivancevich, J. M., J. H. Donnelly, and H. L. Lyon. "A Study of the Impact of Management by Objectives on Perceived Need Satisfaction," *Personnel Psychology,* vol. 23 (1970), 139–151.

25. Kirchoff, B. A. "Using Objectives: The Critical Variable in Effective MBO," *Michigan Business Review,* vol. 26 (1974), 17–21.

26. Kolb, D. A., and R. E. Boyatzis. "Goal Setting and Self-Directed Behavior Change," in D. A. Kolb, I. M. Rubin, and J. M. McIntyre (eds.), *Organizational Psychology: A Book of Readings* (Englewood Cliffs, N.J.: Prentice-Hall, 1971), pp. 317–337.

27. Kolb, D. A., S. Winters, and D. Berlew. "Self-Directed Change: Two Studies," *Journal of Applied Behavioral Science,* vol. 4 (1968), 453–473.

28. Lasagna, J. B. "Make Your MBO Pragmatic," *Harvard Business Review,* vol. 49 (1971), 64–69.

29. Latham, G. P., and J. J. Baldes. "The Practical Significance of Locke's Theory of Goal Setting," *Journal of Applied Psychology,* vol. 60 (1975), 122–124.

30. Latham, G. P., and S. B. Kinne, III. "Improving Job Performance through Training in Goal Setting," *Journal of Applied Psychology,* vol. 59 (1974), 187–191.

31. Latham, G. P., and E. A. Locke. "Increasing Productivity with Decreasing Time Limits: A Field Replication of Parkinson's Law," *Journal of Appplied Psychology,* vol. 60 (1975), 524–526.

32. Latham, G. P., and G. A. Yukl. "Assigned versus Participative Goal Setting with Educated and Uneducated Woods Workers," *Journal of Applied Psychology,* vol. 60 (1975), 299–302.

33. Lawrence, L. C., and P. C. Smith. "Group Decision and Employee Participation," *Journal of Applied Psychology,* vol. 39 (1955), 334–337.

34. Levinson, H. "Management by Whose Objectives?" *Harvard Business Review,* vol. 48, No. 4 (1970), 125–134.

35. Lickert, R. *The Human Organization* (New York: McGraw-Hill, 1967).

36. Locke, E. A. "Toward a Theory of Task Motivation and Incentives," *Organizational Beravior and Human Performance,* vol. 3 (1968), 157–189.

37. Locke, E. A., N. Cartledge, and C. S. Knerr. "Studies of the Relationship between Satisfaction, Goal Setting and Performance," *Organizational Behavior and Human Performance,* vol. 5 (1970), 135–158.

38. Locke, E. A., N. Cartledge, and J. Koeppel. "Motivational Effects of Knowledge of Results: A Goal Setting Phenomenon," *Psychological Bulletin,* vol. 70 (1968), 474–485.

39. Lowin, A. "Participative Decision-Making: A Model, Literature Critique and Prescription for Research," *Organizational Behavior and Human Performance,* vol. 3 (1968), 68–106.

40. Massie, J. L. "Management Theory," in J. G. March (ed.), *Handbook of Organizations* (Chicago: Rand McNally, 1965), pp. 387–422.

41. McGregor, D. *The Human Side of Enterprise* (New York: McGraw-Hill, 1960).

42. Mendleson, J. L. *Managerial Goal Setting: An Exploration into Meaning and Measurement* (Ph.D. dissertation, Michigan State University, 1967).

43. Meyer, H. H., E. Kay, and J. R. P. French. "Split Roles in Performance Appraisal," *Harvard Business Review,* vol. 43 (1965), 123–129.

44. Miller, L. *The Use of Knowledge of Results in Improving the Performance of Hourly Operators* (Crotonville, N.Y.: General Electric Company, Behavioral Research Service, 1965).

45. Morse, J. H., and J. W. Lorsch. "Beyond Theory Y," *Harvard Business Review,* vol. 48 (1970), 61–68.

46. Murray, R. K. "Behavioral Management Objectives," *Personnel Journal,* vol. 52 (1973), 304–306.

47. Prichard, R. D., and M. I. Curtis. "The Influence of Goal Setting and Financial Incentives on Task Performance," *Organizational Behavior and Human Performance,* vol. 10 (1973), 175–183.

48. Raia, A. P. "Goal Setting and Self-Control: An Empirical Study," *Journal of Management Studies,* vol. 2 (1965), 32–53.

49. Raia, A. P. "A Second Look at Management by Goals and Controls," *California Management Review,* vol. 8 (1966), 49–58.

50. Ronan, W. W., G. P. Latham, and S. B. Kinne. "Effects of Goal Setting and Supervision on Worker Behavior in an Industrial Situation," *Journal of Applied Psychology,* vol. 58 (1973), 302–307.

51. Ryan, T. A. *Work and Effort* (New York: Ronald, 1947).

52. Shetty, Y. K., and H. M. Carlisle. "Organizational Correlates of a Management by Objectives Program," *Academy of Management Journal,* vol. 17 (1974), 155–159.

53. Sorcher, M. *Motivating the Hourly Employee* (Crotonville, N.Y.: General Electric Company, Behavioral Research Service, 1967).

54. Stedry, A. C., and E. Kay. "The Effects of Goal Difficulty on Performance," *Behavioral Science,* vol. 11 (1966), 459–470.

55. Steers, R. M. "Task-Goal Attributes, n Achievement, and Supervisory Performance," *Organizational Behavior and Human Performance,* vol. 13 (1975), 392–403.

56. Tannenbaum, R., and W. Schmidt. "How to Choose a Leadership Pattern," *Harvard Business Review,* vol. 36 (1958), 95–101.

57. Vroom, V. H., and P. Yetton. *Leadership and Decision-Making* (Pittsburgh, Pa.: University of Pittsburgh Press, 1973).

58. Wexley, K. N., and W. F. Nemeroff. "Effects of Positive Reinforcement and Goal Setting as Methods of Management Development," *Journal of Applied Psychology,* vol. 60 (1975), 446–450.

59. Wickens, J. D. "Management by Objectives: An Appraisal," *Journal of Management Studies,* vol. 5 (1968), 365–379.

60. Wilsted, W. D., and H. H. Hand. "Determinants of Aspiration Levels in a Simulated Goal Setting Environment of the Firm," *Academy of Management Journal,* vol. 6 (1971), 414–440.

61. Yukl, G. A. "Toward a Behaioral Theory of Leadership," *Organizational Behavior and Human Performance,* vol. 6 (1971), 414–440.

62. Zander, A., and T. T. Newcomb, Jr. "Group Levels of Aspiration in United Fund Campaigns," *Journal of Personality and Social Psychology,* vol. 6 (1967), 157–162.

63. Zander, A., J. Forward, and R. Albert. "Adaptation of Board Members to Repeated Failure or Success by the Organization," *Organizational Behavior and Human Performance,* vol. 4 (1969), 56–76.

Behavior, Structure, and Processes in Two Organizations*

JAMES L. GIBSON, JOHN M. IVANCEVICH,
and JAMES H. DONNELLY, JR.

I T is the purpose of this final article to show that managers have and will undoubtedly continue to utilize many of the concepts discussed throughout this book. Throughout this article we will see that the behavioral sciences are interwoven into the actions of those who manage organizations.

Two organizations, a public utility and a state health agency, have provided us with the necessary materials to examine aspects of the task of managing organizations. They were selected because they provided us with sufficient information and material to make some comparisons. Each of these organizations has undergone extensive organizational development. It is within the context of this similar experience that the comparisons will be made. We will describe the OD programs in each organization and note the changes in behavior, structure, and processes which occurred as a result.

DELTA UTILITY

The Delta Utility is a medium-sized public utility with approximately 2,000 employees. Most of the operating employees (that is, 1,700), lower-level managers, and middle managers are natives of the state; the top-level team of 13 executives comes from outside the state. The managerial cadre and operating group are summarized in Figure 1. According to data collected and analyzed by the company there was evidence that growth and diversification in the industry would necessitate a fresh look at struc-

---

* This material appeared originally as Chapter 17 in James L. Gibson, John M. Ivancevich, and James H. Donnelly, Jr., *Organizations: Behavior, Structure, Processes*, rev. ed. (Dallas: Business Publications, 1976). © 1976 by Business Publications, Inc.

Figure 1
Delta Utility

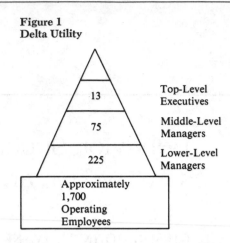

ture, manpower, and development programs. Specifically, customer demands and the total number of customers had increased significantly and were expected to increase at an accelerated rate over the next decade.

The Delta Utility OD Program

A top management committee consisting of the president and four vice presidents met on numerous occasions to discuss the future mannpower plans for Delta. A major conclusion of these sessions was that a systematic program of organizational development was needed. The OD effort was needed according to the committee because of:

1. Rising costs.
2. A turnover of promising management personnel.
3. A need to improve overall organizational effectiveness.
4. A need to improve employee morale.

The committee reached these conclusions after careful deliberation and analysis of records. They did not perform a formal diagnosis of the problem areas but they did examine turnover, cost, and production records. This examination revealed a need to prepare managers for increased demands from customers and closer government observation of Delta's service to the public.

In reviewing the committee's activities we can see that they engaged to some degree in recognizing a need for change and diagnosing problems. The committee after engaging in these activities decided to secure help from an external source.

The external source was a group of organizational development specialists (ODs). The ODs were placed in a position of initiating and monitoring the organizational development program at Delta. The ODs began a formal diagnosis which involved the following steps:

1. Examination of all performance records for the past five years. This was done so that trends could be traced and pinpointed.
2. Interviews with all top- and middle-level and 25 lower-level managers. These interviews enabled the ODs to acquire insight about the overall climate of Delta and improve their understanding of what managers believed was the course for future action.
3. A number of questionnaires administered to the entire management group. The questionnaires were designed to tap the managers' perceptions and attitudes about structure, processes, and behavior.

The formal diagnostic phase provided the ODs with information so that a systematic organizational development program could be implemented. Before any program was initiated the current state of the company had to be plotted and considered. The data revealed that Delta was primarily a rigidly structured and Theory X oriented organization. Each department was primarily concerned with its own set of objectives. The total organization's goals were viewed as some mystery that did not have to be solved at the present time.

The diagnostic phase further indicated that a lack of trust and poor communication existed between the headquarters division and three geographically dispersed units that reported formally to headquarters. An abbreviated version of the top levels of Delta management is presented in Figure 2. Each of the three district managers used the various staff departments for advice and counsel. Officially, the district general managers possessed a high degree of decision-making power. The data, however, indicated that the general managers and their subordinates perceived a low amount of autonomy in reaching decisions and a general climate which discouraged participating in the important decision-making processes of Delta.

Analysis of the historical records, the interview statements, and questionnaire responses led the ODs to conclude that a major organizational development program was needed for Delta if improved organizational effectiveness was to be achieved. A number of alternative development methods were considered such as group discussion methods for identifying problems, leadership training in motivation and group dynamics, and the use of programmed instruction in management and organizational behavior principles. Each of these techniques was eliminated for reasons of incompleteness. That is, they were not designed to accomplish the complete set of minimum development objectives established by Delta top management.

The ODs decided that a management by objectives (MBO) program should be initiated at Delta. It was concluded that a major reeducation of

Figure 2
Abbreviated View of Delta Utility

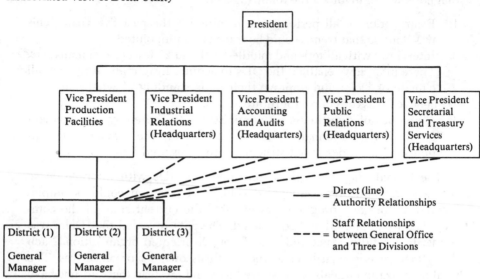

management was necessary if the company was to accomplish the objectives. In summary, the ODs believed that changes in attitudes and a general modification of the behavior of managers were needed.

The ODs recommended the following course of action:

1. Starting at the top of Delta and proceeding to the lowest managerial levels, the ODs would conduct training in the philosophy and practice of MBO.
2. After training there would be a one-year trial period, which would include the implementation of MBO and an evaluation of its impact.
3. After the trial year there would be a feedback session with top management which would examine any improvements in organizational effectiveness.
4. The ODs and top management would then chart the future course of MBO at Delta.

In effect, the ODs recommended that a before-after research design be used to monitor MBO. The Delta research design is presented in Figure 3. The data collected at observation period one would be compared to the data collected at observation period two.

The top management committee agreed to all of the ODs recommendations except the first one. It was their contention that the top managers had sufficient knowledge of MBO and it would be redundant to have them undergo training. The ODs stressed the importance of top management

Figure 3
Delta Research Design for First Year of MBO Program

Observation and measurement Time 1		The experimental treatment		Observation and measurement Time 2
Historical records, questionnaires, and interviews	$\longrightarrow$	Training in philosophy and practice of MBO	$\longrightarrow$	Historical records, questionnaires, and interviews

setting the entire tone for the MBO effort. The importance of taking an active role in what other managers would be engaged in was emphasized many times. Finally, after much debate, the top management committee and the ODs agreed to conduct MBO training for all middle-level managers and to have these managers serve as trainers for the lower-level managers. Thus the stage was set for the training, implementation, and evaluation of MBO at Delta Utility.

The Delta Utility Behavior

Motivation. An often stated assumption is that MBO programs motivate individual participants positively. That is, employees are generally more satisfied with various job aspects and are motivated to strive for higher levels of achievement.

A number of questions concerning the satisfaction of employees were asked in attitude surveys before and after the MBO program was implemented. The responses of managers were classified on the basis of level within the hierarchy. A summary of the general satisfaction of top-, middle-, and lower-level managers is presented in Table 1. There was little improvement, if any, one year after the MBO program was implemented.

Theoretically, the program should have generated positive results for the trained middle managers. This was definitely not the case. Personal interviews conducted by the ODs clearly showed high levels of displeasure among the MBO trainees about the lack of top management commitment to the change program. The top-level executives were criticized because of their failure to undergo MBO training. This had created a generally poor attitude among trainees about the value of the entire program.

In addition to this perceived lack of commitment the trainees also saw little relationship between goal achievement and rewards. For example, managers in the three districts reported on numerous occasions that improved performance was not associated with more autonomy or better salary increments. That is, the first-level outcome, performance, was not instrumental in generating an improved salary evaluation and adjustment.

Table 1
Selected Job Characteristics and Degree of Satisfaction

Level of Management and Job Characteristic	Degree of Satisfaction	
	Before MBO	After MBO*
Top		
A. Autonomy	Moderate†	Moderate
B. Social interaction	Moderate	Moderate
C. Personal growth	Moderate	Moderate
D. Overall satisfaction	High	Moderate
Middle		
A. Autonomy	Low	Low
B. Social interaction	Moderate	Moderate
C. Personal growth	Low	Low
D. Overall satisfaction	Low	Low
Lower		
A. Autonomy	Low	Low
B. Social interaction	Low	Moderate
C. Personal growth	Low	Low
D. Overall satisfaction	Moderate	Moderate

* The after-MBO measures were taken one year after the formal classroom training of the middle-level managers.

† The low, moderate, and high terms are based upon various scales, "1 to 7" and "1 to 10."

Groups. Each of the traditional organizational groups exists in the Delta organization. The *command* groups vary in size from the two supervisors reporting to the vice president of public relations to the seven managers reporting directly to the vice president of production.

The most important *task* group is the top-level committee. This task group often meets on an impromptu basis to discuss organizational development matters. The composition of the task group changes depending upon the problem at hand. For example, in the OD discussions the vice presidents of industrial relations and production are always present, while the other vice presidents attend if they are not busy.

A number of *interest* and *friendship* groups exist throughout the company. The friendship groups include both managerial and nonmanagerial employees. The focal point for some of the more cohesive friendship groups is athletics. The interest groups are more difficult to identify. However, a growing number of managers have joined together who have an interest in continuing their education. The managers have proposed that Delta pay a larger portion of their education fees. The managers interested in furthering their education are from various units throughout the organization.

The cohesiveness characteristic is very evident in some of the groups in Delta. The focal points of cohesiveness are the three districts. These districts are geographically dispersed from headquarters and rely primarily upon their internal know-how to solve problems. This independence from headquarters has resulted in a tendency to join together and work more closely within the district. Headquarters management has perceived this cohesiveness as detrimental to the attainment of overall corporate goals. The district managers and their subordinate managers view the cohesiveness as a force which enables them to perform more effectively. They believe that by working together they can provide better service to customers within the district.

Leadership. In the leadership chapter we discussed trait, personalbehavioral, and situational styles of leadership. Delta management has been described as a system which encourages top-down direction. The predominant leadership style of the firm is somewhat autocratic. The MBO program was designed to encourage a more participative style. Hopefully, this would occur throughout the company. At this time, the ODs has found that only selected units have moved toward more subordinate participation.

The units that have improved the most are the accounting department, some engineering groups, and District 3. These units have reported in interviews and in questionnaire responses that an atmosphere of greater subordinate participation has occurred since the inception of MBO. An examination of the leadership styles via questionnaire responses and interviews of the superiors of these units illustrates that they were inclined to use participation prior to MBO.

The Delta Utility Structure

The MBO program in Delta was introduced into an organization that had an established set of interaction patterns and a specified authority hierarchy. The company was structured according to many of the classical organization principles such as division of labor, unity of command, and relatively centralized decision making. The major decision-making unit was the headquarters division.

Division of Labor. A distinct scalar chain existed at Delta. The president issued directives and objectives to subordinates. These orders were to be followed by all subordinates within the company. He hoped to alter the strict use of the chain of command by introducing MBO. Specifically, he anticipated that subordinates would begin to provide relevant data and information which would aid him in establishing the overall objectives for the firm. That is, he wanted to receive accurate upward flowing communication instead of only dictating downward.

Figure 4 presents an organization chart of the company prior to the implementation of MBO. The vice president of production had a large amount of range and depth. He made decisions that influenced the data processing, marketing, engineering, and direct customer contact activities of the company. Thus, the depth of his job exceeded that of any of the other

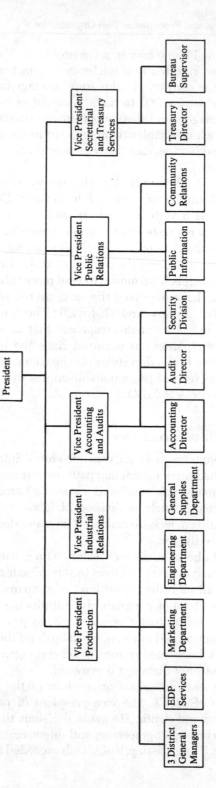

Figure 4
Delta Utility (top and middle levels of management)

vice presidents. Although he was at the same organizational level as the other vice presidents his influence upon the president was significantly greater than his counterparts.

After the MBO program was implemented the firm changed the middle-level management structure. The stated intent was to increase the influence and status of the marketing and engineering departments. The directors of these departments were given more authority (greater depth) and had to perform more job tasks (greater range).

The jobs of operating employees remained the same after MBO as they were before. That is, they had limited range and depth since the employees performed highly specialized job tasks. For example, supply personnel issued only supplies in limited categories, sometimes as few as six to eight items.

Span of Control. The spans of control differed between functional areas. A comparison of before-MBO and after-MBO spans of control is presented in Table 2. In each lower-level position the span of control increased after MBO was introduced. This is not to suggest that MBO caused the increase, but we can state that top management believed that lower-level managers could adequately supervise a larger group of subordinates.

Delta did not utilize a systematic Lockheed-type span of control model to designate superior-subordinate relationships. The top-level committee, however, stated that because the managers were better trained in MBO they probably could manage more subordinates. Other factors, such as co-ordination needed, planning required, and staff assistance received by the superior were not considered in the changes in the spans of control after MBO was implemented.

Table 2
Span of Control for Selected Positions before and after MBO

Position	Before MBO	After MBO
Top management		
President	5	5
Vice president production	7	7
Vice president accounting and audits	3	3
Vice president industrial relations	3	3
Middle management		
District 1 general manager	5	5
Marketing director	11	12
Engineering director	10	10
Accounting director	12	12
Lower-level managers		
District 1 plant supervisor	14	15
District 1 marketing sales manager	4	5
Customer service supervisor	10	11
Plant supply supervisor	6	8

Departmentalization. An examination of the company after the implementation of MBO illustrates that it used various forms of departmentalization. The mixed structural arrangement was designed to meet changing
customer needs and various government regulations.

The company had a territorial arrangement for the three districts. The
district managers reported directly to the vice president and utilized the
headquarters division for staff counseling. In addition there was a functional arrangement. Delta included functions such as production, industrial relations, accounting and audits, public relations, and secretarial
and treasury services.

The customer-oriented structural arrangement is found within the
marketing department. There was a general customer and an industrial
customer department. The members of these units dealt with separate customers and utilized different advertising and marketing research procedures
to assess customer needs. (See Figure 5.)

The structure of Delta was basically one which fostered specialization,
displayed moderately increasing spans of control since the introduction of
MBO, included high degrees of centralization, and had a mixed form of
departmentalization. The company executives anticipated that over an extended period of time the firm would move to an orientation more like
Likert's System 4. The current structural arrangements, however, do not
encourage this type of movement.

Decentralization of Authority. Delta was decentralized to a very limited degree. A measure of a company's decentralization is where the decisions concerning investment and manpower development are made. At
Delta, both before and after MBO, the crucial investment and personnel
decisions were all made in the top-level committee. This committee virtually controlled decisions that involved expenditures and securing and developing personnel.

Figure 5
Delta Marketing Department

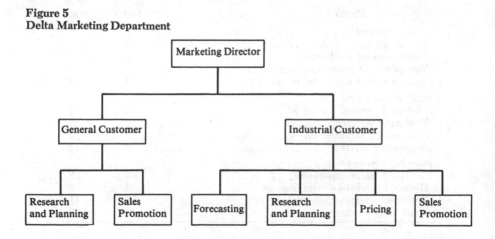

The Delta Utility Process

The ODs assessed the communication and decision-making processes at Delta Utility via observation, interviews, and questionnaire responses. In this section we are only concerned with the formal processes. This does not mean that informal communication flows were not important. In fact they seemed to be especially important in some departments. As we have noted, the communication flow and decision-making mechanisms of an organization are linked to structural and behavioral characteristics.

Communication. The two most important communicators at Delta were the president and the vice president of production. They were the prime initiators of discussions concerning organizational matters. The methods of communication used by these men included discussion with a single subordinate, meetings with more than one subordinate, letters to subordinates, memos, and directives.

Both before and after the implementation of MBO the emphasis in the communications between the president and vice president of production had been upon performance. A large degree of emphasis was placed on providing improved customer service. For example, the vice president of production had established 35 performance criteria which were transmitted to the three district managers. The performance of the district units was based upon these criteria. Included for review were indexes of customer complaint rates, equipment utilization, absenteeism ratios, and 32 other measures. At monthly meetings the three district managers presented the 35 performance measures to the vice president. This feedback enabled him to develop corrective action for the future.

The importance of feedback was also stressed by the other Delta vice presidents. The monthly meeting was a regular event in the accounting and audits and in the secretarial and treasury services departments. The immediate subordinates of the vice president of production also conducted monthly meetings. Thus, a climate of willingness to discuss job-related matters pervaded the company. Figure 6 illustrates this fact. Note that over 50 percent of the managers at Delta reported that they felt completely free to discuss job matters at these monthly meetings.

The value of these monthly meetings was of primary importance to the president. A questionnaire response concerning the value of the meetings illustrated that over 40 percent of the meeting participants rated them only fairly good or not really useful. This is shown in Figure 7.

The predominant formal communication networks at Delta included the vertical and group approaches. These networks were clearly evident in everyday communications. The value of group meetings in Delta is somewhat questionable as shown in Figure 7. Perhaps too many formal meetings (12 a year) are being held.

Figure 6
Frequency Distribution of Responses to the Question: Do
People Feel Free to Talk about Job-Related Matters at
Meetings?

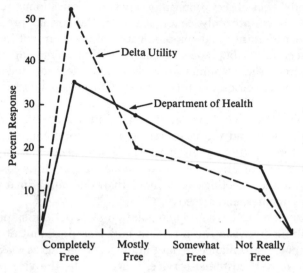

Figure 7
Frequency Distribution of Responses to the Question:
Are Group Meetings Useful Ways to Get Information?

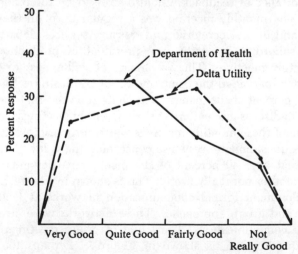

There was also a horizontal flow of communication within Delta. For example, in the preparation of budgets the accounting and audits department provided information throughout the organization concerning the procedures that would be employed. Failure to communicate accurately in the horizontal direction could result in poorer performance. The smoothness of horizontal communications is reviewed in Figure 8. An examination of Figure 8 reveals that communicating with peers was a problem approximately 40 percent of the time.

In summary, the communication flows at Delta prior to the introduction of MBO was top-down and horizontal. Despite the new MBO program this still appears to be the case. Figures 6, 7, and 8 illustrate that some communications problems still exist. There appear to be some problems with the monthly meetings as well as with the flow of horizontal communications. Whether MBO will correct these and other communication problems remains to be seen. Improving upward communications is of major importance to the top management committee at Delta.

Decision Making. The decision-making process was relatively centralized. As stated previously most decisions of any consequence were made by the top-level management committee. An example of this is noted in Table 3. The table indicates the type of decisions made at Delta. It also illustrates that the crucial decisions are made at the top of the organization even after MBO has been implemented. The seven decisions presented in Table 3 were made exactly at the same level as before the implementation of MBO. Thus, there was no change in decision-making authority after the program was implemented.

Figure 8
Frequency Distribution of Responses to the Question: Is There Difficulty Getting Information from People at Your Own Level?

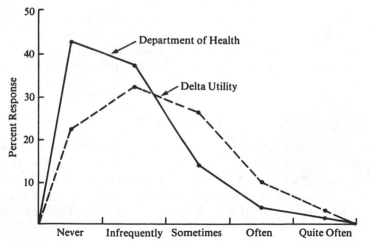

Table 3
Location of Authority to Make Final Decision after MBO

Decision Type	Final Deciders
Equipment for districts	Top-level committee
District budget	Top-level committee
Selection of operating employees at district level	District manager
Selection of managerial cadre for districts	Vice president of production
EDP procedures for districts	Top-level committee
Salary increments for district managers	President and vice president of production
Supplies for district	Vice president of production

The decision process is beginning to become less centralized but it is still basically a top-down process. This is supported to some extent by the location of crucial decision outlined in Table 3. The traditional decision-making process is followed except for the emphasis on control. Throughout the entire process the president and the vice president of production are closely attuned to decisions being made. For example, after the district managers have made a purchasing decision from among various alternatives, the vice president is informed of the choice and either accepts or rejects the decision. This close monitoring is certainly not the intent of an MBO program. The ODs on numerous occasions recommended that the district managers be allowed to present and defend their decisions. Currently they have been allowed to do so in approximately 30 percent of these situations. This is an improvement from their estimate that in about 10 percent of the cases prior to the introduction of MBO they were allowed to present their case.

In summary, the top-level decision makers have set a tone of top-down decision making. This philosophy has resulted in the close monitoring of lower-managerial-level decision making. There appears to be a slight movement toward increased participation in the crucial decisions by lower-level managers.

STATE DEPARTMENT OF HEALTH

The State Department of Health is charged by statute with the responsibility for "administering all provisions of law relating to public health, enforcing all public health laws and regulations of the State Board of Health, supervising and assisting county and regional boards and departments of health, and doing all other things reasonably necessary to protect and improve the health of the people." To discharge this mission, the department has seven major functions:

1. Promote the health of children and adults.
2. Control preventable disease.
3. Control environmental hazards.
4. Provide laboratory services.
5. Develop a statewide system of health facilities and medical services.
6. Provide facilities for treating tuberculosis and respiratory diseases.
7. Act as a repository for all vital statistics.

These seven functions are, in turn, broken down into subfunctions as necessitated by the nature of the major function; these functions are assigned to the divisions of the department for implementation, a sample of which is described in Table 4. As is evident from Table 4, the Department of Health is a complex organization. Resources and administrative effort must be allocated over a range of functions in the context of rapidly shifting priorities and uncertain trade-offs.

Table 4
Major Functions of a Sample of the Divisions of the State Department of Health

The *Medical Licensure* unit maintains the licenses on all physicians and osteopaths in the state.

The *Narcotic and Drug Control* program is directed toward alleviation of the misuse and abuse of narcotics and dangerous drugs.

The *Office of Local Health* provides leadership and direction to each of the local health departments, enforcing all local public health laws, and implementing and evaluating all programs offered through local health departments. It has the responsibility for establishing policies, outlining standards, procedures, and practices of operation of local health departments, and allocating, modifying, and controlling state funds.

The *Division of Administrative Services* coordinates and implements the administrative and fiscal operation of the State Health Department. It provides for the management of federal and state monies, maintains necessary records on administration and fiscal transactions; provides services for all programs of the State Health Department and the county health departments, and supervises the various programs and service units under its jurisdiction.

The *Division of Personnel and Training* coordinates, directs, and supervises the Office of Personnel, Training, and Recruitment and the Local Merit System for county health departments, by maintaining a record of all personnel actions, training activities, and Local Merit System activities.

The *Division of Environmental Services* has three main functions: regulatory, education, and training and evaluation. The division, in cooperation with the local health departments and F.D.A., regulates the sale, serving, and advertising of food, cosmetics, and devices; and inspects all food production, storage and service, schools, and recreational areas. The

Table 4 (*continued*)

division issues operating permits to restaurants, carbonated beverage bottling plants, hotels, motels, trailer coach parks, and septic tank cleaners. It provides educational programs for consumers and industries relative to food laws, regulations, and product safety. It provides training for local sanitarians and industry fieldmen, carries out evaluation of local health department activities, conducts sanitary evaluation of schools, restaurants, and milk processing establishments; and provides certification for interstate shipment of all Grade "A" milk as required by the Interstate Milk Shippers Conference Agreements.

The *Division of Air Pollution* seeks to enhance and protect the state's air resources by controlling air pollution at its source through enforcement of emission standards; reviewing plans and specifications prior to issuance of permits to construct or operate air contaminant sources; registration of sources; answering complaints; making field investigations to determine compliance with emission standards and to gather evidence of violations; conducting legal proceedings against violators; collecting scientific data including measurements of air pollution and meteorological conditions through a statewide monitoring network; collection and analysis of samples and reporting data; carrying out a program of public education and information; and providing technical assistance and advice to others on request.

The *Division of Laboratory Services* provides central public health laboratory facilities to official health agencies and practicing physicians throughout the state. Services include examination of both clinical and environmental health specimens, laboratory consultation, evaluation and certification of local laboratories, and research.

The *Division of Maternal and Child Health* seeks to promote the health of all mothers and children through programs which (1) provide preventive and therapeutic medical services to mothers and babies throughout the state, (2) establish guidelines for standard health procedures observed in all public schools, (3) integrate nutrition with all phases of public health in providing staff for prenatal, well-child, child development, and pediatric clinics, as well as providing education classes in dietary needs and consultation to nursing homes, hospitals, and recipients of food stamps, (4) supervise PKU screening and follow-up, and conduct clinics for children with neurological disorders, (5) set standards and guidelines for statewide family planning clinics, and (6) provide comprehensive health care to "high risk" mothers and their infants.

The financial support for the department's activities comes from federal, state, and county budgets. Federal support is in the form of grants designated for specific programs which Congress has identified as having high national priority. Environmental protection, family planning, and medical care for the aged are examples of activities receiving federal funds in recent years. State support is allocated to the department every two years at the time the legislature meets. State funds are, for the most part, unrestricted and can be designated for use in any of the seven functions; some state funds are restricted for use in designated programs,, such as venereal disease and water pollution control. County funds are designated in county budgets and are used by county health departments to augment federal and state funds.

The relationship between the State Health Department and the 100 county health departments is similar to that of national and regional sales offices. Most of the health programs are delivered through the county health departments just as a national office sells its product through regional offices. From 75 to 90 percent of the programs initiated to promote health of children and adults and to control preventable disease and environmental hazards are implemented through local departments. The State Health Department in these instances provides funds and technical assistance to counties which propose, for example, to hold prenatal, immunization, or family planning clinics. Other activities such as dental care and tuberculin testing are implemented by the State Health Department. There are, however, some dissimilarities in the relationship between the state and county health departments as compared to the relationship between national and regional sales offices.

The most important difference is that the State Health Department has no direct authority over county health departments. Their policies and procedures are determined by county boards of health which consist of health professionals from the county. The composition of the board membership is determined by state statutes and some of its members are appointed by the State Board of Health. Yet the county boards are responsible for determining the scope and content of all public health programs administered through the county health departments. A program devised and funded at the state level can be administered only if deemed desirable by the county boards of health.

Moreover, the personnel of county departments are hired by the county boards. State guidelines prescribe the necessary qualifications for job applicants, but the boards make the final decisions. Employees are accountable to the county boards for the discharge of their job responsibilities. And the county boards evaluate each employee for salary and position advances. Thus, the State Health Department has no direct authority to utilize in supervising the activities of county health departments; its real influence is effected through its control over state funds allocable to support county health programs. The fact that 65 percent of the total funds expended by county health departments are allocated by the State Health Department gives the latter some influence over county health activities.

The public health system of the state operates within a dual authority relationship as shown in Figure 9. The department is a part of the executive branch of the government and, as such, it must implement the laws and regulations of the legislative branch under the direction of the governor. At the same time, health regulations are promulgated by the State Board of Health, the major portion of whose membership is appointed by the governor. The county health departments are supervised by the State Health Department, but they operate within the policies of the county boards of health which, in turn, must operate within the policies of the State Board of Health. As would be expected, this arrangement results in instances of confusion and ambiguity as to who has ultimate authority for an act or decision.

In 1970 the governor, with advice and consent from the State Board of Health, appointed a new commissioner to head the department. The previous commissioner retired from public service after spending the last 15 years of his career as commissioner of health. The newly appointed commissioner was in his late 30s, a licensed physician with considerable experience in health-care administration. He also was a member of the American Management Association and had attended many of the association's training programs. He was familiar with many of the concepts and theories that we have discussed in this text. With this background, the commissioner undertook a major reorganization and development program which had a number of administrative and operational objectives.

The commissioner sought to delegate more authority to the division directors for the operation of their programs. The divisions of the State Health Department parallel closely the seven major functions. He also

Figure 9
The State Public Health Authority
System

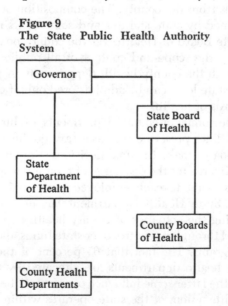

sought to decentralize to an even greater extent the decision making for the expenditure of state funds to the county health departments. Moreover, the current concern for environmental protection suggested increasing the department's commitment to this function.

The State Department of Health OD Program

The development method adopted in the State Health Department was also MBO. However, the MBO training was only one of a number of activities going on. Over a two-year period, the department was reorganized and new people came into positions of authority and a planning system patterned after MBO concepts was instituted among all the county health departments.

The strategy which the new commissioner adopted in managing these development activities followed the *shared approach*. He met with designated groups to formulate reorganization plans and procedures. Early in these discussions he introduced the concepts of MBO appropriate to the problems under discussion. In a real sense the new commissioner acted as a change agent who, though internal to the organization, brought new ideas into the discussion.

The discussions examined the indications that the department was less than optimally effective. For example, there was evidence that it was not delivering the appropriate services to those who needed them. Moreover the costs of many services were considered out of line with reasonable alternatives. These production and efficiency criteria were traceable to the department's policy of delivering the service out of the central office rather than delegating the authority to county health offices. There was evidence that employee satisfaction was less than optimal because of the absence of opportunity for personal development and professional advancement in the organization. Finally, the fact that public demand for increased environmental protection was not being fully met indicated that the department was not as *adaptable* to changing priorities as it should have been. Obviously not all of these problems could be solved by a single OD method, but structural changes seemed to be the first steps to take.

The reorganization was effected, and the major changes are shown in Figures 14 and 15. The formal diagnosis stage continued in executive staff meetings which consisted of the commissioner, deputy commissioners, and division directors. Two primary problems under consideration were (1) the integration and coordination of all departmental activities and programs and (2) the delegation of greater authority for health planning to the county boards of health. The discussion eventually centered on the concepts of MBO as the bases for instituting a planning system which would not only integrate the departmental activities, but also the county department activities. At this point the commissioner indicated his belief that the MBO system should be installed by an external change agent who could devote full time to the training and implementation phases.

It was at this point that he made contact with a university professor. An arrangement was made whereby the professor would diagnose the motivational state of the organization and design a program which would result in the installation of an MBO system. The program was to be over a two-year period with diagnosis and training occurring in the first year and installation during the second year. It was also agreed that the program would be monitored through periodic attitude surveys, the first of which was used as the basis for diagnosis and selection of appropriate training materials.

The initial target group consisted of the entire executive staff. Coincidentally, an in-house planning and training group located in the Office of Local Health initiated a planning process to be installed in each of the county health departments. This process was patterned after MBO concepts and required each county to submit annual plans which specified major objectives in order of priority and estimated costs of each objective. Planning manuals were prepared and training sessions were held in each county to teach the planning concepts to the personnel in the county health departments.

The OD strategy model aptly describes the entire effort.

1. The forces for change were both external and internal. External forces were the demands for greater attention to environmental protection, and internal forces were primarily concerned with uncoordinated programs, the symptoms of which were duplicated and unfocused activities.
2. The recognition of the need for change was precipitated by the appointment of a new commissioner who sought to reorient the thinking of the principal decision makers in the organization.
3. Diagnosis of the problem occurred in group meetings of those who would eventually have to accept and promote the change. Thus the shared strategy was adopted early in the process.
4. The diagnosis indicated a need for both structural and behavioral change. The structure was changed and an MBO training program was initiated to effect behavioral change.
5. The MBO method was introduced at the highest level and was to be introduced at lower levels only after experience indicated actual and potential problems.
6. The entire process was monitored both by direct observation of the results and through periodic attitude surveys.

The State Department of Health Behavior

Motivation.   The State Department of Health employees expressed generally high levels of overall satisfaction, as shown in Figure 10. The survey data also indicated that higher levels of satisfaction were expressed by division directors than by program directors who, in turn, were more satisfied than nonmanagerial employees. This relationship between levels in the hierarchy and satisfaction has been noted in other studies and it points up again the impact of structure on attitudes and behavior.

The differences in perceived need satisfaction between managerial and nonmanagerial personnel are shown in Table 5. As is obvious, managerial personnel perceive greater satisfaction for every need. The greatest differences between the two levels are in authority, goal-setting, and personal growth. Thus, not only are managerial personnel deriving greater overall satisfaction from their jobs, they also derive greater satisfaction of

Figure 10
**Frequency Distribution of Responses to the Question: Considering Everything,
Rate Your Overall Satisfaction at the Present Time**

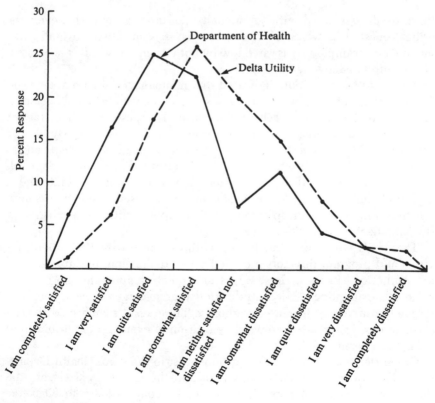

Table 5
Need Satisfaction of Managerial and Nonmanagerial Personnel
in the State Department of Health

Need	Mean Response*	
	Managerial	Non-managerial
Security	5.2	4.6
Accomplishment	5.3	4.5
Self-fulfillment	5.1	4.1
Pay	4.3	3.7
Personal growth	4.6	3.5
Social—friendships	5.3	5.0
Independent thought	5.0	4.1
Social—give help to others	5.4	4.4
Self-esteem	4.7	3.8
Prestige within department	4.9	3.9
Authority	4.8	3.3
Goal-setting	4.8	3.3
Prestige outside department	4.7	3.7

* Based upon a scale of seven points, ranging from "none" (1) to "maximum amount" (7). The mid-point, 4, is labeled "average."

those needs associated with self-actualization and esteem. However, the critical question is which of these needs is associated with overall satisfaction. For example, pay is rated low by both groups, but is this need associated with satisfaction?

The attitude survey data indicated that nonmanagerial employees were motivated by jobs which provided a sense of accomplishment, personal growth and development, self-fulfillment, and self-esteem. These factors are readily identifiable as Maslow's upper-level needs and Herzberg's "motivators." Other needs such as security and social needs were not as closely associated with satisfaction. The interpretation of these data follows the theories of Maslow and Herzberg. These findings indicated a high probability of success for MBO since it is based upon the assumption that employees will respond positively to opportunities for even greater self-actualization and self-esteem.

The needs which were associated with overall satisfaction among division and program directors included self-actualization, but also authority. Authority can be understood as an aspect of autonomy and it is a principal assumption of decentralization that managerial personnel will respond positively to increased authority. These results confirmed the decision to move aggressively toward delegation of even greater authority to managerial personnel.

Group Behavior. A myriad of groups exist in the State Health Department. The usual *command* groups exist and they range in size from the three deputy commissioners reporting to the commissioner to 30 clerks reporting to the Budgets and Accounts section director. In addition to the command groups, a number of *task* groups exist. For example, when county health departments submit requests for funds to support a program, a group consisting of the director of Local Health, division directors who can provide technical assistance for the proposed program, and representatives from departmental service units (laboratory, data processing, and administration) must meet to determine the acceptability of the county's proposal. These task groups change membership depending upon the nature of the proposed programs.

Moreover, the usual *interest* and *friendship* groups form in the department. Friendship groups cut across divisions and programs as their members transfer or are reassigned to other units. These groups interact in the cafeteria during breaks for coffee and lunch; they also attend professional meetings and conferences together. The membership of these groups is not restricted to people at the same hierarchical level; rather, one can find managerial and nonmanagerial personnel in the same groups. The social need, in the sense of making friends, is the most completely satisfied need in relation to other needs as shown in Table 5.

Some indication of the relationships among command and task groups can be observed from Figures 11 and 12. There we see that the sense of cooperation among groups is relatively good in comparison with Delta Utility. This is no doubt due in part to the high level of interaction and communications among and within groups as we noted earlier. In addition, the existence of friendship groups which cut across the organization facilitates communication and cooperation.

Figure 11
Frequency Distribution of Responses to the Question: Rate Cooperation between Your Units and Others Which You Depend Upon

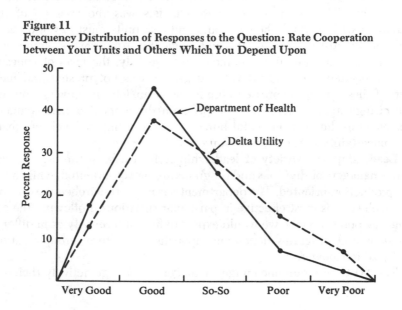

Figure 12
**Frequency Distribution of Responses to the Question: Do People in
Some Units Act to the Detriment of Other Units?**

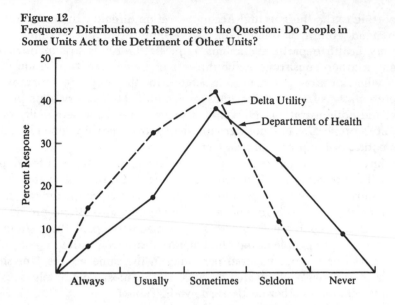

We can also note one example of the way cohesion acts as a reducer of anxiety. As noted, the groups most affected by reorganization were those in the environmental area. Not only were a number of units raised from program to divisional status, but the status of the managers was also raised. This meant they would attend executive staff meetings along with older (in terms of length of employment) division directors; they would report to a deputy commissioner who before reorganization was one of their peers. The net result of these changes was the creation of new situations within which the command and task units must develop. At the time of the attitude survey, the environmental groups were coping with the problems of mutual acceptance. Consequently, the level of cohesiveness associated with fully developed groups was not present and members of these groups expressed high levels of anxiety in conversation with the change agent. Moreover, the program directors and nonmanagerial personnel in the environmental bureau expressed higher levels of anxiety and uncertainty in the attitude survey.

Leadership.   A variety of leadership styles exists in the organization. Some managers of divisions and programs are person-oriented, while others are production-oriented. The department has never researched the question of which style is most effective in particular situations. Following the contingency point of view, we would expect to find different styles in different divisions and programs depending upon task structure, group relations, and position power.

The MBO program encourages managers to engage actively their subordinates in decision making with respect to unit and job goals. And to this extent, the concepts of group decision making and participative management as proposed by Likert are being implemented. Some indication of the likelihood of eventual success of the MBO program can be obtained from the attitude data.

Again we must point out that there may be no relationship between satisfaction and production. But to the extent that overall effectiveness of the unit is enhanced by satisfaction, to that extent should managers be concerned with it. Accordingly, an analysis of selected leader behaviors was made to determine which were associated with employee satisfaction. Among nonmanagerial personnel, satisfaction was highest for those who perceived that their managers encouraged them to set their own work objectives and saw the merit of their ideas even when they were different from the manager's ideas. A comparison of the State Health Department and Delta Utility with respect to work objectives is shown in Figure 13.

The relationship between the managerial styles of division directors and the satisfaction of their subordinates, program directors, follows much the same pattern. Program directors expressed satisfaction to the extent that their managers (1) provided the technical assistance they needed to get their job done, (2) did not insist that they follow standardized procedures, (3) never discouraged them from acting without first checking with their manager, and (4) made them feel that they were part of a team. These behaviors when taken together include a blend of person-oriented and production-oriented factors. We can also see the relationship of these behaviors to the underlying needs for autonomy and self-actualization previously noted.

Figure 13
Frequency Distribution of Responses to the Question: To What Extent Does Your Supervisor Encourage You to Set Your Own Work Objectives?

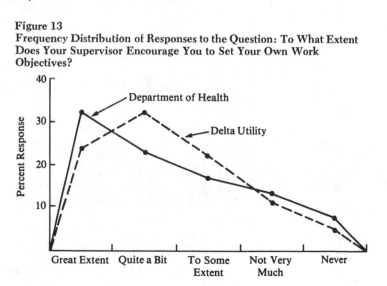

Figure 14
Organization Chart of State Department of Health prior to Reorganization

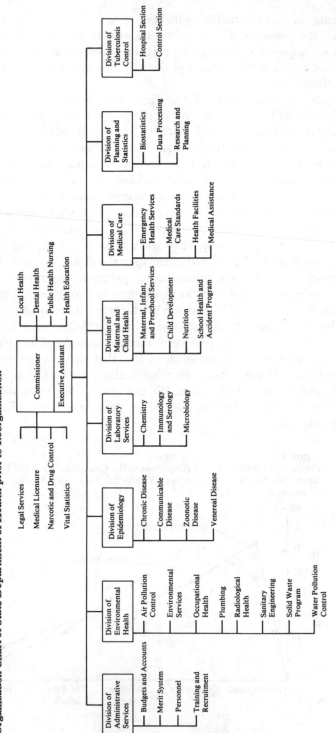

The State Department of Health Structure

The organization prior to reorganization is depicted in Figure 14. There were eight major divisions and within each division from two to eight subunits, commonly termed programs. In addition to the eight division directors, eight program directors reported to the commissioner. After reorganization, as depicted in Figure 15, there were 14 major divisions grouped into three larger units, or bureaus. Heading each of the three bureaus was a deputy commissioner reporting to the commissioner.

Division of Labor. A basic change in the reorganization was to introduce a new level of management specialized according to three functions: administration, environmental protection, and medical services. There were no major changes in the type of specialization implemented at the divisional level, except that the depth of division directors' tasks was increased. They were to be given greater control over the direction of their divisions with coordination achieved at the level of the deputy commissioner.

The depth of the commissioner's task remained unchanged, yet the range of his activities was reduced. Whereas before he had to coordinate

Figure 15
Organization Chart of State Department of Health after Reorganization

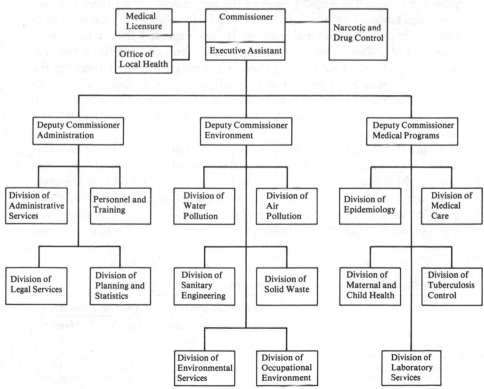

eight divisions, he now would coordinate only the three deputy commissioners. In addition, the eight program directors previously reporting to the commissioner's office were combined so that only three now reported to the commissioner.

The range and depth of nonmanagerial jobs were unchanged as a result of the reorganization. In Lawrence and Lorsch's terminology, the organization was highly *differentiated* at this level with some jobs having little depth and range, such as data processing clerks, laboratory workers, and bookkeepers, while others such as field inspectors, engineering analysts, and medical personnel had considerably more depth and range. This differentiation created the need for a variety of *integrative* techniques including specific job descriptions, rules and procedures, detailed work scheduling, plans, and mutual adjustment.

Departmentalization.   The major change in departmentalization was the identification of environment programs and the consolidation of those programs into one bureau. Six new divisions were created from the previous eight programs in the Division of Environmental Health. There were no significant changes in the basis for other divisions—each reflected one or more of the major functions of the State Health Department.

The establishment of three bureaus was designed to reduce the degree of differentiation at the highest level in the organization. The three bureaus combined basically similar functions and jobs in an effort to deal with integration through hierarchical control. It was expected that MBO would serve as a planning technique to integrate each bureau's activities, but that mutual adjustment would be required to integrate the three bureaus at the deputy commissioner's level. The three deputy commissioners along with the commissioner viewed themselves as an integrating team which would deal with the problems of coordinating administrative, environmental, and medical programs.

Spans of Control.   The changes in spans of control are shown in Table 6. The important change occurred in the span of control of the commissioner, which was reduced from 16 to 6. It was anticipated that the commissioner would be able to direct more attention and time to long-range planning as a result of this change. It also implemented the diagnosed needs to increase the organizational stature and visibility of programs aimed

Table 6
Spans of Control before and after Reorganization

	Before Reorganization		After Reorganization	
	Range	Median	Range	Median
Commissioner		16		6
Deputy commissioners			4–6	5
Division directors	2–8	4	2–8	4

at environmental protection and programs designed to give administrative and staff support to the environmental and medical programs.

The spans of control of program directors were unchanged and varied from 5 to 35. These different spans reflected differences in the basic factors affecting optimal spans, including similarity and complexity of tasks, proximity, and the amount of coordination and direction required of the supervisor. Spans were wider for jobs having low range and depth than for those of high range and depth.

Delegation of Authority. The significant change in the new organization was the delegation of the commissioner's authority to the newly created posts of deputy commissioners. The division directors were delegated greater authority for the operation of their divisions within the framework of integrated objectives to be achieved through the MBO method. The extent to which authority was decentralized varied depending upon the stage of personal development of each division director and the degree of interdependence among the divisions.

MBO when fully implemented would result in the delegation of full authority to each director to allocate assigned resources among the major objectives of the division. This would eventually authorize the directors to acquire, assign, and reassign personnel and to purchase laboratory and data processing services either from in-house staff units or from external sources depending upon where the service could be most economically purchased. These expenditures comprised at least 90 percent of the costs incurred in each division, and thus control over the circumstances of these costs represented considerable authority.

The State Department of Health Processes

Communications. The communication system consisted of two major flows: internal and external. The internal flow consisted of information exchanges flowing upward, downward, and horizontally within the organization. The external flow came from two sources: (1) from other departments and agencies comprising the executive branch of government, and (2) from clients of the organization. Here we will emphasize the internal flow, but we will describe in some detail the external flow because of the interrelationship between the two.

The information flow among departments of the executive branch is primarily concerned with broad policy, resource allocation, and certain administrative constraints. Policy issues have to do with the role of each department in carrying out the priorities as defined by legislative action and the governor's program. These broad policy matters are communicated in cabinet meetings, formal written directives, and informal discussions with the governor and aides. The resource allocations specify the State Health Department's share of available state funds. The administrative constraints concern job classifications, salary schedules, travel regulations, accounting procedures, and other operating matters for which uniformity is desirable. Much time is spent in clarifying and interpreting these policies, decisions, and administrative procedures. Formal documents are filed and codified from time to time in manuals and guides.

The information from clients is formal and informal. The formal flows are in the nature of complaints expressed in public hearings regarding health legislation and regulations. The air and water pollution divisions have regularly scheduled open hearings at which time testimony is taken from clients who favor or oppose environmental regulations. The informal channels consist of letters from clients who express dissatisfaction, or satisfaction, with the operation of state and county health department programs. These complaints are routinely recorded and routed to the appropriate division for corrective action. These information flows from clients are similar to a business firm's market information gathering system.

The internal information flow is upward, downward, and horizontal. It is more aptly described as a network corresponding to what one would expect in a System 4 organization. The popular conceptualization of government organizations as "bureaucracies" with the implication of strictly defined downward communication channels simply does not describe the State Department of Health. In fact, Figures 16 and 17 indicate that the perception of employees with regard to sufficiency and the absence of blocs (noise) in the department's communications flow are more favorable than are the perceptions of Delta Utility managers. The accuracy and clarity of messages among and within units are facilitated through face-to-face discussions.

Of course, some formal communications exist. Operating matters which could be stated in terms of departmental policies were discussed at executive staff meetings and announced as policy. Others matters such as broad organizational aims and proposals for new programs followed formal channels and were initiated at both the top and bottom of the organization. Position papers were prepared and circulated up, down, and across hierarchical lines; few programs of the department could be carried on without the active participation and support of a number of different units. It was thus necessary to involve all relevant units in the discussion of any new program.

The comparative efficiency of upward and horizontal communications can be seen in Figures 16 through 18. Two-way communication in the sense of *obtaining* information from one's supervisor is relatively more efficient in the State Health Department than in Delta Utility. Similarly, horizontal communications (getting information from one's peers) is relatively more efficient as shown in Figure 16.

There were communication difficulties; perfect communication channels simply do not exist. Differences in status and personality contributed to

Figure 16
Frequency Distribution of Responses to the Question: Is There
Enough Communication between Units That You Deal with?

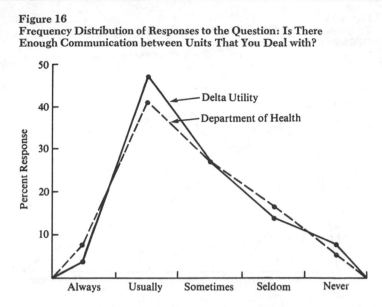

encoding and *decoding* errors. One can readily appreciate the *language* problems when a group consisting of physicians, accountants, statisticians, and engineers must consider and understand the impact of a new program on the operation of their units. And when one adds to this diverse professional group the fact that some are program directors while others are

Figure 17
Frequency Distribution of Responses to the Question: Are There
Blocks in Communications from One Unit to Another?

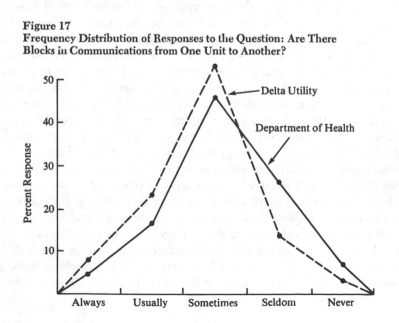

Figure 18
Frequency Distribution of Responses to the Question: Is There
Difficulty Getting Information from Your Supervisor?

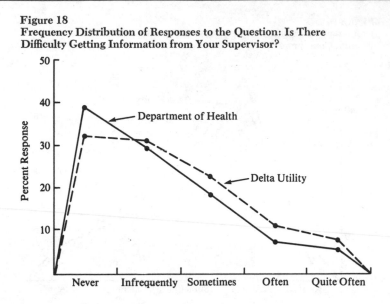

division directors, the potential for communication difficulties is increased. Yet even with these difficulties, or perhaps because of them, the communication channels were relatively efficient as indicated by the attitude survey data.

Decision Making. The decisions, decision makers, and decision processes of the State Health Department are many and varied. The variety of types of decisions made in the organization can be understood from the description of a sample of divisional functions in Table 4. Each division and program director must determine unit goals and the most efficient method for obtaining the stated goals. Yet there exist great differences in the degree of certainty regarding goals and methods among these units. Some divisions have relatively certain objectives and means to those objectives. Laboratory Services, Administrative Services, and the Tuberculosis Division have relatively certain and straightforward objectives and relatively certain methods, that is, *routine technology,* for obtaining those ends. The techniques of laboratory testing, accounting, and tuberculosis diagnosis and treatment are relatively well developed. Other units such as air and water pollution have relatively uncertain objectives, yet relatively certain methods. The uncertainty of objectives in air and water pollution control result from the complex interrelationships between air and water quality and other social priorities, primarily economic in nature. At the same time, the means for reducing air and water polution are well established. We can also recognize units for which objectives are relatively certain, yet means are uncertain; and other units for which both objectives *and* means are uncertain. All of which requires a variety of programmed and nonprogrammed approaches for the evaluation of alternatives.

The decision makers followed different approaches when they were confronted with certain means and objectives. These decisions were highly *programmed* and standardized procedures were adopted to deal with them. The decision, for example, concerning whether and how a premarital blood test would be run in the laboratory was automatically made whenever a specimen was received in the lab. Also entering into the selection of criteria were the value orientations of the decision maker. Although no information exists to indicate which criteria and values were associated with each decision maker, one can well imagine that the variety of professional backgrounds would produce a variety of criteria and values.

The process by which decisions were actually made in the organization parallels closely the communication process. Decisions other than those of a routine nature were seldom made by one person. Rather the decisions were made by groups whose members represented those units which would be affected by the decision. The composition of these groups changed as the substance of the decision changed.